SO YOU WANT
⚜ TO BE A ⚜
GAME MASTER

JUSTIN ALEXANDER

SO YOU WANT TO BE A TO BE A GAME MASTER

EVERYTHING YOU NEED TO START YOUR TABLETOP ADVENTURE— FOR DUNGEONS & DRAGONS®, PATHFINDER® AND OTHER SYSTEMS

PAGE STREET
PUBLISHING CO.

PAGE STREET
PUBLISHING CO.

TO SARAH HOLMBERG,

WITHOUT WHOM THIS BOOK WOULD NOT EXIST.
THANKS, LOVE.

TABLE OF CONTENTS

INTRODUCTION

YOU **HAVE CHOSEN** to enter a world of heroic adventure. More importantly, you have taken your first step toward unlocking those adventures for your friends. Unlike books, movies, or other types of games, a roleplaying game (RPG) offers infinite adventures, limited only by the power of your imagination. And because it's a game of imagination, it can be played almost anywhere. Most games are played around a table, but you can just as easily play via a video call, email, or special programs called virtual tabletops (VTTs).

One member of the group—the one this book is about and whom you've chosen to become—is the game master (GM). In *Dungeons & Dragons*, one of the most popular roleplaying games, the GM is known as the dungeon master (DM). As the DM, you'll be responsible for describing the fantasy world in which the game takes place:

As you come around the corner, you see that the corridor comes to a dead end. Carved in bas-relief upon this wall is a giant face—a face larger than you are tall. As your gaze alights upon it, the face begins to move. Its granite lips form words—words that thunder down the corridor. "WHO DARES TO TRESPASS HERE?"

The other players can now tell you what they're going to do: Will they talk to the face? Try to destroy it? Cast a spell to *silence* it? Or will they try something completely different? The decision is up to them!

But the players don't need to play as themselves. Instead, they'll create the role of a fantasy hero and step into their shoes. Perhaps they'd like to play as a heroic knight pursuing quests of honor. Or as an enigmatic wizard seeking the lost secrets of the cosmos. Or as an ancient elf hoping that the companionship of the younger races will help him to recover the youth he lost centuries ago. In a roleplaying game, you can pretend to be anyone you want!

Playing an RPG is a little like performing in an improvised radio drama. It's as if you were acting in a play or movie, but there's no script and the wonders of your adventure are not limited by even the most extravagant of special effects budgets.

Anything you can imagine is possible in a roleplaying game.

But an RPG isn't just Make-Believe or Let's Pretend. It's also a game. The players' characters will face challenges—monsters, traps, and the like—and their success is not assured. By rolling dice and following the rules of the game, you'll be able to determine the success or failure of your characters' actions. In other words, the players will tell you (the DM) what they want their characters to do, and you'll use the rules (and your own creativity!) to figure out what the result is.

INTO THE DUNGEON

For many of you reading this, nothing I've written here will have come as a surprise. You've either played a roleplaying game before or read a similar introduction in a rulebook or watched an actual play video featuring other people playing the game. That's why you picked up this book in the first place. In fact, you may have already run your first adventure as a DM and are trying to figure out how you can do it better.

But whether you're taking your first steps or taking your game to the next level, let's take a peek at an example of what actually playing a roleplaying game looks like, how that relates to what you'll be doing as a DM, and how this book is going to help you do that.

Jason is serving as the DM for a group of three players. Seth is playing Ranthir, a young apprentice wizard with an endless thirst for knowledge and a penchant for carrying a dozen different bags and satchels packed full of various useful odds and ends. Sarah is playing Tithenmamiwen (Tee), an elven maid rebelling against her elders. Dave is playing Agnarr, a brash barbarian who has little regard for the cares or concerns of the civilized world.

The group, also commonly referred to as a "party," are currently exploring an underground labyrinth once occupied by the Sons of Jade—a group of scholars, loremasters, and magi who sought to unlock the secrets of the ancient and powerful Jade Magi of the Lost City of Shandrala.

JASON (DM): As you emerge through the rubble of the broken wall, you see a large room of cream-colored stone. There are three doors leading out of the room—a tall door of bluish steel directly across from you and two smaller ones off to either side. In the corner of the chamber, a huge mass of debris has been piled high.

Jason is running a dungeon scenario, in which the players' characters (PCs) have descended into an underground vault filled with dangers to overcome and treasure to win. We'll be looking at how to run and create your own dungeons in Part 1, starting on page 21.

SARAH (TEE): I'll go check out the door of blue steel.

DAVE (AGNARR): I'll go dig through the garbage.

SARAH (TEE): There's no pile of filth too large or too small for Agnarr.

JASON (DM): *(laughing)* OK, Agnarr starts digging through the trash. Tee, the door is locked.

SETH (RANTHIR): Does it look like that last door of blue steel we found?

JASON (DM): Virtually identical.

SARAH (TEE): Well, I won't be able to pick the lock then. We'll need the password.

A roleplaying game is a conversation. You'll describe what the PCs see, the players will respond by telling you what their characters do in response or by asking questions to clarify their understanding of the situation, and then you'll respond to them. It's a loop, right? Your topic of conversation is the fictional world of the game, and you'll build that world—and the things that happen in it—by actively engaging with that conversation. You'll listen to each other. You'll build on each other's ideas. You may even get emotional or interrupt or disagree with each other, just like any other conversation.

DAVE (AGNARR): I hate those doors. *(to Jason)* Have I found anything in the trash pile yet?

JASON (DM): Looks like a lot of glass and metal. Small stuff.

SETH (RANTHIR): Anything interesting?

JASON (DM): Give me an Intelligence (Arcana) check.

SETH (RANTHIR): *(rolls some dice)* 13.

JASON (DM): There's a bunch of alchemical equipment. You think it might be the remains of a rather large laboratory. Agnarr's smashing a lot of it, but it doesn't look like it was worth much to begin with.

SETH (RANTHIR): Carry on.

The character is attempting an action and the DM isn't certain of the outcome, so he calls for a skill check, using the mechanics of the game to determine the outcome. The player rolls a 20-sided die, then adds their Intelligence modifier and, because they're proficient in the Arcana skill, their proficiency bonus. The result is 13, which the DM compares to the difficulty of the action. Because the check was equal to or higher than the difficulty, Ranthir succeeded in identifying the alchemical equipment.

*This is called a **ruling**: As the DM, you are figuring out how the rules of the game can be used to determine what happens in the game world. This is more or less the most basic skill of being a DM: When the player says, "I want to do X," how do you respond? We'll break this skill down into a simple procedure, starting on page 24.*

JASON (DM): As you shove aside a particularly large mass of debris, you reveal the corpse of a dead goblin. The sickly sweet smell of decay washes over you in a thick wave. What are you all doing?

SARAH (TEE): Tee doesn't even look. She wants no part of whatever's making that smell. She's going to head over to the door on the left and see if she can get that open.

DAVE (AGNARR): I'll keep digging!

SARAH (TEE): Of course you will . . .

JASON (DM): There are a couple more goblin corpses after the first.

SETH (RANTHIR): How long have they been dead? *(rolls some dice)* I got a 17 on my Wisdom (Medicine) check.

——❧— *Wisdom is a different ability score from Intelligence, and Medicine is a different skill from Arcana. Different characters will have different ability scores and be proficient in different skills. Figuring out which mechanics to use is an important part of making a good ruling.*

JASON (DM): Hard to say for certain. Probably at least a couple of weeks. They're pretty badly decomposed.

SETH (RANTHIR): Okay. I guess I'll keep an eye out over Agnarr's shoulder. If he comes across anything valuable, I'll try to stop him before he destroys it.

JASON (DM): A couple layers down from the corpses, Agnarr suddenly unearths a perfectly preserved box of cherry wood with a mosaic design of inlaid jade. It seems to be completely unmarred—a stark contrast to the broken junk around it.

SETH (RANTHIR): I cast *detect magic*.

——❧— Detect magic *is the name of a magical spell. Some characters, including wizards like Ranthir, are capable of casting powerful dweomers. This spell allows Ranthir to detect the presence of other magical effects.*

JASON (DM): (*to Sarah*) Tee finds the door unlocked.

SARAH (TEE): I'll open it.

JASON (DM): (*to Ranthir*) As soon as your spell comes into effect, you can see a faint magical aura around the box.

SETH (RANTHIR): (*to Dave*) May I please see that, Master Agnarr?

DAVE (AGNARR): (*with a shrug*) Sure. I hand it over.

SETH (RANTHIR): I'll try to open the box.

JASON (DM): (*to Seth*) You open the box to find a perfectly preserved pack of love letters. They appear to have been written by a woman named Athara and are addressed to a man named Oliss. (*to Sarah*) The door swings open with a loud, rusty creak. The narrow hall beyond the door is choked with thick, ropelike webs. The webs nearest to the door have been hacked apart and hang forlornly from the walls in tattered wisps. About 15 feet away, you can see another hall intersecting this one. At the intersection, the hacking of the webs comes to an end and you can see that the corpses of two large spiders—spiders nearly the size of a small cow—lie belly-up on the floor there.

A dungeon adventure is divided into separate **rooms**. *Everything up until this point has taken place in one room, and Jason has known what's in that room—for example, what's hidden inside the pile of garbage—by looking at his notes for that room. We call those notes the* **room key**. *Now Sarah has opened a door and is looking into another room, so Jason flips through his notes to the key for that room and can describe what Sarah sees there.*

Knowing how to create, read, and run a room key is, of course, a fundamental part of running a successful dungeon adventure.

See page 37 for more information on running a room.

SARAH (TEE): Uh, guys, I think you should come over here and look at this. *(to Jason)* Do I see anything unusual about the spider corpses?

JASON (DM): Give me a Perception check.

SETH (RANTHIR): I'll close the box and head over to Tee.

SARAH (TEE): *(rolls some dice)* Awesome! Natural 20 for a total of 28.

JASON (DM): At first everything seems okay. But then one of the corpses starts to twitch.

SARAH (TEE): That's bad.

JASON (DM): Actually, you're pretty sure it's not the corpse itself. Something on the corpse—or inside it?—is crawling and squirming around.

SARAH (TEE): That's very, very bad.

SETH (RANTHIR): *(pretending he doesn't know what only Tee can see)* What's wrong?

SARAH (TEE): Something very, very bad! *(to Jason)* I slam the door shut.

JASON (DM): As you reach for the door you see five smaller spiders—these are only about the size of a large dog—burst out of the larger corpses and start skittering toward you.

SARAH (TEE): I SLAM THE DOOR SHUT!

JASON (DM): You slam the door shut. I need initiative checks.

SARAH (TEE): (*rolls some dice*) 7.

DAVE (AGNARR): (*rolls some dice*) 16.

SETH (RANTHIR): (*rolls some dice*) 10.

In D&D there's a special set of rules used to resolve combat. When combat starts, every character—including the giant spiders being controlled by the DM—rolls for initiative. The highest initiative result goes first, followed by the second highest, and so forth.

By forcing everyone to take turns, the conversation during combat becomes more formal. This will help you (and the players!) keep track of a situation that might otherwise be hopelessly complex. On page 486, we'll dive into techniques that can make running combat even more fun, and we'll also find other situations in which a more formal structure will help you run the game.

JASON (DM): (*rolling dice for the spiders*) Okay, Agnarr, you're first.

DAVE (AGNARR): I throw my shoulder against the door to hold it shut. I've got oil! Anyone got a fire?

SARAH (TEE): Uh . . . You've got your flaming sword.

DAVE (AGNARR): Oh. Right. Well, I don't think I can open the door, throw the oil, and light it before the spiders get through.

SARAH (TEE): Throw the oil over here. (*to Jason*) Can we have him yank the door open while I throw the flask, and then he can hit it with his sword in midair?

JASON (DM): Sure.

DAVE (AGNARR): Awesome. Okay, I toss my flask of oil to Tee and get ready to open the door. FOR THE GLORY!

JASON (DM): All right. As Agnarr shouts the command word for his sword, it bursts into flame. He yanks open the door as Tee throws the oil. The flaming greatsword sweeps through the air, shattering the flask and sending a cascade of burning oil over the bustling mass of spiders just inside the door. Not only the oil but also the thick, dry webs burst into flame. (*rolls some dice*) Two of the spiders—on fire—come bursting out of the conflagration. One crawls up Agnarr's leg and buries its fangs into his thigh.

DAVE (AGNARR): Get it off! Get it off!

JASON (DM): (*rolls some dice*) You take 4 points of damage. And I'll need a Constitution saving throw.

> *Characters have hit points (HP), which represent their vitality. When a character takes damage, they lose hit points. When a character runs out of hit points, they fall unconscious and may die.*

DAVE (AGNARR): (*rolls some dice*) 18.

JASON (DM): Okay, you can feel the acidic burn of the spider's venom, but you manage to shake it loose before it can deliver a full dose. It falls back to the floor at Agnarr's feet. (*to Seth*) The other spider is scuttling straight toward Ranthir. What do you do?

SETH (RANTHIR): I cast *magic missile*. (*rolls some dice*) 3, 4, and 5 points of damage.

JASON (DM): Three blasts of eldritch force lance out from Ranthir's fingertips, striking the spider mid-scuttle. It gives a high-pitched screech as it collapses into a small, smoldering ball. (*to Dave*) It's Agnarr's turn again.

DAVE (AGNARR): With a howl of rage, Agnarr smites the little bastard. (*rolls some dice*) 16 to hit.

JASON (DM): The spider, shaken free from Agnarr's leg, is still skidding across the floor as Agnarr's greatsword smashes down on it. Give me damage.

DAVE (AGNARR): (*rolls some dice*) 14 points of damage plus 3 fire damage.

JASON (DM): Agnarr's sword cleaves the spider in twain. A great gout of greenish ichor geysers into the air.

SARAH (TEE): Are there any other spiders moving in the hallway?

JASON (DM): No. It looks like the flaming oil killed them. But the fire back there is getting quite intense. It's being fueled by the thick webs . . .

SARAH (TEE): I close the door. I say we just wait for it to burn out.

DAVE (AGNARR): Sounds good to me.

SARAH (TEE): Should we try the other door?

SETH (RANTHIR): Actually, I've got an idea. (*to Jason*) I take out the packet of love letters we found. I'm going to stand in front of the door of blue steel and start reading them out loud.

JASON (DM): Umm . . . okay.

SARAH (TEE): What are you doing?

SETH (RANTHIR): If the door of blue steel has a password, then it must have been known to the Sons of Jade when they worked here. And if these letters were written at the same time, the password might be mentioned.

JASON (DM): (*rolls some dice*) How long are you going to keep reading?

SETH (RANTHIR): Until I've finished the letters.

JASON (DM): After 22 minutes of reading, Ranthir begins a new letter: "I am sorry I have not written to you sooner, but the old taskmaster has been working us hard again. Athvor Krassek may think himself to be . . ." But he trails off. At the name of "Athvor Krassek," the door of blue steel begins to swing open . . .

ACTIVE PLAY

One of the coolest things about a roleplaying game—and you can see it happening in this example of play—is that nobody knows what's going to happen until it happens.

If Jason were writing a story for someone else to read, obviously he'd be in complete control. He'd know that A would happen and then B would happen and then C would happen. But Jason isn't an author writing a story. He's a dungeon master playing the game with his friends.

So the players, for example, don't know that there are spider hatchlings hiding inside the mother's corpse (ick!). Jason does, because he created the scenario and plays the nonplayer characters (NPCs), but he doesn't know that the players' characters are going to light the corridor on fire.

Similarly, Jason knows that the password for the blue steel door is "Athvor Krassek," a former administrator of the laboratory, but he wasn't anticipating Ranthir's player deciding to read the love letters in front of the door. Does the name "Athvor Krassek" even appear in those letters? Jason doesn't know that, either, so he decides to roll some dice to figure it out.

Moments like these are created through active play: The players are actively playing their characters. In response, the DM is actively playing all the other characters, and is also constantly putting toys into the fictional world—the love letters, the door, the discarded alchemy equipment—that *everyone* gets to play with.

Active play is the fundamental principle of a roleplaying game. And the secret to being a great dungeon master ultimately boils down to (a) prepping cool toys for you and your players and then (b) playing with them freely and creatively together.

Everything else is just a matter of technique.

TAKING YOUR FIRST STEPS

This book isn't a roleplaying game. It won't teach you the rules. If you want to play *Dungeons & Dragons*, you'll want to pick up either the *D&D Starter Set* (for a quick, playable introduction) or the three rulebooks that contain the full game (the *Player's Handbook, Dungeon Master's Guide,* and *Monster Manual*). In fact, from this point forward I'll be assuming that you're familiar with the rules of D&D.

The rulebooks will teach you how to play, but you want to do more than that. You want to be a dungeon master. You want to create adventures and entire worlds to share with your players. You want to invite them into the wondrous vistas you've imagined and forge unforgettable stories with them. But where do you even begin?

Just turn the page.

Imagining an entire universe may feel daunting right now, but we're going to break this down step by step. Starting in the dungeon, we'll walk through running an adventure. That'll go a lot faster than you might think. You could be DMing your first game tomorrow if you wanted to!

After that, you'll design an adventure for the first time and run that, too. You'll be amazed at just how simple it can be! We'll build on that foundation to make your adventures more dynamic and exciting, and then you'll be ready to choose new types of adventures to explore—heists, mysteries, conspiracies, and more.

OTHER ROLEPLAYING GAMES

Dungeons & Dragons (D&D) is a fantasy RPG set in a world inspired by the works of authors like J. R. R. Tolkien, N. K. Jemisin, George R. R. Martin, and Robert E. Howard. But there are many other RPGs! If you enjoy cyberpunk stories, you might check out *Cyberpunk RED* or *Technoir*. Like horror movies? Check out *Unknown Armies* or *Call of Cthulhu*. You can also find licensed RPGs based directly on fictional universes you already love, like *Star Wars*, *A Song of Ice and Fire*, *Alien*, or *Doctor Who*.

For the sake of simplicity, the examples in the first section of this book are going to assume that you're playing the current edition of *Dungeons & Dragons*. But the vast majority of the book—and the skills you'll learn—will be useful no matter what RPG you've chosen to master.

PART 1

DUNGEONS

DUNGEONS & DRAGONS was born in the dungeon, with Dave Arneson—the creator of the modern roleplaying game—carving out the labyrinths beneath Castle Blackmoor and giving his players the opportunity to delve down into its depths.

As a new dungeon master, you're going to start your adventures in the dungeon, too. The classic dungeon is an underground complex; a maze of corridors linking rooms filled with monsters, traps, and treasure. The heroes in a dungeon adventure enter the maze, defeat the monsters, avoid the traps, and claim the treasure for themselves. (Or maybe they'll flip the script, ally with the monsters, and donate the treasure to the local orphanage. You never really know what will happen during play!)

A dungeon scenario—the adventure that you'll be running for your players—is presented in two parts: the **dungeon map** and the **dungeon key**.

A dungeon map will look something like this:

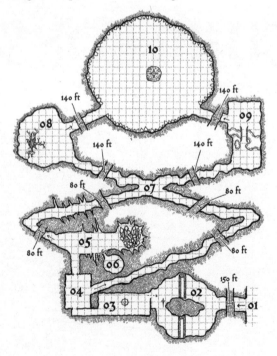

On the map you can see the various rooms that make up the dungeon, and each room has been labeled with a number. In the dungeon key, each numbered room has been given a full description, telling you everything you need to know when the PCs enter that room.

Imagine that you're sitting at a table with your friends and running a dungeon scenario. The PCs are currently standing in one of the rooms of the dungeon, so you look at the dungeon key for that room and describe to the players what their characters see. The players will respond by telling you what they want their characters to do in that room, and you'll tell them what happens as a result. (Think about Agnarr rooting through the garbage pile or Ranthir reading through the love letters.) When the players have done everything they want to do in that room, they'll be able to choose one of the exits from that room—a doorway, an archway, a hallway, a secret passage—and go to a new room, which you can then look up in the dungeon key and describe to them.

And that's it. You just keep repeating that loop—describe the room, resolve the players' actions, go to the next room, describe the room—until the adventure is done. It's very simple. It's also very straightforward for the players because they'll never be left wondering what they should be doing next: Either there'll be something in the current room that they want to do, or they can always pick an exit and go to the next room.

To get ready for running your first dungeon, we're going to break the dungeon loop into two parts and look at each of them separately. First, how you resolve the actions declared by the players, a process that we call a ruling. Second, how the dungeon key works and how you can use it to describe and run each room.

ROLLING DICE

Roleplaying games often refer to dice using an XdY notation, which means that you roll X number of Y-sided dice and add the results together. For example, 3d4 means that you should roll three four-sided dice and 3d6 - 2 means that you should roll three six-sided dice and then subtract two from the result.

⊶ STEP 1: THE RULING ⊷

If playing an RPG is a conversation between you and your friends, then the most basic element of that conversation is the ruling. After you've described what's going on in the game world and a player responds by saying that they want their character to do something, what happens next? As the DM, that's what you get to figure out and create!

Once you do figure it out, of course, you'll describe the outcome to your players. Hearing this updated version of what's going on in the game world will prompt one or more of them to say what the next thing they want to do is. At which point, of course, you'll make another ruling. Which will prompt a response that will prompt a ruling, which will prompt a response, and so on.

It's easy to see that, although a lot of other stuff may happen while you're playing an RPG, this ruling-response cycle really forms the core of your conversation; it's the backbone of everything that happens during the game. This also means that making good rulings is the most basic skill you'll want as a DM.

For example, players might say things like:

- ⬡ "I want to jump over the chasm."
- ⬡ "I open the door."
- ⬡ "I'm going to the library to research parasite demons."
- ⬡ "I attack the orc with my sword!"
- ⬡ "I'm pulling out my thieves' tools. Let's see if I can pick this lock."

Take a moment and think about each of those declarations. You're limited because we don't really have the full context in which these declarations are being made—how wide is the chasm? what type of door is it? who are the characters involved?, etc.—but let whatever first pops into your head roll around for a bit. What would be your response to each declaration? Why? Can you imagine a *different* response to the same declaration?

You might find this exercise easy. (But, no, really. Actually stop reading, take a minute, and do it.) You might find it difficult. You might find it easy for some declarations and tricky for others.

Either way, though, I'm pretty sure you were able to come up with a response for every one of these declarations.

So the first thing to take away from this exercise is that rulings are something you can already do. They're not an arcane ritual and they don't require special skills. They're a basic act of creativity and your imagination has just proven itself equal to the task.

What we do want to do, though, is to make our rulings easier, faster, and more reliable. Since we're playing a game, we'll also want to integrate our rulings with the game mechanics.

There's a fairly basic procedure you can follow for this, and it starts by defaulting to yes.

DEFAULT TO YES

The easiest ruling for a DM to make is "No."

> **PLAYER:** I want to jump over the chasm.
> **DM:** You can't.

> **PLAYER:** I'm going to the library to research parasite demons.
> **DM:** You don't find any information.

> **PLAYER:** I attack the orc with my sword!
> **DM:** You miss.

When you use "No," everything is simple: There are no complications. No consequences. You don't have to create anything.

But that's exactly why you almost never want to use it. "No" stagnates the action. It leaves the situation unchanged. Instead of giving the players a new situation they can react to, you're instead asking them to come up with a new reaction to the same situation.

What you want to do is almost exactly the opposite: Default to yes.

> **PLAYER:** I want to jump over the chasm.
> **DM:** Okay, you're on the other side.

PLAYER: I'm going to the library to research parasite demons.

DM: You find a book of lore written by a scholar named Sagrathea. He reports that parasite demons can be revealed by splashing holy water on their host.

PLAYER: I attack the orc with my sword!

DM: You mercilessly stab the orc. With a shocked look in her eyes, she slumps to the floor in front of you.

"Yes" moves the action forward. It creates a new situation that both you and the players will now be forced to respond to. Now that they're on the other side of the chasm, what will they do? Where are they going to find a supply of holy water? How are they going to hide the orc's corpse?

At a more basic level, defaulting to yes also makes sense because people mostly succeed at the stuff they do. Walk down to the corner store? Say hello to an old friend? Read a book? If someone wants to do those things, they'll almost certainly have no problem doing so, and that also applies to most of the things that the players tell you their characters are going to do.

Another thing to keep in mind is that the players are generally going to propose doing things they *want* to see happen. So if you default to yes, you're really just giving your audience what they want, which is almost always a winning move. Plus, your players probably already know how they want to respond to success. They wanted to jump across the chasm because there was something they wanted to do on the other side.

To boil all that down: Unless you have a specific reason for NOT saying yes, your ruling should always be, "Yes, you do that and this is what happens."

I LIKE BIG BUTS

There are limits to this, however. Saying yes some of the time is good. But the problem with saying yes all the time is that it eliminates the challenge from the game. While we always want to achieve our goals, the truth is that we *also* want to overcome obstacles. It's only by triumphing over adversity that we can truly feel accomplishment, and we can't enjoy the hero's thrilling escape unless we first hang them off the cliff:

PLAYER: I want to jump over the chasm.

DM: You leap across, but come up a little bit short. Slamming into the edge of the abyss, you barely manage to grab onto a thick vine before plummeting into oblivion.

This is the **Yes, but** . . . Yes, you succeed, *but* there's a complication or a consequence or a challenge.

The great thing about, "Yes, but . . ." is that you're not negating the player's contribution to the conversation. They wanted to get to the other side of the chasm, and they've done that. What you've done is add your own contribution to what's happening, creating interest or confronting the player with a new challenge to solve.

The flip side of this coin is the **No, but** . . .

Imagine for a moment that the player says they want to do something that you know is impossible. For example:

PLAYER: I'm going to the library to research parasite demons.

But you know that there's no library in this small town. Or, if there is, that it's too small to have the collection of rare paranormal books necessary to do meaningful research on parasite demons. This is a specific reason for not saying yes, which makes it a perfect time to say no.

When you make a ruling like this, though, it can be useful to take a step back, think about what the player's actual goal is (e.g., finding information about parasite demons), and offer an alternative method for doing that:

DM: No, the local library is too small to have specialized information like that. But you know that the Bodleian Library has a large collection of paranormal texts, so you could take the train up to Oxford.

In practice, the difference between "Yes, but . . ." and "No, but . . ." can be razor-thin or even nonexistent at times. That's fine. We're not trying to classify every ruling we make with scientific precision. We just want to have a few useful rules of thumb that we can use to make effective and entertaining rulings for our players.

MAKING A CHECK

PLAYER: I attack the orc with my sword!

DM: Okay, but you'll need to succeed on an attack roll.

Sometimes the answer you're looking for is neither yes nor no. Instead, it's "maybe" or "I'm not sure" or "Let's find out together!"

When that's the case, you'll want to use the rules of the roleplaying game to determine the character's success or failure. If that's an attack roll in D&D—like trying to stab an orc with your sword—then the rules are very specific about how the action is to be resolved: The difficulty of the roll is equal to the orc's Armor Class (AC), so you simply roll a 20-sided die, add your attack bonus, and compare it to the AC. If you rolled equal to or higher than the difficulty, you successfully stabbed the orc. If you didn't, then you missed the orc.

But what if it's not a combat action? What if the PC is trying to accomplish something else? There are a number of different rules in D&D, but the most basic is an ability or skill check. When in doubt, you can just pick an ability score or skill, set the Difficulty Class (DC) of the check, and ask the player to roll the dice.

Before we pick up the dice, however, let's double-check our check. Should we even be making a check? In fact, how do we know when it's the right time to call for a check?

Well, let's review. If the players ask to do something and success is trivial or certain, then we should default to yes. If success is impossible (there is no local library, there's an invisible wall blocking the far side of the chasm, etc.), then the answer is no. Flipping that around, we can see that a check should be used if success is possible but not certain. (And, equally so, if failure is possible but not certain.)

Let's go one step further, though, and consider the potential failure state. Failure should be meaningful, interesting, or both. If it's neither, then you shouldn't be rolling the dice.

Here's an example where failure *isn't* interesting or meaningful:

PLAYER: I try to pick the lock.

DM: You fail. What do you do?

PLAYER: I try to pick the lock again.

DM: You fail. What do you do?

PLAYER: I try to pick the lock again.

You can see the problem. Because nothing meaningful happens as a result of failing to pick the lock, the game ends up just kind of spinning its wheels.

Does this mean you should never call for an ability check to pick a lock? Not at all. Failing to pick the lock might be meaningful because:

◎ The door is trapped, and failing to pick the lock will trigger the trap.

◎ They're trying to pick the lock during combat, and each time they fail to open the door their companions have to survive another round of enemy attacks.

◎ They're in a hostile area, and if they fail to pick the lock, a guard patrol will discover them in the act.

Failure is meaningful (and interesting) when it creates an obstacle or consequences, forcing the PCs to create a new path to their goals.

There are many ways to achieve this, but the easiest way of implementing meaningful failure is to simply not allow retries on the check: If you failed to pick the lock on the door, that failed check tells us that you'll never be able to pick that lock. You did your best; it didn't work.

Now what? Kick it in? Cast a spell? Look for a different entrance? Look for a key? Seduce the housekeeper? I dunno. You tell me!

As you can see from these alternatives, each new path created from meaningful failure creates interest: The PCs are leaving evidence or engaging in further exploration or creating new relationships. Arguably all of these are, in fact, more interesting than if they'd simply picked the lock and gone through the door!

(With that being said, it's equally true that *success* should be meaningful, interesting, or both. This usually takes care of itself, though, because players rarely try to do something unless they want to see it happen.)

SUCCESS IS STILL GOOD

A trap you can fall into here is thinking, "Well, if failure is better, then I should just force everything to be a failure!" There's a long discussion about all the problems this could create, but the short version is this: Success is also important if, for no other reason, than that the players will become increasingly frustrated if they can never actually accomplish anything. So let the dice fall where they may!

Now that you've chosen to make the skill check, you need to **identify the skill** and **set the difficulty** of the check.

Identifying which skill to use is pretty straightforward. You can usually just scan down the list of skill names and easily spot which one best fits the action the character is attempting. There are, however, a couple of curveballs that a game can throw at you here.

- If there's more than one skill that seems as if it would work, just allow either skill to work. ("Give me an Acrobatics or Athletics check.") Players may also propose an alternative check, and you can usually just default to yes and let them use their preferred skill. ("Can I make a History check to identify the ruined fane instead of Religion?")
- If you don't see a skill that seems appropriate, check the list of tools to see if the character should be making a tool check instead (e.g., using thieves' tools to pick a lock or jeweler's tools to identify a rare gemstone).
- If there's neither a skill nor tool for the check at hand, default to the most appropriate ability check.

If you use the variant rule in D&D for combining skills with different ability scores—which I recommend, because it can give you a lot more flexibility in making rulings—you'll also need to identify which ability score should be used with the skill. For example, you might use Intelligence (Investigation) checks to search a room and Charisma (Investigation) checks to canvass a neighborhood, or use

Wisdom (Animal Handling) to calm or train your triceratops and Dexterity (Animal Handling) when attempting a difficult maneuver while riding the triceratops.

Once you've identified the skill (or tool or ability score), the next step is setting the difficulty of the check. In D&D, there are a couple ways of doing this:

◎ Look at the list of Difficulty Classes on the next page and choose the one whose description best matches your understanding of how hard the action would be. (Is it easy? Hard? Very hard?)

◎ Ask yourself what level of skill someone would need in order to accomplish this task routinely and assign that as the difficulty. (Is this something an apprentice could do more or less at will? A professional? A grand master?)

D&D ABILITY SCORES
◎ Strength
◎ Dexterity
◎ Constitution
◎ Intelligence
◎ Wisdom
◎ Charisma

D&D SKILLS
◎ Acrobatics
◎ Animal Handling
◎ Arcana
◎ Athletics
◎ Deception
◎ History
◎ Insight
◎ Intimidation
◎ Investigation
◎ Medicine
◎ Nature
◎ Perception
◎ Performance
◎ Persuasion
◎ Religion
◎ Sleight of Hand
◎ Stealth
◎ Survival

D&D COMMON ADVENTURING TOOLS
◎ Alchemist's Supplies
◎ Disguise Kit
◎ Forgery Kit
◎ Gaming Set
◎ Herbalism Kit
◎ Jeweler's Tools
◎ Musical Instrument
◎ Navigator's Tools
◎ Thieves' Tools
◎ Tinker's Tools
◎ Vehicle

DIFFICULTY CLASS (DC)	TASK	LEVEL OF TRAINING
5	Trivial	Untrained
8	Very Easy	Apprentice
10	Easy	Professional
15	Challenging	Master
20	Hard	Grand Master
25	Very Hard	Mythic Master
30	Nearly Impossible	Legendary Master

A third option that can work well in other RPGs is to start with a "default" difficulty and then adjust it up or down by considering factors that would logically modify that difficulty.

In D&D, for example, you might start with DC 12 as your default difficulty and, as a rule of thumb, adjust it up or down by two points for every relevant factor. For example, if the PCs were making a Wisdom (Perception) check to see if they spotted an elephant stampede in the distance, you might drop the difficulty by two (because a herd of elephants is quite large and hard to miss) and then another two (because the stampede is also making a lot of noise), resulting in a DC 8 check. If the check was being made in the middle of a thunderstorm, however, you might bump the difficulty back up by a couple of points to DC 10.

This method can get a little muddled in D&D, however, because some of these factors (like the thunderstorm) would be considered situational modifiers and would normally be handled using the advantage/disadvantage system. For now, if you want to keep things simple, just use the Difficulty Class table above to make quick rulings.

NARRATING OUTCOME

To briefly review, after a player has announced their intention to take an action, you'll make a ruling on how the action will be resolved by either:

- defaulting to yes,
- saying yes, but . . . ,

- saying no (and trying to provide the no, but . . .), or
- making a check.

If you choose to make a check, then you

- identify the skill,
- determine the difficulty, and
- roll the dice.

Now, whether you default to yes or make a check, what you'll be left with is the outcome of that action: You know what happened, and you get to describe that to the players! What do they see on the other side of the chasm? What do they learn about parasite demons? If they killed the orc with their attack, what does that look like? Did they skewer the orc? Chop off their head? Knock them into the chasm?

The truth is that narrating outcome is as much art as science. There is no "right" answer as to how the orc died or how you describe this to your players. That's something that you get to create, and the truly great thing is that nobody else will (or can!) create it exactly the way that you do. That's what's so exciting about playing and mastering a roleplaying game.

With that being said, there are two key questions that you need to answer when describing an outcome.

If the result is a **success**, the questions are:

- How does the intention succeed?
- Are there any complications (i.e., unintended side effects)? (There don't need to be and, perhaps, often won't be.)

If the result is a **failure**, the questions are:

- How does the action fail?
- What are the consequences for failure? (There should be consequences, as they are what make failure meaningful.)

We'll explore more advanced techniques for framing and describing outcomes later, but for now I can offer a few quick tips to get you started.

OUTCOME FACTORS

- ⬡ Skill
- ⬡ Knowledge
- ⬡ Power
- ⬡ Finesse
- ⬡ Environment
- ⬡ Time
- ⬡ Luck
- ⬡ The Target
- ⬡ Bystanders
- ⬡ Tools

First, keep it short. Rich, beautiful descriptions are great, but you'll rarely go wrong by throwing the ball back to your players as quickly as you can. Remember that the outcome of the action—whether success or failure—has created a new situation for the players to respond to, and they're likely eager to do so!

Second, you probably already know what the description is! If the character succeeded, they did whatever it was the player said they were trying to do. You can just repeat that back to them: "You leap over the chasm and land on the other side" or "You stab the orc."

On the other hand, if the character failed, then there was a reason you thought failure would be meaningful. (If there wasn't, you would have just defaulted to yes, right?) Was it because they might fall into the chasm? Or get caught by a guard patrol while picking the lock? Whatever it was, you can just tell the player that it happened.

Finally, it can be useful to think in terms of *why* the attempt failed or succeeded. In the sidebar above, you can see a list of factors that can affect the outcome of an action. If you're struggling to come up with a description, just pick one and explain how it caused the outcome.

The character's own skill is often an easy default. "You rolled well" or "You rolled poorly" often gets translated, for whatever reason, to

"Your character did well" or "Your character screwed up." But it can be useful to remember that external factors can play a key role in success or failure. This can be particularly useful when describing failure, because it doesn't belittle the PCs' competency: Your blade strikes the orc right in the chest, but it's turned aside by the orc's breastplate. You know which book you need, but it's been checked out. You cleared the chasm just fine, but the ledge crumbles under your feet as you land.

THE DUNGEON MASTER'S SECRET WEAPON

Now that you've wrapped your head around making a ruling, you're ready for the big secret: Being a dungeon master is easy. It's much easier than being a player.

This might seem absurd right now. Easier? How is that possible? You have an *entire world* to run. The players can ask you almost anything and you always need to have an answer ready to go. What if you don't know what should happen next? Everyone else is depending on you! The whole thing will fall apart!

But it's easy because you have a secret weapon: "Yes, that happens. Now what do you do?"

As the DM, it can feel as if you're the one who's always being put on the spot. That at any time the players can force you to be creative on demand. In reality, though, the exact opposite is true because you control the *entire world*.

When a player says they want to do something, you may have an immediate creative response to it: some interesting twist or obstacle or bit of flavor that leaps into your mind and would enhance and build on what they said. If so, great! Do that.

But if not, then all you need to say is, "Yes, that happens. Now what do you do?"

It's a convenient bit of judo, and it means that the DM is never truly put on the spot, because at any time they can simply flip the player's action back and put the player on the spot. It is, in fact, the *players*, not the DM, who are ultimately responsible for driving the game forward.

Ideally, of course, you'll want to dress up, "Yes, that happens," and make it pretty. So rather than this . . .

PLAYER: I want to jump over the chasm.
DM: Yes, that happens. Now what do you do?

You'd say something like this . . .

PLAYER: I want to jump over the chasm.
DM: You take a running start and leap, easily clearing the gap and landing on the cobblestones on the far side. Now what do you do?

As you're dressing up your default to yes, you may find these two corollaries to your secret weapon useful:

- "How are you doing that?" and
- "What are you trying to do?"

If you can't figure out how the yes happens, it's usually because the players haven't given you enough information about what they're doing. Don't be afraid to ask them.

PLAYER: I want to find out more information about parasite demons.
DM: How are you doing that?
PLAYER: Hmm . . . Maybe I could do some research at the local library?
DM: You can do that. What information are you looking for, exactly?
PLAYER: I'd love to know how we could detect them.
DM: Sure. You find a book of lore written by a scholar named Sagrathea. He reports that parasite demons can be revealed by splashing holy water on their host.

So no matter what happens as you work and play your way through the rest of this book, if you're ever feeling lost, adrift, or overwhelmed, just remember your secret weapon.

STEP 2: HOW TO RUN
+ A ROOM +

Now let's take a peek at the dungeon key. The key describes the dungeon, with each numbered entry in the key describing the associated room on the dungeon map. In a dungeon, therefore, the key provides the environment in which the PCs will take their actions, and provides the raw material you can use to describe the outcomes of those actions.

Let's start by taking a look at a sample dungeon room key:

AREA 15: CRYPTIC LIBRARY

The room is of crimson and dark wood beneath a vaulted ceiling. A set of tall double doors, matching the ones you entered through, faces you on the opposite side of the room. A large pentagonal mahogany table stands in the center of the chamber. There are five large bookcases stuffed full of tomes and scrolls along the paneled walls. Sunlight streams in through bay windows with a built-in bench. The windows are leaded stained glass depicting a subtle pattern of golden florets.

WISDOM (PERCEPTION)-DC 15
To spot the **cloaker** hiding among the shadows on the ceiling.

◉ **GM Note:** This cloaker (a flying, manta ray–like monster) belongs to the colony that can be found in Area 46: The Undercaverns.

INTELLIGENCE (HISTORY)-DC 12
To recognize that the golden florets are the crest of the Klaavian Dynasty of the 14th century, revealing that this was once a royal residence.

(continued)

CLOAKER: *If unnoticed, the cloaker on the ceiling will drop down and attack the first character entering the room. If noticed, it will emit its unnatural moan, affecting all creatures within 60 feet (DC 13 Wisdom saving throw or become frightened), before attacking.*

MAHOGANY TABLE

There are several dark stains on the surface of the table, and the legs are engraved with arcane runes. A DC 10 Wisdom (Medicine) check identifies the stains as blood. A DC 12 Intelligence (Arcana) check identifies the runes as being associated with rites of human sacrifice.

BOOKCASES

The books and other documents here are all of an occult nature. There is a focus on Natharran mythology, particularly an enigmatic figure known as Basp-Attu. A DC 15 Intelligence (Arcana) check identifies Basp-Attu as a dual-bodied demon said to have been born from the mixed ichor of two dead gods during the War of Falling Stars.

WINDOWS

The bay windows look out onto a sun-dappled orchard. A DC 12 Wisdom (Perception) check notices that the apples on the trees are bright blue rather than red.

THE ANATOMY OF A ROOM

Looking at our key for the Cryptic Library, we can see that it's broken down into four parts.

First, the room has a number and a name. The name is useful when you're running the adventure because it will, at a glance, remind you of the room's purpose and content.

Second, there is **boxed text**. This provides an initial description of the room. It can be either read verbatim to the players or summarized in your own words, but the key concept—if you'll pardon the pun—is that it provides the information that anyone walking into the room would instantly perceive.

Immediately following the boxed text, you'll find any **reactive skill checks** for the room. These include information that, like the boxed text, would be instantly perceived by someone walking into the room, but only if they succeed on the check. In this case, a Wisdom (Perception) check should be made to see if the PCs spot the hidden monster. There's also an Intelligence (History) check, because while anyone can notice the golden florets decorating the window, only someone with specialized knowledge will recognize their significance.

The rest of the key is made up of **room elements**, each of which is described in detail.

So what exactly is a room element? Well, it can be almost anything or anyone. Basically, anything interesting in the room that is either hidden or simply has additional details that would not be immediately apparent to someone walking into the room should be described as a room element. If, or when, the PCs investigate that particular element, they can discover these additional details or hidden secrets.

(Other elements, like the cloaker in the Cryptic Library, might decide to investigate the PCs first.)

This ultimately brings us back to the core loop of the dungeon experience: When the PCs enter a room, you use the boxed text to tell them what can be seen at a glance. This provides the players, either directly or indirectly, with a list of the notable things in the room—bookcases, a mahogany table, bay windows. This list may be immediately supplemented by reactive skill checks, after which the players can declare actions to investigate or interact with the various elements in the room.

Their exploration of the room might include additional skill checks to find, access, identify, or otherwise gain treasure or information. If you've added creatures or other characters to the room, then combat or roleplaying (or both) is likely to spontaneously erupt.

One thing to keep in mind through all of this is that the room key does not describe the experience of the room. It merely gives you the raw material. It is by *using* that raw material to actively play in response to the actions of the PCs that the unique experience of the room will emerge during actual play.

When the PCs have finished investigating the room, they can then choose an **exit**—which may, of course, be the same way they came in—and make their way to a new room, at which point the cycle can begin anew.

GM NOTES

Because the goal of a written scenario is for it to be run for players, it's generally good practice to keep the dungeon key focused on what the PCs can discover and interact with. In some cases, however, there will be clarifying details or background information that may be useful for the GM running the scenario—e.g., what the strange footprints the PCs have discovered belong to—but do not have a clear mechanism, at least for the moment, by which the PCs can discover them.

I've found it useful to clearly separate this information from the rest of the key using the "GM Notes" tag. They are best kept brief. If, as you start designing your own dungeons, you find your key becoming overwhelmed by lengthy background information, see if there's a way you can reframe that material so that the PCs can discover it. After all, if the players can never learn something, does it really exist?

✦ HOMEWORK ✦

YOUR FIRST DUNGEON

So running a basic dungeon can be summed up as follows:

- ◈ Describing a room
- ◈ Making reactive skill checks, if any
- ◈ Responding to PC actions by making rulings
- ◈ Repeating until the PCs leave the room
- ◈ Describing the next room

And so forth.

In other words, running rooms and making rulings.

You now know how to do those things, which means you're ready to run your first adventure. (I told you it would happen fast!) On pages 46–64, you'll find Mephits & Magmin, a dungeon adventure I've designed specifically for you.

You'll want to start by reading the full adventure. With a clearly presented dungeon adventure like this, you *could* run it blind by reading each room key when the PCs enter the room for the first time, but I wouldn't recommend it. (And you can't necessarily rely on most published adventures to be clearly presented like this.) You'll have a much better experience if you're familiar with the adventure and are just using the text as a reference or reminder during play. It will let you stay more focused on your players and their experience, giving you the freedom to actively play with them at the table.

In fact, if you're feeling nervous, read the adventure again a couple hours before the game starts. It's the length of a short story, so it shouldn't take too long. But you definitely don't need to memorize the adventure! After all, we write things down so that we don't have to remember them.

WHO DO I PLAY WITH?

Like any other game, the easiest answer to that is "your friends."
Just ask a few of them if they'd like to play a game with you.
You can also check out Finding Players in the Extra Credit
section on page 435.

NAVIGATING THE MAP

The dungeon map for Mephits & Magmin can be found on page 47. Take a look at it now.

Dungeon maps are often drawn on **graph paper**, with each square representing a certain distance. This makes it easy to simply count out distance when that sort of thing matters (during combat, for example, or while leaping over a chasm). The **scale** on this map indicates that 1 square = 5 feet.

Each room in the dungeon, as we've discussed, is labeled with a number that will let you easily identify the entry describing that room in the dungeon key. Most of the rooms in Mephits & Magmin are connected by tunnels. You can use the information in Dungeon Features, page 48, and Corridor Themes, page 49, to describe these tunnels to your players as the PCs move along them. It's generally best to keep this description simple: Indicate the direction of the tunnel, use one or two details to characterize it, and mention how long the tunnel is.

As the PCs approach the entrance to a room, describe it to the players (e.g., "Up ahead you can see the tunnel opening up into a larger cavern" or "There's a door on the left side of the hallway"). This will give the players an opportunity to describe how they're approaching the room, whether they're being stealthy or charging in with a lusty battle cry.

In addition to the walls and halls and rooms, you'll also notice some specific **map symbols** that are used to indicate specific features of the dungeon. We'll discuss these symbols and how you can use them to create your own dungeon maps later (see page 100), but for Mephits & Magmin there are four symbols you'll want to know:

◎ 🔳 indicates the presence of an open pit in the floor. This
adventure includes two open pits, both of which are located in
Area 2 of the dungeon. The key for Area 2 describes how these
specific open pits work.

◎ ━⊂━ indicates a passageway that is concealed or otherwise
not immediately obvious to the PCs. You'll find one in Area 5,
and the key describes how it can be found.

◎ ↘ indicates a change in elevation. You'll see these along various
corridors, indicating that those floors are sloping down in
the direction of the arrow. So, for example, Area 10 is deeper
underground than Areas 8 and 9.

◎ † is a generic marker used to indicate the position of a point of
interest. In Area 2 of the dungeon, for example, it
indicates the specific location of a switch that controls the
release of steaming hot volcanic gas into the open pits.

I recommend making a copy of this map and laying it on the
table in front of you while you're running the adventure. It'll help
you stay oriented and keep track of where the PCs are, and the fact
that you won't need to keep flipping back and forth between the map
and the room descriptions will, in my experience, make running the
adventure infinitely easier. With the map lying flat, you can even use a
small token or coin to keep track of the group's position.

ENDING THE ADVENTURE

Mephits & Magmin reaches its climax when the PCs defeat (or
otherwise deal with) Asuvius, the magmin uraniac in charge of the
sinister activities happening deep within Firebelch Cavern. After you've
finished playing through a conclusion like this—in this or any other
adventure—there'll be a few things you'll want to do to wrap things up.

First, the **epilogue**. Give the players some space to tie off any loose
ends they're still interested in. In a dungeon scenario like this, that will
usually include finishing their exploration of the room where the final
fight took place. It might also include checking out any rooms they
skipped or missed earlier.

That's all great. For this particular scenario, if there are any magmin or mephits remaining after the climax (because the PCs haven't

encountered them yet), I recommend having them flee the caverns and disappear into the night. (The other option would be running additional fights after the climax that will probably just feel pointless and drag the session out for no reason.)

Beyond the purely practical, this period of epilogue can also feature some final roleplaying moments as the PCs interact with each other and the players reflect on what they've accomplished. I recommend encouraging that if you can. (In other scenarios, for example, there might be a convenient NPC who could actually prompt a conversation.)

You might also discover that a time-skip can be an effective part of the epilogue. After the PCs have wrapped things up in Mephits & Magmin, for example, you might cut to them tracking down Elsie Longfoot (see page 48) and have her ask them to describe their adventures as a way of reinforcing what they've experienced and providing a final act of closure.

Or maybe not. This is more art than science. You'll need to play this by ear a bit, and what's right for your adventure will depend on your players, their characters, and what happened at the table. (For example, maybe the PCs all hated Elsie, so that would be a sour note to end things on. Or maybe one of the PCs has fallen madly in love with her, and the epilogue is the two of them going on a date.) If in doubt, you can always ask the players if there are any loose ends or miscellaneous business they want to take care of.

After, and sometimes during, the epilogue, there are a couple bits of key bookkeeping that you'll want to make sure get taken care of.

The PCs will need to **split the treasure**. They'll usually do this themselves (and use any number of bizarre schemes for doing it), but if your players are also new to the game you may need to remind them.

While they're figuring out the treasure, you should take a moment to **calculate experience points**. The default method in D&D is to total the experience points (XP) for each monster defeated and then divide that total evenly between the PCs. For quick reference, here are the XP values for the monsters the PCs may find in Mephits & Magmin:

- 🎲 Mud Mephit—50 XP
- 🎲 Smoke Mephit—50 XP
- 🎲 Steam Mephit—50 XP
- 🎲 Magmin—100 XP
- 🎲 Magma Mephit—100 XP
- 🎲 Animated Armor—200 XP

As an alternative, you can use a milestone award and just tell the players that they advance to second level as the adventure comes to a conclusion.

With all of the rewards taken care of, take care of any other miscellaneous bookkeeping that needs to be sorted. You probably won't have anything like that after running Mephits & Magmin, but if everybody had a good time, you should take a moment to **schedule your next session**.

Don't worry, we'll make sure you're ready for next time!

WHAT ABOUT COMBAT?

Something we haven't taken a close look at yet is what you should do when a fight breaks out. There are a couple reasons for that.

First, the rulebook for your RPG of choice probably describes a very specific procedure for running combat. (In the case of D&D, that's rolling initiative for every participant and then resolving their declared actions in initiative order.) When a fight starts, just follow that procedure. When the fight's done, the PCs will still be in the room and you can continue resolving actions until they decide to leave.

Second, although RPG combat is often highly structured, you're still just resolving actions. You may have a few specialized mechanics like attack and damage rolls, but the same general principles of making a ruling apply. Just use them and you'll be fine!

If combat in your RPG of choice is not highly structured with a specific procedure, then it most likely defaults back to normal action resolution, and the normal guidelines for making rulings will only apply more strongly.

If you want to dive deeper here, check out the Running Combat extra credit on page 486.

⚔ DUNGEON ADVENTURE ⚔
MEPHITS & MAGMIN

BACKGROUND

Firebelch Cavern is an underground system of pyroducts. Also known as lava tubes, these caves are formed when the skin of a lava flow cools and hardens, but the liquid rock within continues to flow through, leaving behind a hollow tube. (Or, more commonly, leaving behind an overlapping network of such tubes built up over the course of multiple and divergent flows.)

The cave is fairly remote from local settlements, but is not unknown to people in the region. Until recently, however, there has been little reason to remark upon it. That changed a little over a month ago when a small band of **magmin** moved in.

Magmin are human-like elementals native to the Plane of Fire. Their cracked and blackened skin, viewed through the flames which continually burn around their bodies, has the appearance of half-cooled lava.

This particular group is led by a **magmin uraniac** named Asuvius. Otherwise identical to their magmin kin, a uraniac's head is studded with chunks of strange silver-white rocks surrounded by an unearthly blue glow. The presence of these uncanny metallic shards cause the uraniac's head to bulge, often reaching a size three or four times larger than normal. This is often accompanied by a super-magmin intelligence (granting a typical uraniac an Intelligence score of 16).

Asuvius has come to Firebelch Cavern in order to take advantage of several key resources—notably geothermal energy, a burnt heartwood tree (Area 8), and unique crystalline growths (Areas 5 and 10)—to conduct technomantic and alchemical experiments. His first goal was the creation of mephits—small but potent elemental spirits who can serve at Asuvius's whims.

In this, Asuvius has already succeeded, and a number of mephits can be found throughout the cave complex, guarding it against intruders who would interrupt Asuvius's efforts to further perfect his techniques.

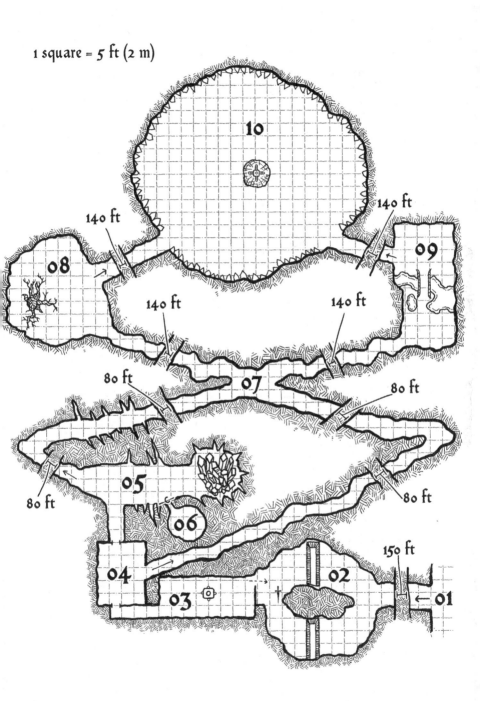

1 square = 5 ft (2 m)

·—✦— **IMPERFECT MEPHITS:** *Due to the mephits in Firebelch Cavern being created instead of summoned, they do NOT have their normal Death Burst effects.*

SCENARIO HOOK

Local hunters and trappers have seen strange lights emanating from Firebelch Cavern. The village provost has asked the PCs to investigate the cave and make sure the lights do not pose a danger. One of the trappers, a halfling named Elsie Longfoot, guides the PCs within sight of the cave entrance but will go no further.

As the DM, you might choose to play through these events. (You could, for example, describe the PCs sharing a drink in a tavern when the village provost sends a messenger asking to speak with them.) But, particularly if this is your first adventure, it's just fine to start things in medias res: Briefly explain to the players how they got to Firebelch Cavern, exactly as described above, and then go to Area 1, below, and describe what they see.

OTHER SCENARIO HOOKS

I'm only offering one scenario hook for Mephits & Magmin here. If you were running this adventure as part of an ongoing game and wanted to offer multiple scenario hooks, or if you just don't like this scenario hook, check out Scenario Hooks on page 498 for a deep dive into how you can create and customize your own scenario hooks.

DUNGEON FEATURES

- ⬡ **Illumination:** None.
- ⬡ **Ceiling Height (Tunnels):** Varies between 4 feet and 11 feet (1d8 + 3 ft.). This can be the result of either the ceiling shifting or the floor rising unevenly. This can become cramped enough to impose disadvantage or difficult terrain on PCs at the DM's discretion.

◈ **Ceiling Height (Finished Area):** Unless otherwise indicated, 6 feet. Designed for magmin (with an average height of 4 ft.) and low enough that tall characters will need to stoop slightly.

◈ **Walls:** Gray or black volcanic rock (AC 17, climb DC 12). Can be either rough or smooth to the touch, and in some places razor-sharp. The walls are often fissured and seamed.

CORRIDOR THEMES

The passages in Firebelch Cavern are lava tubes. They are roughly circular, with walls, floor, and ceiling formed from gray or black volcanic rock. They are usually sloped, although not steeply so.

Features you might use to describe specific sections of the tube include the following:

◈ **Varied Height**, see Dungeon Features on the previous page.

◈ **Difficult Terrain**, as a result of the uneven floor.

◈ **Tree Roots**, growing through the ceiling of the tube in the areas near the surface of the dungeon.

◈ **Lavacicles**, which are stalactites and stalagmites formed from cooling lava. They can include tubular formations (like hollow straws) and also shark tooth stalactites (which have a broad, tapering appearance like the tooth or fin of a shark). These can also be a reason for the total height of a tube to abruptly shrink.

◈ **Iridescence**, where the impurities of the volcanic rock gleam and glimmer with strange colors.

◈ **Fissures**, where the rock has fractured apart (due to cooling or later weathering).

You may find good results with combining two or three of these elements together for each tube, giving each one a unique (yet myriad) character.

AREA 1: CAVE ENTRANCE

You're near the bottom of a steeply sloped, rocky out-cropping in a heavily forested area. Above you a dark mass of stone bulges out of the slope. At its center, partly obscured by verdant green growth sagging from the top of the bulge, is a ragged-edged, black hole that punches back through the rock.

In front of the cave entrance, there's a slag of broken rock forming a kind of natural portico that extends out for perhaps 20 or 25 feet to the edge of the tree line. Three large mounds of wet mud have been heaped at various points on the slag.

WISDOM (PERCEPTION)-DC 15

To notice that one of the "mud heaps" seems to have a nervous twitch. A DC 19 check fully reveals that the three "heaps" are actually small elemental creatures, in which case a DC 14 Intelligence (Arcana or Nature) check identifies them as mud mephits.

> **MUD MEPHITS (4):** *The three mud heaps are* **mud mephits**. *A* **fourth "mud heap"** *is located 40 feet down the lava tube from the cave entrance. Ideally (for the mud mephits), the PCs will enter the tunnel without realizing what the mud heaps are. The mephits will then animate and attack, cutting off their escape.*

CAVE ENTRANCE

Anyone inspecting the cave can make a DC 12 Intelligence (Nature) check to identify this as a lava tube. Formed when the surface of a lava flow cools and hardens but the lava inside continues flowing forward, these caves can extend for dozens of miles. (Given the forest growth surrounding this cave, it is clear that whatever volcanism formed this cave happened long ago.)

AREA 2: FORK IN THE TUBE

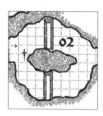

Ahead of you, the slope of the tunnel bottoms out and, a dozen or so feet farther on, it forks, with passages both left and right splitting away from you in concave curves. With the passage leveling out here, it seems some sort of gray gas or smoke has accumulated on the floor.

WISDOM (PERCEPTION)–DC 19

To notice the **smoke mephits**—one on either side of the fork between Area 1 and the open pits—hiding in the smoke. (If the smoke is somehow blown away, the mephits will need to make Stealth checks to remain hidden.)

> **MEPHITS–STEAM (1) & SMOKE (2):** *The smoke mephits are hiding in the smoke. The* **steam mephit** *is waiting at the switch, which activates the steam vents in the open pit. If the PCs reach the far side of a pit, the steam mephit will move to engage them.*

SMOKE

A DC 12 Intelligence (Nature) check will recognize the smoke as dangerous volcanic gas. Anyone inhaling the gas (e.g., by lying prone in it for a full round) must make a DC 12 Constitution saving throw or become poisoned. (The mephits are not affected by this.)

> **POISONED:** *A poisoned creature has disadvantage on attack rolls and ability checks.*

STEAM PITS

As indicated on the map, there are open pits located along both branches of the lava tube. A DC 13 Wisdom (Perception) check reveals the presence of the open pits beneath the smoke.

The pits are 10 feet deep, dealing 1d6 bludgeoning damage to anyone falling in.

The sides of the pits are seamed with deep fissures, through which volcanic gases leak. These have been rigged so that someone throwing a switch at the north end of the fork (indicated with †) will vent steaming hot volcanic gas into the pits. Anyone in a pit when this happens must succeed on a DC 14 Constitution saving throw or suffer 1d8 fire damage and the poisoned condition. (On a success, they take half damage and are not poisoned.)

It takes 1d4 rounds for the volcanic gases to build back up again, at which point the steam can be triggered again.

DO WE REALLY NEED TO FIGHT?

Your players might want to take the diplomatic approach. The encounter here has been designed to discourage that (since the mephits have been instructed to ambush anyone approaching), but whether here or later you can certainly give them a chance to talk things out. These mephits speak Ignan (the magmin tongue) rather than the usual elemental languages, which could be a clue that something unusual is happening here.

How far can diplomacy go? That's up to you, and it will largely depend on the agenda you choose to give Asuvius. Is he just an alien alchemist conducting experiments? Then peaceful negotiations are likely, and maybe the PCs can help him hatch some elemental seeds (see Area 8, page 59).

If you'd rather lean into the simplicity of combat, then Asuvius's true goal might be using his new elemental minions to assert dominion over the local communities. Hard to compromise with that.

AREA 3: PISTON ROOM

The lava tube empties out into a wide square chamber, 15 feet across and perhaps three dozen wide. On the far wall, off to your left, there is an open archway.

The stone here appears to have been carved back, but the walls are not perfectly finished. They have a sort of rough undulation to their surface, which gleams with an iridescent sheen.

In the center of the room there is a large contraption of bolted brass, festooned with a motley collection of pistons that churn endlessly with a hiss of steam. From the top of this contraption an 8-inch pipe runs up to the ceiling, then turns and runs through the wall.

INTELLIGENCE (INVESTIGATION)-DC 12

A close inspection of the floor may reveal that there are small, humanoid footprints that have been burned into the surface. They are difficult to make out against the dark stone and crisscross each other countless times, creating something of a hopeless, visually confusing muddle.

◉ **GM Note:** These footprints are made by the magmin. They are not found in the lava tubes, where the undisturbed volcanic rock is solid enough to not be disturbed by them.

WALLS

Close inspection of the walls will reveal that they were not carved but were instead somehow *melted* into their current configuration.

PISTON CONTRAPTION

The piston assembly is pumping volcanic gases out of the ground here, superheating them, and then passing them over a blue-white stone (embedded within a glass cylinder visible within the contraption), before pumping them, under high pressure, through the brass pipe that passes through the wall.

◎ **Intelligence (Alchemist's Supplies)-DC 12:** The gas is being alchemically infused with the essence of the blue-white stone. A DC 15 check identifies the blue-white stone as a unicorn's bezoar. (Bezoars are growths that can occur within the gastrointestinal tracts of various animals. Unicorn bezoars are particularly rare and said to be infused with life-giving properties.)

STEAM PIPE

The brass pipe is fitted with several valves. Breaking the pipe (AC 16, 10 HP) will cause steam to burst out, filling a 10-foot-square area. Fiddling with the valves will similarly cause steam to vent 1d4-1 rounds later (on a result of 0, it happens immediately). In either case, characters in the area suffer 4d6 fire damage (DC 16 Dexterity saving throw for half damage).

◎ **GM Note:** The steam pipe passes through Areas 5, 7, and 10.

SHORT REST

If your players are also new to D&D, you might want to remind them that this would be a good time to take a short rest (to regain their hit points). It will be very difficult for them to succeed in the adventure if they don't recuperate.

AREA 4: ANTECHAMBER

Two low archways—low enough that the tallest among you need to stoop to pass through—face each other on opposite sides of this long chamber that appears to have been carved out of the stone. Along one of the other walls, a gaping hole leads to a tunnel that slants rapidly down and out of sight.

INTELLIGENCE (INVESTIGATION)-DC 12

A close inspection of the floor may reveal that there are small, humanoid footprints that have been burned into the surface. They are difficult to make out against the dark stone and crisscross each other countless times, but they clearly pass through all three entrances to this chamber.

> **GM Note:** These footprints are made by the magmin. They are not found in the lava tubes, where the undisturbed volcanic rock is solid enough to not be disturbed by them.

WALLS

Close inspection of the walls will reveal that they were not carved but were instead somehow *melted* into their current configuration.

AREA 5: VOLCANIC CRYSTALS

At one end of this long chamber, there is an archway in one corner and a large tunnel slanting down from the opposite corner.

The far end of the chamber from these passages is filled with a huge, crystalline growth. There must be hundreds of individual crystals in the mass, each glowing with a spectral greenish light that casts strange shadows down the fissured walls.

Crossing the room near the crystals is an 8-inch brass pipe that's been fastened to the ceiling.

INTELLIGENCE (INVESTIGATION)-DC 12 (FOOTPRINTS)

A close inspection of the floor may reveal that there are small humanoid footprints that have been **burned** into the surface. They are difficult to make out against the dark stone and crisscross each other countless times, but clearly they pass through the entrances to Area 4 and Area 8. (They do NOT pass into Area 6, which is unknown to the magmin.)

> ⊘ **GM Note:** These footprints are made by the magmin. They are not found in the lava tubes, where the undisturbed volcanic rock is solid enough to not be disturbed by them.

INTELLIGENCE (INVESTIGATION)-DC 15 (CONCEALED PASSAGE)

Although it is not immediately apparent, one of the fissures in the south wall is actually large enough to squeeze through, allowing characters to crawl through to Area 6 with a successful DC 12 Dexterity check. (This check is made with advantage if the character is not wearing armor.)

CRYSTALS

Any inspection of the crystalline mass reveals that a significant number of crystals have been removed. A DC 12 Intelligence (Nature) check indicates that these are volcanic crystals, while a DC 15 Intelligence (Alchemist's Supplies) check reveals these crystals have been adulterated with Stygian gas, granting them their strange illumination and also making them a valuable catalyst for various alchemical procedures.

If properly harvested, a process requiring 10 minutes per crystal and a successful DC 10 Intelligence (Alchemist's Supplies) check, the crystals with the strongest adulteration are worth 10 gold pieces (gp) each. There are 30 such crystals, each weighing roughly 5 pounds and averaging 1 foot in length, remaining.

◎ **GM Note:** The crystals harvested here are being used by Asuvius in Area 10.

WALLS

Close inspection of the walls will reveal that they were not carved, but were instead somehow *melted* into their current configuration.

STEAM PIPE

The brass pipe is fitted with several valves. Breaking the pipe (AC 16, 10 HP) will cause steam to burst out, filling a 10-foot-square area. Fiddling with the valves will similarly cause steam to vent 1d4-1 rounds later (on a result of 0, it happens immediately). In either case, characters in the area suffer 4d6 fire damage (DC 16 Dexterity saving throw for half damage).

◎ **GM Note:** The steam pipe starts in Area 3, passes through here, and continues through Areas 7 and 10.

AREA 6: LAVA NODULE

Scraping through the rough volcanic rock, you scramble into a large, spherical chamber about 15 feet across, as if you were standing inside a kind of rocky bubble, its walls studded with large gypsum crystals that thrust out chaotically in every direction.

GM Note: The magmin are not aware of this area, making it a safe place for the PCs to take a short rest.

AREA 7: CROSSROADS

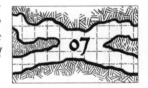

Up ahead the tunnel crosses another, forming an X-shaped intersection. An 8-inch brass pipe angles across the intersection at ceiling height, emerging from one side and passing into the next.

STEAM PIPE

The brass pipe is fitted with several valves. Breaking the pipe (AC 16, 10 HP) will cause steam to burst out, filling a 10-foot-square area. Fiddling with the valves will similarly cause steam to vent 1d4-1 rounds later (on a result of 0, it happens immediately). In either case, characters in the area suffer 4d6 fire damage (DC 16 Dexterity saving throw for half damage).

GM Note: The steam pipe comes from Areas 3 and 5, and continues to Area 10.

AREA 8: THE MEPHIT TREE

A large, globular chamber opens at the end of the tunnel. It's about 40 feet across and almost as high. The ceiling twinkles like starlight. A second tunnel, nearby, leads away from the chamber in another direction. Roughly oppo-site the tunnels, there is a skeletal tree, burnt black, its bark and branches a cracked char-coal. Large glowing pods sprout cyst-like from its dead, obsidian branches.

Two short humanoid figures stand near the tree. They are wreathed in flame, sending strange patterns of light and shadow dancing across the tree and cave walls. Their skin looks like molten lava. They are directing two of the small mud elementals, which are currently in the process of removing one of the glowing pods from the tree.

MAGMIN (2) & MUD MEPHITS (2)

The **magmin** are overseeing the harvesting of elemental seeds from the tree. If combat breaks out, the magmin will direct the **mud mephits** to attack while using their own action each round to use a special Superheat ability. Only when the mephits are destroyed, or if they are forced to engage, will the magmin attack themselves.

SUPERHEAT: *The magmin plunges their hand into a mud mephit within reach. This superheats the mud mephit, causing its body to boil and granting +1d4 fire damage to its fist attacks and mud breath.*

THE TREE

A DC 12 Intelligence (Nature) check will identify this as the remnant of an elven heartwood tree. A physical inspection of the tree combined with a DC 16 check will reveal that the tree was once home to a dryad ovule that's perished in the ancient flames of the lava that created these tunnels.

A DC 12 Intelligence (Investigation) check or any specific investigation of the glowing pods reveals that alchemical stents have been attached to the branches at the points where the pods seem to "sprout" from the tree (see below).

ELEMENTAL SEEDS

A DC 14 Intelligence (Arcana) check reveals that the glowing pods are infused with powerful elemental forces of earth and fire. These appear to be similar to the elemental forces found in mephits.

A DC 16 Intelligence (Alchemist's Supplies) check will indicate the alchemical stents are being used to draw a slow, steady trickle of elemental energy through a matrix of fey energy, which seems to be faintly manifest within the burnt wood of the tree. The elemental seeds are the physical manifestation of this "elemental sieving."

⬦ **GM Note:** These elemental seeds are harvested here and then taken to Area 10, where they hatch (or perhaps "sprout" would be a better term) into mephits.

CEILING

The ceiling twinkles because it's studded with rough chrysoberyls. If collected, the set of small gems has a total value of 150 gp, but this can be doubled with a DC 16 Dexterity (Jeweler's Tools) check to finish them.

CRANK UP THE HEAT
As the PCs head down the long tunnels to Area 10 from Areas 8 or 9, describe the air slowly growing hotter until the heat becomes stifling. (Engage all of the PCs' senses, not just their sight.)

AREA 9: LAVA CANAL

The tunnel widens into a long chamber about 20 feet across. It's lit with a red and garish light emanating from a canal of lava that crosses the middle of the chamber, 20 or 30 feet away. A metal bridge crosses the midpoint of the canal, narrowly accessible between two small pools of lava.

The floor of the chamber is broken basalt. Short pillars of geometric rock thrust up haphazardly at different heights. At one end of the chamber, a 10-foot-wide pillar of long-cooled lava stretches erratically from floor to ceiling.

FLOOR

The broken basalt floor makes this chamber **difficult terrain**.

⚔ DIFFICULT TERRAIN: *Each foot of movement in difficult terrain costs 1 extra foot. (Characters effectively move at half their normal speed.)*

LAVA POOLS/MAGMA MEPHITS (2)

Those approaching the canal will note two small pools of lava, just a couple of feet across, flanking the south side of the bridge. A DC 18 Wisdom (Perception) check reveals that these lava pools are, in fact, **magma mephits**. They'll wait for the PCs to begin crossing the bridge and then animate, preferably cutting the group in half and separating them from each other.

BRIDGE

The metal is superheated by the proximity of the lava canal. Those touching it with their bare skin must make a DC 12 Constitution saving throw or suffer 1d2 fire damage.

AREA 10: ELEMENTAL GEODE

You're looking into the interior of a giant, glittering geode, nearly 100 feet across. Pulses of light pass through the crystals of the geode in waves; you can pick out two or three distinct waves, each circling around the geode.

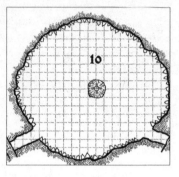

A brass pipe punches through the skein of the geode and crosses to the far side, where it's connected to a technomantic apparatus that appears to be partially extruded from the geode's crystals. A huge clockwork, humanoid figure has been strapped into this apparatus.

In the center of the geode is an inflationary rift—a dome of black, volcanic rock that has pushed up through the geode. A red-hot glow oozes from a cracked rift that crosses the top of this dome. Above this rift, more technomantic machinery has been built, with various pipes piercing down into the molten, steaming rock.

Atop this machinery is a squat, humanoid figure whose skin appears to be formed from red-hot lava. Bathed in flame, the figure's head is curiously bulbous—grotesquely distended to perhaps three or four times that of a human and studded with strange silver-white rocks surrounded by an unearthly blue glow.

There are two more of the lava-skinned humanoids—these without the bulbous heads. Above, circling around the top of the geode, are two imp-like creatures with bodies composed entirely from steam.

DIFFICULT TERRAIN: *The curved, crystalline "floor" of the geode makes the interior* **difficult terrain**.

CREATURES

◉ Asuvius, the magmin uraniac (use **magmin** stats, but with Intelligence 16 and proficiency in Alchemist's Supplies and Arcana)

- 2 **magmin**
- 2 **smoke mephits**
- Steampowered construct (use **animated armor** stats, see page 45)

ASUVIUS'S TECHNOMANTIC PERCH

From his perch, Asuvius will spend his first action initiating the activation sequence for the steampowered construct (see page 64). He will use his bonus action on that round, and subsequent rounds, locking in targets for the construct (i.e., the PCs), one per bonus action.

STEAMBLAST: *As an action taken by someone at the controls, the technomantic device emits a blast of steam in a 30-foot cone. Creatures within the cone must make a DC 10 Constitution saving throw, taking 2d6 fire damage on a failed save, or half as much on a successful one. Recharge 5-6.*

RECHARGE: The Steamblast has Recharge 5-6. This means that after it has been used the first time, you should roll 1d6 each round. If you roll a 5 or 6, Asuvius can use the Steamblast again.

Someone in the perch can take an action to attempt a DC 14 Intelligence (Arcana) check to figure out how the controls work. On a success, they can take an action to shut down the initiation sequence for the steampowered construct or use bonus actions to cancel or reassign targets (and set target priority).

- **Alchemical Nests:** On the back side of the perch (where they can't be seen from the entrances), there are three alchemical nests. Each nest is an oval-shaped concavity filled with alchemical fluids. In one of them is nestled an elemental seed.

- **Elemental Seed:** A DC 14 Intelligence (Arcana) check reveals that the glowing pod is infused with powerful elemental forces of earth and fire. These appear to be similar to the elemental forces found in mephits.

⬡ **GM Note:** These nests are used by Asuvius to bring the elemental seeds to "term," at which point they split open and hatch a mephit. By controlling the alchemical mixture, Asuvius can control what type of mephit emerges.

STEAMPOWERED CONSTRUCT

After someone on the technomantic perch begins the activation sequence, it takes five rounds for the steampowered construct to come online. Once online, it will attack whatever targets have been indicated by the controls on the perch.

FORESHADOW THE CONSTRUCT

Don't wait until the steampowered construct has fully activated to roll initiative for it. Each round, on its initiative count, describe how it's "booting up"—the ratcheting sound of its gears spinning; its eyes begin to glow; it emits little bursts of steam from its joints.

STEAM PIPE

The brass pipe crossing the geode is fitted with several valves. Breaking the pipe (AC 16, 10 HP) will cause steam to burst out, filling a 10-foot-square area. Fiddling with the valves will similarly cause steam to vent 1d4-1 rounds later (on a result of 0, it happens immediately). In either case, characters in the area suffer 4d6 fire damage (DC 16 Dexterity saving throw for half damage).

⬡ **GM Note:** The steam pipe originates in Area 3, passing through Areas 5 and 7 before arriving here.

TREASURE

Asuvius is carrying a small pouch containing 157 silver pieces (sp), 34 gold pieces, and 200 gps' worth of helenite gem-coins (a green gemstone currency used by magmin, created by baking volcanic dust and ash in a furnace with glass).

STEP 3: HOW TO RUN
⟶ A DUNGEON ⟵

You're a dungeon master now!

Or, if you're reading ahead, you will be soon.

In running your first adventure, you've used a very simple structure of rulings and rooms. Simple, but powerful. There's a lot you can do with just rulings and rooms. I've run entire campaigns using nothing but rulings and rooms.

So far we've focused on the classic dungeon scenario: the underground labyrinth filled with traps and treasure. But the basic structure of a dungeon scenario, also known as a **dungeon crawl**, can be used to run a lot of different adventures, such as

- a haunted mansion,
- a smuggler's warehouse,
- a half-sunken shipwreck,

- a transdimensional maze,
- the skull of a dead god, or
- a zombie-ravaged inn.

What will your next adventure be? That's entirely up to you! Although there are other published scenarios you could purchase and run for your players, RPGs are designed for you to create your own. It's fun to do this, and it gives you the opportunity to customize your adventures to the stuff that your players enjoy and want to do. You can create literally anything you can imagine. That's the whole point!

CAMPAIGNS

The heroes have gone on an adventure. With that adventure done, what happens next? Another adventure! The sequence or collection of adventures the PCs play through is referred to as a campaign. Kind of like how a TV series is made up of many episodes, an RPG campaign is made up of many scenarios.

Before we get down to creating your first dungeon, though, we're going to start expanding the simple rulings-and-rooms structure by adding a **dungeon procedure**. Over the next several chapters, we'll be looking at a lot of new options and fun twists for how dungeons can be built and played. These new options, of course, will add complexity. The more complexity you add, the easier it will be to become confused, overwhelmed, or simply lose track of stuff. A procedure will help you manage the complexity by organizing it into a semi-formal sequence.

When you were running your first adventure, for example, you were actually following a very simple procedure:

1. Track the movement of the PCs.

2. When they enter a room, describe it to them.

When they were done doing stuff in the room, they'd pick an exit and you'd go back to your procedure. It's just a different way of thinking about rooms and rulings, right?

To take the next step, though, you'll want to start using a **dungeon turn**.

THE DUNGEON TURN

A dungeon turn is kind of like a turn in any other game: Everyone gets a chance to do something, you resolve the outcome while keeping an eye on anything else that needs to be tracked, and then you start a new turn and do it again.

During each dungeon turn, you'll do the following:

1. Mark **ticks** (to track time, resources, etc.).

2. Make an **encounter check**.

3. Declare actions.

4. Make **Perception-type checks** as necessary.

5. Resolve actions, including tracking movement on the map.

A dungeon turn lasts roughly 10 minutes in the game world, but this is best understood as a fairly amorphous figure. For example, what if the party moved 150 feet during the last dungeon turn, but they moved only 50 feet this turn before reaching a point of interest where they wanted to do something else (and, therefore, started a new turn)? Don't sweat it. One of the reasons we use dungeon turns, in fact, is to average this sort of stuff out into a "good enough" approximation.

On a similar note, you may sometimes find it useful to really formalize this procedure, explaining to the players exactly how the dungeon turns work and systematically collecting their action declarations each turn. For example, let's say you ask your characters to mark one tick for every turn they use their lit torches. That might look like this during actual play:

JASON (DM): Okay, it's a new turn. Tick your torches.

SETH (RANTHIR): My torch has burned out.

JASON (DM): What is everyone doing?

SETH (RANTHIR): Well, I'm lighting a new torch.

JASON (DM): That's an incidental action. What's your dungeon action?

SETH (RANTHIR): I'm going to cast *detect magic* and Search the statue.

DAVE (AGNARR): I'll stay by the door we came in and be the Lookout.

SARAH (TEE): I'll pick the lock on the opposite door.

And so forth.

This can work fine, and there are likely many situations in which it might be the best way to handle things. (Particularly if you're just getting started and trying to get a grip on how dungeon turns work.) But it can also lead to very stilted forms of play:

JASON (DM): Okay, you've gone another 100 feet down the passage. That ends this turn. Now what?

PREETI (ELESTRA): We continue walking down the corridor.

JASON (DM): Okay, you've gone another 100 feet. New turn. Now what?

This sort of thing can make the dungeon turn more of a liability than a useful tool. Personally, I find the dungeon turn most useful as a tool that the DM can privately use to organize and keep track of things without the players being aware of it. I refer to these as **player-unknown structures**: They leave the players free to interact directly and naturally with the game world, while giving the DM the tools they need behind the screen to keep that world running smoothly.

When you're using a dungeon turn as a player-unknown structure, you're more likely to end up with play that looks like this:

JASON (DM): As you enter the room, Ranthir's torch starts to sputter. Looks like it's about to go out.

SETH (RANTHIR): I'll pull out a new one.

Jason makes a note about the new torch. He knows that lighting the torch is an incidental action (see page 74), so Ranthir is still free to do something more substantial during this dungeon turn.

JASON (DM): Great. Now what?

SETH (RANTHIR): I'm going to cast *detect magic* and see if there's anything weird about that statue.

JASON (DM): What's everyone else doing while Ranthir is doing that?

DAVE (AGNARR): I'll stay by the door and keep an eye out for any trouble.

SARAH (TEE): I'll pick the lock on the opposite door.

The question, "What's everyone else doing while so-and-so does that?" is a very powerful tool. It prompts an action declaration, but also encourages everyone to get involved instead of just watching from the sidelines. Dungeon turns cover big chunks of time, so there's plenty of room for everyone to actively engage with the situation.

TRACKING ALL THAT ACTION

Keeping track of what four or five different players have said they're doing can be tricky. One option is to jot down a quick note, then just work through the list you've made resolving in whatever order makes the most sense.

Alternatively, you don't have to collect the full list. You can resolve as you go. For example, Jason could tell Ranthir what he sees with his detect magic *spell and then ask everyone else what they're doing. The important thing is to make sure everyone gets a turn! It can be surprisingly easy to just keep resolving stuff with Ranthir, for example, and forget that the other PCs have all frozen in place because you've forgotten about them.*

DUNGEON RUNNING SHEET

On page 71 you'll find the Dungeon Running Sheet. You can make copies of this sheet and use it for your own dungeon adventures, but it's also easy to duplicate its functionality using a sheet of scratch paper.

Party Name provides a convenient label for the sheet. This might be the "Red Elks" or the "Cabal of Black Night" or just the "Thursday Night Group."

Turn Tracker gives multiple slots for tracking effect durations. Its use is described in more detail under "Ticks," on page 72.

Marching Order provides a template for tracking the current or standard positioning of the PC. Each square is a 5-foot square on the map, allowing you to easily list relative positions that can be directly transferred onto a battlemap. The template provides space for the PCs to travel three across, but can easily be used for single-file lines or 10-foot-wide corridors (where the PCs can only walk two abreast).

You should ask your players what their marching order will be—i.e., who'll be in front, who'll be in the middle, who'll be at the back, etc.—at the beginning of the session and write it down here. Whenever the PCs are moving through the dungeon, you can simply assume that this will be their relative positioning and use it to adjudicate outcomes accordingly (who triggers traps, who's in a position to spot the ambush, and so forth). You may find that you and your players start referring to a "standard marching order," diverging from it only when special circumstances make it necessary. This saves a lot of time and busywork at the table and lets you focus on more interesting stuff in the game world.

If the PCs are journeying into a dark environment (which is hardly unheard of when it comes to dungeons), it can also be a good idea to determine which PCs are carrying **light sources** and indicate these on the marching order. I recommend a simple symbol, such as ☆, and you might also find it useful to indicate the range of the light for easy reference. So a torch, for example, would be ☆ 20/40 (meaning bright light in a 20-foot radius and dim light out to 40 feet).

Here's an example of what a completed marching order looks like:

Front

		Tee	
Agnarr ☆			
Ranthir	Nasira		
Elestra	Tor		

Back

The **Movement** section of the running sheet includes three slots. **Party Speed** is almost always equal to the speed of whichever party member is the slowest. The group's **Dungeon Pace** is equal to the party's speed x 5 (see the Movement dungeon action, page 77, for details). Finally, **Fast Pace** is equal to the party's speed x 100.

DUNGEON RUNNING SHEET

Party Name	Party Speed	Dungeon Pace	Fast Pace

TURN TRACKER

EFFECT	DURATION	TRACKERS		
		☐☐☐☐☐☐ ☐☐☐☐☐☐	☐☐☐☐☐☐ ☐☐☐☐☐☐	☐☐☐☐☐ ☐☐☐☐☐
		☐☐☐☐☐☐ ☐☐☐☐☐☐	☐☐☐☐☐☐ ☐☐☐☐☐☐	☐☐☐☐☐ ☐☐☐☐☐
		☐☐☐☐☐☐ ☐☐☐☐☐☐	☐☐☐☐☐☐ ☐☐☐☐☐☐	☐☐☐☐☐☐ ☐☐☐☐☐☐
		☐☐☐☐☐☐ ☐☐☐☐☐☐	☐☐☐☐☐☐ ☐☐☐☐☐☐	☐☐☐☐☐☐ ☐☐☐☐☐☐
		☐☐☐☐☐☐ ☐☐☐☐☐☐	☐☐☐☐☐☐ ☐☐☐☐☐☐	☐☐☐☐☐☐ ☐☐☐☐☐☐
		☐☐☐☐☐☐ ☐☐☐☐☐☐	☐☐☐☐☐☐ ☐☐☐☐☐☐	☐☐☐☐☐☐ ☐☐☐☐☐☐
		☐☐☐☐☐☐ ☐☐☐☐☐☐	☐☐☐☐☐☐ ☐☐☐☐☐☐	☐☐☐☐☐☐ ☐☐☐☐☐☐

MARCHING ORDER

Front

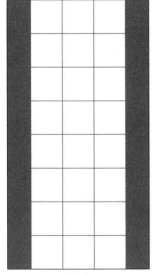

Back

DUNGEON TURNS

1. Mark ticks (to track time, resources, etc.).
2. Make an encounter check.
3. Declare actions.
4. Make Perception-type checks as necessary.
5. Resolve actions and track movement.

ENCOUNTER CHECK

1. Roll 1d8. 1 = Encounter.
2. If encounter, roll on encounter table.
3. Determine encounter distance. 2d6 x 10 feet.
4. Make a reaction check.
5. Determine surprise, if any.

REACTION TABLE

2D6	REACTION
2–3	Immediate Attack
4–5	Hostile
6–8	Cautious/ Threatening
9–10	Neutral
11–12	Amiable

DUNGEON ACTIONS

- Movement
- Combat
- Conversation
- Helping
- Lookout
- Overcome Obstacle
- Ritual Casting
- Search
- Other Actions

TICKS

Items and spells have **durations**. You'll want to track these durations so that you'll know when they come to an end in the game world.

Using your running sheet, simply list each effect and its duration in dungeon turns. At the beginning of each dungeon turn, mark each track with a **tick**. When the number of ticks equals the duration, the effect expires.

It's your choice at what point during the turn the effect expires, but more often than not it will be easiest to describe it at the beginning of the turn when you mark the tick.

I recommend making your ticks in pencil. When Ranthir's torch burns out, for example, he'll likely want to immediately light a new one. Instead of starting a new line, you can just erase the current ticks and start over.

If you're using a running sheet with preprinted ticks, like the one in this book, then there are a couple more tricks you might find useful. (You can also use graph paper to this effect.)

First, when starting a new track you can mark the spot on the track where the duration expires. You could circle it, for example:

Alter Self   1 hr   ⬛⬜⬜⬜⬜⭕
                              ⬜⬜⬜⬜⬜⬜

Now you don't have to keep counting ticks to see if you've reached the duration. Once you've reached the indicated tick, you know the torch or spell or trap timer has expired.

Alternatively, instead of marking multiple tracks each turn, you can make the top track on your sheet a master track. The master track is ticked each turn, as usual. On the other tracks, however, you indicate duration relative to the master track tick. (So if the current master track is on tick 7 and a new torch with a duration of six dungeon turns is lit, you'd indicate that its duration ends on tick 13.) Each time you tick the master track, simply scan down the column to see which effect ends.

Your master track will likely fill up at some point: Simply erase the track or start a second master track in the first available slot and cycle the duration indicators appropriately.

SHORT EFFECTS

Some effects, of course, have a duration shorter than a dungeon turn. For example, a *bless* spell only lasts for up to 1 minute. You don't need to track these. Or, at least, you don't need to track them using dungeon turns.

LONG EFFECTS

Other effects are quite long. A lantern, for example, can burn for 36 turns. For these long timers, it can be good practice to periodically update the players on its status. So, for example, you could make an additional duration mark at every 12 turns for the lantern, making a point of mentioning how much oil has been depleted as you hit those milestones. This not only helps manage the length of your duration track for these longer items, it also helps the players feel the passage of time in the game world.

ENCOUNTER CHECK

The dungeon turn is a looping procedure. Within that loop, the process of generating a random encounter is its own little mini-procedure. Let's break this **encounter procedure** down into its specific steps:

1. Make an **encounter check** by rolling 1d8. A roll of 1 indicates that an encounter will occur.

2. Roll on the dungeon's **random encounter table** to determine the random encounter. (You can see an example table on the next page.)

3. Determine the **encounter distance** by rolling 2d6 x 10 feet.

4. Make a **reaction check** by rolling 2d6 and consulting the reaction table (on the next page).

5. Determine surprise, if any. In D&D, this will usually be done with opposing **Dexterity (Stealth)** and **Wisdom (Perception)** checks.

EXAMPLE: ENCOUNTER TABLE

DIO	ENCOUNTER
1–3	1d4 + 4 goblins
4–5	1d2 giant spiders
6–7	1d4 goblins + 1 giant spider
8	Ogre
9	Ettercap
10	Roll again twice, combine the encounters.

REACTION TABLE

2D6	REACTION
2–3	Immediate Attack
4–5	Hostile
6–8	Cautious/Threatening
9–10	Neutral
11–12	Amiable

If an encounter is indicated, the encounter you generate using the encounter procedure should appear at some point during the dungeon turn.

Running a successful random encounter can be tricky. We'll take a closer look at some of the best practices in Running Random Encounters on page 80.

DUNGEON ACTIONS

During each dungeon turn, each PC can take one dungeon action.

Not everything a PC does in the dungeon should be considered a dungeon action. Some of the things players say their characters are doing will be considered **incidental actions**. Incidental actions happen during the dungeon turn, often at the same time that the character is doing their dungeon action. Examples of incidental actions include:

◎ talking while doing other tasks

◎ minor amounts of movement, up to a character's speed

◎ a quick item interaction (e.g., lighting a torch, pulling a switch, or opening an unlocked door)

◎ anything else that isn't time-consuming

At your discretion, if characters are taking a whole bunch of incidental actions all at once, you can declare that the amalgamation is equivalent to a full dungeon action. For example, opening an unlocked chest would normally be an incidental action. Checking 50 chests to find the missing travel documents? That's probably chewing up a full turn. Same thing if they're chatting for a bit, then opening a chest, then walking to the far side of the room, then checking out the mural on the wall, then appraising the value of the mithril sconces, and then . . . and then . . . and then . . . Somewhere in there they've spent 5 to 10 minutes doing all that miscellaneous stuff and you should feel free to start a new dungeon turn.

If players are aware of the dungeon turn structure, they may declare specific actions. If you're running the dungeon turn as a player-unknown structure, then you'll be interpreting the players' declarations conceptually through the dungeon actions.

JASON (DM): You've reached a T-intersection. About 40 feet to your left you can see a door made from gold; it glints in the light from Agnarr's flaming sword. To the right, at about the same distance, there's a plainer door of weatherworn oak.

·—🗡► *The group has been marching down the corridor, using a Movement action.*

SARAH (TEE): Let's head toward the gold door, but I want to check the last 20 feet for traps.

·—🗡► *They still had 40 feet of distance left in their Movement action, so even after the navigational decision, Jason still counts this additional movement as part of the same Movement action. He then starts a new dungeon turn with Tee taking the Search action.*

JASON (DM): Okay, you head a little closer to the door and then Tee gives the hand signal for everyone else to stop where they are. Tee, give me an Intelligence (Investigation) check.

While Sarah makes her check, Jason marks ticks and makes an encounter check for the current turn. The check is negative, so no monsters appear.

JASON (DM): What is everyone else doing while Tee checks the hall?

DAVE (AGNARR): I'll actually hold back at the intersection. Play rear guard.

Even though Dave hasn't explicitly said he's taking the Lookout action (see page 78), that's clearly what Agnarr is doing, and so Jason counts that as Agnarr's action for this turn and resolves it accordingly.

JASON (DM): Okay, give me a Wisdom (Perception) check.

SETH (RANTHIR): I'll take the time to read a few more pages of Sagrathea's journal.

Reading an enigmatic sorcerer's diary isn't covered by a specific dungeon action, but it's clearly a time-consuming activity and, therefore, not an incidental action. It's an Other Action (see page 79) and Jason counts it as Ranthir's action for the turn.

Either way, it won't be unusual for the PCs to all be doing the same action, particularly when movement is involved (e.g., the whole group walks down the hall together in marching order). You can usually just roll with this; there's no need to bog things down by checking with every single player every single time to make sure they're still moving with the group.

It's also quite possible that some or all of the PCs will choose to just stand around and wait while other PCs are doing stuff. While you want to give everyone an opportunity to participate, it's just fine if they choose not to. If you're feeling charitable, you might assume such characters are on Lookout. Alternatively, when it feels appropriate, you may want to ask them if they want to Help the PCs who are taking action.

DUNGEON ACTIONS
- Movement
- Combat
- Conversation
- Helping
- Lookout
- Overcome Obstacle
- Ritual Casting
- Search
- Other Actions

DUNGEON ACTION: MOVEMENT

Characters can move up to their **dungeon pace** (which is speed x 5) in one dungeon turn. At these distances, usually all of the characters will be moving together, and you can assume they're simply moving at the party's dungeon pace.

Characters can perform **incidental movement** while performing other dungeon actions. If you need a rule of thumb, assume a character can move up to their speed before the movement requires a full dungeon turn.

The calculation for dungeon pace assumes that the characters are exploring the environment: examining their surroundings, discussing their options, making notes, updating their map, hesitating before making navigational decisions, and so forth.

If characters are simply trying to move as quickly as possible through an area they're familiar with, they can travel at a **fast pace** (speed x 100). While doing so, they suffer disadvantage on Perception and Stealth checks; they also cannot map or take notes. It's generally not possible to move at a fast pace through unfamiliar tunnels, although there may be exceptions at your discretion.

DUNGEON ACTION: COMBAT

When a fight breaks out in the dungeon, Combat becomes the dungeon action for all combatants during that dungeon turn. In effect, this just means that a new dungeon turn begins when combat wraps up (so mark your ticks, make a fresh encounter check, and so forth).

COMBAT & LOUD NOISES

If the PCs are being particularly noisy—and combat would certainly qualify!—you may choose to make an additional encounter check for the turn, representing the increased likelihood of other denizens being drawn to the disturbance.

DUNGEON ACTION: CONVERSATION

Talking as an incidental action is obviously common no matter what the PCs are doing, but sometimes the party hunkers down for a lengthy debate about what their next course of action should be. A long conversation like this should probably be counted as a dungeon action, so where's the line?

Basically, just look at the clock: Have the players been talking for about 10 minutes or so? Then it's time to start a new dungeon turn: Make your ticks and checks.

DUNGEON ACTION: HELPING

Characters can Help the actions of their allies. In some cases, this just means that both characters are taking the action (e.g., they're each searching a different section of a particularly large room). In other cases, the helper will grant advantage to the character they're helping.

DUNGEON ACTION: LOOKOUT

A character on Lookout is focused on observing their surroundings, usually keeping an eye out for anything dangerous. Characters on Lookout make Perception-type checks normally, whereas characters taking other non-Movement dungeon actions suffer disadvantage on their Perception-type checks due to distraction.

DUNGEON ACTION: OVERCOME OBSTACLE

Opening an unlocked door is easy enough and would be considered an incidental action, but if the door is locked or stuck, it becomes a more significant obstacle. Examples of overcoming such obstacles can include:

- picking a lock
- forcing open a door
- disabling a trap
- climbing out of a pit trap
- moving a heavy log
- solving a riddle
- repairing an object

Ultimately, where the line lies between getting hit by an arrow trap (instantaneous and probably best considered an incidental action resolved as part of a larger dungeon turn) and puzzling out the precise pattern of steps required to cross a booby-trapped mosaic floor through trial and error by throwing a heavy weight around (probably a full dungeon action) is a ruling for you to make.

DUNGEON ACTION: RITUAL CASTING

Some spells, and all spells that are ritually cast, have a casting time of 10 minutes. Casting any such spell is a dungeon action.

DUNGEON ACTION: SEARCH

Characters can search a typical room or up to 50 feet of hallway as a dungeon action. Colossal rooms may, at your discretion, require multiple actions to search fully.

DUNGEON ACTION: OTHER ACTIONS

This list of dungeon actions should cover most activities in the dungeon, but it's hardly encyclopedic. If a PC takes an action that feels like it should take at least 5 or 10 minutes, that probably counts as a dungeon action. Handle it as such.

DUNGEON PERCEPTION

You don't need to make Perception-type checks every single turn (that would quickly become mind-numbing and monotonous), but the question of who sees what and when they see it is so pervasive in the dungeon—happening so often as part of another action—that it's worthwhile to call it out as its own step in our dungeon procedure.

In D&D, these checks will usually be Wisdom (Perception) or Intelligence (Investigation) checks, but could also include Wisdom (Survival), Wisdom (Insight), or any number of knowledge checks depending on the current situation.

Remember that Perception-type checks are resolved normally by characters Moving at dungeon pace or taking the Lookout action. All other characters make Perception-type checks with disadvantage due to distraction.

RUNNING RANDOM ENCOUNTERS

The encounter procedure detailed previously should give you all the raw material you need to run a random encounter, but there's a great deal of art that can go into playing the encounter to its best effect.

The key thing is that the function of the random encounter is to *keep the world in motion*. While running Mephits & Magmin, you may have noticed how all the bad guys politely waited in their room for the PCs to show up. In fact, if the PCs ever stopped and just waited around somewhere in that adventure, they would never be disturbed. It's as if the monsters were all freeze-framed until the PCs walked through the door.

Now, this rarely causes a big, dramatic problem. The illusion usually works and the players, more often than not, probably won't notice the conceit. But it can be a lot more fun if the dungeon feels like a real place with creatures on the prowl and evil cultists going about their business! It can immerse the players more deeply in the world, ratchet up the tension (you never know who might walk around the corner!), and force creative problem-solving.

Random encounter checks are the easiest mechanism you can use for making a dungeon feel alive like this: They can simulate everything from daily routines to regular guard patrols, allowing you to stay tightly focused on running the current room (instead of trying to juggle the entire dungeon all at once) while the dungeon nevertheless continues to pulse and thrum with life. Life. That's a really important concept here. Where random encounters can fail is when they're reduced to nothing more than the bare bones of the procedure: Roll dice. Random monsters walk through the door. The PCs stab them a bunch. The game continues as if the encounter had never occurred.

Random encounters are a form of **procedural content generation**. The term comes from computer gaming. There it refers to the programmatic creation of content—a procedure algorithmically generates data that would otherwise need to be manually created. For example, instead of having a human developer place every tree in a forest, you can instead have the program follow a certain set of rules and place all the trees in the forest for you. You can see how the same concept applies here: Our procedure (i.e., the encounter check) generates content (i.e., the creatures) and we inject that content into our game.

In a computer game, there are some fairly severe limitations to procedural content generation. Although these systems get better every year, they tend to create carbon-copy results and can often be rife with logical problems. They lack the "human touch."

The great thing about a roleplaying game, of course, is *you*. As the DM, you, unlike a computer game programmer, are sitting right there at the table. You can—and must!—take the raw material provided by our simplistic procedural content generator and give it the human touch, investing it with your rational judgment and unbridled creativity.

When our random encounter procedure generates 1d4 + 4 goblins, for example, the 1d4 + 4 goblins *are not the encounter*. The encounter is what you do with those goblins. The 1d4 + 4 goblins are just the improv seed that you get to riff off of.

For example, when you roll up those 1d4 + 4 goblins, you might decide that:

◎ They're Orcus worshippers who have all flayed the skin from their right hands, leaving a motile skeleton that remains animate even after the goblins have died.

(continued)

◎ They're religious zealots who have been converted to the worship of Apollo and preach about the "glorious scourge of sunlight" to fellow travelers.

◎ Three of the goblins are being attacked and brutalized by the others; the victims will beg for help from the PCs.

◎ They're mercenaries who are looking for a good paycheck. Are the PCs hiring?

You can see how each of these is not only a completely different encounter—every version of "1d4 + 4 goblins" can be unique—but that each encounter is deeply infused with life.

To find this life in your own encounters, you need to **contextualize the encounter**. The procedure has generated something random. It's your job to explain why it *isn't*. You want to connect this encounter to the current environment and situation of the PCs. This will also connect the encounter to the scenario, making it a significant part of the game instead of irrelevant fluff that's just chewing up table time.

When you roll up an encounter, ask yourself four questions:

1. What makes these monsters unique?

2. Where are they coming from?

3. What are they doing?

4. How do they react to the PCs?

These answers do not need to be elaborate or some Herculean feat of jaw-dropping creativity. They don't even need to be full sentences. It only takes a little nudge to make the encounter specific and interesting (instead of generic and boring).

WHAT MAKES THE MONSTERS UNIQUE?
◎ **Appearance** (scars, hair-/scale-style, clothing, size)
◎ **Rank** (lieutenants vs. galley cooks)
◎ **Distinctive Ability** (special power, magic item)
◎ **Behavior/Personality** (unusual vulnerability or hostility)
◎ **Visible Treasure** (large amulet, bejeweled diadem, bulging coin purse, etc.)

WHERE ARE THEY COMING FROM?

This obviously depends on the scenario you're running, so take a look at your dungeon map. Broadly speaking, you can either think in terms of **where monsters of this type are keyed** (e.g., this encounter is with goblins and goblins are keyed to Area 8, so that's where these goblins are coming from) or **somewhere nearby** (so look at rooms near the PCs' current location for inspiration).

It's also possible that the encounter is coming from *outside* the current scenario. For example, these might be goblins from another tribe who have just arrived with a giant riding spider that they're delivering to the local tribe.

Either way, where the encounter is coming from is also informed by what their destination is, and that's usually connected to the next question . . .

WHAT ARE THE MONSTERS DOING?

The possibilities here are almost limitless, and the more specific you can make it to the scenario the better.

- Working guard patrol
- Escorting prisoners or valuables
- Moving raw goods or supplies
- Performing a ritual
- Heading home for the night or going to work
- Running an errand
- Delivering a message
- Going to meet someone
- Eating or relaxing
- Crafting or mining
- Singing songs
- Training
- Performing an experiment
- Building or expanding the dungeon

What they're doing also helps determine where they're going, which generally takes one of four forms:

◎ **Passing by** (e.g., the PCs are in a room and the encounter is walking down the hall outside)

◎ **Passing through** (e.g., they're going to walk through the room the PCs are in)

◎ **Coming to the PCs** (which means that whatever they're doing is in this room)

◎ **Remaining stationary** (the encounter is doing something in a room or hall that the PCs are approaching, so the PCs come to the encounter rather than vice versa)

This also means you can flip this around: If you're trying to figure out what the encounter is doing, just look at where the PCs are (and the rooms near them) and ask yourself what the encounter would be doing there. For example, if the PCs are in the kitchen, it's more likely the goblins are coming to grab some food.

Also: Have the PCs done anything that could explain what the encounter is doing here?

Has there been a fight recently? Then maybe the noise attracted the encounter. Did they fail a Stealth check earlier? Maybe the encounter is following their tracks. Did they leave a bunch of bodies lying around? Then the encounter might be actively searching for them or heading to the armory to get geared up.

Connecting random encounters to the actions of the PCs is a great way of showing them how their actions have consequences (and, therefore, that their choices are meaningful) while simultaneously grounding that encounter in such a specific context that it doesn't feel random at all.

USING ENCOUNTER DISTANCE

An easy habit to fall into, when an encounter check indicates a random encounter, is to simply say, "You see a monster and the monster sees you; roll initiative." There are a lot of variations of this—the monster opens a door, the PCs open the door, the monster walks around the corner, etc.—but they all boil down to the same thing.

The encounter distance check can help you break this habit by prompting easy alternatives.

◉   Is the distance farther than the current line of sight (e.g., the monster must be outside the room)? Make appropriate Perception and Stealth tests to see if the monster notices the PCs, the PCs notice the monster, or both.

◉   Is the distance closer than line of sight (e.g., the roll indicates 20 feet, but the PCs are in the middle of a 50-foot-square room)? You can default to the logical line of sight (although Stealth and Perception checks might still be appropriate), but also ask yourself what else could explain the discrepancy. (This is how you get moments like xenomorphs climbing through ceiling panels.)

There may, of course, be times when this simple dice prompt produces nonsensical results. It's a good thing that you, as the dungeon master, are right there to override it when necessary!

HOW DO THEY REACT TO THE PCS?

Not all encounters need to be combat encounters.

The reaction check in our encounter procedure is designed, in part, to gently push us away from defaulting to combat.

Defaulting to combat is really common. I think we're partly influenced by video games where "stomp the Koopa" and "shoot the cacodemon" is the default action. But on a more fundamental level, it's because combat is *easy*. Most RPGs include robust rules for combat, including a very specific procedure for resolving it. Just follow the procedure and the rules will take care of the rest.

(This is, ironically, *also* why combat has been a default action for video games from *Space Invaders* to *Call of Duty*. It's a lot easier to implement a loop of combat mechanics than it is to run a unique encounter.)

Punching somebody in the face (or stabbing them with a *+2 longsword*) is not, of course, the totality of human (or elven or even Klingon) experience. But if everything reacts to the PCs walking into a room by snarling and drawing their blades, then it can very easily become so.

The reaction table (see page 74) provides a basic prompt you can use to shape the initial moments of the encounter across a broad spectrum of experiences, but it's also a good example of a general principle when it comes to procedural content generators: If you already know what the answer should be, you don't have to ask the dice.

For example, if all the goblins in this tribe have sworn a blood oath to slay the PCs and you roll up a random encounter with goblins . . . well, you already know they're going to be hostile, right?

(Although, for the sake of argument, you could still choose to roll a reaction check and use a result of "Amiable" to suggest that these goblins *aren't* part of the hostile tribe: Maybe they're visitors or prisoners or dissidents. These are all tools for you to use; not for you to be used by.)

On a similar note, the outcome of the reaction check is deliberately vague. This is necessary because it can be applied to a wide variety of intelligent, semi-intelligent, and unintelligent creatures, but it's also expected that you'll use your creativity and knowledge of the setting to make the general result specific. A Hostile encounter, for example, might be a group of starving wolves; slavers looking to capture the PCs; or a group of paladins who mistakenly think the PCs are slavers.

The indicated reaction is also only a starting point. It's possible the encounter's attitude won't shift ("We fight to the death!"), but there's no reason, for example, that the PCs can't convince the paladins that they've made a mistake.

Where the encounter goes from there is entirely up to you (and your players)!

RUNNING TRAPS

Traps are a staple of pulp adventure and a classic element of dungeon adventures. Down in the dark places of the earth, there is danger lurking everywhere. These hazards can take a wide variety of forms.

- Pit traps (spikes at the bottom optional)
- Boulders chasing you down corridors
- Ceilings collapsing
- A fusillade of arrows shooting from the wall
- Poison gas filling the chamber
- Huge blades scything out of walls
- Human-sized snares in the jungle
- Poison needles jabbing those who unlock a chest
- A bear trap snapping shut on your leg

A magical milieu unlocks even more fantastical varieties. In addition to simply imagining the impossible, you can take almost any spell in the rulebook and use it as the seed for a memorable trap.

- A *lightning bolt* lancing down the hall
- A *fireball* that explodes when you open a door
- A strange mist that *charms* all those within it
- A monster *summoned* when you fail to pick a lock
- *Explosive runes* when opening the wrong book
- A room where gravity reverses
- Floating bubbles that envelop and suffocate
- Teleportation traps (sending you to places unknown)
- A magical *alarm* alerting guardians

Traps are tricky, though, and I don't just mean for the PCs. Running a trap in a way that's satisfying and entertaining for the whole table can be a challenge. It's a process that can be broken down into three parts:

- ⬡ Finding the trap
- ⬡ Triggering the trap
- ⬡ Playing the trap

In order to **find a trap**, a player must declare that they're actively searching—i.e., taking the Search dungeon action. They might be specifically looking for traps, but not necessarily. The default method for resolving this in D&D would typically be an Intelligence (Investigation) check, but players may come up with clever ideas, so don't be afraid to call for alternative checks or even default to yes if it seems appropriate. (For example, the players might pour water on the floor so that it would run down the seams around a covered pit trap.)

If a PC isn't actively searching, then you might allow successful Perception-type checks to notice *evidence* of the trap's existence—scorch marks, an arrow sticking out of the wall, water pooling oddly on the floor, bits of blasted bone scattered around, etc. This is **trap-sign** and it may give the players an opportunity to realize their danger and begin an active search (which can be resolved normally).

SO PERCEPTIVE!

If a PC has an incredible success on their Perception-type test—e.g., rolling 10 points higher than the DC of a Wisdom (Perception) check—you might still allow them to detect a trap even if they're not actively searching. The character is just that good!

If the PCs don't detect a trap, then it's quite likely that they will **trigger the trap**. Broadly speaking, a trap will have either a proximity trigger or an action trigger.

A **proximity trigger** can take a number of forms in the game world: a magical alarm, a pressure plate on the floor, a trip wire, an infrared sensor, etc. When a character passes through an area with a proximity trigger, roll 1d4. On a roll of 1, the trap triggers. This roll simulates the uncertainty of stepping on exactly the right spot to activate the trigger. (Sometimes you step over the trip wire thanks to dumb luck.) It also means, since you'll roll for each character separately, that it won't always be the character at the front of the party who triggers the trap, which creates some nice variety and uncertainty in the game. (It's even possible the entire group will luck their way past a trigger, which can *really* surprise them when they double back and—wham!)

A trap with an **action trigger** goes off when a specific action is taken: a poison needle jabs you in the thumb when you try to open a chest; the ceiling collapses when you open the false door; lightning bolts crisscross the room if you pick up the jade idol. You usually won't make a check for these triggers; they'll automatically go off if anybody does the indicated action.

Finally, if a PC **fails a check when searching for a trap**, this might also trigger the trap. Depending on the circumstances, you'll need to make a ruling on whether it definitely goes off, it doesn't go off, or there's just a risk of it going off (i.e., rolling a 1 on a 1d4).

Whether the PCs find a trap or trigger a trap, that's not the end of the trap. Either way, you still need to **play the trap**.

The key thing here is that your description of the trap should not be limited to its mechanical effect. Yes, the arrow trap will make a +5 attack roll for 1d6 + 4 damage against all characters in the hall. But where are the arrows coming from? The walls? The ceiling? Are they shooting out of holes or through an illusory surface? How is the trap being triggered? A trip wire? A pressure plate? An *alarm* spell keyed to a magical rune inscribed on the ceiling?

For example, if the PCs find a trap before it triggers—or if it resets and can be triggered over and over again—they'll likely want to disarm or disable it. The rote mechanical resolution for disabling a trap is to make a Dexterity (Thieves' Tools) check. But if you understand *how* the trap works, it will allow the players to get creative with their work-arounds—to get their "Indiana Jones" on, so to speak.

These work-arounds might include alternative skill checks (perhaps made with advantage to reward clever thinking), or they might bypass the mechanical resolution entirely: walking around a pit trap, opening a trapped door from a distance with *mage hand*, using a shield to block the arrow trap in the wall, or just commando crawling under the line of fire.

Even when the players default to the rote mechanical resolution, knowing how the trap works will still let you ask them *how* they're disabling it, or describe it yourself in narrating the resolution. When they disable the pit trap, do they force it open? Do they nail a board over the top of it? Do they wedge it with iron spikes so that it can support their weight one at a time? The difference will matter if they end up getting chased back down this hallway by goblins riding spiders!

On the other hand, let's say that the trap is triggered. The rote resolution here is, once again, jumping straight to a mechanical effect: You've stepped on the pressure plate, therefore make a Dexterity saving throw or suffer damage.

But it can be more fun if you give the players a chance to react!

SARAH (TEE): I very slowly make my way down the corridor, checking carefully for traps.

JASON (DM): Give me an Intelligence (Investigation) check.

SARAH (TEE): 8.

That's a failure. There's a fireball trap in the corridor activated by a pressure plate. That's a proximity trigger, so Jason rolls 1d4 and gets a 2. Tee has avoided the pressure plate. Jason rolls again for Agnarr, the next person in the marching order, and this time rolls a 1.

JASON (DM): Agnarr, as you're following behind Tee, a section of the floor depresses under your foot and you hear a sharp click. What do you do?

DAVE (AGNARR): I freeze! Tee! I think you missed something!

JASON (DM): Okay. Nothing seems to happen.

SARAH (TEE): With a heavy sigh I come back and check out his foot. Let's see if I can figure out what Agnarr has stepped in this time.

Giving players a **trigger reaction** like this can be effective even if their proposed actions are likely to all be resolved the same way (e.g., whether you're diving for cover or hitting the deck, you're probably making a Dexterity saving throw). Sometimes they'll surprise you, but even if they don't, you'll still end up with a scene that is more vividly detailed and with which the players are more actively engaged.

Another way of doing this is to design traps with **ongoing effects**, which can turn the environment into a challenge or puzzle. ("Okay, so we've accidentally hit a switch that is periodically blasting the entire hallway with fire. How do we get to the other side?" or "Ranthir has been knocked out by sleeping gas and anyone entering the room is likely to *also* get knocked out. So how do we get him out?")

It can also be really effective to **combine traps with monsters**, either to create a dynamic environment for the fight or to give the monsters a unique tactical advantage (e.g., if they know where the traps are located and can trigger them to wreak havoc with the PCs).

HOW NOT TO RUN A TRAP

Here's how you should NOT run traps in your game:

⊚   Use passive Wisdom (Perception) to determine if they spot a trap.

⊚   Make an Intelligence (Investigation) check to see if the character can figure out how to disable it.

⊚   Make a Dexterity (Thieves' Tools) check to determine if they disable the trap.

⊚   If any of the checks fail, the trap is triggered and inflicts a random amount of damage.

The problem with this sequence is that at no point did the players make an interesting choice. Or any choice at all. It's an entirely automatic sequence of mechanical interactions that the players don't even choose to initiate.

TEN-FOOT POLES

A common anti-trap tactic is to use a 10-foot pole to probe the ground ahead. This has the normal 1 in 4 chance of triggering proximity traps (but hopefully at a safe distance). It has the advantage over normal searching in that it can be done as part of the Movement action, although it does impose disadvantage on Stealth checks (since the tap-tap-tapping of the pole isn't exactly discreet).

Your players may propose similar "be cautious without actively searching" approaches. Sometimes these are still best handled using the Search dungeon action. In other cases, some variation of this 10-foot-pole procedure can probably be employed.

NEXT STEPS

To recap, our big focus here was adding a dungeon procedure to help you keep track of everything while running the dungeon. This included structures for keeping track of time and juggling the PCs' actions, but the random encounters are the really big add-on.

In fact, if you want to keep things simpler, you might consider skipping the random encounter checks for your next adventure. Get comfortable with the rhythms of dungeon actions and keeping track of time, then bring in the random encounters when you're ready to make your dungeons more exciting.

Speaking of the next adventure, that's your next step in becoming a dungeon master! In the next chapter, we'll walk through the process of creating your first dungeon adventure. Once it's ready to go, you can use everything you've learned so far to run it for your players and continue their campaign.

If you'd like, it's actually not a bad idea to do that several times, designing additional adventures and continuing to run them as you grow more comfortable in your role as the DM. There's no rush. After all, as we've discovered, there's really no limit to the number of adventures you can have with nothing more than a simple dungeon.

When you're ready to expand the scope of your adventures, we can begin exploring Advanced Dungeons together, starting on page 138.

✦ HOMEWORK ✦

DESIGN A DUNGEON

Are you ready to design your first adventure?

I promise you that you are, even if it doesn't feel like it right now. The great thing about a dungeon scenario is that it ultimately boils down to just two essential elements:

- ◈ The dungeon map
- ◈ The dungeon key

And that's it! That's all you need! Whether you're feeling excited or trepidatious right now (or maybe a little bit of both), we're going to work through a simple step-by-step process for prepping your key and map.

Of course, you've already used a key and map while running your first scenario. So once you're done making your own, you'll already be ready to run your adventure!

BRAINSTORMING YOUR DUNGEON

Should you start with your key or with your map?

This can be a kind of chicken-and-egg problem. If you start by drawing the map, then you're just kind of sketching random room shapes and hoping that you'll be inspired to fill them later. If you try to start with the key, on the other hand, there's the obvious problem that you don't actually have any rooms to describe yet. This can naturally lead you to try doing them sort of both simultaneously—maybe drawing a room and then keying it and then drawing the next room—but I've found that this can be very confusing in practice, and can lead to a lot of frustration when any mistake on the map may precipitate erasing big chunks of your key and vice versa.

So I like to start with a brainstorming session. This gives me the freedom to experiment, steer clear of false starts, and lay out the elements of the adventure in broad strokes before committing to the specific details of map and key.

Let's begin with the **scenario concept**. There are an infinite variety of dungeon adventures you could design. What is the *specific* dungeon that you're designing today?

We can think of the scenario concept as being made up of the dungeon's **location**, **denizens**, and **goal**. To at least some extent, these will all be connected to each other: If the PCs are hunting the dwarven pirate Wee Willow Whipwater, it follows that the location is likely to be her ship and its denizens will be her crew.

You may already have a concept in mind. If so, great! Use it as a seed to flesh out the other two elements. Do you want to run an adventure in a haunted house? Use that location to figure out who lives in the house (owners and ghosts alike) and what the PCs' goal likely is (probably getting rid of the ghosts . . . unless the ghosts are fine and it's the owners who are the problem). Do you want to run an adventure featuring giant ants? Then I'm guessing it'll be set in a giant anthill. (Now: What could motivate the PCs to visit the anthill?) Do the PCs want to go explore the local mountain range? What types of dangerous creatures might live in those mountains? And where do they live?

If you don't have a concept in mind, then I recommend focusing—just momentarily—exclusively on either the location, the denizens, or the goal. This will give you the initial seed and, as we've seen, everything else can flow from that.

Denizens are a great place to find inspiration because there'll often be a big list of them in your RPG of choice. In D&D, for example, you can just flip through the *Monster Manual* looking for a cool illustration that catches your eye. In games that don't have a bunch of different creatures—like a game set in the real world, for example— you can usually get a similar utility by looking at the different factions in the setting instead.

THE CHALLENGE RATING MENU

In the *Dungeon Master's Guide* there is a list of "Monsters by Challenge Rating." This is basically a menu that you can order your scenario denizens from.

"Ah, yes, garçon. I'd like a killer whale with a swarm of quippers on the side."

There are a couple ways you can think about this. First, you can think about who the **big boss** of your adventure might be. For that, take a peek at the list of monsters with a challenge rating equal to the PCs' current level. Alternatively, you can think about the **horde**. Who are the typical denizens in this location whom the PCs are likely to meet in groups? For the horde, you want to look at creatures with a challenge rating lower than the PCs' current level. (I usually go at least a couple levels lower, because it gives me more flexibility in building encounters.)

Instead of picking just one denizen when you're looking for inspiration, it can be even more effective to pick two. For example, a ruined castle full of goblins can be fun, but what happens if you pair those goblins with another creature?

- goblins and ogres
- goblins and blink dogs
- goblins and tieflings
- goblins and owlbears

Just reading through that list probably started sparking your imagination. You can *see* what a clan of goblin blink-dog riders looks like, and it's completely different from a tribe of goblins worshipping an ogre "god" or one with "sacred" bloodlines descended from the demon lord Skarnak.

Putting two creatures together like this forces an act of creative closure: We reflexively *need* to explain why these two creatures coexist, and we instinctively create that explanation, closing the gap between them by forging something thrillingly original.

Even better, the creative frisson will continue spinning out new ideas, like radioactive isotopes knocked free during a nuclear reaction: The opulent bedchambers of the Ogre God. The dark fane dedicated to his worship. The heretic cages where disobedient goblins are locked up until they repent. These provide raw fodder for your dungeon key, filling it with cool rooms that will give your adventure a unique identity.

Of course, the seed for your scenario concept can also come from the **location** itself.

I find this often boils down to asking myself, "What would make for a really cool map?" Or, to look at it from a slightly different angle, "What would be a really cool place to explore?"

SAMPLE DUNGEON LOCATIONS

- Cave
- Ruins
- Castle's oubliette
- Subterranean city
- Crypt or catacombs
- Mine
- Mansion
- Pyramid
- Tower
- Ship or shipwreck
- Colossal body
- City building or business
- Security vault
- Stronghold or fortress
- Cliff dwellings
- Treetop buildings
- Subaquatic complex
- Pocket dimension
- Cloud cities
- Prison

In a fantastical world, such locations are only limited by your imagination. But if you're looking for inspiration, it's always worth looking to the world around you: The megamall, with its cavernous byways and twisting back corridors, transforms into a dwarven city. What would your local library look like if the librarian was a sorcerer? If you sunk your church beneath the earth, how would it be transformed? Would its stained glass become phosphorescent fungi? Take the real world, give it a fantastical twist, and you can never be sure exactly where you'll end up.

For me, personally, the third element of the scenario concept—the **goal**—rarely serves as the font of inspiration when it comes to adventure design. Your mileage may vary, though. Which is an important point in itself, I think. What we're talking about here is a creative process, and creative processes are inherently personal experiences. There's no One True Way™, and you'll probably find your path to be a little different for every adventure you create.

As you start running a campaign, though, you may find that the players are setting goals for themselves. They might ask questions like, "Where did these magmin come from?" or say things like, "If there's one uraniac, there might be more. We need to figure out what they're up to." This is a gift! You can just take their goal, add a location and denizens (which are often strongly implied by the goal), and have your next adventure.

If you're looking for more generic goal-based brainstorming, then I recommend magic items. They're big and shiny and it's usually pretty easy to motivate the PCs to go after them just because they're awesome. Alternatively, you can also have the PCs get hired by somebody who wants the item retrieved, whether just because they're a rich collector or because the item's power naturally suggests their motivation (e.g., "I need this *ring of regeneration* because my daughter lost her leg in a terrible accident"). In D&D, just like monsters, you've also conveniently got a huge list of magic items that you can just scan through looking for inspiration.

A big ol' pile of gold coins can also provide motivation, of course, but the advantage of a magic item is that it can become an active part of the scenario, with its powers combining with other elements of the scenario to create a unique dungeon key. How are the goblins using that *ring of regeneration*? Is it worn by their ogre lord to reinforce his "divinity"? Do they use it in a grotesque ritual, initiating their warriors by chopping off their limbs and having them regrow? Items like *demon armor* or *staff of fire* can give a unique twist to a boss fight, while others can explain phantasmagorical alterations of the environment.

Now that we've sketched in our scenario concept, we're going to finish our brainstorming session by listing ideas for the individual rooms in our dungeon.

One of the great things about a dungeon is that you can pour almost any awesome idea you might have into a dungeon room.

It's a very flexible scenario structure, so we're free to imagine almost anything. We're not looking for fully fleshed out rooms, though. Quite the opposite. We're making a short, punchy list that's a mixture of cool ideas and stuff that "needs" to be in the dungeon. Here's a sample of what my **brainstorming sheet** looked like when I was creating Mephits & Magmin:

- lava canal
- steampunk construct finale
- crystals
- broken basaltic floor
- iridescent volcanic tunnel
- inside a geode
- mud mephits guarding the entrance
- magmin "supercharging" mud mephits
- inflationary rift, red hot glow oozing from crack across the top of the dome

If we were to continue developing that idea of a blink dog–riders adventure I mentioned on page 95, we could perhaps imagine a goblin border fort and start making a list like this:

- barracks
- mess hall
- upper levels accessible only by blinking
- den mother's cave
- pup warrens
- blink practice range
- armory
- taxidermied displacer beast
- smithy
- saddler specializing in blink tack

And so forth.

Don't feel like you need to capture every single room that will (or could) end up in the final dungeon. You're capturing broad needs and cool concepts. It's not unusual for me to walk away from this list, maybe grab a sandwich, and then come back with a fresh mind to add more stuff to it. But when you feel like you've given yourself a goodly bag of tricks, it'll be time to move on to your map.

As you're working on your brainstorming sheet, think about the following questions:

◈ What challenges need to be overcome to achieve the goal?

◈ What logically needs to exist in this location? (e.g., where and how do the monsters sleep?)

◈ What cool things can the denizens do, and what environments would make that even more fun?

◈ What are some common features of a location like this? (e.g., castles have throne rooms and lava tubes have crystalline growths.)

◈ What fantastical twist could you apply to common rooms?

◈ How might the special abilities (e.g., flight or fire immunity or teleportation) create unique needs or alter the functions of common rooms?

COMBINING IDEAS

Not everything on your brainstorming sheet needs to make it into the final dungeon. The purpose of brainstorming, after all, is to generate lots and lots of possibilities; to create a big supply of raw ideas. An important part of the creative process is refining those raw ideas, polishing them into something special.

Later in this chapter we'll be creating a 5 + 5 Dungeon, a simple recipe you can follow to create a great adventure. Following this recipe, you will naturally boil your brainstorming down, selecting the five or ten best ideas you had for dungeon rooms. Even when you start designing larger dungeons, though, it will still be a good idea to sort the wheat from the chaff and focus on your best stuff.

Before you toss out the rooms that didn't make the cut, though, see if there's a way to *combine* those ideas with the rooms you chose. Remember that you want your rooms to have multiple points of interest, and the interactions between different elements—whether planned ahead of time or emerging from the actions of the PCs—will add depth to the dungeon experience. Rooms are cooler with combos.

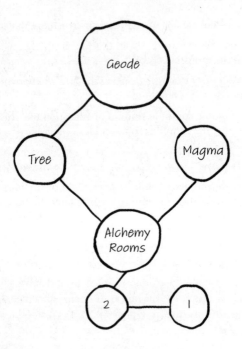

MAPPING

All you need to make your own dungeon map is some paper and a pencil. (Graph paper is ideal, but even that's optional.) Alternatively, there are a lot of different software tools you can easily search for online and use for dungeon mapping, with options ranging from the utilitarian to the opulent. This software is particularly useful if you want to create a map that you can scale up and use as a battlemap, either online or with miniatures at the table.

Whichever mapping method you choose, however, you're going to want to start simple. We're going to sketch a **connection map**.

The basic idea is that, without worrying about precise measurements or geometry, you're laying out the rough arrangement of the rooms and how they connect to each other. In some cases, you're not even concerned with individual rooms, instead grouping rooms together that you know will be clustered in the final dungeon and for which you're primarily interested in how that cluster will be linked to the rest of the complex.

Working with this sketchy connection map makes it a lot easier to experiment, make mistakes, and shift things around. It's not, of course, a binding contract: As you begin working on your final map, you'll almost certainly find that stuff continues to shift and change as you refine and hash out the details. But by figuring out the broad strokes first, you'll save yourself a lot of tears and wasted time later.

Once you've got everything in roughly the right place, you can start work on the **final map**. Graph paper is your best option here, and the first thing you'll want to do is set a **scale**. For a dungeon, you'll generally want to use a scale of either 1 square = 5' x 5' area (which will translate directly to a battlemap if you choose to use one) or 1 square = 10' x 10' area (which will let you fit larger complexes on a single sheet).

If your dungeon is a building or other structure, like a ship or the body of a dead god, you may want to start by sketching in the outline of the floorplan. More often than not, though, I'll just pick a spot on the page and start drawing: toward the center if the PCs are entering via staircase; toward the edge if it's the mouth of a cave or the front door or something like that.

As you're drawing, there are a lot of ways to make a map pretty, but the most important thing, in my opinion, is getting a map that *works*. For your walls, you don't need anything more than simple black lines, and you can use a handful of other simple symbols, as shown in the Map Key Symbols on page 103, to add any additional utility you might need.

Make sure to **number your rooms**. It's generally good practice to keep the numbers of rooms near each other in the dungeon close to each other in the key, too, since it will make it easier to reference things during play, but you can use whatever sequencing makes the most sense to you.

Later, when you start making larger dungeons with multiple levels, you may want to experiment with alternative numbers using level prefixes—e.g., A-13, C-34, 4-46, 5-3, etc. These will, once again, make it easier for you to reference your key during play. (It also means that if you decide to add a new section to Level D, it won't cascade into your numbering on Level F.)

Once you start making dungeons with multiple levels, also make sure to **label your stairs** and other level connectors, indicating what level and room they go to. Believe me when I say that the last thing you want to be doing in the middle of a session is flipping through your maps, trying to figure out where the stairs on Level 3 go to.

KEYING

As you're drawing, of course, you'll be pulling the ideas from your brainstorming sheet, creating the corresponding rooms, and adding them to your maps. You'll also likely be discovering new ideas as you go! Putting pencil to paper and developing your sketchy concepts into something concrete is going to get your creativity flowing. Follow that flow, adding details to existing rooms or entirely new rooms as the inspiration strikes you.

Either way, make sure you're keeping notes. You might do this directly on your brainstorming sheet or connection map, but while mapping I'll often have my laptop on the table next to me with the dungeon key open in a word processor. I don't recommend trying to write down the full key as you map. I find it more rewarding to stay focused on each task, and you're likely going to be revising stuff as you work on the map anyway. But what I will do is number the rooms, transfer notes from my brainstorming documents, and jot down any other details that occur to me while mapping.

This means that by the time I'm done mapping, I already have a functional outline of the entire dungeon. The next step, of course, is to fill in the key.

DUNGEON MAP KEY SYMBOLS

DOORS			
	Door		Concealed Door
	Double Door		False Door
	Arch	F	Trapdoor in Floor
	Portcullis	c	Trapdoor in Ceiling
	Secret Door	S	Secret Trapdoor
WALL FEATURES			
	Window		Arrow Slit
STAIRS AND CONNECTORS			
	Stairs	u	Ladder Up
	Natural Stairs	d	Ladder Down
	Spiral Stairs	m	Magic Portal
TRAPS			
T		Trap	
T		Pit Trap	
		Open Pit	

(continued)

FURNITURE

[icon]	Altar	[icon]	Rug
[icon]	Fireplace	[icon]	Chair
[icon]	Table	[icon]	Throne
[icon]	Chest	[icon]	Bookshelf
[icon]	Barrel	[icon]	Coffin
[icon]	Bed	[icon]	Statue/Suit of Armor

WATER

[icon]	Water
[icon]	Well
[icon]	Pool
[icon]	Stream

OTHER FEATURES

[icon]	Incline Down Arrow
[icon]	Point of Interest
[icon]	Dais
[icon]	Natural Platform
[icon]	Bridge
[icon] 20	Light Source (Including Range)

KEYING: DUNGEON ROOMS

While working on your dungeon key, use the format described in The Anatomy of a Room on page 38, and shown in Mephits & Magmin for each room:

- The room's **name**, a quick reminder of the room's purpose and content
- **Boxed text**, an initial description of the room
- **Reactive skill checks**, providing additional description in response to a skill check
- **Room elements**, describing contents of the room in detail

This format gives you a container to pour your ideas into and tries to give you the tools to organize your notes so that they can be easily referenced and used while playing the game. But you shouldn't feel constrained by it. For example, if there's a room that doesn't have any reactive skill checks in it, don't feel like you need to force one in. You definitely don't.

In keying the dungeon, it can be useful to think in terms of featured rooms and scenic rooms. A good rule of thumb, in fact, is to have a roughly even split between the two.

Featured rooms are the meat of the dungeon. They're where most of the action will be and where you'll be putting most of your coolest ideas. To design an awesome featured room, start by making sure that it includes multiple elements—the stuff that either requires or rewards the players for doing more than just looking at it.

I, personally, have a rule of thumb to include at least *three* interactive elements. By including multiple elements you encourage the group to split up and check out different stuff at the same time.

SETH (RANTHIR): I'm going to look through the papers on the desk, see if I can figure out what they've been researching here.

SARAH (TEE): I'll check out the chests. Make sure they're not trapped.

JASON (DM): Go ahead and give me an Intelligence (Investigation) check for that. Dave, what's Agnarr doing while they do that?

DAVE (AGNARR): I'll cautiously open the wardrobe.

It can be tempting to put just one cool thing in a room and declare it done, but if each room only has one interactive element it will often cause the group to default to having one character become The Guy Who Checks Out the Room. (In D&D, it's usually the rogue.)

Not every single player needs to be engaged in every single room. (That would be overkill, honestly.) But if you offer multiple options in each featured room, break things up a bit, and get more people involved, then over the course of the entire scenario it's likely that everyone at the table will feel engaged with the exploration of the dungeon, and that will improve the experience for the whole table. Not just because it's fairer for everyone to have a turn but also because it will give an opportunity for everyone to unleash their creativity.

Scenic rooms, on the other hand, are the ones that basically break this rule of thumb. They often don't have any interactive elements. If they do, then it's probably just one that's easily resolved. They're the rooms you look at and swiftly pass through on your way to the featured rooms.

You can perhaps think of them as "empty rooms," but I find this label to be more deceptive than revealing. You might occasionally have a legitimately barren chamber, but for the most part these rooms aren't *boring*. They can—and should!—still have cool stuff in them, even stuff that's of vital importance to the scenario. Examples include

- a fossilized dinosaur on display,
- a tapestry revealing the history of the ruined monastery,
- a trail of blood leading to a murder victim in the next room,
- strange runes floating in midair, or
- the invisible sensor of a *clairvoyance* spell.

These rooms offer a moment of appreciation or analysis, after which the PCs can quickly move on, because while scenic rooms aren't necessarily empty, what they provide is negative space—a contrast to the featured rooms; a moment of calm to emphasize the frenetic chase; the unsurprising baseline that allows true surprise to exist. If every time the PCs opened a door in the dungeon there was something shocking or amazing behind it, the players would quickly grow numb to the experience. You need the quiet to give meaning to the loud, and that's what scenic rooms offer.

AWESOME DESCRIPTIONS

Whether a room is featured, scenic, or maybe somewhere in between, you'll need to describe it. There are a few rules of thumb I find useful when trying to create **awesome descriptions**.

Three of Five: Think about your five senses. Try to include at least three of them in your descriptions. Sight is a gimme and Taste will rarely apply (although sometimes you can taste the air), so that means picking a couple out of Hearing, Smell, and Touch. (It can be useful to remember that you don't actually have to touch something to intuit what it might feel like if you did. Touch can also include things like wind and temperature.)

Including the full sensorium of the characters will help to immerse the players in the game world. If you feel like getting fancy, consider other senses, such as:

- balance (vestibular sense)
- movement (kinesthesia)
- temperature (thermoception)
- pain (nociception)
- ultrahuman (provided by magic or technology; e.g., a *detect magic* spell or night vision goggles)

You can get a lot of mileage here by just listing things in the scene—a wardrobe, a bookshelf, a goblin—and dropping a descriptive tag on each one while following the Three of Five rule.

Two Cool Details: Try to include two irrelevant-but-cool details. These are details that aren't essential to the encounter or room or NPC, but are still nifty and distinct. It's the broken cuckoo clock in the corner, the slightly noxious odor with no identifiable source, the graffiti scrawled on the wall, or the bioluminescent fungus.

These "superfluous" details help the world feel like a real place, a place where people live and things exist that aren't centered on the PCs' experience. Plus, you never know when a clever player will find some insanely creative way to use these details to add something truly special to the game.

Three-by-Three: By rule of thumb, each featured room should have three elements. Describe each of those elements with at least three details. (So it's not just "a bookshelf." It's a "tall bookshelf in the corner, its shelves crammed with scrolls and books.")

For a scenic room, you can simplify this down a bit by just including three details total—either of the room in general if it's relatively barren, or of its primary point of interest. Whatever works.

More so than the other guidelines I'm suggesting here, this one is likely to lead you astray if you treat it as too much of a holy commandment. The point, though, is to get you into the ballpark of effective detail. You want to take the generic ("there's a bookshelf") and bring the world to life by helping the players to imagine a specific bookshelf in a specific space. On the other hand, you don't want to overwhelm the players and exhaust them with needless exposition. The three-by-three guideline encourages you to (a) prioritize the most important elements of the room and (b) give each of those elements the focus it deserves. Of course, there will be the occasional epic room with more than three things you need to establish, and maybe in those rooms you dial back the number of details per element to keep your initial description manageable.

All of this is an art, not a science.

EXITS & DIMENSIONS

There are a couple of essential substrates when describing dungeon rooms. First, you need to establish the size and shape of the room. You'll likely find that this needs to happen at or near the beginning of your description, providing a blank slate that you—and your players' imaginations—will fill with each additional element you detail.

The dimensions can be clinical ("The room is 40 feet long and 20 feet wide"), but this is often not required. "Large chambers," "small rooms," and the like will be quite common. Sometimes you can get away with establishing size in a more descriptive way—e.g., seeing "a comfortable study" or "a typical bedroom" or "a modest kitchen" will similarly cement the scene.

Although it doesn't have to be mentioned every time, don't forget the third dimension: Have cramped, low ceilings and breathtaking vaults that vanish into the darkness above the PCs.

Second, make sure you mention all the exits from the room. Remember that the core structure of a dungeon adventure is to "do stuff in a room until you run out of stuff to do, then pick an exit and go to the next room." It's vital for the players to know what their navigational choices are . . . and surprisingly easy to forget the doors because you're focused on all the cool stuff inside the room.

For clarity, I recommend grouping all the exits together ("There's a set of double doors on the far side of the room, an archway to the right, and a little tiny door—only about three feet high—on your left"). I've found it usually works best to either incorporate these into the description of the room's dimensions ("You see a large room with a door on the opposite side") or to list them at the end of your description, where recency bias will help your players keep track of their options.

KEEP IT PITHY

Having just dropped a big ol' list of things to include in your descriptions—cool details and exits and dimensions and three-by-three and three of five—it's a good time to paradoxically point out that length is your enemy when it comes to room descriptions. Players have a limited attention span, they can only keep track of so many things at one time, and, most importantly, they want to be *doing something*, not listening to exposition. In fact, the more effective and evocative your descriptions are, the *more* your players will be champing at the bit to start doing stuff in response to them. (That's kind of the whole goal of an awesome room description.)

So keep it pithy. What you want is a handful of evocative images, providing just enough seed and scaffold that the players will perform creative closure and conjure the totality of the scene in their own minds. (If I describe "bookshelves crammed with tomes and scrolls," I don't need to describe every book. Each player will fill those shelves all by themselves.) This not only prevents the players from "tuning out" a long description, but the act of closure itself will draw them into and immerse them in the game. They become silent partners in the creation of the world, and thus become invested in it and captured by it.

OUT OF THE BOX DESCRIPTIONS

The trap of boxed text is that it can create a subconscious belief that you describe a room up front and then, after that, the players are just taking actions within the pre-established environment.

But that's an artificial dynamic. It's much more effective to let the details of the setting continue flowing through the description of the action: the crunch of broken glass beneath their feet as they move across the room. The coppery smell of blood as they draw near the corpse. The sudden chill from the wind whipping through the shattered window.

This can also be useful to keep in mind if you're struggling to keep your room descriptions pithy: The impulse to crowd too much stuff into your boxed text is partly driven by a perceived need to describe everything as thoroughly as possible. But once you realize that the room's description will continue beyond the boxed text, it becomes a lot easier to say, "I'll save this bit for later."

Often you can include these additional details in your notes by incorporating them into the interactive elements in the room.

THAT'S A LOT OF THUMBS

You may have noticed that the phrase "rule of thumb" got used quite a bit while we've been discussing room keys and descriptions. How many thumbs do I have, exactly?

Hopefully enough thumbs to really emphasize that these are all guidelines. They're tips that will help you unlock your imagination and bring your world to vivid life. If you treat them like a straitjacket, though, they'll do the opposite. The important thing is to do what's right for the current scene and what's most effective for you and your players.

KEYING: DUNGEON FEATURES

Whether it's an abandoned dwarven city, a border fortress, or a hive of giant bees, a particular dungeon will typically have traits or features shared by many or all of its rooms. For example, the honeycomb material that makes up the walls of the beehive or the blue glowgems, faint and oft-cracked with age, that illuminate the halls of Khunbaral.

You could, of course, include these elements in every room key where they're relevant, no matter how many room keys that might be, but this is a lot of duplicated effort and wasted space, and it can actively debilitate the utility of a room key by cluttering it up with a lot of extraneous noise. When looking at the description of a room, you want the big, important stuff to pop out at you. You don't want it buried under mundane or routine details.

The Dungeon Features section of the key is designed to conveniently summarize these common elements of the dungeon's rooms, while keeping those details separate from the individual room keys. Common things to describe in your dungeon features include:

- Illumination
- Ceiling Height
- Walls
- Doors

But you shouldn't feel limited to these categories. If a dozen different rooms in your dungeon have large, identical clockwork spheres floating in the middle of them (for whatever reason), it may be appropriate to describe them in detail in your dungeon features.

In larger dungeons, you might have several distinct sections (the castle vs. the dungeon beneath it; the caves vs. the submerged tunnels; the dwarven armories vs. the fungal farms). You might want to include a separate set of Dungeon Features for each section, or your single Dungeon Features section might just distinguish each section appropriately. (You can see an example of this in the Mephits & Magmin adventure on page 48, where the ceiling height of the tunnels and finished areas are different from each other.)

However, don't fall into the trap of trying to capture every nuance of, for example, ceiling height in your dungeon features. The point is to capture material that is broadly true in your dungeon so that you don't have to copy-and-paste that material into every key entry. If a particular room or door is different from the dungeon's norm, there's no need to make a big deal out of it: Just describe it normally in the key.

This also means that it's frequently not necessary to include every category of information in your Dungeon Features section. If there is no common type of door or ceiling height in the dungeon, for example, that's just fine.

KEYING: CORRIDOR THEMES

So you have a dungeon map depicting rooms that are linked to each other either directly or via corridors. And you have a dungeon key that describes the rooms.

But what about the corridors?

Corridors can, of course, be any number of things: hallways, tunnels, courtyards, passages, shafts, stairs, etc. Because they typically don't appear on the dungeon key, however, they can often default to blank ciphers or generic mush—just empty expanses of gray stone or featureless utility spaces.

To avoid this, of course, you could just add every hallway to your key. In practice, however, this becomes quite laborsome and tends to bloat your dungeon key in ways that aren't particularly useful.

Instead, you can add a Corridor Themes section to your dungeon key. The goal here is to provide a palette you can draw from to flexibly describe hallways on the fly as the PCs pass down them. For example, in a haunted house your corridor theme might be

- torn red carpets
- a painting with eyes that follow you
- broken furniture
- cobwebs
- broken glass on the floor
- creaking floorboards

In a megacorp's skyscraper, on the other hand, you might have

- potted plants
- security cameras
- motivational propaganda posters
- color-coded section stripes on the wall
- navigational signs
- touchscreen directories
- maintenance drones
- vending machines

Brief bullet points giving plug-and-play options you can drop in might be all you need, or some of these elements might need additional explanation (e.g., how the color-coding in the arcology works). You could even key these elements to a random table if you'd like to procedurally generate your descriptions of PCs creeping between rooms. Whatever works for you and for the dungeon.

HOMEBREW KEYS VS. PUBLISHED KEYS

This whole time I've been telling you to write down your key, but what does that actually look like?

You might think that looks like the keys you see in published adventures, but that's not entirely accurate. A published key, like the one you used while running Mephits & Magmin, may show you the general form and the type of content you might prep for your own dungeons, but it's also far more verbose and polished.

This is because when I, for example, wrote Mephits & Magmin,

KEYING A HALLWAY

"But I have a reason to key this specific hallway!" Great. Do it. Corridor themes are a way of focusing your prep, but if you have some specific need that's better served with a different tool, you should follow that need.

One-off traps located in hallways are a good example of this. Special doors that need to be resolved before entering the room on the other side are another (whether they're trapped, cursed, or just have a *magic mouth* that asks you riddles).

I needed the key to communicate my intentions to you. You obviously don't live inside my head, and so I had to clearly explain not only what I was putting in the key, but also, to at least some extent, *why* I was putting it into the key. There are also certain standards of style and grammar that one simply expects in a professional publication.

When you're keying a dungeon for yourself, on the other hand, you *don't* need to explain yourself clearly to someone else. You want to put together complete, well-organized notes for your future self, but you are, ultimately, talking to yourself.

For example, take a look at the key for Area 1 of Mephits & Magmin on page 50. If I were keying that same room for use in my personal game, it might look something like this:

AREA 1: CAVE ENTRANCE

◎ rocky outcropping
◎ cave entrance in the middle of a slag of broken rock
◎ three mounds of mud visible

Wisdom (Perception)-DC 15: Spot mud mephit moving. DC 14 Arcana/Nature=mud mephits.
4 mud mephits, one hiding in tunnel. Ambush as PCs enter cave.
Intelligence (Nature)-DC 12: Cave is a lava tube. Very old.

You can easily see the rough simplicity here. I already know what the cave entrance looks like in my own head, so I only need a brief list of the major points to refresh my memory, and from that I can weave a full description at the table. Similarly, I know why I've placed the fourth mephit inside the tunnel, so I only need a brief reminder ("ambush as PCs enter cave") to orient me.

The particular details of the version of the key you see here won't necessarily be ideal for you, either. For example, you might like to pre-script more of the boxed text. On the other hand, maybe you wouldn't feel the need to write down the Wisdom (Perception) check to spot the hidden mephits. (That is, after all, the standard mechanic for doing so.)

The point is that you're writing your key for an audience of one: yourself. If you write it accordingly, without belaboring unnecessary details or polishing your presentation, you'll not only save prep time but you'll also likely end up with a better key that's easier to use.

COMBAT ENCOUNTER DESIGN

Combat is an important part of many roleplaying games, and while creating scenarios you'll often find yourself supplying bad guys for the PCs to punch, stab, eviscerate, or otherwise dispatch with physical violence. The trick with designing these combat encounters is that you want them to be difficult enough that the players feel a risk of failure, but not so difficult that the PCs can't possibly win.

For D&D, the *Dungeon Master's Guide* includes detailed guidelines for creating Easy, Medium, Hard, and Deadly encounters. You'll often find similar guidelines in other RPGs, too. These guidelines are useful, but it's also important to understand their limitations. Encounter guidelines can only take into account the known abilities of an NPC and compare them to the abilities of a typical group of PCs. But the potential encounter space for an RPG is effectively infinite and limited only by circumstance and imagination, and there are a wide variety of variables that will affect the actual difficulty of any specific encounter:

- The players' tactical decisions
- The tactical decisions you make for the NPCs
- The PCs' abilities
- The PCs' equipment
- The size of the battlefield
- The terrain
- The luck of the dice

And so forth. In my experience, the best an encounter design system can do is ballpark a specific encounter's difficulty and outcome. Which, to be clear, is still incredibly useful.

Because of this, however, there's a principle of encounter design that I think you'll find useful whether it's your first RPG, the first time you're running a new RPG, or even just the first time you're running for a new group of players: When it comes to encounter difficulty, you have to miss by a lot and for a fairly long time for "too easy" to ruin your campaign. On the other hand, you only need to miss once and by very little for "too hard" to kill all the PCs and end your campaign immediately.

In other words, as you're wrestling with encounter difficulty, aim low. You can always dial it up over time to find the sweet spot for your group.

The entertainment value of a combat encounter doesn't entirely derive from the risk of absolute failure in any case. For example, PCs come equipped with lots of cool toys. It's fun to use your awesome powers and abilities to good effect, even if you're just tossing minions around on your way to the big boss.

Of course, if every fight is trivial the fun will wear out pretty quickly. But you only need the challenge of a fight to be high enough that there are consequences for making bad tactical decisions. The possibility of a bad decision will incentivize players to find the good decisions and to feel rewarded when they do.

There are entire books written on strategy and tactics, and an encyclopedic discussion of the topic is probably somewhat beyond the scope of introductory adventure design. But there are a few tricks you can use to get the ball rolling.

First, look at the stat blocks in the encounter. What abilities does the opponent have? Then think about how those abilities could be enhanced through the use of terrain. This isn't limited to fantastical abilities, either. If an opponent has a potent ranged attack, for example, could they be positioned in a way that would make it difficult for the PCs to engage them in melee (e.g., on an upper level or on the opposite side of a chasm)? What are the opponent's strengths? How can those be enhanced? What are its weaknesses? How can those be protected?

You can either answer these questions based on the map you've already designed, or you can flip it around and make sure to design your rooms so that your bad guys can take tactical advantage of them. (Don't worry. The players will figure out how to turn the tables and use the terrain to their own advantage soon enough.)

Second, build encounters that include multiple stat blocks. Not just goblins, but:

◎ goblins and ogres
◎ goblins and blink dogs
◎ goblins and tieflings
◎ goblins and owlbears

Déjà vu, right? This ties conveniently into the principles we've discussed for creating your scenario concept, but you can also use one-off companions, pets, and the like to spike individual encounters. You can also include multiple stat blocks using variants of the same creature type. These might be extraordinary individuals (e.g., a goblin magi or chief), but can also be larger divisions within a society or species (e.g., goblin shadowstalkers vs. blood warriors).

Having two different stat blocks in the same encounter automatically gives the players a meaningful choice in target selection regardless of the specific tactical situation: If you're fighting six blood warriors, it doesn't matter which one you hit first. If you're fighting three blood warriors and three shadowstalkers, on the other hand, you'll have to figure out which one needs to be prioritized.

Multiple stat blocks also give you, as the DM, the ability to combine the abilities of those opponents in interesting ways. Six blood warriors can do what blood warriors can do. But if they form a defensive line blocking the corridor and the goblin magi lays down a *grease* spell that forces the PC melee fighters to make Dexterity saving throws while fighting on the front line, then fighting the blood warriors has instantly become a novel tactical dilemma for the players to solve.

I've generally found that you get most of the potential benefits here when you add the second stat block. Although much larger encounters could certainly benefit from three or four or even more stat block varieties, this quickly becomes complexity for the sake of complexity, resulting in diminishing or even negative returns.

Novelty in general can often be overrated here. Yes, it can be exciting to get a constant stream of new stuff, but it also comes at a cost and can even backfire.

The reason for this is mastery: As you spend more time playing goblin shadowstalkers, for example, you will quickly become familiar with their mechanics. You'll memorize their AC and attack bonuses so that you don't have to keep looking them up all the time. This will speed up the pace of combat and free you to focus on improving other aspects of play. You'll also be learning how to use the shadowstalkers' abilities to their best effect, improving your tactical mastery, and finding new ways to challenge the PCs.

Even more importantly, the players will *also* be mastering the shadowstalkers. They'll be learning what they can do and figuring out the best way to, for example, guard against their *shadow step*. They'll start casting *protection from poison* spells to give them an advantage against their asp-tipped blades.

If every single goblin in your dungeon is a special snowflake with a package of unique abilities that aren't shared by any other goblin, neither you nor your players would get the pleasure of learning what a goblin can do and then *applying that knowledge*.

Chess doesn't become a more interesting game if you only play it once and then toss it aside for another game; it becomes *less* interesting because you never learn its tactical and strategic depths. A constant, never-ending stream of novelty doesn't make for a richer experience. It flattens the experience.

Of course, if the *only* thing the PCs ever fought were goblin shadowstalkers, the shadowstalkers would soon wear out their welcome. Fortunately, you can have the best of both worlds. As we've already seen, you can get a lot of variety—while also leveraging mastery—by combining a small variety of stat blocks into a bunch of different combinations over the course of a dungeon: A goblin magi with shadowstalkers will have a different tactical impact than a goblin magi with a squad of blood warriors, or blood warriors and shadowstalkers together, or any of the three in a squad by themselves.

And then, when the PCs move on to a new scenario or the next level of a larger dungeon, you can mix things up with a fresh selection of foes.

WHAT ABOUT A RANDOM ENCOUNTER TABLE?

If you're eager to add random encounter checks to your dungeon procedure, you'll need to build a random encounter table for your adventure. You can skip ahead to Random Encounter Tables in Advanced Dungeons on page 160 for a step-by-step guide to designing one.

---

5 + 5 DUNGEONS

At this point you're hopefully bubbling over with ideas for what your first dungeon will be, but it might still feel a little overwhelming as you try to figure out how to take all of this stuff—scenario concepts, keys, maps, encounters, dungeon features, oh my!—and develop it into a playable adventure.

To get started, therefore, I recommend creating a 5 + 5 Dungeon.

The 5 + 5 Dungeon is an **adventure recipe**. These recipes work a lot like any other recipe: They detail a proven template for a successful adventure and a list of required ingredients. Simply provide the **adventure ingredients**, follow the recipe to add them to your adventure, and you'll be good to go!

STEP 1: THE SCENARIO CONCEPT

As with any dungeon, you'll want to start your 5 + 5 Dungeon with a strong scenario concept: location, denizens, and goal. What type of dungeon is it? Who will the PCs be confronting there? What are the PCs trying to do?

We discussed how to find inspiration for your scenario concept on page 94.

STEP 2: DUNGEON FEATURES & CORRIDOR THEMES

Take a blank page—whether that's paper, in your word processor, a link in your campaign wiki, or whatever else works for you—and write "DUNGEON FEATURES" at the top of it. Then grab another one and label it "CORRIDOR THEMES."

If there are details that you immediately think should be added to these lists, you should go for it. But your primary goal right now is to give yourself a space to jot down notes and features that occur to you while keying.

Additional details on dungeon features can be found on page 111, and corridor themes are on page 112.

STEP 3: FIVE FEATURED ROOMS

Your 5 + 5 Dungeon will include five featured rooms. Create:

- 1 challenge (see page 125)
- 1 fight (see page 129)
- 1 twist (see page 132)
- 1 reward (see page 134)
- Pick a second challenge, fight, twist, or reward.

So, for example, you might have a dungeon with two fights, a challenge, a twist, and a reward. Or two rewards, a fight, a twist, and a challenge.

These room archetypes are described on pages 125 to 136.

THE FIFTH ROOM

Having a fifth room that doubles one of the others is a way to mix things up so that your 5 + 5 Dungeons all feel a little unique from each other in pacing and structure. You don't want your adventures to feel rote or predictable, even if the players only notice it subconsciously.

The fifth room also gives you an opportunity to tailor content to a PC who might not have a lot to do in the rest of the dungeon. Or, alternatively, to give the whole group an extra helping of the game play you know they like the most.

5 + 5 BRAINSTORMING

As you're brainstorming for your 5 + 5 Dungeon, you'll likely end up doing steps 2 and 3 at the same time. Heck, you'll probably end up doing a good chunk of your brainstorming during step 1. That's okay. The adventure police are not going to kick down your door for skipping around in whatever way makes sense to you: The 5 + 5 Dungeon recipe is flexible. And I'm pretty sure the adventure police don't even exist.

STEP 4: SCENIC ROOMS

Next, add five scenic rooms to your dungeon. Scenic room archetypes are described on page 123.

Having a total of ten rooms in your 5 + 5 Dungeon (five scenic rooms plus five featured rooms) is designed to pace the dungeon and provide enough material for a typical four-hour session of play.

STEP 5: MAPPING & KEYING

Review the tips and tricks for mapping on page 100, creating a connection map to work out the relationships between your scenic and featured rooms before executing your final map on graph paper.

Give the players interesting navigational choices to make by including

- forks in corridors,
- rooms with more than one exit,
- secret doors and passages, and
- crossroads.

The even balance between scenic and featured rooms is designed to give the players room to explore, so don't clump all the scenic rooms together in one half of the dungeon and all the featured rooms together in the other half. But you also don't want to just alternate between scenic and featured rooms, because that will become very predictable for the players.

STEP 6: FINISHING TOUCHES

With your map and key done, revisit your corridor theme and dungeon features. Clean up your notes and add any additional details to finish fleshing them out.

The last thing to consider is the **scenario hook**: Why do the PCs want to explore this dungeon and how do they learn of its existence?

A few widely applicable scenario hooks are as follows:

- Someone hired them to go to the dungeon and do something.
- The PCs found a treasure map or heard locals talking about something valuable in the dungeon.
- The PCs were attacked and tracked their attackers back to the dungeon.

For your first few adventures, as with Mephits & Magmin, you may want to start the adventure in medias res: At the beginning of the session, the PCs are standing at the dungeon entrance and you briefly explain how they got there and what their goal is. But, when you're ready, it can also be a good idea (and quite fun!) to actually play through these events.

If you'd like to get more ambitious with your scenario hooks, check out Extra Credit: Scenario Hooks on page 498.

DUNGEON ROOMS

Scenic
- Themed
- Utility
- Fantastic Feature

Challenge
- Trap
- Environmental
- Skill
- Puzzle
- Social

Fight
- Guardian
- Sentry
- Mooks
- Boss

Twist
- Trick
- Secret Area
- Remix
- Combo
- Unexpected Ending

Rewards
- Treasure
- Clue
- Sanctuary
- Boon
- Scenario Goal

DUNGEON ROOMS: SCENIC

Scenic rooms, as we've discussed, are designed to be passed through with minimal interaction. If the PCs stop to examine anything at all, it should be quickly resolved and they will be on their way again. While a scenic room can be pedestrian, mundane, or even completely empty, don't hesitate for a moment to fill it with eye candy. Keying a scenic room can often be about identifying the "one cool thing" it contains, with such features serving as landmarks, inspiring awe, or even invoking terror. (Or all of the above.)

THEMED

Dungeons have themes—of place, character, concept, ideology, mood, or composition. The themed room establishes, develops, or manipulates those themes.

At the most basic level, simply look to your scenario concept: How can the themed room reflect the location, denizens, or goal? If the PCs are exploring a gothic mansion, this could be a dining room with strange décor or a bedroom draped in black veils. If the bandits keep a pack of trained wolves, this could be their empty kennels. If the party is here to steal Lord Denton's gold, then it might be the sitting room where he has proudly displayed his old prospecting map.

In this way the themed room can also act as foreshadowing or provide clues for what the rest of the dungeon might contain.

UTILITY

If you think of the dungeon as a real place, then there are often rooms that should logically just exist. The bandit fort should have barracks; the abandoned dwarven city's forges should be long cold; the haunted zeppelin should have ghosts on the flight deck.

Such rooms can also serve as the set pieces for challenges, fights, or the like. But, if not, they can (and often should!) be included as scenic rooms.

FANTASTIC FEATURE

Magic makes all things possible. Take the opportunity to imagine the impossible and feature it in a scenic room, evoking a sense of wonder in the players as they explore your setting.

Fantastic features can include stuff like:

- a levitation sculpture formed from floating amethysts
- magical paintings that come to life
- an oracular spirit frozen in a block of rune-carved amber
- a tree with metallic leaves
- a room where all the furniture is limned in faerie fire

- ◎ a taxidermied unicorn
- ◎ a waterfall of black acid
- ◎ a room of magical portals leading to other rooms in the dungeon
- ◎ an observatory that shows the sky of some other alien world
- ◎ a shrine dedicated to unknown gods

This isn't limited to fantasy games, of course. Science fiction, horror, and other speculative genres all offer a palette for creating the exotic and awe-inspiring. In fact, you could interpret this more broadly as an opportunity to highlight your chosen genre.

DUNGEON ROOMS: CHALLENGE

A dungeon should be about more than just fights. (We'll get to those in a moment.) There are many other challenges that can be featured, and including stuff that can't be automatically responded to with eldritch blasts and pointy steel will encourage the players to creatively engage with the adventure and actively think about what their course of action should be. In fact, challenges can be most effective when they're presented in the form of a **dilemma**—a tough choice between two options.

TRAP

A trap is often seen as the default non-combat challenge in a dungeon. Like combat, a trap threatens the PCs with damage or a debilitating effect, often blocking their journey until they have figured out how to bypass or overcome it.

We discussed how to design and run traps extensively in the last chapter. See Running Traps on page 87.

ENVIRONMENTAL

Hazardous environments—volcanic eruptions, toxic gas, pools of acid, rotten floorboards, rock slides, etc.—usually work like traps, but there are other forms of environmental challenge, too.

Examples of environmental challenges could include:

- a broken bridge over a vast chasm
- debilitating heat that exhausts over time unless preventative measures are taken
- force fields blocking a hallway
- a tall cliff that must be climbed
- a polluted river that needs to be cleaned
- needing shelter during a sudden blizzard
- swimming across a rapids-filled river
- navigating through an area of magical darkness
- a drawbridge that needs to be lowered to access the castle

Environmental challenges evoke the dungeon location, making it an active part of play instead of just scenery that the group glides past.

SKILL

You will, of course, use skill checks throughout the entire game, including when you're resolving other types of challenge rooms. Sometimes, however, it can be useful to think of challenges from a skill-first perspective, if for no other reason than that it allows you to use the list of skills in your game of choice as a source of inspiration.

A good skill-based challenge, however, isn't just about targeting the character's skill. It's also about the player's skill. Much like a trap, if a challenge simply boils down to the DM telling the player to, "Make such and such a skill check," the player rolling the dice, and the outcome being declared, that's hardly exciting or engaging game play.

Ideally, you want to present a situation in the game world that challenges the player to figure out the solution before executing it (with a successful skill check or otherwise). It's even better if the player is able to create their own solution to the problem. Complex challenges that require several steps or simultaneous problems to be overcome are also a great way to increase interest.

PUZZLE

Riddles, ciphers, logic puzzles, and similar challenges are another great way of engaging player skill, but they can be tricky to pull off successfully. First, puzzles often require someone to have just the right bit of insight to solve them. This can make them quite fragile in practice, and if none of the players can figure out the solution to your puzzle, the entire session can grind to a painful and frustrating halt.

To avoid this, puzzles should almost always be optional. Instead of blocking access to the next section of the adventure, for example, the puzzle can instead grant access to an optional reward. For puzzles that *do* give access to the next section of the adventure, make sure to include alternatives. If you have a door that can be opened by answering a riddle, for example, then you might include an alternative route that will force the PCs to face something dangerous. Or simply make sure that the PCs can also hack the door open with their axe or cast a *knock* spell to get through.

Players may also want to use a skill check to simply have their characters solve the puzzle for them. From a certain point of view, this makes sense ("My wizard is much smarter than me!"), but it tends to defeat the reason for including the puzzle in the first place. Instead of providing the solution on a successful check, consider giving the player a hint to help them solve the puzzle. Clues to a puzzle's solution can also be hidden in other rooms of the dungeon, allowing clever players to solve the puzzle directly, while others piece it together through exploration.

In order for many types of puzzles to be solvable by the players, though, they may need to be able to actually see what their characters see. Puzzles, therefore, often benefit from prepping physical handouts. There are many different forms that a puzzle can take:

- a riddle posed by a sphinx
- an encoded letter that must be deciphered
- a shattered clay tablet that must be pieced back together
- a set of colored statues that must be arranged on plinths according to the color wheel

(continued)

- ⬡ a maze the PCs must successfully navigate
- ⬡ a lock with a combination the PCs must figure out
- ⬡ a secret message that's been encoded on the gravestones in a cemetery
- ⬡ flashes of light containing a hidden message in Morse code
- ⬡ four shrines each containing a statue dedicated to one of the four elements; the PCs must expose each statue to the appropriate element
- ⬡ a room in which only specific tiles on the mosaic floor are safe to stand on

SOCIAL

In a social challenge, the PCs have to accomplish their goals by interacting with the NPCs in the dungeon. That might be the bad guys of the scenario, but there will often be other characters in the dungeon, creating a wide variety of possible social interactions.

In practice, a social challenge may devolve into combat. Conversely, there are many would-be combat encounters that can be bypassed with clever diplomacy. This is a good reminder that these room archetypes are not hard-and-fast categories. There's a lot of overlap in what you design, and the really great rooms will, in any case, invite the players to think outside the box and create their own solutions, taking the dungeon in directions you never could have anticipated.

Examples of social challenges include:

- ⬡ The palace majordomo expects a bribe.
- ⬡ The undead courtesan doesn't realize that she's long dead.
- ⬡ Another faction in the dungeon must be convinced to help the PCs defeat a common foe.
- ⬡ The bandit king will help the PCs, but only if they do something morally questionable.
- ⬡ The PCs are interrogating a prisoner.
- ⬡ A rival band of adventurers could share what they've learned about the dungeon, if the PCs can make it worth their while.
- ⬡ Two NPCs have a feud and they want the PCs to adjudicate it.

- The PCs convince the "bad guys" that they've been tricked into attacking innocents.

- The bandits mistake the PCs as being emissaries sent by the local necromancer—can they keep up the bluff and avoid detection?

- A devil attempts to trick the PCs into signing a contract for their souls.

ROLEPLAYING IS EVERYTHING

Some DMs will refer to social challenges as "roleplaying challenges." Personally, I try to avoid this because it creates the impression that "roleplaying" is only the bit of the game where your character is talking.

Roleplaying, though, is much more than that. It's about playing a role. It's about making choices as if you were your character.

Combat, for example, isn't the place where you should be hitting the pause button on roleplaying. Exactly the opposite, in fact. Combat is where your character is making *life or death* decisions. It's the ultimate crucible where character is tested and defined. Think about movies like *Saving Private Ryan*, *Bullet in the Head*, *Black Hawk Down*, or *Avengers: Infinity War*.

This extends to the entire dungeon. There aren't "roleplaying rooms" and "not roleplaying rooms." Every single room is a chance for players to express themselves and develop their characters.

DUNGEON ROOMS: FIGHT

Rooms with a fight archetype are designed to be resolved with the combat mechanics. The vast panoply of possible opponents, which can be mixed together in any number of combinations, creates an almost infinite variety of encounters, while the formal combat mechanics found in most roleplaying games create a comfortable familiarity and security in running them at the table.

Check out Combat Encounter Design, page 115, for an in-depth look at designing these encounters.

GUARDIAN

A guardian encounter seeks to protect something—a room, a treasure, a character, the entire dungeon, or maybe just itself/themselves. You can probably think of this as a "typical" combat encounter. There'll be a bunch of opponents in a room and they'll stand and fight until the fight is done.

SENTRY

A sentry encounter, on the other hand, is designed to raise the alarm. Rather than standing and fighting, a sentry will attempt to run and fetch help, ring a bell, activate an *alarm* spell, or the like. A common variant is for some opponents in the encounter to stand and fight while others run to raise the alarm.

A sentry room will generally be designed as an easier encounter, giving the PCs a chance to stop the alarm from being raised if they can act quickly, stealthily, and/or decisively.

When designing a sentry encounter, of course, you'll want to give some thought to what the consequences will be if the alarm *is* raised.

MOOKS

Mooks are henchmen, foot soldiers, minions, petty street gangs, and similar *fireball* fodder. They're the guys Jackie Chan or John Wick throw around to fill the scene with furious action and look like bad-asses. Such encounters shouldn't be completely trivial in an RPG, but these are the easy fights that the PCs will usually steamroll (unless they suffer a spate of ill fortune or have already been badly injured). That's okay! Easier fights not only provide a change of pace, the contrast between Mook encounters and Guardian or Boss encounters will also make the tough fights feel tougher.

In more advanced dungeons (see page 138), Mook encounters also make great reinforcements that can be summoned by Sentry encounters and similar alarums.

MOOKS ARE EVERYWHERE

*Mook-type opponents, of course, can be used in any combat
encounter, not just Mook encounters. In Guardian and Boss
rooms, they provide ablative shielding and crank up the action.
They can also make good Sentries, with the PCs needing to mow
them down before they can scatter and alert the big bads.*

BOSS

Bosses are the big, significant bad guys. There are lots of different
concepts for bosses—end bosses, mini-bosses, optional super-bosses,
puzzle bosses, recurring bosses, dual bosses, summoned bosses, staged
bosses—but the key thing is that these are the tough fights. They feature
an opponent with a stat block that's a whole lot nastier than everybody
else in the dungeon, and the PCs are going to have their limits tested in
the fight. (Unless, of course, they get clever about things.)

Boss encounters should usually feature other opponents in addition to the boss. In most roleplaying games, having four, five, or six
PCs all gang up on a solo opponent usually doesn't make for a great
encounter. There are exceptions, but even if the action economy of
having a bunch of PCs all focus fire on a single opponent doesn't
turn the boss into a mook, the tactics of such an encounter are rarely
interesting. (PCs with melee attacks will just swarm the boss and then
the rest of the fight turns into a dice-rolling slog.)

Since the boss is the most dangerous combat encounter in the
area, it's not unusual to assume that they're the one in charge. But
that's not necessarily true—they might be the real leader's champion,
enslaved demon, loyal sister, summoned creature, or any number of
other possibilities.

It's also easy to make the opposite assumption: If someone's
in charge, then they *must* be a boss (i.e., bigger and stronger than
everybody else). That's also not necessarily true, either. In Mephits &
Magmin, for example, Asuvius has essentially the same stat block as
the other magmin.

Bosses are cool, but they're not a necessity. Don't feel as if you're obligated to include them in your adventure. It'll make them feel even more special when you *do* want to use one.

DUNGEON ROOMS: TWIST

A complication, a surprise, an inversion of expectation. As the players fall into a rhythm and start to feel as if they've got everything figured out, a good Twist room will throw them for a loop and force them to actively reengage with the dungeon until they can get back on top of things again.

TRICK

A good trick room appears to be one thing, but is actually another:

- A shrouded maiden chained to the wall is actually a medusa, waiting to strike.
- An illusory feast is disguising food that is actually rotten and disgusting.
- A fake treasure is used to lure the PCs into a trap.
- A lowly servant seems ready to turn on his cruel masters but is actually the bandit king in disguise.
- A rotating room designed to disorient the PC and thwart their mapping.
- Escher-like chambers with non-Euclidean geometry.
- A false door leaves the PCs trapped.
- Teleportation areas seamlessly move the PCs to a different location in the dungeon.
- A treasure map shows a false version of the dungeon's layout.
- A "ghost" that is actually just an elaborate hoax.

In some cases it's the whole dungeon that's a trick, and this room is actually the revelation of what's really going on. This is the moment when the PCs realize that the goblins are actually the good guys and the villainous villagers tricked them, or that the legendary treasure they seek has been cursed and the entire dungeon is a prison seeking to keep its great evil contained.

SECRET AREA

Secret rooms make for great bonus areas, while secret corridors can provide shortcuts through the dungeon or allow PCs to outflank their enemy's defenses.

REMIX

Take one of the other rooms in the dungeon and find a way to twist it or invert it, so that the players will be able to leverage their experience with the other chamber while simultaneously needing to puzzle out the differences. (Or vice versa, since they may often be able to encounter the rooms in either order.)

If the other room was scenic, then perhaps this room only superficially appears the same while actually concealing some hidden danger (e.g., the suits of armor in this hallway are animated and will attack intruders). If it's a challenge, then the solution that worked in the other room won't work in this one (e.g., a waterfall cascades down the rocks here, making them slippery and more difficult to climb; or there's a riddle that seems identical if you don't listen carefully, but it requires a different answer). If it's a fight, then the terrain is radically different or perhaps the enemies have a unique set of abilities, spells, or magical items (e.g., surprise flamethrower!). And so forth.

COMBO

Take two different room archetypes and combine them together in one room. (This can include other Trick room archetypes.)

When looking for a combo, try to find a room that's greater than the sum of its parts. Fortunately, you may be surprised at how often this just sort of automatically happens as a result of putting two different things in the same place: Ogres in a trapped room can use that trap to their advantage, while ogres assaulting the room where the PCs are trying to get across a chasm immediately add the pressure of time to the skill challenge.

Another thing to keep in mind when building a combo is that the two elements can be tightly interwoven. Rather than just having a boss and a puzzle in the same room, for example, you could have a boss who *is* a puzzle—e.g., they can only be harmed if exposed to sunlight.

UNEXPECTED ENDING

A very specific type of twist is the unexpected ending, when the PCs think they've wrapped everything up but things suddenly slip away from them.

This might be the revelation that the ogres were working for Prince Rupert the whole time, revealing the true boss that they still need to defeat! Or maybe they discover that the princess they sought to rescue is actually being held in a different château, creating a link to their next adventure.

DUNGEON ROOMS: REWARDS

Rewards! Why are we even in this dungeon stabbing and shooting and blasting things? The loot!

Some rewards will be purely mechanical in nature (e.g., experience points), but most will be grounded in the narrative of the game world. Some of these will be mechanically tokenized to one degree or another (gold pieces, blessings, charms, and epic boons in D&D, for example), whereas others will flow entirely from and be significant only because of the fictional reality of our characters, including their goals, aspirations, and fears.

TREASURE

Wealth! Some treasure is useful in its own right, while other treasure will give the PCs funds to pursue their dreams and achieve their agendas:

- Glittering piles of gold and silver coins
- Marvelous magic items
- Sparkling gems and precious jewels
- Beautiful works of art
- Historical artifacts
- Antique furniture
- Lost technology
- Rare books and manuscripts
- Armories filled with weapons
- Valuable trade goods

While coinage is simple, making treasure more specific can make it memorable and feel more special while also inviting the players to come up with clever ways of using or leveraging the treasure. The process of liquidating treasure can also be used as the hook for future scenarios, while putting treasure in a bulky form can make the process of actually removing it from the dungeon a unique challenge in its own right.

CLUE

The room's reward might be a vital piece of information. This clue might reveal something about another room in the dungeon (e.g., there's a secret passage in the library or the shadowstalkers are vulnerable to sunlight). Alternatively, it might be the scenario hook for a whole new adventure (e.g., a treasure map revealing the location of another dungeon).

SANCTUARY

This place provides a place of safety within the dungeon where the PCs can safely rest or find some other form of respite. Examples include:

- a secret chamber the denizens of the dungeon are ignorant of
- a room that can be made secure if magical wards are activated
- a sanctified chapel shunned by the undead
- a mystic font that provides magical healing
- the clan caves of friendly goblins who welcome the PCs

False sanctuaries can offer an interesting twist, but they generally work best if it's possible for the PCs to realize the truth before being caught off guard.

BOON

These rooms contain some resource or benefit that will aid the PCs. These advantages can be generic in nature (PCs can always use another *potion of healing*), but are often more compelling if they're more specifically tied to the present scenario. For example:

- *potions of fire resistance* in a dungeon filled with magma mephits
- a blessing, charm, or other supernatural gift
- a potential ally who might be willing to fight alongside the PCs
- a silver salve for the eyes that can reveal which goblins have been corrupted by the shadow maggots
- uniforms that the PCs can use to disguise themselves as guards

The effectiveness of many boons may be limited to the current scenario, but others may persist long after the scenario has come to an end.

SCENARIO GOAL

This room contains whatever it is that the PCs are trying to achieve or retrieve in the dungeon.

It's not unusual for this to be a room with a combo twist, combining the scenario reward with a guardian or challenge that must be overcome to claim it. (But it's also possible those protections are in the next room over and this room simply serves as the denouement of the adventure.) Scenario twists may also mean that the scenario goal isn't what the PCs thought it would be when they first entered the dungeon.

In other cases, the scenario goal might be one and the same as overcoming some other room type. (For example, defeating Prince Rupert in combat or cleansing the goblins' water supply as a skill challenge.) You can consider that sort of goal to be a combo twist if that's useful to you, but I wouldn't worry too much about trying to achieve some sort of perfect classification.

Along these same lines, it's not unusual for a scenario goal to be one of the other reward types: claiming the Sword of Fatherfall (treasure), finding the map revealing the location of the Lost City of Shandrala (clue), bringing the refugees to a place of safety (sanctuary), or waking the Sleeping Knights to join their crusade (boon).

RUN YOUR SCENARIO

Now that you've created your first scenario, it's time to bring it to the table and share it with your players!

For the most part, you're going to find that this works almost exactly like the first dungeon scenario that you ran. (Except you created it!) To incorporate the new techniques from the How to Run a Dungeon chapter, start by making a copy of the Dungeon Running Sheet. Then, a few hours before the game is scheduled to start, take a few minutes to review the dungeon turn, dungeon actions, and random encounter checks.

If you're feeling overwhelmed, remember that you don't need to add all these procedures in at once. For example, you could use dungeon turns but wait before introducing random encounters.

If you have several hours to play, the players will likely finish your entire dungeon. But if not, that's okay! When it's getting close to the time you need to quit playing, find a good stopping point (ideally one where everyone is eager to see what happens next!) and then schedule another session when everyone can come back and finish the adventure!

...AND FOR YOUR NEXT ADVENTURE

Now that you've created and run your first dungeon, you may be wondering, "What comes next?" The most immediate answer to that question is likely, "Do it again."

Dungeon crawl scenarios are also known as **location crawls**, and as we've seen, these locations can be almost anything. The 5 + 5 Dungeon recipe is also very versatile, allowing you to pour almost any idea you might have into a tried-and-true formula. So there's no reason you shouldn't keep running these adventures while you and your players grow more comfortable with the game. It really is possible to run an entire campaign armed with nothing more than these simple dungeons.

Once you've become comfortable and confident, though—or maybe even a session or two before that happens—you'll eventually want to start expanding your adventures beyond the confines of the 5 + 5 Dungeon. To do that, we'll begin by taking our dungeons to the next level. (If you'll pardon the pun.) The Advanced Dungeons (see page 138) and Dynamic Dungeons (see page 176) chapters will give you a lot of new tools and options for this, but don't feel like you need to use them all at once! With each new adventure you create and run, pick and choose what you want to explore next.

⁘ ADVANCED DUNGEONS ⁘

Dungeons come in a variety of sizes. The 5 + 5 Dungeon recipe in the last chapter creates a fairly typical example, with enough content to fill roughly four hours of play—one or two sessions for a typical group.

Micro-dungeons are smaller, with only one or two featured rooms and a similar number of scenic rooms. Probably no more than five rooms at most. These dungeons lack the dynamic elements and opportunities for exploration found in larger dungeons. (In most micro-dungeons, you probably don't even need to bother using dungeon turns.) But the great thing about a micro-dungeon is that it can be incorporated into a larger adventure without taking up a full session.

A **large dungeon**, on the other hand, is at least three times the size of a typical 5 + 5 Dungeon. Large dungeons will have at least thirty rooms or so, and often even more than that. A lot of published dungeon adventures feature large dungeons, with the expectation that exploring the dungeon will take up several sessions of play.

The key difference of the large dungeon, however, is not simply its size or playing time. It's the expectation that clearing the dungeon will require multiple **expeditions**. In other words, the PCs will enter the dungeon, explore a portion of it, but then be forced to retreat (or otherwise find respite) for a long rest and resupply, returning to the dungeon later to renew the exploration in a new expedition.

This core concept of visiting and revisiting the dungeon—as opposed to simply bulling your way forward until you reach the "end"—fundamentally changes the pace of play. Which is good, because the simplistic "kick down the door" style of play, where the PCs systematically go from one door to the next clearing each room they find, can become terribly monotonous in larger dungeons.

To run a successful large dungeon—and, indeed, what makes a large dungeon a special experience—the players have to be able to make strategic choices using the knowledge they've gleaned from previous expeditions to improve their chances of success on their current expedition. This means some combination of the following:

◈ **Having goals other than "kill all the monsters."** Because RPGs often have detailed combat systems, it can be easy to default to "clear the dungeon" as a default goal, particularly for a dungeon adventure. But if the goal is just "kill all the monsters," then most of the strategy goes out the window and the PCs are reduced to mindless drones kicking down every door. We're ahead of the game here, because we already discussed setting dungeon goals in our scenario concept (see page 136).

◈ **Having non-linear, xandered dungeon design** (see page 150). If there's only one route through the dungeon, then it's impossible for the PCs to learn the dungeon geography and make strategic choices. This also defaults the dungeon back to "kill all the monsters" (because there's no way for the PCs to strategically avoid any of them).

◈ **Having varied experiences in the dungeon,** not only because variety is the spice of life but also because it will provide strategic choice. ("I'd rather try to ride the rapids of the Dark River than fight the orcs" is a richer choice than "I'd rather fight the goblins than fight the orcs," although there's nothing inherently wrong with the latter by any means.) Using a mixture of different featured rooms (see page 105) and reaction checks (see page 85) will go a long way here.

◈ **Having the dungeon come to life as an active environment.** This makes each expedition into the dungeon a fresh and slightly different experience, as the PCs make strategic choices in an evolving fog of war and can directly apply the lessons learned—particularly geographic lessons—from previous expeditions in new contexts and in response to new challenges. To achieve this effect, we'll start by using random encounters (see page 160), restocking procedures (see page 165), and updating the dungeon key (see page 171). Then, when you're ready to take these techniques to the next level, you can check out Dynamic Dungeons (see page 176).

Some of these are, as you can see, things you're already doing. The rest of this chapter, and the next, is going to give you the tools to do everything else.

EXPEDITION-BASED PLAY

The basic dynamic of expedition-based play is that the party gathers a set of resources and then goes forth to pursue a goal. (In other words, they plan the expedition and then go on the expedition.) This goal might be something generic (e.g., "Get as much gold as possible") or it might be something terribly specific (e.g., "Get revenge by slaying Orok the Minotaur").

Some of the resources gathered for the expedition will be mechanical in nature (e.g., hit points, spell slots, etc.), but it's likely that the PCs will also gather other resources (e.g., magic potions, rations, ammunition, etc.). Either way, the PCs will expend these resources over the course of the expedition until they run out of resources, at which point they will have to withdraw to some form of base camp at which they can replenish their resources in preparation for their next expedition.

What makes expedition-based play interesting is that the players are trying to maximize the return on their investment. In other words, they want to achieve as much as possible—to get the most gold, to clear out the maximum number of Orok's minions, to achieve as many milestones as possible on the way to their goal—with the resources that they have. This creates a crucible in which their strategic and tactical decisions become extremely meaningful and, therefore, extremely interesting.

To make expedition-based play really work, you want a cost associated with abandoning the current expedition and starting a new one. This is often the money spent on new supplies, but it can also be in the difficulty level of getting back to the point where they left off (which can be achieved in dungeon scenarios with random encounters and restocking, as discussed later in this chapter).

Beyond the large dungeon, there is another category: the **megadungeon**.

There are three defining characteristics of the megadungeon, each of which is only tangentially related to its size:

⊘ It must have enough content to support a full campaign. (For D&D, we might say that it has to be able to support two full tiers of play, with each tier being roughly five levels.)

⊘ It must be large enough that "clear the dungeon" cannot be an achievable goal. In other words, you can play the entire campaign in the megadungeon and, when you are done, the megadungeon will still be there, waiting for you (or someone else) to continue exploring its depths.

⊘ It must, in some way, contain multiple "scenarios." This usually takes the form of either having multiple distinct goals that can be independently, or semi-independently, pursued in the megadungeon and/or having disparate factions, each of which controls a chunk of the dungeon and poses a unique collection of challenges. (In some ways, you can even think of the megadungeon as being made up of a number of individual dungeon experiences that are simply connected or intermeshed with each other.)

The earliest D&D campaigns, including those that existed even before D&D did—like Dave Arneson's Castle Blackmoor and, later, Gary Gygax's Castle Greyhawk—were originally megadungeon campaigns. They provide a surprisingly robust and diverse play experience, emphasizing a goal-oriented style of play, and, like dungeons in general, are not limited to underground warrens: They could be a derelict, alien colony ship in a science fiction game or a vast garden maze in Wonderland.

The tools you'll use to run a megadungeon will mostly be the same as the ones you'll use for large dungeons, although the scope and scale of the megadungeon may, as we'll see, alter your best practices a bit.

LEAVING THE MEGADUNGEON

Although a megadungeon can support an entire campaign, that doesn't mean it needs to be the entire campaign. It can be quite useful to break up the megadungeon experience with other scenarios. There are a number of ways you can set this up, but a fairly straightforward method is to just include clues in the dungeon that point to adventures outside of the dungeon. Treasure maps are a great way to do this!

CUSTOMIZING THE DUNGEON TURN

As you become more comfortable running your dungeons and begin exploring a wider array of dungeon types, one of the first things you may want to start experimenting with is the dungeon procedure itself.

As an extreme example, you might have a dungeon that's completely abandoned, perhaps protected only with ancient booby traps or with guardians that are all automatons limited to individual rooms. For such an adventure, you might not want to use dungeon turns at all. Dungeon turns, after all, are designed to track time and trigger effects, like random encounters, accordingly. If a dungeon doesn't have any time-based effects or pressure, there may be no advantage to mucking about with the extra bookkeeping of the dungeon turn.

The point is that there's nothing sacrosanct about the default dungeon turn procedure. It's not the One True Way™ of running a dungeon. It can—and should!—be modified.

Encounter frequency is a good example of this. The default encounter check is 1 in 1d8, but maybe you're running an adventure in an abandoned city in the middle of the desert and you really want to emphasize how barren and desolate the location is. In that case you might decide to only check for an encounter every other turn, or make a 1 in 1d12 or 1 in 1d20 check instead.

Conversely, if you were running an adventure in a highly secured goblin fortress with regular guard patrols, you might want to crank up the rate of random encounters. Or make a second encounter check each turn specifically for the guard patrols.

Similarly, you can vary the encounter frequency and/or the encounter tables used depending on where the PCs are located in the dungeon. (This can, for example, create high-risk areas. It could also create less populated regions where the PCs might be able to risk taking a rest.)

You can also **bias reaction checks**. For example, rolling 2d6 + 2 for a reaction check would eliminate the possibility of dungeon denizens immediately attacking the PCs on sight. Conversely, a 2d6-2 check would increase the average hostility of the dungeon. You could also create custom tables and checks to achieve whatever spread of probability feels appropriate.

In addition to encounter checks and reaction checks, you might introduce **custom checks** for the dungeon. For example, in the faerie warrens of the Snow Queen you might have a 1 in 6 check each turn to see if blizzard conditions begin. If the PCs have left corpses lying around, you might do a 1 in 8 check each turn to see if they've been discovered (and an active search for intruders has begun). And so forth.

Although the list of dungeon actions is fairly comprehensive for the typical activities of adventurers, your players are creative and the characters they're playing are unique, so it's quite possible they'll come up with some new exploration technique and start using it regularly. If that's the case, you may find it useful to formally create a **new dungeon action** to handle it.

You can actually find an example of this way back in the original 1974 edition of D&D: Some characters had the ability to use ESP (extrasensory perception) and would attempt to detect the thoughts of monsters lurking around corners or on the far side of doors or walls. Doing so was time-consuming, however, requiring a dungeon turn.

More accurately, it required a quarter-turn. You can similarly introduce **half-turn** and **quarter-turn actions** (with characters being able to take two of the former or four of the latter each turn). This will obviously increase the amount of bookkeeping you need to juggle during play, but you may find that it's worth the extra complexity to be able to handle a broader range of discrete actions with greater precision within the dungeon turn structure.

Personally, I don't. But that's really the point: You should play around and find what works for you, for your group, and for the adventure that you're designing.

REWRITE THE RECIPE

Having a flexible, tried-and-true adventure recipe like the 5 + 5 Dungeon in your pocket is always useful, but it's still just *one* recipe. You don't have the same thing for dinner every night, right? So as you grow more familiar and comfortable with the dungeon experience, you should feel empowered to start experimenting with the recipe.

The ultimate goal, really, is to move beyond the 5 + 5 Dungeon recipe entirely. With practice, you'll eventually reach a place where you can confidently create dungeons without any guidance at all, just following the whim of your creative muse. As you're looking for your first steps along that road, however, you might want to start out by tweaking the recipe a little bit here and there, just to see what happens. (Add a little paprika to the egg salad, y'know?)

You could **vary the number of rooms**, maybe dropping rooms from the recipe until you're left with a fast-paced micro-dungeon that the PCs can perform a fast hit-and-run on. Or you could add extra rooms, perhaps to make the warlord's headquarters feel more important than the regional outposts the PCs have been chewing their way through.

You can also play around with the **archetype ratio**. Maybe this dungeon is tightly packed with featured rooms and fewer scenic rooms, making it more of a 7 + 3 dungeon. (Or vice versa.) You could double or triple up certain archetypes—having more fights or more challenge rooms than usual—while dropping others.

Will you make mistakes while doing this? Absolutely. But you'll also learn a lot. Every dungeon you create and run will teach you new lessons about dungeon design, about the game you're playing, and about what you and your players like.

DUNGEON LEVELS & THE 5 + 5 SEGMENT

As you begin designing larger dungeons, however, the 5 + 5 Dungeon recipe can still come in useful, because you can conceptualize the dungeon as a collection of 5 + 5 Dungeons. Each set of rooms becomes a segment, and these 5 + 5 segments can be linked together in any number of ways.

A fairly straightforward method of doing this is to simply make each 5 + 5 segment a separate **level** of the dungeon. Larger dungeons frequently have multiple levels like this, with both dangers and treasures traditionally increasing the deeper one delves. Separate levels also often provide a natural demarcation between different sections of the dungeon, which neatly correlates with the idea of using separate 5 + 5 segments for each level. In other words, even though there may be limited connections between them, you can often think of each level as a "separate" dungeon, making it much easier to organize and run them.

Once your dungeon has multiple levels, of course, you'll need to find ways to connect them so that the PCs can move up and down between them. There are, fortunately, many different types of **level connectors** you can use.

STAIRS

You know what stairs are. Let's not be silly. But there are so many different types to consider! Straight, spiral, L-shaped, U-shaped, and helical. And that's before you get really exotic with split stairs, invisible stairs, folding stairs, inverted stairs, non-Euclidean stairs, and anything else you might imagine of a fantastical nature.

SLOPES

Similar to stairs, but without the stairs. This sounds simple enough, but in the absence of stairs, a long and gentle slope can transition PCs between levels without them necessarily realizing they've shifted elevation.

CHUTES

Vertical passages that cannot be traversed on foot. Chutes require either climbing or flight.

LADDERS

Like a chute, but with a climbing aid already onsite. Variants of the ladder include ropes, poles, pre-driven pitons, and antigravity fields.

TRAPDOORS

Trapdoors may lead to stairs, slopes, chutes, or ladders, but they may also taunt PCs from the middle of a ceiling or drop down directly into a lower chamber.

WINDOWS

Imagine a window looking down into a lower level of the dungeon. (Perhaps with something looking back up at you!) You could also have a vertical dungeon in which the PCs could fly up and find an alternative entrance to an upper level by smashing through a more traditional window.

The Mines of Xartok

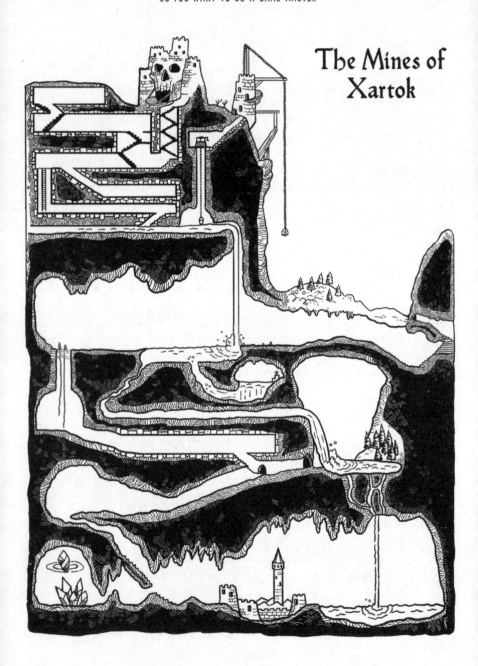

TELEPORTS

Teleportation effects allow for rapid transit through larger dungeon complexes, but they also have the potential to leave PCs disoriented until they can figure out where they are at the other end. Teleports can notably be either one-way or two-way.

TRAPS

Pit traps that drop PCs into an underground river three levels below. One-way teleportation traps that leave them unexpectedly stranded in a far corner of the dungeon (or staring at a familiar entrance, all their progress lost). Greased slides that send them shooting down to lower levels. Moving walls that shove them off subterranean cliffs. Traps that force the PCs to enter a new level are usually designed to be one-way trips, but sometimes resourceful characters can find a way to reverse the journey nonetheless.

MULTI-LEVEL CHAMBERS

Large, vertical chambers can contain entrances leading to different levels within the dungeon. For example, one might imagine subterranean gorges or cliffs. Or an obsidian pyramid squatting in a massive cavern, its steps leading to a burial chamber connecting to an upper level.

ELEVATORS

In their most basic configuration, elevators are chutes with a self-propelling means of passage, but taking a page from *Star Trek*'s turbolifts or Wonka's Chocolate Factory suggests that elevators don't always have to be limited to a vertical plane. Others may require the PCs to provide the means of propulsion. (A grinding wheel? Magical fuel? Blood sacrifices? Mystic keys?) Another common variant is the "sinking room," reminding us that fantasy elevators don't need to feel like the Empire State Building, and may not exist to serve the interests or comforts of their passengers.

BASKET & PULLEY

These are similar to elevators in their operation, but have the distinction of allowing their passengers to directly observe their surroundings for the duration of the trip. (The small size of the "basket" might also suggest that entire adventuring parties may not be able to take the journey at the same time.)

ETHEREAL TRAVEL

Sections of the dungeon may be designed such that normally solid obstacles (like the floor) can be moved through by way of the Ethereal Plane (or similarly transdimensional/non-Euclidean egress).

RIVERS

A natural variant of the slope. If the river runs flush with the walls, however, getting back upstream may require some tricky swimming. (And if it runs flush with the ceiling, navigating the river may require some deep breaths.)

UNDERWATER

In the real world, the fluid level in any connected system has to be the same, which means that underwater journeys will be most useful in moving PCs to different sections of the same level (or, at least, different "levels" on the same horizontal plane). However, magic, alchemy, steampunk technology, and science fiction gravity manipulation can all provide any number of airlocks and semi-permeable barriers allowing for underwater dives to the depths of an otherwise dry dungeon.

Or possibly the PCs will be responsible for flooding those lower levels when they breach a sealed door. (In a minor way if they've just swum down a stagnant, submerged shaft. In a major way if they dump an entire subterranean lake into the eighth level of the dungeon.)

5 + 5 VALLEYS

Another classic formula for linking 5 + 5 Dungeon segments is the 5 + 5 Valley: The PCs enter a valley, gorge, canyon, or the like and they see that it's lined with caves. There might be three or six or twelve different caves, and each cave is a 5 + 5 Dungeon.

Many, but probably not all, of these cave mouths can be linked to each other via underground tunnels and secret passages, forming a much larger complex than is at first apparent.

One of the great things about a 5 + 5 Valley is that it really emphasizes the importance of player choice in a compact environment: They can see all of those cave entrances and it's entirely their choice which one they're going to explore first. They are masters of their own destiny.

This also makes it a good idea to distinguish at least some of the cave entrances from each other so that the players have some meaningful basis for making that decision. (If they don't have any way of distinguishing the cave entrances, it's basically just random.) That might be bloodstains, a foul smell emanating from the mouth of the cave, strange pictorial decorations, heads of the last party of adventurers foolish enough to come this way displayed on spikes, an incomplete treasure map, or any number of other possibilities.

COLLAPSED PASSAGES

A variant on the chute, stairs, shaft, slope, or passage. Or, rather, where there used to be a chute, staircase, shaft, slope, or passage. Its former existence may be obvious or it may be obfuscated, but it's going to require some excavation before the passage will be usable again.

A common variant on this theme is the doorway that has been deliberately bricked up or plastered over. It's not unusual for such passages to be obvious from one side but not the other.

TRANSPORT

Think Charon on the River Styx. Or harpies willing to carry women (or men disguised as women; their eyesight is very poor) up a shaft. Or a PC being sucked bodily into a fist-sized ruby, which is then carried aloft by a silver raven. This form of connector has an essentially limitless variety, but the basic idea is that the PCs are being transported through the agency of an NPC or monster.

BEING SWALLOWED

"The cave is collapsing!" "This is no cave." Esophageal jaunts to the lower reaches of the dungeon should probably be used sparingly, but will certainly be memorable when employed. (The vomitous method of ascension is less pleasant, but no less memorable.)

BRUTE FORCE

Tunneling through walls using a *stone shape* spell. Levitating or flying through "unreachable" vertical passages. Using *gaseous form* to traverse "impassable" air vents. Blind or scry-prepped teleports. Casting *etherealness* to phase through solid stone. This category is basically a catchall for any and all methods PCs might use to find paths where no paths were meant to be. This isn't something you can plan for (although you might encourage it by giving the PCs maps as part of their treasure), but you should try to keep in mind that they're not cheating when they do it.

This attitude may be easier to hold on to, of course, if the dungeon already has multiple paths to success designed into its non-linear structure.

XANDERED DUNGEONS

To understand the importance of non-linear dungeon design, we need to start by looking at the exact opposite—the linear dungeon.

Imagine a dungeon in which each room has exactly one entrance and one exit. The size of the dungeon doesn't really matter, because it's going to play the same way no matter what: You enter Room A, then go through the only exit into Room B, then Room C, Room D, and so on forever.

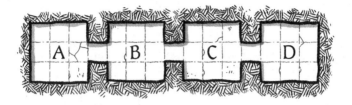

The sequence in which you encounter these rooms can never be changed. More importantly, if you enter a room with an obstacle, you have no choice but to overcome that obstacle before you can continue exploring the dungeon: You can't find an alternate route. Or seek out resources that might help you. Or forge an alliance with the beleaguered kobolds on Level 2 to help you overthrow the tyrannical goblin gloomcaster!

Lost in this linearity is the true spirit of exploration. Such a dungeon acts as a road. It's a route planned by another. And whereas Lewis and Clark were explorers, when I head down I-94, I am merely a driver.

Also lost is the entire strategic component of the game, and with it a great deal of the player creativity and spontaneity that make the very best experiences at the gaming table. In many ways, in fact, the players are no longer playing the game: They're often reduced to just doing what you tell them to do.

This, in turn, will put an enormous amount of pressure on you as the dungeon master! If you're going to force the players to do specific things in a very specific order, then you'd better make sure you literally *never* make a mistake. You give them a puzzle they can't solve? Or a monster that, for whatever reason, proves too difficult for them to defeat? Then they're stuck. The entire adventure breaks.

But if the PCs can choose a different path? Then getting stuck in Room B isn't a problem. They can retreat, circle around, rush ahead, go back over old ground, poke around, sneak through, interrogate the locals for secret routes . . . The possibilities are endless because the environment isn't forcing them along a predesigned path. The group instead becomes actively engaged in making the dungeon their own, and through it all, instead of experiencing the canned script of a theme park ride, they are living the thrill of true exploration and discovery.

These complex, interwoven adventures are known as **xandered dungeons**—dungeons that, being built on a non-linear foundation, can support complex, creative, and strategic play. Designing such a dungeon can seem daunting at first, but the reality is that xandering a dungeon can be done by simply applying a few straightforward techniques. Some of these techniques are designed to create complex geographic scenarios (out of which meaningful choices can naturally arise). Others are designed to confuse the players' mapping of the dungeon (or, more generally, their understanding of how the dungeon is structured). The point is not necessarily to create a maze-like environment (although it can be) but rather to create an environment of sufficient complexity so that the "hand of the author" is obfuscated.

A xandered dungeon doesn't just lack an intended path, it is incapable of having one. This not only implicitly tells the players that their choices are meaningful (because *they* are the ones charged with creating their path), it also deepens the illusion of the game world as a real place. Although the xandered dungeon is no more difficult to run than any other dungeon, the emergent complexity of its non-linear design will take the adventure in directions that you, as the DM, could never have anticipated. Seeing this and knowing it to be true, the players will perceive the things happening in the game as being "real" events, not scripted contrivances.

XANDERING TECHNIQUES

The techniques used to xander a dungeon are a diverse collection, ranging from those commonly and often used to the rare and exotic options that are likely to define a dungeon experience. They should not be mistaken for a features checklist. Your goal is not to cram them all into every dungeon that you create. In fact, that may create such a clamor that it will be difficult for the players to hear any signal through the noise.

Instead, the next time you sit down to create a dungeon, consider picking one or two of these techniques and really focusing on them. You can go further, actually, and narrow your design theme down to a specific, flavorful variant of a particular technique.

For example, perhaps the PCs are exploring an ancient city studded with arcane brass elevators. Operating the elevators requires inputting specific strings of strange symbols on keypads, which correspond to the level the occupants wish to go to. The PCs will be able to learn various symbol combinations via exploration or experimentation. These would be a very specific example of an unusual, discontinuous level connector (see page 154).

Whether common or exotic, the structural theming of the chosen techniques will give the players something to latch on to. As they figure out "how this dungeon works," a very different form of dungeon mastery will emerge, along with the satisfaction of being able to use their knowledge to unlock secrets, gain strategic advantage, solve puzzles, and avoid potential pitfalls.

XANDERING TECHNIQUES

- Loops
- Multiple Entrances
- Multiple Level Connections
- Discontinuous Level Connections
- Secret & Unusual Paths
- Sub-Levels
- Divided Levels
- Minor Elevation Shifts
- Midpoint Entry

LOOPS

Branching paths in a dungeon allow for choice but are still functionally linear in their design. (In practice, the PCs will follow a branch to its end, backtrack, and then go down a different branch. But each branch still presents an independent linear experience.) Where things start to get interesting is when you grab a couple of those branches and hook them together into a loop so that Room A leads to Room B that leads to Room C and so forth until you eventually end up back in Room A. These loops are the basic building blocks for xandered dungeons: They provide meaningful strategic and tactical choices, make exploration impactful, and allow PCs to find alternative routes around or through potential threats.

LOOPS WITHIN LOOPS: *One loop is nice. It lets you approach the goblin caverns from both directions. But it's really when you have multiple loops intersecting each other—loops within loops—that truly dynamic navigation becomes possible in the dungeon.*

MULTIPLE ENTRANCES

Multiple entrances give the PCs an immediate strategic choice as they approach the dungeon complex. Hidden secondary entrances also reward exploration both inside and outside the dungeon, allowing for favorable approaches and quick escapes. Each entrance allows the PCs to engage the dungeon in a different way, creating unique experiences.

In terms of structure, multiple entrances effectively create an additional "loop" through the surface above the dungeon.

MULTIPLE LEVEL CONNECTIONS

If there is only a single route leading to the next level of the dungeon, then the complexity of the current level is collapsed into a chokepoint. But if you introduce multiple connections between the levels of a dungeon, you create a synergy between complex level designs. Just as you create new structural loops by including multiple entrances to the dungeon, each additional connection you draw between levels creates new looping paths through the dungeon.

DISCONTINUOUS LEVEL CONNECTIONS

In a linear design, the levels of a dungeon must proceed in their predetermined order. Level 1 leads to Level 2. Level 2 leads to Level 3. Level 3 leads to Level 4.

But once you introduce multiple connections between levels, you are free to have some of those connections skip levels. For example, there might be a chute on Level 1 that takes you down to Level 3. Or a hidden tunnel on Level 4 that takes you back to the surface a half mile away from the dungeon's main entrance.

From the players' perspective, these discontinuous connections obfuscate the geography of the dungeon. They know the chute goes down . . . but does it go down to the same level as the stairs they found earlier? This sort of confusion turns the navigation of the dungeon into a puzzle to be solved. Will the maps they're making at the bottom of the chute connect to the map they made after going down the stairs? Can they use what they learned via one route to inform their explorations along another?

SECRET & UNUSUAL PATHS

These are fairly self-explanatory. They reward curiosity and exploration, and secret and unusual paths can also breathe fresh life into areas of the dungeon that have already been traversed. Examples include:

- camouflaged doorways
- caved-in tunnels
- traps that drop you to lower levels
- archaic teleportation systems that must be decoded
- rope bridges that cross over caverns that can be explored from below
- submerged bypasses connecting two seemingly unrelated lakes

Here, too, you will benefit from the non-linear design of the xandered dungeon: Because there are other viable paths for the PCs to explore, you can include truly esoteric, unusual, and flavorful paths that may be missed by the unwary (and, therefore, appreciated all the more by those who do discover them).

SUB-LEVELS

The distinction between a "level" and a "sub-level" of a dungeon is somewhat arbitrary, but perhaps the defining characteristic is that it departs from the main "sequence" of the dungeon. It may be smaller than the other levels of the dungeon, difficult to reach, or both. As such, sub-levels serve as boulevards of discovery or elaborate shortcuts (or both).

Like discontinuous level connections, a sub-level interferes with the players' ability to intuit the structure of the dungeon. ("Wait . . . is *this* the fourth level? Then where were we before?") Your maps and keys for the dungeon are all neatly numbered and organized for ease of use and reference, but there should usually be nothing neat or easy in exploring the dark places beneath the earth.

DIVIDED LEVELS

Similar to the concept of the sub-level is the divided level. While existing within the main "sequence" of the dungeon, a divided level cannot be completely traversed without going through the levels above it or below it.

For example, on the third level of the dungeon you might find two staircases going down to the fourth level. But on the fourth level itself, there will be no path that connects the two staircases. (Or, if there is such a path, it may be incredibly well hidden or difficult to traverse.) The only way to get from one staircase to the other is to either go back up to the third level or, alternatively, go farther down and work your way back up. In your notes, such a level might be labeled as Level 4A and 4B.

MINOR ELEVATION SHIFTS

When the PCs come to a staircase they may naturally assume that they are going up or down to a new level of the dungeon. But by including minor elevation shifts within the topography of a single dungeon level, you can confound these expectations. For an extreme example of this, look at the map on the next page.

In addition to short stairways and misleading slopes, you can also include tunnels that loop under each other while technically remaining on the same "level" of the dungeon in your map and key. It's also important to "think vertically" within rooms as well, including a variety of ceiling heights, balconies, galleries, and the like.

These techniques aren't just a matter of confusing your players' mapping. Once again, you're disrupting their ability to deduce the organization of your maps by analyzing the reality of the game world. The entire concept of a dungeon "level" is really just for your convenience as a DM; by understanding that and including things like minor elevation shifts, you're creating a world that not only seems more dynamic and complex but actually *is* more dynamic and complex.

Basically, don't fall into the trap of thinking that because your map is two-dimensional it means that the world should be two-dimensional.

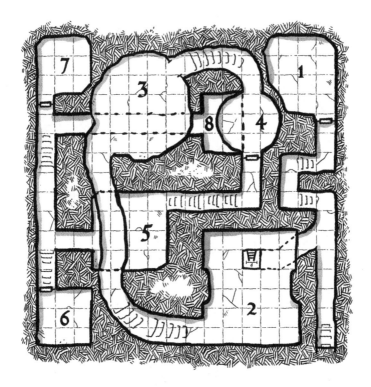

MIDPOINT ENTRY

You can also complicate the players' approach to a dungeon by creating immediate bilateral exploration. In other words, PCs entering a dungeon are usually only faced with one navigational question at the macro level: "How do we get down to Level 2?"

But if the PCs are instead entering in the middle of the dungeon (even if they don't realize that's the case)—with levels above *and* below them—then they're first faced with a tougher question: "Which way do we go?"

Note that this decision point is similar to the one faced by PCs who have "skipped" a level as a result of a discontinuous level connection. It's also similar to the situation faced by PCs who have taken advantage of a hidden entrance leading to a lower level of the dungeon.

The distinction of the midpoint entry is that it's the expected, default entry point to the dungeon.

XANDERING IN PRACTICE

We've mostly been discussing xandering in the context of large dungeons with multiple levels, but these principles are just as valuable in making smaller dungeons, too. In fact, a smaller scale can make the choices offered by xandering clearer and more sharply focused for the players.

There can also be an impression that xandering the dungeon is an artificial conceit—something that has to be "forced" into a scenario. But in my experience exactly the opposite is true. Think about the house where you live, the office building where you go to work, or the mall where you do your shopping. Do any of these spaces have only one possible entrance? Are they linear strings of rooms that can only be entered in sequence? Prisons, banks, museums, schools. The world around us is intensely xandered, and effortlessly so.

There are dangers, though, in overly xandering a dungeon. There's a point at which endless loops and countless connections within the dungeon result in meaningless choice instead of meaningful choice, and the goal is not that you should *never* use branching paths or create chokepoints for accessing the lower levels of the dungeon. Rather, such features should be used purposefully instead of by default. Xandering techniques should be used for specific effect, and you should beware the featureless sprawl of looping corridors that can result from careless excess.

Here are a couple useful self-checks you can use.

DIFFICULT VS. EASY

Looking at your map, there should be areas of the dungeon that are difficult to reach and areas that are easy to reach. I don't just mean isolated secret rooms (although there's nothing wrong with those), but rather large, significant regions of the dungeon.

In making this assessment, you're diagnosing whether you've made the dungeon too boring by making the choice of path through the dungeon irrelevant. You want the dungeon to benefit from being interconnected, but if everything in the dungeon trivially connects to everything else then navigation becomes meaningless.

FAR VS. NEAR

Similarly, have the interconnections made your dungeon too shallow? Look at where the PCs will be entering the dungeon. There should be areas of the dungeon that feel far away from these entrances. If everything in the dungeon feels equidistant, break some of those connections or delve a little deeper in your design.

Note that "near" and "easy to reach" portions of the dungeon aren't problems to be eliminated. What you're looking for is an effective balance in the mix between all four of these design elements (difficult, easy, near, and far).

DUNGEON LANDMARKS

The complexity of a properly xandered dungeon can leave players feeling adrift, with one corridor of gray stone blending seamlessly into every other. In some cases, this can be a deliberate design decision and used to good effect, but most of the time it's more of a bug than a feature.

The solution is to include big, notable landmarks. When lost, stumbling across a known landmark can help to reorient the group. More importantly, such landmarks will help the players form their mental map and, thus, their understanding of the dungeon.

If you're designing a dungeon with lots of unique, interesting features, this will largely just take care of itself: The players will glom on to whatever details particularly resonate with them, and use those details to guide themselves. (On the other hand, it can never hurt to do another quick pass through your design and add in a few deliberate landmarks: a large bloodstain. A unique statue. A room of strange runes.)

RANDOM ENCOUNTER TABLES

Random encounters are useful in any dungeon, but they become particularly vital in large dungeons, where the conceit of monsters all quietly waiting in their rooms for the PCs to show up can become painfully apparent. Having integrated the encounter check into our dungeon turn (see page 73) and discussed how to run encounters when they're generated (see page 80), it's time to look at how you can create your own random encounter tables.

The size of a random encounter table can vary quite a bit, and is fairly dependent on the dungeon (or the section of the dungeon) that you're designing it for. I've designed dungeons that have four entries on their random encounter table and I've designed dungeons that have a hundred different encounters, although somewhere between six and twenty encounters is far more common.

Once you know how many encounters will be on the table, you just need to assign an appropriate die type. This is usually pretty straightforward: If you've got six encounters, roll 1d6. If you've got twenty encounters, roll 1d20. If you've got five encounters, then either eliminate one (so you can roll 1d4), add one (so you can roll 1d6), or have one of the encounters occur on multiple dice results (e.g., both 5 and 6).

If you'd like some encounters to occur more frequently than others, you can either use a larger die type and assign those encounters to multiple results or you can roll multiple dice in order to generate a bell curve of probability (and then assign your frequent encounters to the middle of the chamber). You can search online for the probability of any combination of dice, but as an example of what I mean, see the following page for the probability table when rolling 2d6.

2D6 PROBABILITY TABLE

					6					
			5	⚁⚀		5				
		4	⚀⚂	⚁⚁	⚂⚀	4				
	3	⚀⚃	⚁⚂	⚂⚁	⚃⚀	⚄⚁	3			
2	⚀⚄	⚁⚃	⚂⚂	⚃⚁	⚄⚀	⚄⚁	⚄⚁	2		
1	⚀⚅	⚁⚄	⚂⚃	⚃⚂	⚄⚁	⚄⚁	⚄⚁	⚄⚁	⚄⚁	1
⚀⚀	⚁⚀	⚂⚀	⚃⚀	⚄⚀	⚀⚅	⚁⚅	⚂⚅	⚃⚅	⚄⚅	⚅⚅

2	3	4	5	6	7	8	9	10	11	12
2.77	5.56	8.33	11.11	13.89	16.67	13.89	11.11	8.33	5.56	2.77

You can easily see how the encounter assigned to a roll of 5 (11.11%) is roughly four times more likely to occur than an encounter assigned to a roll of 2.

Since the ends of this table become very unlikely to occur, it's not unusual for me to construct a table like this:

2D6	ENCOUNTER PROBABILITY
2-3	8.33%
4	8.33%
5	11.11%
6	13.89%
7	16.67%
8	13.89%
9	11.11%
10	8.33%
11-12	8.33%

This still provides a bump for the encounters at the center of the curve, but it evens out the odds of the least likely encounters. (Plus, nine total encounters is a perfectly nice number of encounters to have for a dungeon. Often more than enough.)

The real secret, though, is that you don't really need to worry about it that much. When in doubt, just use a flat die roll and call it a day.

Far more important are the encounters you're actually stocking the table with. You can either prep bespoke encounters or procedurally generated encounters.

Bespoke encounters, broadly speaking, are prepped just like any other encounter in the dungeon: They are specific creatures who are doing specific, predesigned things. For example:

> **COMPETITIVE ORCS:** *These five* **orcs** *are heading to the archery range. Each is boasting about how well they will shoot and making bets about which of them will score the most "eyeholes." (It appears their archery targets are made from skulls.) They are accompanied by two* **goblins** *who are overburdened carrying their bows, arrows, and other equipment. The group makes their Dexterity (Stealth) and Wisdom (Perception) checks at disadvantage due to their vociferous arguing.*

Such encounters are less flexible and, once encountered, are usually used up. (The PCs are not going to just keep encountering more orcs arguing about their archery performance.) They are also time-consuming to create and often result in a lot of wasted prep (since you will likely end up creating bespoke encounters that don't get used).

The advantage of a bespoke encounter, however, is that it's plug and play. By spending the time to design the details of the encounter before play begins, you don't need to improvise those details during play. Bespoke encounters also allow you to encode specific rituals, events, or routines into the life of the dungeon.

Procedurally generated encounters, on the other hand, provide you with the raw building blocks of an encounter, but then require you to improvise the specific encounter based on the current circumstances of the PCs and what's happening in the dungeon at that moment. (See Running Random Encounters on page 80.) If you roll an encounter with "1d6 orcs + 1d4 goblins," for example, then those orcs might be on their way to the archery range; but they could also be overseers escorting goblin miners to their duties or a guard patrol or chefs delivering food to the mess hall.

Because these encounters can, in practice, be any number of things, they are usually not used up. You can keep rolling "1d6 orcs + 1d4 goblins" forever, and each time the encounter can be something fresh and new.

One common error, however, is to assume that this means procedurally generated encounters can't feature specific, named NPCs. This is not the case. You could easily include a procedurally generated encounter like "Warchief Skaglock + 1d4 orcs" on your random encounter table, with the specific details of how and why the warchief is being encountered being determined during play.

Whether using bespoke or procedurally generated encounters, you'll generally want to keep the difficulty manageable—what D&D refers to as an Easy or Medium encounter. Random encounters, by their nature, are generally scene setters, not the big finales.

This is easy to do if the encounter has a set number of monsters (e.g., "five orcs and two goblins"). If you want to randomize the number of creature encounters, it can get a little trickier.

1. Choose the creature type (e.g., orcs).

2. Determine how many of those creatures would qualify as an Easy, Medium, and Hard encounter for the PCs. (With five 3rd-level PCs, for example, these would be encounters with two orcs, four orcs, and six orcs.)

3. Identify a dice range that fits your vision for the encounter. It can cover the Easy and Medium ranges but should ideally not drift into Hard unless it has a low probability of happening. If you're using multiple dice with a bell curve, I would generally try to get the middle of that bell curve lined up with a Medium encounter. (For our orcs, 1d4 or even 1d4 + 1 would seem to work well.)

If the encounter includes multiple creature types, this obviously gets even trickier to juggle. I usually find it easiest to divide the XP budget between the two creature types first and then determine the appropriate range for each creature type.

Another option is to include **combined encounters** on your encounter table. A common example is, "Roll again twice." If you do this, you'll want to make really sure your encounters are landing in the Easy/Medium range, because when multiple encounters combine they'll end up in Hard (and you don't want them routinely drifting into or past Deadly). Alternatively, keep your encounters entirely in the Easy range, but make it very common (or even the default) to combine multiple encounters.

The great thing about combined encounters is that they add an even greater dynamic range to what can be procedurally generated: Orcs + goblins inspires one encounter; orcs + pseudodragon a different one.

WHERE DO THESE MONSTERS COME FROM?

When you roll up a random encounter in the dungeon, where are these monsters coming from? I mean, it's a fantasy game, so they might be literally materializing out of thin air, but that's not likely to be a common scenario.

Option #1: They're the monsters that appear on your dungeon key; they just happen to be wandering around at the moment. So if the PCs kill five orcs in a random encounter, then you should delete them from a keyed encounter. (It can be useful to list which keyed areas the random encounter "belongs" to on your random encounter table.) If all the orcs in the dungeon have been killed, then there are none to be randomly encountered and you can ignore those results.

Option #2: There's a separate pool of "wandering monsters" who are just assumed to be moving around the dungeon at any particular time. When the PCs kill five orcs in a random encounter, delete them from the wandering monster pool. If the pool runs out of wandering orcs, then you could either choose to source them from keyed areas or, once again, ignore those encounters.

Option #3: Wandering monsters are either not tracked or they are explicitly "bonus" encounters. In a larger dungeon (particularly a megadungeon), they might just be passing through the area. In other situations you might rationalize the variation in local population as drones returning to the hive or some similar explanation. It's also possible to just embrace the quantum uncertainty: There is no definitive answer for exactly how many goblins or giant bees or whatever live here until the dice determine it through the course of play.

RESTOCKING THE DUNGEON

Let's say that some people move out of their house. That house won't stay vacant forever, right? It probably won't even stay vacant for long. That's just what you'd expect from a real, living world.

Similarly, when the PCs clear the gibbering-mouther infestation out of the Rainbow Grotto, they leave behind a perfectly nice set of caves that could later be reinhabited by

- tiefling bandits,
- goblin nomads,
- a fairy incursion from the Feywild,
- a pack of blink dogs, or
- giant fireflies.

Each poses an entirely new problem for the PCs to deal with.

But why would you do this? Why not create an entirely new dungeon for every scenario?

First, you've got a perfectly good map of the Rainbow Grotto. Reusing it can save you a bunch of work. This makes restocking a particularly great option if your game starts in a couple of hours and you haven't had time to prep anything yet.

Second, the persistence of the world—and the consequences of the PCs actions—will make the events of the campaign feel more real. (If the PCs had taken the time to properly dispose of those gargoyle corpses at the ruins of the cathedral, then the necromancer never would have moved in and made gargoyle zombies.)

HELLO, NEIGHBOR!

Restocking a dungeon doesn't always mean a new threat moving in. In one of my campaigns, for example, the PCs cleared out a haunted château and then took possession of the property. They weren't sure what to do with it, but a few sessions later they'd become allies with a group of knights who were suddenly being wrongfully hunted as outlaws. The PCs offered the château as a hideout, and it soon transformed into the headquarters for the rebellion.

You could similarly imagine a friendly elementalist moving into the ruined tower outside the village and fixing it up. Or the PCs' smuggler friends using the old goblin caves to stash their goods.

These benevolent repurposings are equally effective at making the world feel like a real, persistent place where the PCs' actions are meaningful and impactful.

Finally, and perhaps most importantly, it's fun. Restocking a linear dungeon with new monsters is often boring because you're just repeating the same mandatory grind. Restocking a non-linear dungeon, on the other hand, gives the players a chance to leverage their existing knowledge of the dungeon in myriad ways. ("Oh! I know where we can set up an ambush for these goblins! Remember that ledge where the tieflings were hiding?")

Restocking a regular or micro-dungeon, while it can save you some work, is largely similar to creating a whole new scenario. Since the PCs will have likely "finished" the dungeon during their first visit, they'll have no reason to return, so you'll need a fresh scenario concept and scenario hook to pull them back in.

With bigger dungeons, on the other hand, restocking can become part of the scenario. Because the PCs are making multiple expeditions into the dungeon, the dungeon can evolve and change between each expedition. This can be useful in large dungeons, but really comes into its own with a megadungeon, where it becomes an integral part of breathing life and fresh scenarios into the dungeon environment. It also prevents, in combination with random encounters, a "return to save point" mentality where the PCs, after retreating from the dungeon, are free to just pick up from where they left off, encouraging them to push forward and make as much progress as they can on each expedition.

When thinking about restocking, I find it useful to break the dungeon into **zones**. Methods for doing this can include:

- ◉ **Segments.** If your dungeon is a collection of 5 + 5 Dungeon segments, then you can treat each segment as a separate zone.

- ◉ **Levels.** Each level of the dungeon can be treated as a separate zone. If this ends up being too large to be useful, you could break each level into **quadrants** (or some similar regular division).

- ◉ **Chokepoints.** Look for the points in the dungeon that form bottlenecks. The area between two or three chokepoints can form natural zones, defined at least in part by the defensibility of those rooms.

- ◉ **Lairs.** In your original key, where were the different factions of monsters living? Even once these have been cleared out (or abandoned by their original inhabitants), they're likely still logical places for new creatures to potentially take up residence.

But the most important thing is that the dungeon's zones make sense to you. Not every room in the dungeon needs to belong to a zone and, indeed, the zones may change and shift over time, but there will be an internal logic to the dungeon and, once you understand it, the zones will usually become obvious to you.

With your zones identified, you'll make **restocking checks**. You'll usually make a check between each expedition into the dungeon, but at your discretion you might also make a check if the PCs take a long rest inside the dungeon.

The next thing to determine is which zones to check. There are three options:

◎ **Empty Zones.** Any zone that has been completely cleared by the PCs (e.g., there are no denizens left in it) can be checked to see if it becomes reinhabited.

◎ **Disrupted Zones.** Check any zones the PCs entered or passed through during their last expedition, including those that are still inhabited (suggesting reinforcements, etc.). You might check only disrupted zones (including empty zones the PCs entered), or you might check disrupted zones in addition to all empty zones.

◎ **All Zones.** Alternatively, you could check every single zone in the dungeon, but this is usually not a good idea. It's time-consuming and will often result in the dungeon filling up with monsters at a silly/ruinous rate. In addition, constantly churning, replacing, or changing content that the players haven't even seen yet is a waste of time. (If they haven't been to Level 5 of the dungeon yet, it's virtually always fine to leave everything down there in a state of stasis until the PCs actually arrive and start interacting with it. You can imagine that there's a constant flurry of activity down there just out of sight; but whatever you designed for Level 5 will be the current state of things the first time the players arrive.)

As you check the zones, you can start with **custom restocking**. This basically means doing cool stuff that spontaneously occurs to you and/or developments that proceed logically from the events of the game. For example, the PCs have been attacking the goblin lairs on Level 2, and you think to yourself, "The goblins would probably try to get help. Maybe they could hire some of the lizardmen mercenaries from Level 4?" (Or from the far side of the mountain. Restocking will often come from outside the confines of the dungeon. It's also quite possible that these lizardmen didn't previously exist in your campaign notes, but now you've created them because you needed an answer to the question, "Where could the goblins go for help?" This is one of the ways that restocking can provide depth to your game world.)

You can also think of this as unprompted stocking, but that's not strictly accurate because it's being prompted by literally everything that happens during your game.

Once you run out of clever (or obvious) ideas, you can switch to **procedural restocking**. As with random encounter checks, you can customize your restocking procedure in a bunch of different ways, but here's a basic version you can start with:

1. Make a **restocking check** for each zone by rolling 1d8. A roll of 1 indicates that the zone will be restocked.

2. Roll on a **stocking table** to determine what denizens the zone will be stocked with. Place these denizens where you feel it's appropriate. (If you don't have a stocking table, you can often use the random encounter table for the dungeon to similar effect. Alternatively, just pick an appropriate denizen.)

3. Add appropriate **minor treasure** to the zone (usually carried by the new denizens). Then roll 1d8, adding a **major treasure** on a roll of 1. (Some games will have systems for randomly generating treasure, in which case you can use those. If not, you'll have to create bespoke treasure hordes using your best judgment.)

A common variant to this procedure is to make a zone-based check to see if the zone should be restocked, but then making stocking checks and/or treasure checks for each individual room. (If you generate treasure in an unoccupied room, that usually means it will be hidden or secured in some way.)

But why use procedural stocking at all? Why not just have events in the dungeon proceed logically? Well, what I like about stocking checks—just like random encounters—is that they act as improv seeds. It can be a little too easy to just say that nothing will happen in an empty dungeon zone. The procedural stocking will provide the push to keep things in motion and inject the unexpected into your creative process.

POOR MAN'S STOCKING TABLE

As I mentioned, procedural stocking is a lot easier if the game you're playing includes stocking tables—i.e., tables for randomly generating dungeon denizens and/or treasure. Unfortunately, there are many RPGs that lack these tools.

With a little effort you can create your own tables for any game, but I'm quite lazy, so there are a couple of improvised techniques I've used to good effect.

First, you can often use a random encounter table to similar effect. If possible, I usually get better results from going one step up from whatever I'm trying to stock. For example, if I'm restocking a dungeon level, I could use the random encounter table for that level, but I might get better results if I were to randomly choose a dungeon level's encounter table to roll on or, instead, use the wilderness encounter tables (see page 402) for the region the dungeon is located in. (These options allow the region around the area I'm restocking to influence the outcome.)

Second, you can transform almost any monster book into a random table by randomly rolling a page number and, if necessary, then randomly choosing a monster on the matching page. (Online dice rollers make it easy to randomly generate a number in any given range.)

In games like D&D, which can have opponents spread across a wide range of difficulties, you probably don't want to randomly select *any* creature, but it's usually pretty easy to narrow the range. In D&D, for example, you can use the "Monsters by Challenge Rating" list, select a target challenge rating, and then randomly select a monster from the list. For a broader range, choose a target challenge rating (usually two CRs lower than the average party level) and then roll 1d3-1d3 to select a specific CR.

The *Dungeon Master's Guide* also includes a list of creatures by terrain type, which can be used to similar effect.

UPDATING THE DUNGEON KEY

Updating the dungeon key is often done hand in hand with restocking: As new denizens move into an area, they'll clean up the wreckage left in the wake of the PCs, reset the traps, change the décor, set up a dark fane harnessing necromantic energies to open a nethergate to the Null Realms . . . you know, the usual.

But updating your key is also about reflecting the actions of the PCs. It *is* the wreckage they leave behind—the bodies, the graffiti on the walls, the smashed doors, and looted tombs. It's a reference so that, when they circle back through this area again, they can see the impact that their actions have had.

During play, I find it useful to quickly jot down notable additions or changes to the key right in my notes. In some cases, this **marginalia** is sufficient by itself, but I usually find it useful to spend a couple minutes after a session briefly reviewing everything that happened and making sure I've taken notes on everything relevant.

When the required notes exceed the marginalia, I'll prep a **scenario update**, which works kind of like a diff file. This document just lists each altered room of the dungeon and the things that have been changed in that room. For example, if the PCs were in Area 5 of Mephits & Magmin (see page 56) and they looted the Stygian crystals, I'd write something like:

AREA 5
◎   crystals looted

You don't need to get any more complicated than that. The idea is that you can check the diff file, see that the crystals have been removed, and then modify your description of the room while primarily referring to the original key entry.

(Mephits & Magmin is a small enough dungeon that I probably wouldn't need to actually do this, but it serves as an easy example. And if some new denizens were to move into the dungeon in the future, perhaps it would be relevant!)

Maintaining a collection of these diff files for your various dungeons and dungeon levels may be the beginning of maintaining a **campaign status document**. For more information and best practices for these, check out the extra credit on page 448.

A more comprehensive option is to create a **new dungeon key**. I'll generally do this only if the diff file is chewing up too much space or has become too onerous to use smoothly and accurately. Basically, though, you just take your notes from the diff file and rewrite the key, creating a completely fresh document that's more or less indistinguishable from a brand-new adventure.

For example, using the same update to Area 5 of Mephits & Magmin, I might rewrite the key for that room as:

AREA 5: VOLCANIC CRYSTALS

At one end of this long chamber there is an archway in one corner and a large tunnel slanting down from the opposite corner.

The far end of the chamber from these passages is filled with a huge, crystalline growth. Although it appears a number of crystals have been damaged, there are still hundreds of individual crystals in the mass, each glowing with a spectral, greenish light that casts strange shadows down the fissured walls.

INTELLIGENCE (INVESTIGATION)-DC 12 (FOOTPRINTS)

A close inspection of the floor may reveal that there are small, humanoid footprints that have been burned into the surface. They are difficult to make out against the dark stone and crisscross each other countless times, but clearly pass through the entrances to Area 4 and Area 8. (They do NOT pass into Area 6, which is unknown to the magmin.)

⍟ **GM Note:** These footprints are made by the magmin. They are not found in the lava tubes, where the undisturbed volcanic rock is solid enough to not be disturbed by them.

INTELLIGENCE (INVESTIGATION)-DC 15 (CONCEALED PASSAGE)

Although it is not immediately apparent, one of the fissures in the south wall is actually large enough to squeeze through, allowing characters to crawl through to Area 6 with a successful DC 12 Dexterity check. (This check is made with advantage if the character is not wearing armor.)

CRYSTALS

A DC 12 Intelligence (Nature) check indicates that these are volcanic crystals, while a DC 15 Intelligence (Alchemist's Supplies) check reveals these crystals have been adulterated with Stygian gas, granting them their strange illumination and also making them a valuable catalyst for various alchemical procedures. It appears that all of the crystals with adulterations strong enough for alchemical work—several dozen in all—have been removed.

⊘ **GM Note:** The crystals were harvested by Asuvius and, later, the Red Elk adventuring party.

WALLS

Close inspection of the walls will reveal that they were not carved but rather somehow melted into their current configuration.

Compare this to the original key entry on page 56 and note the subtle differences. Obviously, it's quite common for dungeon rooms to have much more radical changes: The crystals were completely smashed apart and scattered across the floor, the narrow entrance to Area 6 has been blasted open, or the magmin have draped the body of the PCs' dead companion over the crystalline mass as a warning.

STARTING A MEGADUNGEON

Large dungeons aren't that different from single-session dungeons, and it's pretty easy to slowly expand your dungeon scenarios as you explore their new dynamics.

A megadungeon, on the other hand, can feel like a completely different beast altogether. Enough adventures to fill an entire campaign? A dozen or more levels? Hundreds of rooms? How can you possibly come to grips with all that?

The secret is that you don't have to. You really only need to prep enough of the megadungeon to run your first session. Then you can expand the megadungeon only as you need to, slowly delving deeper and deeper into the netherworld.

The generic rule of thumb is that you should start by prepping the first three levels of your megadungeon, but I find it useful to understand *why* that's a good rule of thumb: You want enough material that the PCs aren't likely to simply skip their way into an area you haven't prepped in the first session.

In short, take a look at your maps and assume a worst-case scenario in which the PCs make a beeline directly from the entrance to the nearest set of stairs, then from those stairs to the next. In a single session, it's likely they'll chew through a dozen rooms or so. You'll want a healthy margin of error, though, just in case, so assume they might make it through a couple dozen. How far can they get?

For your first session, the answer is likely to be, "Somewhere on the third level." (Hence the rule of thumb.) In practice, they probably won't. But they *could*. And sometimes they will. Even if they don't, knowing what the next chunk of the dungeon contains is usually valuable context for running the current chunk of dungeon (e.g., the goblins can talk about the lizardmen mercenaries on the next level).

Where this analysis becomes even more useful, though, is after the first session. Look at how far the PCs penetrated last time. Assume that they continue their exploration of the dungeon from that point and ask yourself, once again, "How far can they get?" That's the chunk

MEGADUNGEON LEVELS = DIFFICULTY

In the traditional megadungeon, each level would correspond to a matching level of difficulty. So the first level of the megadungeon would have challenges appropriate for 1st-level characters, the second level would have challenges for 2nd-level characters, and so forth.

There's no reason to strictly adhere to this concept, but it's not a bad guideline—for both practical and thematic reasons—that the deeper you go into the megadungeon, the more difficult and dangerous it will become. This can give you guidelines for the types of creatures to be found on each level, and it's also a useful limiter when you're prepping your megadungeon starter: Even if the 1st-level PCs want to do (or, through dumb luck, stumble into doing) a speedrun down to the third level of the dungeon, they won't be able to make much progress down there against high-CR challenges (and would be well advised to retreat and spend some time exploring the upper levels).

you need to prep next, and you can continue biting off chunks of the dungeon like this until, sooner than you might think, you'll start hitting sessions where the answer to "How far can they get?" is "No farther than I've already prepped." And that's a great moment, because it's at that moment that the megadungeon settles down and you'll find the momentum of the campaign driving itself forward, with you only needing to apply the slightest bit of steering to keep things rolling.

Going in blind as you create your megadungeon and kind of exploring it the same way the PCs will (so that, for example, you don't know what's on Level 6 until your maps delve down to that depth) can be a lot of fun, but you can also lay out a grand plan of your megadungeon, even if you're prepping it in chunks.

The most basic way to do this is to list the levels of the megadungeon. For example:

- **Level 1:** Goblin Warrens
- **Level 2:** Lakes of the Sahuagin
- **Level 3:** Nothic Druids
- **Level 4:** Chaos Caverns
- **Level 5:** Hobgoblins & Hell Hounds
- **Level 6:** The Nymphaeum Gates
- **Level 6A:** Mastaba of the Mephit Lords
- **Level 7:** Four Elemental Sacraria
- **Level 8:** Sepulcher of Gloom

From this list you could even sketch a rough side view of the dungeons, using xandering techniques to rough out the connections between levels.

⟶ DYNAMIC DUNGEONS ⟵

We've added scale and complexity to our dungeons, but that's not the only way to add depth to a scenario. We can also create dynamic dungeons in which the denizens actively respond to what the PCs are doing.

One of the great things about a location crawl is that each keyed area is effectively "firewalled." By default, the only thing you need to think about while running the scenario is the room that the PCs are currently in. This makes running a location crawl incredibly easy, because everything you need can be right at your fingertips.

The drawback, of course, is that this results in a very static scenario. If the PCs are fighting the goblins in Area 43, it feels like the goblins in Area 44 should hear them and come rushing over to help their compatriots. But because they're behind the firewall—because the DM is only focusing on Area 43—they don't.

So you think to yourself, "Okay. When there's a fight, I should scan nearby rooms to see if there's anyone who might hear what's happening." And if you've gained enough experience as a DM, and if there are only one or two rooms nearby, you can probably make that work. It's definitely harder—you're having to flip back and forth between different room keys—but it's manageable.

But what if there are more than a couple rooms? What if there are five or six or ten rooms within potential earshot? And what if, instead of being Areas 43 and 44, right next to each other in your notes, they're Areas 43, 44, 52, 53, 57, and 84?

Oof. That's getting a lot harder to juggle, and we've just gotten started. So far we've only considered the simple case of having the bad guys hear the fight and then come rushing to help. What if the modron in Area 57 decides the most logical course of action would be to fetch additional reinforcements? Where would it go to find them? Now you're not just flipping around trying to find nearby denizens to activate, you're flipping through the whole dungeon trying to figure out where the nearest barracks is. And what would the response of the goblins in the barracks be? And what other areas will they affect or be affected by?

You can see how quickly this becomes completely untenable, even for the most experienced DMs. To run truly dynamic dungeons and bring them to life, we can't just try to run all the rooms in the dungeon at once. The firewall is too valuable. Instead, we need a fundamentally different approach and a new set of tools to make it work.

We've actually already taken our first steps in this direction by using random encounters, and these will remain a useful part of our arsenal even as we add more weapons to it.

ADVERSARY ROSTERS

It's virtually impossible to keep track of all the denizens in a dungeon of even moderate size because the information describing them has been scattered across the key and embedded into dozens of room descriptions. We do this because we think of the denizens as "belonging" to a particular room. They're "the goblins in the library" or "the security guards in the ops center."

Of course, our whole goal with a dynamic dungeon is to *not* have the denizens tied down to a specific room. We want them free to move around the dungeon and respond to events in the way that real people do. So what we need is a different way of keying denizens and tracking them in the scenario.

We can do this with an **adversary roster**, a list of the dungeon denizens separate from the room key. If we were to build a roster for Mephits & Magmin, for example, it would look like this:

EXAMPLE MEPHITS & MAGMIN-ADVERSARY ROSTER

ACTION GROUP	AREA	NOTES
4 mud mephits	Area 1	
2 smoke mephits + 1 steam mephit	Area 2	
Work Crew: 2 magmin + 2 mud mephits	Area 8	(moving between Areas 8 & 10)
2 magma mephits	Area 9	
Asuvius + 2 magmin + 2 smoke mephits	Area 10	
Steampowered Construct	Area 10	(needs to be fully charged)

If you're using an adversary roster, the denizens listed on the roster should NOT be included in the location key. In practice, you'll have the adversary roster on a separate sheet of paper—ideally placed off to one side for easy reference—and use it to keep track of where the adversaries are. For example, when the PCs enter Area 9, you'd flip to the room key but also cross-reference the adversary roster, see that there are two magma mephits there, and add them to the room description.

More than that, you can use the adversary roster to move denizens around the dungeon in real time. Maybe the steam mephit in Area 2 flees the PCs and bolts to Asuvius in Area 10 to report the intruders. You notice the work crew cycling between Area 8 and Area 10, so you have Asuvius call them over as they deliver their elemental seeds and send them out as a patrol to locate the PCs. Or maybe something completely different. These aren't scripted events. The point is that the adversary roster empowers you to actively play the dungeon in response to the PCs' actions.

This does increase the complexity of running the scenario, but it's not the exponential, cascading increase that we saw earlier. You're no longer strictly looking at the current room key, but rather than trying to juggle five dozen location keys all at once, you can generally limit yourself to looking at just the current room key and the adversary roster. In other words, two discrete chunks of organized information instead of a chaotic multitude.

THE FOG OF WAR

One pitfall you can fall into when using an adversary roster is having everybody in the dungeon immediately swarm the PCs. Sometimes that's the logical outcome of the PCs' actions and that's fine. (They'll quickly learn to take approaches that don't result in that outcome and retreat and regroup if it does.) But you should bear the fog of war in mind: Even if the PCs attack one action group, it doesn't necessarily mean that everyone in the location will immediately know what's happening, and even if the alarm does go up, some action groups may be assigned to guard other areas or simply have no idea exactly where the crisis is happening.

The adversary roster gives you the opportunity to roleplay the entire dungeon. Seize that opportunity! Really think about what each denizen—or group of denizens—knows, and what they would do with that knowledge.

The fundamental building block of the adversary roster is the **action group**. You rarely want to track every single individual in the dungeon separately, so you group them together for easy management. (Although some of your action groups can, of course, consist of a single individual if that's appropriate.) Most of the time, an action group will consist of all the adversaries in a single location at the beginning of a scenario, but sometimes you'll want to take a particularly large group and split them into smaller units. You can think about this in purely utilitarian terms: Do you think that the group is likely to split up and take independent action? Then it should be two action groups.

For example, if you've got twenty orcs bunking in the barracks, you might split them up into four action groups with five orcs each so that they can split up or be sent as guards to different areas of the compound.

For ease of use and reference, you can also **label** and/or **number** each group. A label is mostly useful as a keyword and reminder: If you see a Death Squad and a Perimeter Guard on your adversary roster, it'll be a helpful reminder of how each group will behave and respond.

ACTION GROUP STAT SHEETS

You might find it useful to prep stat sheets for some or all of your action groups. Just put the stat blocks for all the denizens in the group on a single sheet of paper. When the PCs run into an action group, simply grab the matching stat sheet for easy reference during play. That way you won't need to flip back and forth between multiple pages in your books and notes—all the information you need will be right at your fingertips.

ACTION GROUP TYPES

Action groups tend to fall into one of four types, defined by their typical behavior. Classifying them like this on your roster will make it easier for you to quickly figure out how each group should behave during play.

Patrols make regular circuits through a location. This can be indicated by keying their route (Patrol Areas 1, 5, 7, 8, 9, 2, 1). In some cases, I find it useful to create a separate Patrol Roster (if there are multiple patrols or if their routes are particularly complicated for some reason).

Mobile groups are the default. These are keyed to a specific location, but are generally willing and able to respond to the activities of the PCs.

Mostly Stationary groups, on the other hand, are unlikely to leave the area they're keyed to. This might be a choice on their part (they won't respond when the alarm is raised for whatever reason) or it may not (they're dire wolves locked in a kennel). Adversaries waiting in ambush are another common example of this type. Because there is the possibility for these action groups to become mobile (e.g., someone releases the dire wolves), however, I will include them on the adversary roster, but indent their entries to clearly distinguish them from more active elements.

Stationary adversaries will *never* leave the location they're in. As a result, these adversaries are NOT included on the roster and, instead, still appear in the room key. (Because they will *only* be encountered in that location, there's no reason to clutter up the roster with them.) This might include literally immobile creatures, those simply uninterested in the rest of the complex, or creatures that are sealed away until the PCs disturb them (at which point, if they aren't immediately destroyed, you might choose to add them to the roster).

These distinctions—particularly those between Mostly Stationary and Stationary—are purely utilitarian. They don't represent some deep or universal truth about the game world. Think about how you want to use a particular group of adversaries during play and then classify them appropriately. (If it turns out you were wrong, it's easy enough to just ignore the indentation, right?)

ADVANCED ADVERSARY ROSTERS

I recommend running some typical dungeons using the basic adversary rosters described above to get a feel for how they can be played with at the table. Then you can add in some of these advanced options when you need them.

VARIABLE AREAS

Action groups don't need to be limited to a specific area. The feudal lord might be in his throne room or his bedchambers. A wizard might be studying in the library or working in his laboratory. An orc sergeant might rotate through the barracks of his minions.

ROSTERS ON THE MAP

In addition to the roster, you can also lay the dungeon map out in front of you like a table mat. (You could even print the roster on the same sheet as your map if there's room.)

If you've numbered your action groups, you can now grab matching tokens, put them on the map, and manage your adversaries in real time. Just move them around the map as the situation demands.

(Numbered counters are fairly easy to find. You can also make your own by printing out numbers and affixing them to washers or quarters or the like.)

If you're using a virtual tabletop, it can be even easier to set this up: If you do the prep work to place all of your monsters on the scenario map before play begins, you can just zoom out and manage them in real time.

There are a few ways to show this on the adversary roster:

◎ **Area 21 or Area 40.** Here you simply list the options and can choose whichever one feels appropriate or dramatic during play. (Or, perhaps, they'll just be in whatever area the PCs affect or explore first.)

◎ **Area 21 (1-2) or Area 40 (4-6).** The location is randomly determined, in this case by rolling 1d6.

◎ **Area 21 (day) or Area 40 (night).** The group's location is dependent on the listed circumstances. A division of night and day is common.

A trap to avoid falling into here is attempting to minutely script every detail of the daily lives of every NPC. You really want to focus on establishing a typical starting condition for the location and let all those minor details flow out during play, using variable areas for NPCs only when it's particularly significant.

Another thing to keep in mind is that you can often simulate the activities of a compound without complicating the roster. For example, if the guards at the front gate of the mansion work six-hour shifts and then get relieved, you probably don't need to include all four shifts of guards. Functionally speaking, the mansion has one guard (although the name of that guard might be different depending on what time of day the PCs show up).

NOTES/FOOTNOTES

You can include additional information or cross-referencing by adding notes as a third column on your adversary roster, using footnotes, or both. This can include:

⬦ Adversaries carrying a specific piece of equipment. (This is useful when you have a bunch of cultists all using the same stat block, but only some of them—or one of them—is holding the Red Key of Hrathlar. Otherwise, of course, you'd just list their common equipment in their stat block.)

⬦ Brief tactical notes. (Stuff like "can be telepathically summoned by the mind flayer" or "will usually wait to launch prepared ambush" or "can see through walls.")

⬦ If they've been classified as Mostly Stationary, why they've been classified that way (sleeping, in ambush, indifferent, etc.).

⬦ Other notes regarding their activities (*polymorphed* to look like prisoners, playing poker, torturing Sebastian, etc.).

I generally use a notes column if the notes are brief enough to fit on one line. I use footnotes for longer stuff, or if they only apply to individual characters in larger action groups.

MULTIPLE ROSTERS

For some scenarios, you may want to prep multiple rosters. For example, you might have one roster for Day and another for Night. Or a Normal status and an Alert status.

Creating multiple rosters is usually only worth the effort if the location radically shifts as a result. If the differences are minor or isolated to a handful of characters, then you can probably stick to using conditionals for individual action groups. It's also useful to double-check and make sure there's some sort of player-facing significance to the different roster states. If the players are unlikely to ever notice the difference between Lord Duchamp's Mansion in the Morning and Lord Duchamp's Mansion in the Midafternoon, that's probably a good indication that you only need one roster that captures a "good enough" estimation of a typical day at Lord Duchamp's mansion.

SPLIT ROSTERS

There's a practical limit to how large an adversary roster can become. Once you get a sufficiently large number of action groups, it becomes difficult to manage them. Personally, I find that number to be around 15 to 20 (and by the time I reach 25, I've usually reached my limit). Your mileage may vary, but there'll eventually be a breaking point.

Larger complexes can sometimes be broken down into smaller sections to make them manageable. (You could have different adversary rosters for each level of a dungeon, for example, if there's limited movement between the levels.) There can also be conceptual breakdowns that you can use to divide your adversary roster into more usable chunks. (For example, you might separate the VIPs from the Security Patrols, making it easier to spot and use the active response teams.)

ROSTERS & RANDOM ENCOUNTERS

In location crawls, I will generally choose to use either random encounters or adversary rosters, but not both. After all, I don't need to randomly determine if the security guards stumble on the PCs if I'm tracking the precise location of the security guards in real time.

For smaller location crawls, I usually prefer adversary rosters. It's just more fun and, in my experience, more effective to actively play the entire scenario with real-time strategy. When a location becomes large enough that the adversary roster becomes unmanageable, though, I'll often swap back to random encounters as a more efficient way of modeling the dynamic life of the complex.

Hybrid approaches, where you use an adversary roster but also make random encounter checks, can also be useful, particularly in situations where you're using split rosters. For example, if the PCs are on Level 4 of a large dungeon and you're using a split adversary roster that only includes the monsters on that level, you might use a random encounter check with a low encounter chance to generate any monsters "passing through" from another area of the dungeon.

An example of another hybrid approach from my own campaign was the Bloodpool Labyrinth. In this dungeon there were a limited number of monstrous patrols, but the focus of the scenario was on navigating the labyrinth and its many nonmobile hazards keyed to specific rooms. As a result, I chose to run the patrols using a random encounter table instead of trying to track them in real time.

One thing to keep in mind is that random encounters put pressure on the PCs. If you find that pressure fading away because your adversary roster is too passive, you can also use a random encounter check to prompt you, on a successful check, to have one of the action groups become active (i.e., move to a new location). You can also design patrols into your adversary roster, moving them along their paths once per dungeon turn at the same time as (or in place of) your encounter checks.

ROSTER RESTOCKING

Using adversary rosters can also make it fairly trivial to restock your dungeons (see page 165) as the denizens are killed, replaced, or re-tasked. Because you've separated the denizens from the key, you don't need to go through and re-key every room to update the denizens. You can just create a new adversary roster, often using the exact same key (with perhaps minimal changes to reflect other changes to the complex).

PASSIVE LOCATIONS

As a final note, adversary rosters are a technique for locations with active bad guys. Not every dungeon needs a roster. Sometimes the PCs really are cracking open dusty tombs that have lain undisturbed for centuries and they have only themselves to blame when they awaken the eldritch horrors within. Variety is the spice of life, and good scenario design is often about finding the right tool for the job.

DYNAMIC ENCOUNTER DESIGN

Once you start running dynamic dungeons, you'll need a different methodology for encounter design.

When you're running static dungeons with isolated encounters, you need each individual encounter to be challenging in its own right. Because the players are more or less free to reset their resources after each encounter, every fight needs to push the PCs to the brink and threaten disastrous defeat, because what would be the point otherwise?

When you're running a dynamic dungeon, on the other hand, the primary challenge comes not from the tactics of the individual encounter (although those are still important), but from the strategy of the entire dungeon. It's not enough to win the battle; you have to win the war. It's a richer and deeper style of play.

A core concept here is **combining encounters**. An obvious consequence of running a dynamic location with adversary rosters or similar tools is that multiple action groups can join a single encounter. If you design each action group as if it were a skin-of-your-teeth static encounter, then when two or more of those action groups merge into a single dynamic encounter, they'll annihilate the PCs.

What you generally want instead are action groups that, if encountered alone, are relatively easy encounters, but that can become increasingly dangerous encounters *if they are allowed to join together*. This means that you, as the DM, don't need to pull the bad guys' punches, which, in turn, creates a strategically interesting scenario, baking in the default strategic goal of "don't let them gang up on us." (This is a fairly basic goal, but one that invites multiple potential solutions depending on circumstance—stealth, overwhelming strikes, negotiation, etc. And it forms a firm foundation on which more complicated strategic goals can be built.)

Here are the **principles of dynamic encounter design**:

◈ You rarely want an encounter with One Big Bad Guy™. (These can be a nice change of pace, but single opponents are difficult to keep balanced and tactically interesting against a gaggle of PCs.)

◈ It's better to have encounters with lots of opponents in order to provide tactical complexity.

- Encounters with a single action group will likely have little immediate risk, but they still require some strategic ablation of resources. (The PCs should lose a few hit points, need to cast some of their spells for the day, etc. In other words, these encounters should be able to wear them down over time.)

- Two or three action groups should be able to join together and be a challenging encounter, but rarely a risky one.

- If four or five action groups join together, the PCs should still be able to win the fight, but it may be touch and go and/or require some clever thinking by the players. (You'll be helped here because such encounters often develop over time, with the fourth or fifth action groups joining in the middle of combat, which means the PCs won't be facing all the bad guys at the same time.)

What you can see from these principles is that a dynamic dungeon empowers you to have a larger range of potential encounters (ranging from the easy to the extremely difficult) without any of those encounters becoming meaningless filler.

Exactly how these principles will apply in a specific roleplaying game will vary depending on exactly how that game is designed. In the current edition of D&D, it boils down like this:

- Most of your action groups should be designed as Easy encounters, spiked with the occasional Medium action group. A ratio of 2:1 or 3:1 is probably right most of the time.

- Use Hard action groups sparingly. (The key thing to remember is that a couple of Hard action groups joining up together can very easily become an ultra-lethal encounter.)

- Deadly action groups should almost never be used. You're almost always better off letting such encounters emerge from the strategic flow of the scenario. (But this does mean that when you roll out the very rare Deadly encounter, particularly in non-dynamic situations, you'll get real bang for your buck.)

If the game you're looking to apply these principles to gives you concrete guidelines for gauging difficulty, you can probably use those as a basis for dialing in the encounter design that you need. If it doesn't, then you may need to do some experimentation to figure out what easy, challenging, and potentially overwhelming encounters look like and the various ways you can split them apart into effective action groups.

As always, your group's mileage may vary. Clever and resourceful players, in particular, may find ways to dominate your dungeons. If that's happening regularly at your table, feel free to crank things up a bit until you find the sweet spot for you and yours (keeping in mind, as always, that you have to miss by a lot and for a fairly long time for "too easy" to ruin your campaign). It may also be useful to remember that successfully slipping through a situation unscathed that you know *could* have turned into a complete clusterfuck can be a thrilling, edge-of-your-seat experience in its own right. (And a perhaps welcome change of pace from all the clusterfucks that will inevitably happen in other scenarios.)

One of the key things to really grok about a dynamic dungeon is that, to at least some extent, it gives the *players* a degree of control over the encounters they face. With sufficient strategic cleverness, they can even "design" their own encounters—keeping encounters easy by preventing action groups from joining up, luring enemies to locations of their choosing, and so forth. This is very different from a static dungeon where the encounters are locked to specific rooms and you, as the DM, are solely responsible for designing every aspect of them. In a dynamic dungeon, it's not your job to crush the PCs; it's your job to set the stakes high and give them the opportunity to screw up and push themselves to the breaking point.

PRECIOUS ENCOUNTER DESIGN

Some RPGs are not designed for strategic-based play and, therefore, struggle with dynamic encounter design. These are sometimes referred to as tactics-based or tactical RPGs, and you can usually identify them because they provide mechanics that trivially allow the PCs to fully restore their resources at the end of each fight. (The game becomes tactics-based because, mechanically at least, it's designed to isolate each encounter with no long-term strategic impact as a result of how a particular encounter is resolved.) The fourth edition of D&D, unlike other versions of the game, was designed like this.

The problem is that without the strategic ablation of resources, encounters that don't carry some significant risk of wiping out the PCs become meaningless (since any losses incurred will just reset when the encounter is finished). Conversely, of course, encounters that are too difficult and would wipe the PCs out remain nonviable. The result is that tactical RPGs have a very narrow and very specific difficulty that has to be hit with every single encounter, and this is simply incompatible with having multiple action groups fluidly moving around and combining with each other. When your encounters are balanced on a knife's edge, unexpected reinforcements are always ruinous.

If you're running a tactical RPG, therefore, you won't be able to use dynamic dungeons. Such games instead focus on **precious encounter design**, in which enemies and terrain are carefully designed in static, prefabricated packages to create maximum tactical interest. The better tactical RPGs will give you guidelines on how best to do that for their specific mechanics.

1ST–LEVEL FRAGILITY

When running dynamic dungeons in D&D, something to be particularly conscious of is the fragility of 1st-level characters. Their limited resources combined with the high probability of any single hit reducing them to 0 HP (or even killing them outright) makes them particularly vulnerable to the large groups of opponents that are usually desirable in action groups.

For a 1st-level adventure, I recommend using only Easy action groups with one or two opponents. Alternatively, simply limit your scenarios to static dungeons until the PCs level up.

DUNGEON FACTIONS

Many dungeons will be the demesne of a single faction:

- The caves where the Skullface goblins live
- The grotto fortress of the drow
- The mansion belonging to the Donatello crime family
- The hive filled with giant bees
- The sunken reef villa of the sahuagin lord

Such dungeons are referred to as **lairs**. You might run into the occasional prisoner, dissatisfied minion, or competing party of adventurers within such dungeons, but for the most part everyone you meet in a lair is working for the same "team."

Other dungeons, however, aren't so simple. Within their vaulted halls, there are multiple factions at work. It's possible that they're working together in a temporary alliance or living with some rickety détente, but it's also possible that they're actively hostile with each other—Montagues and Capulets, drow and svirfneblin, liches and beholders, Eloi and Morlocks.

Adding faction means adding action. A lair will usually settle down into some form of status quo, its denizens going through their normal routines. Just living their lives. But once you add multiple factions—once you add giant wasps to the giant beehive—the conflict and competing interests between those factions will drive events forward. Having multiple factions also means opportunity. They give the PCs a chance to sow division, forge alliances, seek refuge, play both ends against the middle, and otherwise take advantage of the more complex strategic tapestry afforded by the fault lines between factions.

As play continues, the PCs' actions will disrupt whatever balance of power previously existed in the dungeon. Between sessions, as you're doing your restocking checks and updating your dungeon key, the factions become a framework for figuring out what happens next.

"Okay, the PCs killed seventy percent of the orc population on Level 3. Who can take advantage of that, and what will the Orc King's response be? Actually, wait, they just killed the Orc King. Have the orcs broken up into factions? Could the Red Prince"—I just made that name up, potentially personalizing one of the nameless orcs on the adversary roster—"have allied with the goblins on Level 2 to push his claims? How will the other orcs feel about being asked to coexist with lowly goblins? Will they turn to the Voodoo Necromancer of the Southern Hills"—a character I just made up out of whole cloth— "who was once the Orc King's adviser?"

That's 15 seconds of brainstorming. Follow it up with a few minutes of actual prep and you've got orc-and-goblin warbands with faces painted bright crimson squaring off against orc warriors 'roided out on alchemical strength boosters wearing the bone fetishes of the Voodoo Necromancer. It doesn't even really matter if the PCs don't get directly involved in the actual politics here: Even if they just slash their way through these orcish factions, they'll recognize that the dungeon has changed in their absence and get some unique and interesting hacking out of it.

CREATING FACTIONS

For each faction in the dungeon, you'll want to prep the

- ⬡ faction roster,
- ⬡ faction territory,
- ⬡ faction agenda, and
- ⬡ faction reaction.

The **faction roster** is simply part of the dungeon's adversary roster, identifying the dungeon denizens who belong to or are closely allied with the faction. You may find it convenient to prep a separate roster for each faction, or, depending on the dungeon, you may find it better to indicate each action group's faction alliance in the notes column of a single adversary roster.

The **faction territory** is simply whatever section of the dungeon the faction controls. I often find it useful to color-code each faction, and then outline each territory in the matching color. In some cases, I find it can be clearer to make a copy of the dungeon map and literally color in each faction's territory.

Not every section of a dungeon needs to belong to one of the factions. In fact, having no-man's-lands between the factions can be quite effective. It gives space for nonaligned denizens to lurk, for the PCs to find sanctuary, and/or for the factions to fight each other.

Giving each faction a **faction agenda**—something they specifically want or want to achieve—will provide a motivation for their actions, and thereby help inspire you in figuring out what those actions should be.

The **faction reaction** is how they will likely respond to the PCs. Remember reaction checks? This is the same thing: Immediate Attack, Hostile, Cautious/Threatening, Neutral, or Amiable. By default, in fact, this will be determined by the random chance of the reaction check the first time the PCs encounter members of the faction. (First impressions are very important!) Alternatively, you could preset each faction's reaction as part of your prep. (The gricks will attack on sight and the goblins are Hostile, but the kobolds are Cautious and the dark dwarves are Neutral.) An option that splits the difference is to give each faction a bias to their reaction check. Of course, over time, the actions of the PCs may influence and change the faction reaction to them.

RANDOM FACTION CONFLICT

With your factions in place, you may find it useful to use a procedural content generator to develop the relationships between factions over time. As always, your personal inspiration should take precedence, but if you find yourself looking for a little inspiration, you can follow this procedure between sessions.

You'll first need to construct a **random faction table** for your dungeon. To do this, simply list the factions in your dungeon and assign an appropriate die. There are three additional entries that can be fun to add to this table:

- ◎ **Wandering Adventurers**, representing any competing adventuring groups that might also be exploring the dungeon.

- ◎ **Outsiders**, providing a prompt that some faction outside of the dungeon has become interested in its affairs. (This could be a completely new faction, in which case you'd obviously need to create it. Alternatively, it might be some other faction that's been established in a previous adventure, binding the campaign together.)

- ◎ **Roll Again Twice**, creating the possibility of multi-party faction conflicts.

With your random faction table in hand, use the following procedure:

1. Make a **faction conflict check** by rolling 1d6. A roll of 1 indicates that conflict has broken out between the factions.

2. Determine the factions involved by rolling twice on your **random faction table**. (If you roll the same number twice, either reroll or assume some sort of civil strife.)

3. Roll on the **faction conflict table** on the next page to determine the outcome of the conflict.

Finally, interpret this result and translate it into the appropriate updates to your adversary roster and key.

EXAMPLE: RANDOM FACTION TABLE

DIE ROLL (D12)	FACTION
1	Skullface Goblins
2	Red Goblins
3	Sahuagin
4	Nothic Druids
5	Dreadwood Ents
6	Asmodean Hobgoblins
7	Oberonic Hegemony
8	Court of Waves
9	Court of Fire
10	Wandering Adventurers
11	Outsiders
12	Roll Again Twice

FACTION CONFLICT TABLE

DIE ROLL (D8)	OUTCOME
1	Stalemate Skirmish
2	1 Faction Damaged
3	1 Faction Crippled
4	1 Faction Destroyed
5	Both Factions Damaged
6	Both Factions Crippled
7	Both Factions Destroyed
8	Factions Unite

- **Stalemate Skirmish:** The factions are largely unaffected by the conflict. Their defensive positions may have been reinforced, or you may wish to subtract one or two members from one of their encounters or action groups. (The conflict may leave them ripe for alliances against their recent foes, or leave a chamber showing recent signs of conflict, or a couple of new graves have been dug in the cemetery at the entrance of the dungeon.)

- **Faction Damaged:** A damaged faction has suffered losses equal to roughly 25 percent of their strength. (You might eliminate entire encounters or action groups, or perhaps subtract 1d4 members from each encounter or action group for that faction.)

- **Faction Crippled:** A crippled faction has suffered losses equal to roughly 50 percent of their strength. (This makes it very likely that entire action groups have been lost. Consider also modifying their territory, or leaving chunks of it undefended.)

- **Faction Destroyed:** A destroyed faction has been eliminated. Their lair may lie empty, be occupied by the other faction involved in the conflict, or restocked randomly. Their population has been killed, driven off, or enslaved.

- **Factions Unite:** The two factions have allied with each other. (One of their leaders may have been killed or subjugated, uniting the factions under a single leader. Or the alliance may be for some short-term goal. Or the populations might be fully intermixed between their lairs.)

EXAMPLE: FACTION CONFLICT

Like a random encounter check, the output of random faction conflict is designed to be flexibly and creatively interpreted. Let's take a look at what it might look like in practice if you rolled a successful faction conflict check.

- ◎ **Determine Factions:** I roll 1d12 twice, generating 6 and 8. That's the Asmodean Hobgoblins and the Court of Waves.
- ◎ **Determine Outcome:** I roll 1d8 and get 5. That's Both Factions Damaged.
- ◎ **Interpret Results:** I know that the hobgoblins have been in conflict with the sahuagin lakefolk. The sahuagin have been able to use their water magic to ward against the hobgoblin fire magic and hell hounds. So there are a couple possibilities here: I could imagine the sahuagin going to the Court of Waves and making pledges of fealty to the feyish powers in exchange for their assistance against the hobgoblins. Or, alternatively, the hobgoblins could be the supplicants to the Court, asking them to use their powerful elemental magic to create a destructive tidal wave in the sahuagin's underground lakes that would ruin their defenses.

The latter seems more intriguing to me. (You could easily decide otherwise or come up with some other explanation entirely.) But how did this result in the hobgoblins and the Court of Waves ending up damaged? Hmm . . . What if the ritual went horribly awry, unleashing uncontrolled elementals who ran rampant through the Courts and slew the hobgoblin leaders who were in attendance for the ritual?

Now you've got a leadership crisis on Level 5, blasted chaos on Level 7, and rampaging elementals added to the random encounter tables throughout the entire dungeon.

See how easy this is? Let's do it again.

⬡ **Determine Factions:** I roll 10 and 6. That's Wandering Adventurers and the Asmodean Hobgoblins again.

⬡ **Determine Outcome:** I roll 7 for Both Factions Destroyed.

⬡ **Interpret Results:** This one is pretty easy to figure out. A group of adventurers (or perhaps mercenaries hired by the sahuagin?) invaded Level 5 and wiped out the still highly disorganized hobgoblin cultists. Ironically, the surviving adventurers were then killed by one of the rampaging elementals.

Let's go one step further here and suggest that sahuagin wave-casters have descended into the now-abandoned hobgoblin warrens and are trying to pacify the rogue elemental.

I think you can see how this simple system can be used to add a little quick spice to a large dungeon or megadungeon between PC visitations.

NOW YOU ARE
✦ THE MASTER! ✦

You've learned a lot! And, if all's gone well, you've run your first adventure. Ideally, you've run several of them. You're starting to get comfortable as a DM, and you've started experimenting with larger, more complicated, and more dynamic scenarios.

What's next?

That's up to you!

The location crawls you've been running so far are an incredibly versatile scenario structure, and you'll find them cropping up in almost every adventure you ever run. (It turns out no matter where you go . . . there's a location.) But it probably won't surprise you to learn that they're not the *only* scenario structure. There are many other types of adventures to be had!

The rest of this book is an instruction manual for several different scenario structures you can use to prep and run these adventures:

- ◎ **Mysteries** (see page 201)
- ◎ **Raids and Heists** (see page 267)
- ◎ **Urban Adventures** (see page 315), including urbancrawls, social events, and conspiracies
- ◎ **Wilderness Adventures** (see page 363), including hexcrawls and pointcrawls

You'll likely recognize many of these concepts from the movies, books, graphic novels, and other media you enjoy. If there's one that looks particularly exciting or enticing to you, you can skip straight to that section.

Alternatively, you might want to check out the Extra Credit section at the back of the book. These specialized tools and techniques can be added to your game at any time, and will often enhance many different scenario structures. So you should feel free to reach out and grab anything that looks useful whenever the fancy strikes you:

- **Creating Your Campaign** (see page 435), including how you can find players, pitch your game, create characters, and learn new roleplaying games.

- **Campaign Status Documents** (see page 448), a tool for organizing your campaign notes.

- **The Open Table** (see page 463), an alternative way of running a campaign that can make playing an RPG as easy as a board game.

- **Quick-and-Dirty Worldbuilding** (see page 471), with guidance for the essential material you need to start running games in a world of your own creation.

- **Running Combat** (see page 486), a grab bag of tips and tricks for improving your combat encounters.

- **Scenario Hooks** (see page 498), aka how you get the players to play your adventures.

- **Supporting Cast** (see page 506), another grab bag of tools and tricks for creating and running memorable NPCs.

- **Splitting the Party** (see page 525), or what to do when the PCs want to do multiple things at the same time.

Of course, you can also just keep reading the book from cover to cover by simply turning the page! That'll work just fine and nobody is going to stop you.

Whichever path you choose, remember the most important lesson: Have fun!

PART 2

MYSTERIES

ROLEPLAYING GAMES WERE born in the dungeon, but they didn't stay there for long. In 1981, Chaosium, Inc., published *Call of Cthulhu*, an RPG based on the horror fiction of H. P. Lovecraft in which the players took on the roles of investigators seeking to unravel eldritch mysteries.

Call of Cthulhu wasn't the first time someone had run a mystery scenario in an RPG, but it was the first time an RPG had been made in which mysteries were the primary focus. The hobby has never looked back, and you can find mystery scenarios almost everywhere you look.

This is likely because mysteries are an incredibly versatile scenario structure. Your mind might immediately leap to Agatha Christie whodunnits, the flair of Holmesian deductions, or the antics of private detectives in film noir, but as the example of *Call of Cthulhu* demonstrates, that's really only scratching the surface. You've got police procedurals ranging from the lurid sensationalism of the *CSI* franchise to the gritty realism of *The Wire*, but you've also got newspaper dramas like *All the President's Men* or *Spotlight*, political thrillers, spy stories, legal thrillers, and conspiracy fiction, to name just a few. Mysteries creep in around the edges of epic fantasy ("What exactly is this magic ring the halfling found?") and superhero comics (Batman is the world's greatest detective), and they're the basis for any number of pulp adventure stories: Who's rustling the cattle? Where is the Spear of Destiny? Why did this strange island suddenly appear in the middle of the Pacific Ocean? What happened to Will Byers?

Mystery scenarios, of course, work differently from dungeon scenarios. Where the dungeon is made up of rooms connected by corridors, the mystery is made up of **scenes** (or nodes) connected by **clues**. To unlock the power of the mystery scenario for our campaigns, we'll first have to understand how these new tools work at the table and in our prep.

✦ SCENES ✦

One of the things that makes a dungeon easy to run is that, in the dungeon, every moment of the experience is usually (a) relevant, (b) interesting, and therefore (c) part of the game.

If you try to do the same thing outside of the dungeon, though, it's usually a car wreck.

> **GM:** Okay, what are you doing now?
>
> **PLAYER:** Let's head over to the Courvier Estate in the Nobles' District. I want to see what Lady Isabella has to say about this.
>
> **GM:** How are you getting there?
>
> **PLAYER:** We'll ride our horses.
>
> **GM:** Okay, you get your horses out of the stables and begin riding up Moonlight Lane. You reach the T-intersection with Guildsman Road. Do you want to go right or left?
>
> **PLAYER:** Left.
>
> **GM:** Okay, you go another block down to Almond Street. Which way do you want to go?
>
> **PLAYER:** Straight.

That's obviously not right, is it?

You could similarly imagine trying to navigate through a forest by describing every tree or trying to stake out a tavern to see if Lord Arundel will show up in disguise only to have the GM describe every single person who walks in or out of the tavern for six hours.

What this should probably look like instead is something like this:

> **PLAYER:** Let's head over to the Courvier Estate in the Nobles' District. I want to see what Lady Isabella has to say about this.
>
> **GM:** Okay, when you arrive at the Courvier Estate, you are ushered into Lady Isabella's private study. A few moments later, she comes sweeping into the room. "What do you want? I'm very busy."

Or, alternatively:

PLAYER: Let's head over to the Courvier Estate in the Nobles' District. I want to see what Lady Isabella has to say about this.

GM: (*rolls some dice*) As you're heading up Guildsman Road toward the Nobles' District, an arrow suddenly flies past Natasha's head before skipping off the cobblestones. Her horse whinnies in alarm. Give me initiative checks!

In both cases we've skipped over the boring bits and jumped ahead to the next interesting bit.

EMPTY TIME

We refer to the boring bits as **empty time**. The stuff that happens during empty time isn't necessarily irrelevant or unimportant, it's just that the characters aren't making **meaningful choices** during that time. The choices that the PCs are making during empty time either won't change the outcome, they're not choices that we, as players, are interested in, or both.

For example, a badly injured character might need to undergo weeks of physical therapy at Lincoln Memorial to recover or a group of galactic diplomats might need to travel for days through hyperspace to reach the capital of the Seven Star Imperium. These are not unimportant tasks—the injured character must do the therapy to recover and the diplomats may be rushing to prevent an interstellar war—but unless we're interested in roleplaying specific moments in the struggle of therapy or exploring inter-character drama in the quiet moments on board the starlight courier (and we very well could be!), the ultimate outcome of recovery or arrival at the foreign capital is a foregone conclusion and the intervening span is empty time.

The interesting bits, on the other hand—the fight that crippled the character, the negotiations with the Seven Star Imperium—are **scenes**. They float like islands in the sea of empty time, and they're connected by **intention**.

In fact, I find it easiest to identify empty time—the bit we skip over—by looking at the players' current intention. What is it that they want to do? The intention creates a **vector**. All you need to do is look along that vector and ask yourself, "Where's the next meaningful choice?" For example, the PCs' intention is to go to the Courvier Estate. Is the choice of route significant?

Maybe it is! Maybe that ambush only happens if the PCs go up Guildsman Road. If they take the scenic route along Old Dragon Gorge Road instead, they'd avoid the ambush and arrive at the Courvier Estate without incident. (Or maybe with a different incident.)

But more likely the choice of route isn't significant. Almond Street? Walnut Street? Macadamia Way? It doesn't matter. It's not a meaningful choice, so we can skip past it and continue following the vector until we find a choice that *is* meaningful.

Broadly speaking, if the PCs declare an intention, they'll either achieve that intention (e.g., they reach the Courvier Estate and speak with Lady Isabella) or they'll encounter an obstacle. Following the vector, we could imagine it being interrupted in any number of ways:

- They get ambushed on the way.
- The bridge over Dragon Gorge has been washed out and they'll need to take a different route (or help repair the bridge).
- The Nobles' District has been quarantined due to an outbreak of arcano-plague.
- The doorman at the Courvier Estate refuses them entry.
- Lady Isabella is not home at the moment because she's attending a meeting of the Lords' Council to discuss the recent outbreak of war in the Lowlands.

Spotting interruptions like these in a vector may be based on what you know about the world and its current situation. (For example, you know that insectoid assassins have been hunting the PCs. Or your notes indicate that the Dragon Gorge bridge was washed out during the flooding caused by the recent siege of the Aquanautic Titans. Or it's just logical that the PCs would be challenged by a noble's doorman.) But it can just as easily be a moment of creative inspiration as you hear the players declare their intention and immediately think, "Wouldn't it be cool if they got ambushed by an insectoid hit squad?" or "I think it would be fun to roleplay a scene with that ornery

Courvier doorman." You might even have a random encounter check or similar mechanic that would systemically inject interruptions.

More often than not, though, you'll find that vectors take you all the way to their destination without interruption: If the PCs want to do research at the library, they'll arrive at the library. If they want to meet with an NPC, they'll find the NPC. If they want to go back to the dungeon, they'll get there and start delving.

CONTEXT IS MEANINGFUL

Something that can be easy to forget is that a choice can be meaningful even if it only changes the context of an outcome.

For example, maybe the PCs are going to get ambushed by insectoids no matter what route they choose to the Courvier Estate. (Because an insectoid scout is lurking outside of their inn and will summon the assassin swarm when they see the PCs leave.) But this can actually make the choice of route meaningful, because an ambush on Guildsman Street would be framed differently than one along Old Dragon Gorge Road!

Deciding when context is or isn't sufficiently meaningful is, of course, more art than science.

TRANSITIONS

Having identified the empty time and, therefore, what the next scene will be, how do we actually transition from the current scene to the new one? What does "skipping the empty time" actually look like?

The first option is a **sharp cut**. You simply jump directly from the current scene to the beginning of the next scene.

PLAYER: Let's head over to the Courvier Estate in the Nobles' District. I want to see what Lady Isabella has to say about this.

GM: Okay, we cut to all of you waiting in Lady Isabella's private study. The door slams open and she comes sweeping into the room. "What do you want? I'm very busy."

This uses the language of film, and you may even find it useful to literally say things like, "We cut to . . ." But you'll see the same technique in every storytelling medium, from novels to comic books. The current scene is done; let's move directly to where the next interesting bit is.

A softer option is **abstract time**. It generally takes the form of an eliding narration. Stuff like, "Several days pass as you cross the Great Plain . . ." or "You leave the Docks and head across town . . ."

> **PLAYER:** Let's head over to the Courvier Estate in the Nobles' District. I want to see what Lady Isabella has to say about this.
>
> **GM:** Okay, you leave the Hogshead Tavern and head up Guildsman Street into the Nobles' District. After a brief and somewhat rancorous exchange with the doorman at the Courvier Estate, you're ushered into Lady Isabella's private study. A few moments later, she comes sweeping into the room. "What do you want? I'm very busy."

I frequently default to this style because it never fully disengages from the players. With practice it becomes easy to read a table's reaction to eliding narration and "know" when you need to drop out of it and back into a scene. In other cases, the players will just speak up and tell you. (For example, maybe the players would actually like to ask the doorman a few questions while he's escorting them to the study.)

The advantage of sharp cuts, on the other hand, is a punchier pacing and the ability to put really strong frames on the scenes you choose. (More on that in a moment.)

A blended approach is also possible, featuring a sharp cut to a point much closer to the new scene and then using eliding narration to set the scene up.

> **PLAYER:** Let's head over to the Courvier Estate in the Nobles' District. I want to see what Lady Isabella has to say about this.
>
> **GM:** Okay, when you arrive at the Courvier Estate, you have a brief and somewhat rancorous exchange with the doorman before being ushered into Lady Isabella's private study. A few moments later, she comes sweeping into the room. "What do you want? I'm very busy."

This blended approach can give you some flexibility in setting up the given circumstances of the scene—i.e., the stuff the players need to know in order for the scene to make sense—and also gives the players an opportunity to course correct how their characters would enter the scene. ("Wait! I don't want to knock on the door. I want to sneak in and surprise Lady Isabella!")

FRAMING THE SCENE

There are a bunch of different ways you can think about setting up or "framing" a scene, but it largely boils down to rapidly establishing the initial moment of the scene (the who, what, where, and when) and then giving things a short, sharp push to put things in motion.

Start by identifying the **agenda** of the scene. This is essentially *why* you chose this scene. What was the meaningful choice you identified? Why is it important? Why do we care? Agendas don't have to be incredibly clever or of earth-shattering significance, but there has to be some sort of reason for why we're playing out the events of this scene.

Consider what a scene without an agenda looks like:

PLAYER: Let's head over to the Courvier Estate in the Nobles' District. I want to see what Lady Isabella has to say about this.

GM: Okay, we cut to: Guildsman Street. You're riding your horses toward the Nobles' District and you're approaching Walnut Street. What are you going to do?

PLAYER: Ride straight through the intersection.

End of scene.

Without an agenda—without a reason to focus on the events at the intersection of Guildsman and Walnut—that's clearly a waste of time.

You can think of an agenda either in terms of the scene's **stakes** (literally what's at stake in the scene) or as a **question** that the scene is going to answer.

For example, imagine that the PCs are about to encounter an ogre. The agenda might be:

◈ Can the PCs kill the ogre? (At stake are the lives of the PCs and the life of the ogre.)

◈ How are the PCs going to get past the ogre? (This makes the scene more open-ended. It might still be resolved through combat, but that's not the only possibility.)

◈ Can the ogre convince the PCs to help him fight the goblins? (This is a completely different scene!)

Other agendas might include:

◈ Can Antoine stop the angry mob from burning down the necromancer's tower?

◈ Can Hammett find the bloodstained glove?

◈ Will LaPadite betray the Jewish family living in his secret attic?

◈ Will Annie take the heroin?

◈ How much of Case's sanity will be lost gazing through the portal?

These are not, it should be noted, questions that you need to know the answer to. Quite the opposite, in fact. You're playing the scene to *find* the answer, and you can only find it in collaboration with your players. By creating the scene together and seeing what happens.

As you play the scene, in fact, you may discover that it's actually about a completely different question than you thought. (You framed the scene as, "Can the PCs kill the ogre?" but then the bard starts seducing the ogre.) That's okay. More than okay, in fact. Those often end up being the very best scenes.

RUNNING AWESOME SCENES

The trick to running an awesome scene is making sure that the agenda of the scene can't be trivially resolved.

Think about a combat scene. Most RPGs feature a big, robust combat system, and so a combat scene is rarely trivial to resolve: The players have to make lots of meaningful tactical choices and figure out how to maneuver their way to victory.

Once you start framing non-combat scenes, however, they can easily end up being short and unsatisfying: The PCs have an objective. They briefly interact with the environment or an NPC. And then the scene is abruptly done.

What the scene needs is an obstacle that will block the PCs from achieving their objective. (A combat scene, you'll note, inherently provides this obstacle: the bad guys you need to defeat.) You'll get even better results if there are multiple objectives, multiple obstacles, or both. If there are multiple objectives, you can get a lot of mileage by setting up the scene so that they conflict with each other (and, therefore, also become the obstacles of the scene).

In framing scenes, we talked about identifying the vector of an intention and looking at the point where that vector intersected an obstacle. You can (and should!) continue that into the scene itself: The PCs can't just jump directly to an "I solve the problem" die roll. Instead, they'll need to take some preparatory actions to establish an unobstructed vector to the thing they want.

Example 1: You want to shoot Victor at his club. But you can't just drive up outside the club and shoot him. You'll have to start by finding a way to get inside (sneaking or fast-talking your way past the bouncers or casting a *teleport* spell), then track him down, and *then* take your shot.

> **Example 2:** You want to convince Michael to sell you the data chip. But first you need to get him to admit that he has it. Then you've got to convince him that there's another way to save his sister. And then you've got to convince him that you're offering him something worth the risk.
>
> The great thing is that you don't even need to know *how* these obstacles will be overcome. Instead, just set up the obstacles:
>
> ◎ Michael doesn't want to admit he has the data chip.
>
> ◎ Michael needs it to save his sister.
>
> ◎ Michael has hidden the data chip in a locker at the bus station.
>
> It's up to the players to figure out the solutions!
>
> (Not every scene needs to be awesome, though! Don't push it. Sometimes you really do want to just get in, answer a quick question, and get out.)

THE BANG

Now that you know what the scene is about, you need the **bang**—the explosive moment that forces the PCs to start making meaningful choices (or at least provokes them with the opportunity to do so), propelling the scene into motion. In that explosion, a bang defines the agenda of the scene and reveals it to the players.

This is the arrow in the wall or the noblewoman barging through the door and demanding answers. It's the torches of the mob coming over the hill or the Nazi knocking on your door.

The design of your bang will usually have a big impact on how the scene plays out. For example, consider a scene where the PCs encounter an ogre. Does the scene start when the ogre jumps out and snarls in their face? Or when they're still approaching its chamber and they can hear the crunching of bones? Or when they see a goblin strung up on a rack with its intestines hanging around its ankles . . . and then the deep thudding of heavy footsteps fills the corridor behind them as the ogre returns for its meal?

Other bangs might look like this:

- You return home, but your wife isn't there. As you enter your bedchambers, you see a large bloodstain on the ground.
- You're riding through the Blue Hills when the sun sets and the full moon begins to rise. In the distance, you hear the howl of wolves. The howls are getting closer.
- You rip open the envelope. There is only a single sheet of parchment within, and there are no words on it. Only a single, large, black spot.

Choosing the "right" bang is often more art than science, but a rule of thumb I've found useful is the quicker you get to the bang and the larger the number of interesting choices that can be made in response to the bang, the better the bang is.

With that being said, while bangs launch scenes, that doesn't always mean that they're the first thing that happens in a scene. It's often useful to give yourself a little breathing room to establish the scene before kicking things into high gear. Consider the letter with the black spot, for example. You could cut from some previous scene directly to the PC ripping open a letter they received, but it might be more effective if you took a step back and, for example, described the messenger arriving to hand the letter to the PC (or the PCs finding the letter lying on their bed or slipped into their pocket or whatever the delivery mechanism might be) and then letting the player announce that they're opening the letter.

In fact, bangs can often land better if you've properly set the scene. If the players are confused or trying to get their bearings in the new scene, they may not be able to understand the full importance—and, therefore, the full impact—of the bang.

SETTING THE SCENE: LOCATION & CHARACTER

Now that you've framed the scene, you need to fill the frame with all the specific details that will bring that scene to life. My philosophy is to take all the elements of the scene—the who, what, where, and when—and fill those elements with all sorts of toys that both you and the PCs can play with. Once again, the more flexible these toys are, the more useful they become and the more potential the scene will have. If you include something that only has one potential use, that's good. But an element that can be used in eight different ways? That's S-tier.

The good news is that you don't need to make eight different plans for how to use an element. In fact, you almost certainly shouldn't. The priority is just including stuff that's fun to play with. Even better, your players are a gaggle of creativity, and if you let them, they'll take even the most boring stuff and spin it in ways you could scarcely imagine. So as you're filling the frame, remember this all-important maxim:

You may know where the scene begins, but you don't know where it ends.

You're not writing a book or filming a movie. Unlike a traditional author, you may know where you're starting, but you've got no idea where the journey will end. That can sound intimidating, but in practice it's liberating. You just need to set the pins up. Your players will be the ones to knock them down.

As you're setting things up, the **location** is the When and Where of the scene. It's the immediate environment for the actions of the scene and it can range from the claustrophobic ("the back room at the Red Hand") to the absurdly panoramic ("racing down the dusty slopes of Olympus Mons").

We talked about how to describe a room in Keying: Dungeon Rooms (see page 105) and the truth is that a dungeon room is often just a hyper-specific type of scene, so pretty much all of that advice also applies when you're describing other scenes:

◈ Three of Five

◈ Two Cool Details

◈ Three-by-Three

And just like a dungeon room, you want to keep all of this as pithy as possible.

The other major elements in the scene are the **characters**, the Who of the scene. I find it useful to think about the characters in a scene in three categories: leads, features, and extras.

Leads are the major characters in the scene. They're the characters who are most affected by the agenda of the scene or who are capable of having the greatest impact on the agenda of the scene.

Features are the supporting cast of the scene. They wield influence over the leads or provide crucial information or are important resources in whatever conflict is being fought.

Extras are scene-dressing. They might be taken hostage or appealed to for mob justice, but they can usually just be thought of as part of the location instead of as active agents in the scene.

PCs in a scene are almost always leads. You may find it useful to think of some PCs as being the leads in the scene and other PCs as features (because the agenda of the scene is primarily of interest to the former and of less interest to the latter), but if you've got a scene where *none* of the PCs are leads, you might want to take a moment and triple-check what you're doing. Unless you've got some amazingly good reason for sidelining the PCs, it's almost always a good idea to find a way to reframe the agenda of the scene so that it's about the PCs.

The only situation in which I would consider framing a scene in which the PCs aren't leads is one in which the PCs are *deliberately* choosing to not participate. For example, maybe they're eavesdropping on a conversation. (But even then, I'd double-check to make sure that a secondary agenda in the scene isn't about the PCs avoiding detection. And then triple-check to make sure that the scene isn't *really* about something like "Will the PCs stop Roberta from confessing her love to Charles?")

GIVEN CIRCUMSTANCES

*The **given circumstances** of a scene include all the elements of the scene itself, but also all of the relevant events and continuity that have led up to the scene. Confronting the villain who killed your beloved horse or fighting a climactic battle in a burning house when your own parents were killed in a fire packs an extra punch.*

ENDING THE SCENE

We leave a scene the same way we entered it: by cutting to a new scene. The trick, of course, is knowing *when* you should cut away. The facile answer is that the scene is over when the characters are done making meaningful choices (and you, therefore, establish the vector to the next meaningful choice and frame the next scene), but let's take a closer look at what that means in practice.

FINISHING THE AGENDA

If the agenda of a scene is defined by a question, a really obvious place to cut from is the point where that question has been answered.

This line of thinking, though, can become a trap if you think that it's the *only* way for a scene to end, largely because it will also mean that you'll feel pressured to conclusively resolve the agenda in every scene. Some of the most interesting agendas actually develop over multiple scenes before being resolved. (Think about will-they-won't-they romances, for example.) Other conflicts literally *can't* be resolved until some other event has occurred. Staying mired in a scene that has reached an impasse is a quick exercise in boredom, and you'll want to identify other moments that indicate when it's time to move on.

THE SECOND LULL

As you roleplay through scenes, you'll start to get a feel for how they flow—the back-and-forth between characters; the rise and fall of tension. As a scene kicks off, things will often move fast and hard, as all of the leads push hard on achieving their objectives. And then there'll often come a moment when things slow down, when people seem uncertain in their actions, when things seem to be coasting a little bit. That's okay. Don't cut away! The characters in the scene—and the players around the table—need that moment to reflect on what's happened, think about what it means to them, and then figure out how they're going to adjust their strategy.

But what you generally want to avoid is the second lull. As things start to slow down again, either cut away or introduce a new bang to bring a new scene to them.

ON THE EXIT

If all the PCs leave, that's a pretty clear-cut signal that the scene is over. But often even a single lead leaving (whether that's a PC or NPC) will indicate that the scene is drawing to a close.

Much like the second lull, a good rule of thumb here can be the second exit: The exit of the first lead makes it clear the scene is coming to an end, giving everyone else a chance to wrap things up. When the second lead leaves, it means that either the agenda has been resolved or interest in the scene is waning fast and it's time to cut away.

SCENE TO SCENE

As one scene ends, it's time for a new scene to begin. All conversations are loops and it's time to close this one: Identify the next scene, then shift to abstract time or cut hard to the next bang.

THE THREE CLUE
RULE

We can now take our scenes and turn them into a mystery scenario. The key building block of a mystery is the **investigation scene**, in which the PCs discover a **clue** that points them in the direction of another scene in which they can continue their investigation. The clue, in other words, creates the vector between the current scene and the next scene. (For example, the letters found partially burned in the fireplace reveal that Claudette was exchanging regular correspondence with Lord Denton. The next scene, therefore, can be the PCs meeting with Lord Denton to ask him a few questions.)

The most basic structure for a mystery scenario is the **breadcrumb trail**: Scene A has a clue pointing to Scene B; Scene B has a clue pointing to Scene C; and so forth, until the penultimate scene contains a clue pointing to the final scene of the adventure, where the truth is discovered, the bad guy is confronted, or both.

For example, if Claudette was slain by a vampire, then the final clue might reveal the location of the vampire's crypt. If she faked her own death in order to escape with the Summerville Diamond, then the final clue could point to the hunting lodge where both she and the jewel are hidden away.

The breadcrumb trail, however, has a fatal flaw. In order for the scenario to work, each clue must lead to the next, and that means there must be an unbroken chain of clues from the beginning of the scenario until the end. If the PCs were to miss *any* of the clues, they would become lost and the scenario would break.

Each clue becomes a chokepoint in the scenario, and each chokepoint increases the fragility of the scenario. The more clues your scenario has, the more fragile it becomes. In fact, it's even *worse* than that, because each clue is actually *multiple* chokepoints:

◎ The PCs need to look for the clue.

◎ The PCs need to find the clue.

◎ The PCs need to interpret the clue and reach the correct conclusion.

For example, consider Claudette's burned letters. Although it seems obvious to you that the PCs should search her room, they might never think to do that or even deliberately choose not to do it. ("We've troubled her mother enough.") If they do search the room, they might never look in the fireplace, or perhaps they fail their Intelligence (Investigation) check to find the letters. Having found the burned scraps of paper, they have to choose to read them (which, again, seems obvious, but might not be to the players for any number of reasons) and, having read them, they need to correctly conclude that they should seek out the Lord Denton mentioned in the letters.

Remember: If any one of these steps—searching the room, finding the letters, reading the letters, realizing they should talk to Lord Denton—fails to happen, the scenario would break and the PCs would have no way of finishing it. Or even continuing. Your whole session just slams into a wall.

And that's just one clue!

This kind of tight, bare-bones, clue-to-clue-to-clue plotting can work in noninteractive mediums because the writers control the characters and can ensure they always reach the right conclusion at the right time. In reality, though, it's not even the way most detective stories work. It can be slightly more common in TV procedurals, likely due to the limitations of time, but the next time you're reading a mystery novel or watching a whodunnit film, pay attention to how often a detective's deduction will be based on not one clue, but several.

For example, consider this exchange from *A Study in Scarlet*, the first Sherlock Holmes mystery:

WATSON: "That seems simple enough, said I; but how about the other man's height?"

HOLMES: "Why, the height of a man, in nine cases out of ten, can be told from the length of his stride. It is a simple calculation enough, though there is no use my boring you with figures. I had this fellow's stride both on the clay outside and on the dust within. Then I had a way of checking my calculation. When a man writes on a wall, his instinct leads him to write above the level of his own eyes. Now that writing was just over 6 feet from the ground. It was child's play."

This is just one small deduction in a much larger mystery, but Holmes has taken several pieces of information—the tracks outside, the tracks inside, the writing on the wall—studied them, and then drawn his conclusion from them. And just like the Great Detective gathering a body of evidence until, ultimately, a conclusion emerges, we can follow this trail of clues until it leads us inexorably to the solution for transforming the fragility of our breadcrumb mysteries into a robust scenario structure:

For any conclusion you want the PCs to make, include at least three clues.

This is the Three Clue Rule.

Why three clues? Because the PCs will probably miss the first, ignore the second, and misinterpret the third, before synthesizing all of them in some incredible leap of logic that you never anticipated, but somehow gets them exactly where they were supposed to go the whole time.

(I'm only slightly joking.)

If you think of each clue as a plan (the PCs will find A, conclude B, and go to C), then when you have three clues you not only have a plan; you've also got two backup plans. It's all about redundancy.

In a best-case scenario, the PCs will find all three clues. There's nothing wrong with this! The players can use the additional clues they find to confirm and reinforce their conclusions. For the players, this sort of positive feedback feels great. ("I *knew* there was something fishy about Lord Denton!") And it only serves to make the scenario robust.

Even better, remember that one of our potential failure points comes from the players finding a clue but then misinterpreting what it means. For example, they find a coat check receipt signed by Lord Denton, but become convinced that it means they should stake out the coat check at the Hotel du Chat Noir. Additional clues can help push the players off these erroneous conclusions and get them back on track. ("The letters mention a Lord Denton. Wasn't that also the name on the coat check receipt?")

In a worst-case scenario, of course, the PCs may completely miss (or misinterpret) two of the clues, but they'll still have at least one clue in hand that will keep the mystery moving forward.

A corollary here is that there are NO exceptions to the Three Clue Rule.

"But this clue is really obvious! There's no way the players won't figure it out!"

In my experience, you're probably wrong. The reality is that you're the one designing the scenario, which means that you already know the solution. That makes it almost impossible for you to judge whether or not the clue is "obvious." It's like answering a riddle that you already know the answer to.

More importantly, even if you're right and the solution *is* obvious . . . so what? We already know that having extra clues to confirm and reinforce this "obvious" solution isn't going to cause any problems. So why not be safe rather than sorry?

Now, if three clues are good, why not more? Why not five? Or eight? Or twenty?

There's nothing wrong with more clues, but in my experience, three clues is the sweet spot. With three clues you have enough redundancy that the PCs will almost never completely miss all the clues they need, and they also provide enough complexity that the players will be able to combine information, confirm their hypotheses, and enjoy some positive reinforcement that makes the whole mystery feel tight and satisfying.

LEADS VS. EVIDENCE

There are actually two types of clues in a mystery scenario.

First, there are **leads** that tell you where you can go to find more clues. These are the procedural clues that will move the PCs from one scene to the next.

Second, there's **evidence** that will help you understand what's happening (e.g., who the murderer is).

For example, when the PCs find Claudette's body they might find identification papers that include her address. This is a lead that points them toward searching her rooms (where they can find the burnt letters, which are another lead pointing to Lord Denton).

RED HERRINGS ARE OVERRATED

Red herrings are a classic element of the mystery genre: All the evidence points toward *X*, but it's a red herring! The real murderer is *Y*!

When it comes to designing an RPG scenario, though, I've found that red herrings are overrated. I'm not going to go so far as to say you should never use them, but I will go so far as to say that you should only use them with *extreme* caution.

First, getting players to make the deductions they're supposed to make is hard enough. Throwing in a red herring (i.e., a clue pointing to a false deduction) just makes that harder. Even worse, once the players have reached a conclusion, they tend to latch on to it. It can be extremely difficult to convince the group to let it go and reassess the evidence.

The key way to make a red herring work in a mystery story, after all, is have some piece of evidence that absolutely and incontrovertibly refutes it. ("Harold couldn't have murdered Judy; he was at the bar when she was murdered!") Unfortunately, your concept of "incontrovertible refutation" may hold just as much water as your concept of "really obvious clue that cannot be missed." (So if you do decide to include a red herring, make sure to include at least three clues refuting it!)

Second, there's really no need for you to prep a red herring. The players are almost certainly going to take care of it for you. If you fill your adventure with nothing but clues pointing conclusively and decisively at the real killer, I can virtually guarantee you that the players will become suspicious of at least three other people before they figure out who's really behind it all. They will, in fact, become very attached to these suspicions and begin weaving complicated theories explaining how the evidence they have fits the suspect they want. (This is a classic example of how a clue can be misinterpreted, which is why the Three Clue Rule is so important to begin with!)

But in investigating her body, the PCs might also discover that it's been drained of blood. That's evidence pointing toward the conclusion that a vampire is responsible for her death. (Similarly, in the burnt letters, Claudette might mention seeing an unusually large bat in the tree outside her window at night, the malevolent red glare of its eyes seeming to burn their way into her soul.)

Both evidence and leads should follow the Three Clue Rule, but they can do so in slightly different ways.

In order to get out of one scene and into the next, the players need to have enough leads pointing them to another scene where they can look for more clues. That generally means that every scene is going to need to have three leads in it.

The evidence that points to the solution of the mystery, on the other hand, can be spread out across multiple scenes. There might even be entire scenes, particularly early in the adventure, that include no such clues! In such scenarios, the players would need to follow several leads in order to get deep enough into the mystery to start uncovering the truth.

PERMISSIVE CLUE-FINDING

The maxim "more clues are always better" is an important one. There can be a natural impulse when designing a mystery to hold back information. After all, a mystery is essentially defined by a lack of information. The detective doesn't know who the murderer is, right?

As GMs, this can give us a subconscious bias toward trying to hide information from the players. If a clue wasn't planned ahead of time— if it wasn't parsimoniously assigned to them in our notes—then the PCs shouldn't be allowed to have it! It would ruin the mystery!

But although we may be tempted to fixate on the enigma that motivates the PCs, mysteries are actually defined by the *acquisition* of knowledge, not its lack. So what we need to do is exactly the opposite. As we run our mystery scenarios, we need to consciously choose to be permissive in clue-finding.

Of course, there's a difference between having lots of clues and having the murderer write his home address in blood on the wall. But whenever you hold back a piece of information, you're closing off a path toward potential success. So unless you have a good reason to block it off, your first impulse should be to keep the path open.

In other words, **default to yes**. If the players go looking for information, default to the idea that they find something useful, unless their method of investigation is completely unrelated. (Like, say, staking out the coat check at a random hotel.)

Here's another way of thinking about it: Don't treat the list of clues you came up with during your prep as a straitjacket. Instead, think of that prep work as your safety net.

I used to get really attached to the particularly clever solutions I designed. I would emotionally invest in the idea of my players discovering this clever solution that I had created. As a result, I would tend to veto other potential solutions the players came up with—after all, if those other solutions worked they would never discover MY clever solution!

Over time, I've learned that it's actually a lot more fun when the players surprise me. So now I try to think of my predesigned solution as a worst-case scenario—the safety net that snaps into place when my players fail to come up with anything more interesting.

To be open to permissive clue-finding, however, you first have to understand the underlying situation: Who is the vampire? How did he kill this victim? Why did he kill them? When did he kill them? Then embrace the unexpected ideas and approaches proposed by the players and figure out how they can be used to point them toward your revelations.

PROACTIVE CLUES

Sometimes, despite your best efforts, the players will work themselves into a dead end: They don't know what the clues mean or they're ignoring the clues or they've used the clues to reach an incorrect conclusion and are now heading in completely the wrong direction. (When I'm using the Three Clue Rule, I find this will most often happen when the PCs don't realize that there's actually a mystery that needs to be solved—not every mystery is as obvious as a dead body, after all.)

This is when having a backup plan is useful. The problem in this scenario is that the PCs are being too passive—either because they don't have the information they need or because they're using the information in the wrong way. The solution, therefore, is to have something active happen to them.

Raymond Chandler's advice for this kind of impasse was "Have a guy with a gun walk through the door."

Or, more generally: The bad guy finds out they're being investigated and they take some kind of action against the PCs (sending someone to kill them or bribe them or dig up blackmail on them or kidnap their loved ones, etc.).

Or, alternatively: The next part of the bad guy's plan happens. For example, they rob another bank. Or kill another victim. (This has the effect of proactively creating a new location or event for the PCs to interact with.)

The idea with all of these, of course, is not simply to have something happen. What you're really doing is giving the PCs a new avenue for obtaining a clue that they need: That's either a new crime scene for them to investigate, or it's a matchbook in the thug's pocket that will point them at the bar they need to investigate.

In a worst-case scenario, though, you can also design a final "Get Out of Jail Free" card that you can use to bring the scenario to a satisfactory close no matter how badly the PCs get bollixed up. For example, in our vampire mystery—if the PCs get completely lost—you could simply have the vampire show up and try to kill them (because she thinks they're "getting too close"). This is usually less satisfactory than actually hunting the vampire down in her lair, but at least it gets you out of a bad situation. It's the final backup when all other backups have failed.

LOGIC CLUES AREN'T CONCLUSIONS!

One common error that a lot of people make when using the Three Clue Rule for the first time is to mistake it for a kind of logic puzzle:

- ⬡ This clue indicates that the killer was wearing a green sweater.

- ⬡ This clue indicates that the killer was taller than 6 feet.

- ⬡ This clue indicates that the killer had gray hair.

If you combine those together, you know that the only person with gray hair who was taller than 6 feet who was also wearing a green sweater was Peter, so Peter is the killer!

This can work if each of these clues points uniquely to Peter: He was the only one wearing a green sweater, the only one taller than 6 feet, and the only one with gray hair. (These are then three different clues all pointing to the same conclusion.)

But if you need all three pieces of information to eliminate other people with green sweaters or gray hair or whatever, then these are actually three *different* conclusions and each one needs three different clues pointing to it.

—+· HOMEWORK ·+—

YOUR FIRST MYSTERY

The great thing about a mystery scenario is that, once you know how they work, they're super simple to put together. For your first mystery scenario, we're going to construct a basic mystery chain—a series of scenes with each scene connected to the next by a set of clues.

STEP 1: THE SCENARIO CONCEPT

Start by figuring out what the mystery is about. Was someone murdered or kidnapped? Was something stolen or destroyed? Is someone being threatened? Who did it? Why? Are there weird phenomena? Where are they coming from? Are they dangerous and need to be stopped, or benign and in need of protection?

STEP 2: THE HOOK

How do the PCs become aware that there's a mystery to be solved? If it's a crime, there'll usually be a crime scene. It can also just be something like "the place where weird stuff is happening." Or maybe someone or something comes *to* the PCs and brings the mystery with them. (Thugs kicking down the door is a classic, but so is, "We just got attacked by something weird out on Route 6," and "My name is Miss Johnson and I'd like to hire you for a job.")

The hook is your first scene.

STEP 3: THE ENDING

What's the conclusion? Where do the PCs learn the ultimate answers and/or get into a big fight with the bad guy? (Big fights with bad guys are a really easy way to manufacture a satisfying conclusion.)

The ending, of course, is the last scene of the scenario.

STEP 4: INVESTIGATION SCENES

Brainstorm cool locations or people related to the mystery. Ex-wife of the bad guy? Abandoned mansion on the mist-shrouded heath? Stone circle that serves as a teleport gate? Follow your imagination wherever it takes you.

A mystery chain can be extended to any length, but five scenes is a good length for a scenario you want to play through in a single session. Since you already have a hook and an ending, that means you're aiming for three more scenes, but I recommend brainstorming more than three items and then picking the three coolest ideas. You'll end up with better stuff. (Also: Before you toss the other ideas, see if there's any way you can combine them with the three you picked and make them even cooler.)

Scenes that consist only of the PCs talking to a single NPC are likely to run a little shorter than other scenes. That's just fine, but if you have a lot of these scenes, you may want to add a few more to make sure the players don't speedrun your scenario. (If you need a rule of thumb, assume a social-only scene is only worth a "half" scene for the purposes of hitting your quota of five scenes.)

STEP 5: A PROACTIVE ELEMENT

Remember the guy with a gun? Add one of these proactive elements to your adventure, giving yourself a scene that you can trigger at any time if you need to get things back on track or, alternatively, add a little extra content if the PCs are making short work of your scenario.

As we've discussed, the two big options here are (a) the bad guy figuring out the PCs are trouble and sending someone (or something) to get them to lay off or (b) the next part of the bad guy's plan happens (and the PCs learn of it).

Either way, remember that the primary goal is for this proactive scene to drop additional clues that the PCs can follow to hop back onto the mystery chain, so make sure you figure out what those leads look like. You might even want to prep multiple leads, using whichever one is most appropriate for where the PCs are currently located on the chain.

DUNGEONS IN YOUR MYSTERIES

Think about including a micro-dungeon (see page 138) as one of the locations in your mystery chain. (In practice, this means you might have multiple scenes at that one location, but that's just fine: You just plant your three clues in the various rooms of the dungeon.)

This can include both your hook (the PCs explore a dungeon and find clues leading into a mystery scenario) and your conclusion (e.g., they have to fight their way through a crypt or a penthouse or a container ship to confront the bad guy).

Particularly for your first mystery adventure, including one—or two!—micro-dungeon(s) is a great way to give yourself some rock-steady islands of familiarity as you chart your way through unfamiliar waters.

You can also do this with other scenario structures, like raids (see page 268) or heists (see page 307). For example, clues might inform the PCs that they need to obtain the Jade Eagle of Chang'an, but the only way they can do that is by stealing it from the Guatemalan mansion of Luisa Fernanda Pérez Rodríguez.

STEP 6: CONNECT THEM WITH CLUES

Now that you have your list of five investigation scenes, you just need to connect them. Figure out what order the scenes should be in—based on either what's logical or what's most dramatic (or both)—and then add three clues to each scene pointing to the next scene.

As you're doing this, I recommend making a **revelation list**. To get started, simply list each investigation scene the PCs need to find. Each of these is a revelation (or conclusion) that the players need to have while playing the scenario, so under each one you should list the required three clues. For example:

SCENE 2: CLAUDETTE'S RESIDENCE

◈ Claudette's Identification Papers (*Scene 1*)
◈ Canvass the Neighborhood (*Scene 1*)
◈ Madame Rosette's Identification of the Body (*Scene 1*)

SCENE 3: SPEAK TO LORD DENTON

◈ Claudette's Burnt Letters (*Scene 2*)
◈ Lord Denton's Coat Check Receipt (*Scene 2*)
◈ Questioning the Staff (*Scene 2*)

STEP 7: ANCILLARY REVELATIONS

With the essential procedural revelations listed along with their clues, you can now flesh out your revelation list with all of the conclusions that are based on evidence. For example, in our investigation of Claudette's murder, we have the evidence pointing to a vampire being responsible:

CLAUDETTE'S KILLER IS A VAMPIRE

◈ Claudette's body is drained of blood (*Scene 1*).
◈ Burnt letters reference a bat haunting her (*Scene 2*).
◈ Lord Denton mentions her irrational fear of bats (*Scene 3*).
◈ Large wolf stalks PCs, turns to mist (*Proactive Scene*).

You'll note that I've included more than three clues for this revelation, which is, of course, just fine. I've also indicated in which scene each clue can be found, which is useful because the clues for these types of evidence-based discoveries can be spread across multiple scenes.

It's not that this sort of **ancillary revelation** isn't actionable (the PCs could, for example, stock up on stakes, mirrors, and garlic), but rather that it won't lead the PCs to a new scene where they can continue their investigation.

This step is technically optional, since you can theoretically have a purely procedural mystery in which the PCs follow leads from one scene to the next until they reach the conclusion. In practice, however, you'll almost always find that there are other enigmas that you want the players to unravel. In fact, it's really recommended, since it will add a lot of depth and interest to your players' experience.

STEP 8: FLESH OUT YOUR SCENES

Finally, take a look at your list of investigation scenes and flesh them out.

If it's a simple location, you can use an approach similar to a dungeon room: a description you can use when the players arrive at the location, followed by important elements (including, for example, the clues the PCs can find there).

More elaborate locations may have multiple rooms (e.g., both the bar and the manager's office in the back). Some locations might even be full-fledged location crawls embedded in your mystery scenario, but don't fall into the trap of treating every location as if it were a dungeon: If the PCs aren't crawling from one room to the next and exploring most rooms in detail, prepping that location as if it were a dungeon will probably be a waste of your time.

For example, when the PCs arrive at the mansion where Claudette lived, they're likely to be greeted by her mother, Madame Rosette. It's not likely that they'll meticulously search every room in the mansion as if it were a dungeon, and if they did it wouldn't be very productive, since none of those rooms contain clues. (So even if the players wanted to search the mansion from roof to basement, their search would be empty time and you should frame past it, probably by saying something like, "You spend the afternoon going over the mansion with a fine-tooth comb but don't find anything outside of Claudette's room. As you open the door to her room, you see . . .")

So in this case you'd want notes that would let you introduce the mansion and Madame Rosette, and then probably detailed notes on Claudette's room where the PCs will focus their investigation (or, at the very least, where their investigation will bear fruit).

If your investigation scene is focused on an NPC, or if an NPC is of particular importance within a larger scene, you'll want to prep the material you need to feel confident roleplaying them. We talk about this in more detail in the Supporting Cast extra credit starting on page 506. If the NPC has a clue the PCs need, make sure to note that as key info so that you don't forget to give it to them.

PREPPING SCENES VS. RUNNING SCENES

We've talked about framing scenes during play and we've talked about prepping scenes for your scenario. These are not precisely the same thing, although there's *a lot* of overlap between them.

Framing a scene involves setting the agenda, describing the environment, introducing the characters, and throwing a bang.

The trick is that if you prep a very specific frame before play begins, you can accidentally deprotagonize the PCs by stealing the players' agency.

For example, the PCs identify Claudette and where she lived. What happens next? Well, they might head over to the mansion in the afternoon, speak with Madame Rosette, and then investigate Claudette's room. But they could also decide that they need to:

◎ Execute a search warrant, barging past the confused and mourning Madame Rosette.

◎ Sneak into the mansion and investigate Claudette's room in the dead of night.

◎ Threaten Madame Rosette and try to intimidate her into revealing something.

And each of those scenes have distinctly different agendas and bangs. They even have slightly different environments and characters.

So I find it useful, when prepping a scene, to think of it like a toybox that I'm filling with toys. I'll be able to play with those toys while running the session and use them to frame my scenes, but I won't be locked into a specific script with them.

Now, in practice, you'll be able to make some educated guesses about how scenes are *likely* to get framed during play, and you can use those guesses to help you figure out what toys you can prep. You don't need to turn your brain off. You just need to leave yourself open to play.

As you flesh out your scenes, whether they're locations or characters (or both), you'll likely discover new opportunities to plant clues that didn't previously occur to you. That's great! Don't hesitate to do so! Sometimes these new clues will emerge logically and organically from what you're creating; in other cases they'll just be cool ideas that seem to be spontaneously sparked by your creative engagement. Either way, they'll only deepen your scenario and make it more robust. Just make sure to add them to your revelation list for easy reference!

MAKING CLUES

"Now just connect them with clues!"

It may feel like we skipped a couple of steps there ("Just 'make a clue' he says!"), but you'll quickly find that's not true. It really does boil down to making a revelation list and then filling in three clues (or more) under each revelation.

With that being said, let me share a few practical tips I've learned about making clues. First, there are some broad categories into which clues can fall:

- Physical Artifacts
- Glyphs/Data
- Biosignatures
- Interrogation
- Surveillance

These categories aren't exactly comprehensive, and the boundaries between them aren't exactly razor-sharp, but they can get you started. If you're looking for something a little more specific, here are some examples from scenarios I've designed:

- Correspondence (letters, email, etc.)
- Diaries
- Ephemera from a location (matchbooks, theatrical posters, tickets, etc.)
- Official reports
- Tracks (to be followed)
- Tailing someone
- Business cards
- Fingerprints
- DNA
- Blood type (including fantastical types like "Vulcan")
- Graffiti
- Financial records
- Tattoos
- Canvassing
- Video/audio recordings
- Mystic visions/strange dreams
- Shipping information (tracking, postmarks, return addresses, etc.)
- Books (including inscriptions, bookmarks, and marginalia)
- Bureaucratic records/background checks

Again, not a comprehensive list, but if you're struggling to fill in a clue, running down this list and seeing if there's anything that fits the scenario can really save the day. Particularly because, as you're designing clues for your scenario, you'll want to make sure to include a wide variety of them.

This is partly about creating a more engaging investigation. (If the PCs are just doing the same thing over and over and over again, that's less interesting than an adventure where they're doing lots of different things. And a puzzle isn't really puzzling if the solution is always the same thing.) But it's also structurally important: If all the clues are fundamentally similar, then it's not just that the players are doing the same thing over and over again; it's that the players *must* do that thing. And if they don't think to do it, then they'll miss ALL the clues.

The Three Clue Rule is built on redundancy, but clues that are overly similar to each other only provide a superficial redundancy. It's kind of like monoclonal agriculture: When all the bananas are clones of each other, they're all susceptible to the same pests and can be universally wiped out by a single disease. Just so with monoclonal clues, which can all fail simultaneously.

For example, if the PCs need to figure out that Tony is hiding out at the Silver Rodeo, you might say:

◎ They can ask Tony's girlfriend, Susan.
◎ They can ask Tony's partner, Silvester.
◎ They can ask Tony's mother, Sara.

Those are three different clues. But if the players, for whatever reason, don't ask the people in Tony's life where Tony is hiding—because they don't want to risk tipping him off, because they erroneously conclude that Tony wouldn't have told anyone where he was going, or just because they don't think to do it—then that one failure will wipe out all of those clues.

The principle of permissive clues means that you shouldn't necessarily get rid of all these "redundant" clues, but for structural purposes, they can be grouped together and only "count" as a single clue on your revelation list for the purposes of the Three Clue Rule. (You could even list it as "Question Susan, Silvester, or Sara," for example.)

As a final note, remember that the problem of monoclonal clues is limited to the clues pointing to a single revelation. It's fine to design a scenario with lots and lots and lots of clues coming from talking to people, as long as those clues are spread out across a bunch of different revelations (each of which has varied clues of different types also pointing to them).

Another good way to keep your clues varied is to **work from the skill list**. If you're looking for inspiration in creating your clues, look at the skill list for the RPG you're running. Pick any skill. How could the PCs use that skill to get the information they need?

For example, let's say you need a clue that points the PCs to Cai Lijuan:

◎ Cryptography? Cai's left his diary, which he writes in a personal code, in the drawer of the bedside table.

◎ Locksmith? There must be something Cai locked up here. Let's say there's a safe hidden behind a picture frame with documents identifying Cai inside.

◎ Photography? There's a USB stick with photos. There's nothing that identifies Cai in the photos themselves, but you could check the EXIF data.

Obviously not every skill will be relevant to every conclusion, but if you have a particular piece of information in mind, running down the skill list will probably make specific skills jump out and provide ideas.

You can also **work from the conclusion**. This is why I recommend starting with the revelation list for the scenario. It allows you to focus very specifically on what in the current scene can indicate the conclusions they need to make.

This may seem obvious, but I can get lost a surprising amount of the time floating around in a haze of, "What clues would they find here?" or "What clues would the bad guys have left?" You really want to flip that around: Instead of thinking about what clues might be in the scene, focus on what you *need* the current scene to tell the PCs and then treat that as a puzzle or a problem to solve.

For example, imagine that the PCs are investigating a cabin on the lake. If you start by asking yourself, "What clues would be in the cabin?" that's too broad. It's too vague.

But if you instead say, "I need a clue that points the PCs to Cai Lijuan," that's far more actionable:

◎ There's a crumpled envelope in the wastebasket addressed to Cai.

◎ The property owner can identify Cai as the person who was renting the cabin.

◎ There's a box of cold pizza in the fridge. Cai's name is printed on the delivery label.

◎ The family vacationing in the next cabin down the lake met Cai and knows his name.

◎ Cai's car is still parked at the cabin; the PCs can run the license plate or VIN.

Something else along these same lines that can trip you up is the **fallacy of the perfect crime**.

For example, let's say that the PCs find an incriminating note that gives them a vital clue . . . but wait! Why would the conspiracy let the PCs find the note? Why wouldn't they destroy it?!

Well, in some cases it's carelessness or bad luck. In others, they're holding on to incriminating evidence that can give them leverage over their fellow conspirators. Sometimes they're planning to destroy it, but they just haven't yet. Sometimes the note has information they need for a job, so they hold on to it until the job is done. Maybe they have a sentimental attachment to the note because it was written by their dead wife. And so forth.

Of course, this logic extends beyond incriminating notes.

Wouldn't it make sense for the murderer to wear gloves or wipe away their fingerprints? (Maybe they did and the clue is something else. Or they tried, but missed a partial. Or they're dumb. Or they panicked. Or they wanted to, but got interrupted.)

Wouldn't they have disabled the cameras? (Maybe they didn't spot the camera. Maybe they *did* hack the cameras and deleted the footage, but left traces from their hack that can be traced instead. And so forth.)

The perfect crime or conspiracy, of course, would have flawless operational security and leave no evidence. As a GM designing scenarios you can be particularly susceptible to the fallacy of the perfect crime: Obviously if the bad guy knew they were leaving a clue, they would destroy it. You just thought of how the criminal could have left the clue, so obviously the criminal would have realized that, too!

But that's not how it usually plays out in reality, and doesn't really make for a great scenario in any case. You actually want to do the opposite: If you're thinking about the crime and can't find a clue that gives the PCs the information you need to give them . . . well, what extra mistake did the criminal make that will let you give the PCs that information?

NON-ESSENTIAL REVELATIONS

In addition to your revelation list, there may be a lot of other information that PCs can discover or deduce in the course of their investigation: that the villain beats her husband; the particular effects of the poison the killer is using; the cult's beliefs on the wisdom of cats.

If these are **essential revelations** (i.e., it's important or necessary for the PCs to learn this fact in order for the scenario to work), then they should go on your revelation list and should follow the Three Clue Rule.

But a lot of this information will be **non-essential revelations**. (For example, the fact that the villain beats her husband is interesting—and maybe the PCs could even figure out some way to use that to their advantage—but it's not something the PCs need to know in order to track her down and bring her to justice.) Non-essential revelations don't need to follow the Three Clue Rule (although they certainly can), and it's up to you whether you think it's useful to keep a non-essential revelations list. (I generally don't, and if you do decide to keep such a list, I recommend keeping it separate from your main revelations list. You really want to keep your focus on that essential structure.)

RUNNING YOUR MYSTERY

You've now carefully laid out a scenario in which there are multiple paths to the solution and the players will always be flush with the clues they need to keep the mystery moving forward. You've even got a proactive backup plan designed to get the PCs back on track if anything should go awry!

Nothing could possibly go wrong!

. . . why do we even say things like that?

Most of the time, if you follow the Three Clue Rule, your mystery scenarios are going to work out just fine. But the truth is that you are either a mouse or a man (probably the latter) and, sooner or later, your best-laid plans are going to go awry. When that happens, you're going to want to be prepared for the possibility of spinning out new backup plans on the fly.

To make this a little easier, you can use your revelation list as a checklist, tracking which clues the PCs have found. As they grab each clue, simply check them off the list or cross them out entirely, whichever works best for you. If they miss a clue, circle it or put a star next to it or something like that. (They might still circle back later and find it after all, but you should assume that they won't.)

This will let you see, at a glance, if there are conclusions where the PCs are in jeopardy because they've missed two clues: If there are three clues pointing them toward the dwarven alchemy lab, for example, and they've missed two of them, then you'll want to keep a close eye on that third and final clue to make sure the PCs find it.

Finally, listen carefully to what the players are saying to each other. When they've actually reached a particular conclusion, you can check that whole conclusion off your list and stop worrying about it. (But be careful not to cross it off as soon as the players discuss it as a possibility. Only check it off if they've actually concluded that it's true.)

If you see that too many clues for a conclusion are being missed, or that all the clues have been found but the players still haven't figured it out, then you'll know it's probably time to start thinking about new clues that can be worked into the adventure. (This is where your proactive elements will come in handy!)

NODE-BASED
✦ ADVENTURES ✦

A mystery chain is a great way to design your first mystery adventure because the linear sequence of investigation scenes simplifies and makes very clear what's required in each scene for a robust scenario, but the reality is that the chain is a rather restrictive set of training wheels. If you've done your homework, you've probably already felt yourself chafing against its limitations.

The primary problem, of course, is its lack of flexibility. It's very similar to our example of a linear dungeon:

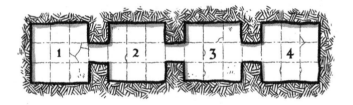

Like the linear dungeon, it drastically constrains not only our design options, but the players' ability to make dynamic and interesting choices during play. Even with the Three Clue Rule, the linearity makes the scenario more fragile than it needs to be as each scene becomes a chokepoint, and any scene that goes awry or proves more challenging than you'd anticipated becomes a roadblock.

Even fulfilling the Three Clue Rule within the strictures of the mystery chain is more challenging than it needs to be. It can be very hard to force three leads all pointing to the same conclusion into the same scene—but absolutely no leads pointing to any other locations or people associated with the mystery!—and have it feel natural. In many ways, you're simultaneously trying to cram too much information into a single scene AND artificially limiting the information the PCs are allowed to access.

So once you've made one or two adventures using the mystery chain recipe and learned what you need to from it, it'll be time to break the bondage of the chain. And you can do that by taking everything we've learned about mystery scenarios and flipping it on its head.

INVERTING THE THREE CLUE RULE

The Three Clue Rule states:

> *For any conclusion you want the PCs to make, include at least three clues.*

The underlying theory, as you know, is that having three distinct options provides sufficient redundancy to create a robust scenario: Even if the PCs miss the first clue and misinterpret the second, the third clue provides a final safety net to keep the scenario on track.

But you can also invert this logic:

> *If the PCs have access to ANY three clues, they will reach at least ONE conclusion.*

This is true if all three clues point to the same conclusion, but it's also true if the three clues point to *different* conclusions. In other words, if the PCs need to reach three conclusions (A, B, and C) and the PCs have access to three clues, each of which could theoretically allow them to reach one of those conclusions, then it's very likely that they will, in fact, reach at least one of those conclusions. (They could, of course, also make all three conclusions.)

Assume for the moment that each of those conclusions is an investigation scene—which we're now going to refer to as a **node**—and the clues are leads pointing to those nodes. The diagram on the facing page illustrates a simple example.

The scenario starts in the **initial node** of Node 1, which contains three leads—one pointing to Node A, one pointing to Node B, and one pointing to Node C. Following the Inverse Three Clue Rule, we can be fairly certain that the PCs will be able to successfully conclude that they need to go to at least one of these nodes.

Let's assume they go to Node A. Node A contains two additional clues—one pointing to Node B and the other pointing to Node C.

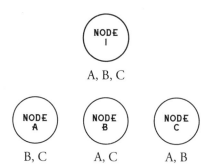

At this point the PCs have access to five different clues. One of these has successfully led them to Node A and is no longer important, but this still leaves them with four clues (two pointing to Node B and two pointing to Node C), and the Inverse Three Clue Rule once again shows us that they have more than enough information to proceed in their investigation.

Let's assume they now go to Node C. Here they can find clues to Node A and Node B. They now have access to a total of seven clues, and even though four of these clues now point to nodes they've already visited, that still leaves them with three clues pointing them to Node B. The Three Clue Rule itself shows that they now have access to enough information to finish the scenario.

(Note that we're only talking about clue *access* here. This doesn't mean that they're guaranteed to find or correctly interpret every clue. In fact, we're still assuming that they don't.)

NODES

What makes node-based scenario design so powerful is the almost infinite flexibility of what a node can be.

LOCATIONS

A place where the PCs can physically go. If you think of a lead as being anything that tells you where to go next, telling the PCs about a specific place that they're supposed to go is the most literal interpretation of the concept. Once PCs arrive at a location, they'll usually find more clues by searching the place.

PEOPLE

A specific individual that the PCs should pay attention to. It may be someone they've already met or it may be someone they'll have to track down. PCs will usually get clues from people by either observing them or questioning them.

ORGANIZATIONS

Organizations can often be thought of as a collection of locations and people, but it's not unusual for a particular organization to come collectively within the PCs' sights (e.g., "It looks like the Oberon Trust is involved in all this"). Organizations can be both formal and informal; acknowledged and unacknowledged.

EVENTS

Something that happens at a specific time and, more often than not, a specific place. Although PCs will often be tasked with preventing a particular event from happening, when events are used as nodes (i.e., something from which clues can be gathered), it's more typical for the PCs to actually attend the event, whether openly or surreptitiously. (On the other hand, learning about an event may lead the PCs to the location where it's being held; the organization responsible for holding it; or the people attending it.)

ACTIVITIES

An activity is something that the PCs are supposed to do. If the PCs are supposed to learn about a cult's plan to perform a binding ritual, that's an event. If they're supposed to perform a binding ritual themselves, that's an activity. Activities are often ancillary revelations, but if the activity would result in the PCs gaining clues, then it counts as a node. (For example, the PCs might gain leads telling them that they need to cast a *legend lore* spell in front of a specific painting.)

NON-LINEAR DESIGN

Let's revisit the murder of Claudette:

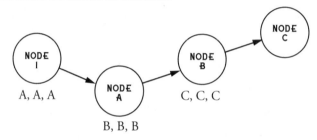

In the linear mystery chain version of this scenario, the PCs discover Claudette's body (NODE 1) and are able to identify her, leading them to Claudette's home (NODE A). At the mansion, they discover burnt letters hinting at a secret affair with Lord Denton, a suspicion that is confirmed when they question the maid! Rushing over to Lord Denton's mansion (NODE B), they confront him with the scandalous evidence. A distraught Lord Denton reveals that he and Claudette would meet at the Old Forsyth Crypt (NODE C) in New Hope Cemetery. They were supposed to meet there yesterday, but he was detained in a cabinet meeting and, by the time he arrived, Claudette was no longer there. The PCs thank Lord Denton and promise him whatever discretion they can, and then head toward the cemetery, hoping to find more clues . . .

This scenario obviously works. Everything flows logically and the clues come hot and heavy, keeping the PCs in the chase. (Again, there's nothing wrong with a well-designed mystery chain.) But what if we designed this same scenario as a node-based adventure?

As the PCs investigate Claudette's body (NODE 1), we don't need all of the clues to point to Claudette's house. Instead, we could have three different clues point to three different nodes:

- **Node A-Claudette's Home:** Searching the alley near where the body is found will turn up Claudette's identification.
- **Node B-Lord Denton:** In the pocket of Claudette's coat is a coat check receipt signed by Lord Denton.
- **Node C-Old Forsyth's Crypt:** In Claudette's purse is a charcoal rubbing. Research can reveal that it was taken from the wall of the Old Forsyth Crypt at New Hope Cemetery.

With no additional effort (you're still just prepping three clues, right?), there are suddenly many different ways that the adventure could play out. The PCs might still go to Claudette's house first and discover her affair with Lord Denton, but decide that he's too powerful and they should pursue their other leads first.

Or maybe they go to Lord Denton first, but without concrete proof (and maybe a flubbed Persuasion check) Denton gives them the cold shoulder. After discovering the burnt letters in Claudette's room, however, the PCs return and furiously demand answers!

Or perhaps they miss both the identification papers and the coat check receipt in the first scene, leaving them with no choice but to check out the Old Forsyth Crypt. There they find where Claudette has recently and impetuously carved "Claudette + Mountblanc" in a tree just outside the crypt. They don't know who Claudette is, but "Mountblanc" leads them to Lord Denton Mountblanc, who breaks down in tears when he learns that Claudette has been killed.

My point here is that when you create interesting nodes, you'll generally find that those nodes can be shuffled into virtually any order and you'll still end up with an interesting result. Importantly, these variations aren't just a matter of random noise. Given a broader context, the players are able to strategize their investigation, and the choices they make will have a meaningful impact on how events play out. The PCs might even decide to split up and pursue two leads at the same time.

Up to this point, we've also only looked at these choices in the context of relatively static nodes, but we can also imagine more dynamic scenarios in which the players' choices of when and how to pursue their investigation become even more meaningful. For example, if they strong-arm Lord Denton before they have evidence, then when they circle back later they might discover that he's disappeared. Now add a proactive node to this scenario: How might the PCs' actions tip off the vampire and when does she dispatch her consorts to deal with them? In other scenarios you might find ways to add different consequences to different leads, for example by introducing a deadline: Will the PCs choose a safer-but-longer course of action, or will they pursue the lead that's quicker but risks tipping off Boss Boar that he's under investigation?

As a GM, I find these types of scenarios more interesting to run because I'm also being surprised and delighted by how events play out at the table. And as a player I find them more interesting because I'm being allowed to make meaningful choices.

Furthermore, when an individual scenario is placed within the context of a large campaign, it allows the choices made within that scenario to have a wider impact. For example, if they expose Lord Denton's affair and ruin his engagement, he could easily return as an antagonist in future scenarios. If Lord Denton owes them a favor and becomes their patron, that's a completely different campaign. If they screw up and Lord Denton gets turned into a vampiric consort, that's yet another campaign.

On a more basic level, the fact that the players are being offered the driver's seat is meaningful in its own right. Even if the choice doesn't have any lasting impact on the final conclusion of "good guys win, bad guys lose," the fact that the *players* were the ones who decided *how* the good guys were going to win is important. If for no other reason than that, in my experience, it's more fun for everybody involved. And more memorable.

STRUCTURING NODE-BASED SCENARIOS

As we talk about the various paths that the PCs can take through a node-based scenario, it's important to remember that we're not prepping the paths, we're prepping the destinations. We're not writing a

Choose Your Own Adventure novel and we don't need to plan out every choice (or, worse yet, sequence of choices) the players might make. It's much more like building a playground: You're installing the equipment, but it's ultimately the kids who decide where they're going to run, what they're going to play with, and, importantly, how they're going to play with it.

With that being said, just like a theme park designer (in this increasingly tortured analogy), there is still a great deal of structure that you *can* control in node-based scenario design. If you put something in the front of the "park," for example, it's far more likely to be one of the first things the PCs experience than something that you put all the way at the back of the park. Because node-based scenario design is primarily about the flow of information, the "front" and "back" of the park—the "near" nodes and the "far" nodes, if you will—is about which clues are placed in which nodes, and how many of those nodes the PCs will need to maneuver their investigation through to reach the clues, location, and/or person that will bring the scenario to a close.

So let's take a peek at some of these node structures.

CONCLUSIONS
Conclusions can be achieved by funneling leads toward a specific node.

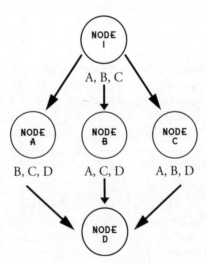

In this design, for example, each node in the second layer contains a third clue that points to the concluding Node D. The function should be fairly self-explanatory: The PCs can chart their own course through Nodes A, B, and C while being gently directed toward their goal, which is located at Node D.

One potential "problem" with this structure is that it allows the PCs to potentially bypass content: They could easily go to Node A, find the clue for Node D, and finish the adventure without ever visiting Nodes B or C.

I put the word "problem" in quotes here, though, because in node-based scenario design this is often desirable. When the PCs make a choice to avoid something—either because they don't want to deal with it or because they don't want to invest the resources needed to engage with it—and figure out a way to bypass it or make do without it, that's almost always fodder for an interesting moment at the gaming table. For example, the choice to deliberately not approach Lord Denton is an interesting and significant choice, and it makes the existence of the Lord Denton node meaningful to the scenario even though (and, in fact, *because*) the PCs never meet him.

In practice, there will often be an incentive for the PCs to investigate the other nodes instead of skipping them. I've found this to be true to at least some degree even if you don't deliberately design those incentives, but of course you can do that, too, with a mixture of carrots and sticks. For example, the lead in Node A might be a map of Node D (useful for planning tactical assaults), the clue in Node B might be a snitch who can tell them about a secret entrance that doesn't appear on the map (another carrot), and Node C might include a goon squad that will reinforce Node D if they aren't mopped up ahead of time (a stick).

In other scenarios like this, the PCs won't necessarily know right away that Node D is where they need to go. So with multiple clues in hand after Node A, they might still semi-randomly decide to check out Node B or Node C before following their lead to Node D. In other cases, they'll simply miss the first lead to Node D they have an opportunity to find. After leaving the initial node and investigating Node A, after all, they're twice as likely to have found a clue pointing to Node B or Node C.

All of this means that the PCs doing a speedrun straight to Node D—even though it looks so incredibly trivial if you have the privilege of looking at the node list (which, of course, the players do not)—is a lot less common than you might think, and it's rarely a problem even when it does happen. In practice, I never really think about it, and everything works out just fine. (It's one of the benefits of the immense flexibility of node-based scenario design.)

FUNNELS

Funnels take the basic structure of the conclusion and simply expand it:

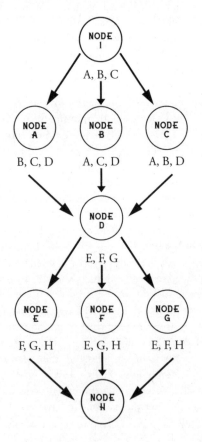

Each layer in the funnel—e.g., Nodes A, B, and C; or Nodes E, F, and G—is a free-form environment for investigation or exploration that gradually leads toward the neck of the funnel (Nodes D or H). The neck then contains the clues leading them into the next free-form environment.

I find this structure useful for campaigns where an escalation of stakes or opposition is desirable. For example, the PCs might start out investigating local drug dealers (Nodes A, B, C) in an effort to find out who's supplying drugs to the neighborhood. When they identify the local distributor (Node D), his contacts lead them into a wider investigation of citywide gangs (Nodes E, F, G). Investigating the gangs takes them to the Tyrell crime family (Node H), and mopping up the crime family gets them tapped for a national Mafia task force (another layer of free-form investigation), culminating in the discovery that the Mafia are actually being run by the Illuminati (another funnel neck).

(The Illuminati, of course, are being run by alien reptoids. The reptoids by Celestials. And the Celestials by the sentient network of black holes at the center of our galaxy. The black-hole consciousness, meanwhile, has suffered a schizoid bifurcation due to an incursion by the Andromedan Alliance . . . wait, where was I?)

In other words, there's always a bigger fish! This funnel structure is well suited for D&D campaigns. You don't want 1st-level characters suddenly "skipping ahead" to mind flayers, so you can use the chokepoints or gateways of the funnel structure to move them from one power level to the next. And if they hit a gateway that's too tough for them right now, that's okay: They'll simply be forced to back off, gather their resources (level up), and come back when they're ready.

Another advantage of the funnel structure is that, in terms of prep, it gives you manageable chunks to work on: Since the PCs can't proceed to the next layer until they reach the funnel neck, you only need to prep the current "layer" of the campaign.

LAYER CAKES

Layer cakes achieve the same general sense of progression that a funnel structure gives you, but allow you to use a lighter and looser touch in structuring the scenario.

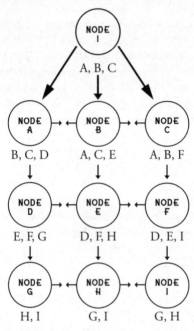

As illustrated, the most basic structure of the layer cake is that each node in a particular "layer" gives you clues that lead to other nodes on the same layer plus one clue pointing to a node in the next layer. Although a full exploration of the first layer won't give the PCs three clues to any single node on the second layer, they'll have three clues pointing to the second layer collectively. Therefore, the Inverted Three Clue Rule means that they'll reach at least one node in the second layer, and from there they can begin collecting additional second layer clues.

An interesting feature of the layer cake, in practice, is that whereas PCs in a funnel design are unlikely to back up past the last funnel neck (e.g., once they reach Node E, they generally won't back to Node C because it has nothing to offer them), in a layer cake design such interlayer, back-and-forth movement is quite common.

Layer cakes, therefore, have a slightly larger design profile than funnels, but allow the GM to curtail the scope of their prep work (i.e., you only need to design the current and next layer of the cake) while allowing the PCs to move through a more realistic environment. You'll often find the underlying structure of the layer cake arising naturally out of the game world.

LARGE LAYERS

In case it hasn't been clear, I've been using three-node layers in these examples because it's a convenient number for showing structure. But there's nothing magical about the number. A "layer" can be made up of any number of nodes; their defining characteristic is simply that they contain clues pointing to other nodes in the same layer and/or the next layer down (whether that next layer is a conclusion, the neck of a funnel, or another full layer of nodes).

As long as

- each node has a minimum of three leads in it,

- each node has a minimum of three leads pointing to it, and

- each layer has at least three leads pointing to it from the "layer" above it,

then the Three Clue Rule and its inversion will be naturally satisfied and guarantee you a sufficiently robust flow through the layer.

Larger layers, of course, require more prep, but that larger scale can be a feature in itself. They also give you the opportunity to vary the number of clues in each node, creating a greater range of node experiences. (Particularly dense clue locations could have six or eight or ten clues all pointing in different directions.)

LOOPS

Loops are a different way of thinking about how nodes can connect to each other. The other node structures we've looked at are all focused on a forward momentum: The PCs are moving toward the conclusion or the neck of the funnel or the next layer of nodes (or all of the above). Loops, on the other hand, can be a more naturalistic arrangement, where nodes are related to each other but not necessarily as a hierarchy or progression.

For example, here's a simple loop:

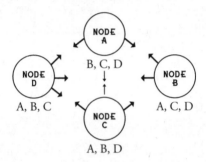

In this example, all four nodes contain three clues pointing to the other three nodes. The advantage of this structure is that the PCs can enter the scenario at any point and navigate it completely. (Whereas a PC entering Node D in our layer cake example would never find their way back to Nodes A, B, or C.)

Obviously, this is only really useful if the PCs have multiple ways of getting led into the loop. If the loop constitutes the entire adventure, then that would mean seeding different scenario hooks (see page 498) into your campaign, each pointing at a different node.

DEAD ENDS

Dead ends in a linear scenario are generally disasters. They mean that the PCs have taken a wrong turn or failed to draw the right conclusions and now they're going to crash into a wall: There should be a clue for them to follow, but they're not seeing it, so there's nowhere to go, and the whole adventure is going to fall apart.

But handled properly in a node-based scenario, dead ends aren't a problem: This lead may not have panned out, but the PCs still have other clues to follow.

Such dead ends can emerge naturally: The PCs go to Node A, but for whatever reason fail to find any of the clues there, so they pick up one of the other clues they found earlier and head over to Node B hoping to have better luck.

But you can also deliberately put dead ends in your scenarios:

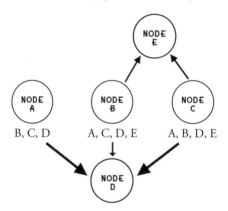

In this example, Node E is the dead end. Clues at Node B and Node C suggest that it should be checked out, but there's nothing to be found there. Maybe the clues were just wrong; or the bad guys have already cleared out; or it looked like a good idea, but it didn't pan out into usable information; or it's a trap deliberately laid to catch the PCs off guard. Alternatively, the location can contain valuable evidence, even though it doesn't have any leads to other nodes. The possibilities of a dead end are pretty much limitless.

The trick to implementing a dead end is to think of the leads pointing to the dead end as "bonus clues." They don't count toward the maxim that each node needs to include three different clues. (Otherwise you risk creating paths through the scenario that could result in the PCs being left with less than three clues. This is not necessarily disastrous in practice, but, according to the Inverse Three Clue Rule, might be.)

On the other hand, as you can see, you don't need to include three leads pointing to the dead end, either. It's a dead end, so if the PCs don't see it, there's nothing to worry about. It's what we referred to as a non-essential revelation (see page 237).

Of course, if you include less than three leads pointing to the dead end, you're increasing the chances that you're prepping content that will never be seen. But this also means that the discovery of the dead end might constitute a special reward—extra treasure, lost lore, a special weapon attuned to their enemy, etc.

This is also a good reminder that dead ends may be logistical blind alleys, but that doesn't mean they should be boring or meaningless. Quite the opposite, in fact.

PROACTIVE NODES

Just like you can have proactive scenes in a mystery chain scenario, you can have proactive nodes. These are the nodes that come to the PCs and interact with them.

Proactive nodes are usually characters. I often think of them as the "response teams" of a scenario. This is frequently literal, with my proactive nodes being the people who are sent to deal with the PCs once the bad guys realize they're snooping around. But it's also a useful metaphor: Proactive nodes are the easiest tools you, as the GM, can use to take action at the table instead of just reacting to what the players are doing.

What about other proactive nodes?

Well, locations tend to be stationary and rarely follow people around . . . unless you apply sufficiently advanced technology and/ or magic. The technology doesn't really need to be all *that* advanced, either: An abandoned ghost ship drifting into the town's harbor can easily be a proactive node.

Organizations can be proactive in their responses, but the response usually takes the form of a specific response team.

Events can be proactive if they're of a sufficiently large scale or if they're specifically targeted at the PCs: A citywide festival or a ritual that causes all the trees in the forest to start weeping blood count as the former. A series of enigmatic phone calls that ring up a PC's cell phone would be an example of the latter.

Almost anything can be a proactive node if it can be framed as information being pushed on the PCs. For example, if the PCs are cops investigating a series of bank robberies, they would be automatically notified if a new bank robbery takes place. (Is this an event or a location? Both? Does it matter? Don't get too obsessed with categories here.)

Don't forget to add a clue or three to your proactive nodes: They can be used to create a living world where there are both long-term and short-term reactions to the PCs' choices, but they also have the practical function of getting the scenario back on track.

THINKING BEYOND THE DIAGRAMS

The various node structures we've looked at can all be used together in an almost infinite variety of ways. After all, any node can be linked to any other node by simply including an appropriate lead, right? So you can easily glue these structures to each other. A funnel is basically just a conclusion with another conclusion pasted onto its final node. And you can easily design a layer cake of any length and then have its final layer terminate in a conclusion, or have a different layer cake narrow into a funnel before expanding back out into another layer cake. (Feel free to paste a dead end onto any of these pretty much anywhere you'd like.)

As you begin experimenting with nodes, you also need to quickly start thinking outside of the diagrams. I've used diagrams to illustrate how leads can be distributed between scenes and how that distribution can affect the flow of a scenario, but they'll prove quite deceptive if you try to use them as a basis for your scenario design.

First, the diagrams already "cheat" in terms of showing all the leads involved. If you look at the diagram for the conclusion structure on page 241, for example, you'll note that the leads linking Nodes A, B, and C to each other are not indicated with arrows.

The diagrams also feature a perfect symmetry, which should almost certainly be honored more in the breach than the observance. It's, again, useful for clearly illustrating certain concepts, but it's usually a little too trite and a little too constraining if it limits your actual adventure design.

I may occasionally sketch out diagrams like this to help conceptualize the broad strokes of an adventure ("the street gangs can funnel into the local distributor, and then the distributor can have leads to . . ."), but once I'm in the trenches the utility rapidly fades.

So if it's not flowcharts and diagrams, what tool *do* you use to design node-based scenarios?

The good ol' revelation list.

Here's an example of a node-based revelation list:

SCENE 1: ELVEN CORPSES

- The Duke's Map (*Scenario Hook*)
- Encountering Mutilated Corpses (*Adventure 3: The Old Forest*)
- Reports of Mutilated Corpses (*Adventure 2, Scene 4*)

SCENE 2: THE BLACK TREE

- Tracking Drow Scouts (*Proactive 1: Drow Scouts/Scene 1: Elven Corpses*)
- Map to the Black Tree (*Scene 3: The Drow Camp*)
- Elven Retaliation Scrolls (*Proactive 2: Elven Retaliation Squad*)

SCENE 3: THE DROW CAMP

- Tracking Drow Scouts (*Proactive 1: Drow Scouts*)
- Elven Retaliation Scrolls (*Proactive 2: Elven Retaliation Squad*)
- Map of the Old Forest (*Scene 4: Drow Citadel*)
- Questioning Prisoners (*Scene 2: The Black Tree*)

SCENE 4: DROW CITADEL

- Questioning Prisoners (*Scene 2: The Black Tree*)
- Subverting the Crystal Ball (*Scene 3: The Drow Camp*)
- Following the Slave Train (*Scene 3: The Drow Camp*)

Like the revelation list from a mystery chain on page 229, you'll note that I've indicated where the clue can be found in parentheses after the clue. (This notably includes leads found in other adventures that point to Scene 1 of this adventure. These cross-scenario leads serve as scenario hooks—in this case, additional scenario hooks—for the adventure.)

There are actually two ways you can organize lists like this: You can list all the clues a node contains or you can list all the clues that point to the node. We refer to the former as a **clue list** and the latter as a **revelation list**.

The revelation list, as we've seen, is most useful when we're running a scenario. It also makes it easy to confirm that you've honored the Three Clue Rule for all of your revelations.

When outlining or developing a scenario, however, the clue list is often more useful. After coming up with the "big concept" for a scenario, my design process usually starts with writing down cool ideas for various nodes. Then I'll think about what kind of information a node might naturally contain to point at the other nodes. For example, I might jot down:

SCENE 2: THE BLACK TREE

- ◎ Questioning Prisoners (to the Drow Citadel)
- ◎ Questioning Prisoners (to the Drow Camp)
- ◎ Drow Scouts might show up here (track to Scene 1 or Scene 3)

Once I've done that for all the nodes, I'll do a quick audit of each node and make sure I've included three clues. If I haven't, I'll get proactive figuring out how I can creatively include more clues.

As I write up the full version of each node, though, I'll assemble the revelation list: Each clue I include in the full write-up gets listed in the revelation list under the node it's pointing to (with a cross-reference back to where it's found).

This allows me to double-check my design process to make sure I've got all the clues I need. But it's also important because, when it comes time to run the scenario, it's the revelation list that's essential.

CLUE LISTS AT THE TABLE?

Wouldn't it be useful to have a clue list at the table, too?

Not as much as you might think. The trick is that the clues are baked into the key for your adventure (the description of the investigation scenes, locations, NPCs, etc.). If your key is properly and clearly organized, then when you're running a location or NPC or whatever, the associated clues should be obvious and easily accessible, so you don't need a separate checklist for them.

If your key isn't well organized (and, therefore, you might miss the clues), you should, of course, fix it. It'll cause a lot more problems than just missed clues.

In terms of really understanding how a particular scenario "works," though, the revelation list can feel confusing if you're not familiar with it. It can feel more intuitive to look at a list of clues in a node and then follow where they lead. (This is, after all, how the PCs will conceptually work their way through the scenario.) But you can get that same sense of flow from a revelation list: You just need to work backward.

Look at a node and ask, "How would the PCs get there?" In other words, follow one of the clues on the revelation list back to its source node. Then repeat the process from there.

For example, how would the PCs get to the Drow Citadel in the scenario on page 256? Well, let's pick a random clue: Following the Slave Train from Scene 3: The Drow Camp. So we look at Scene 3 and pick a random node there: Tracking Drow Scouts from their proactive scene. Since that's a proactive scene, it's essentially a scenario origin point. It's the trailhead, so to speak, and from the trail we've followed we can see that "tracking bad guys through the Old Forest" is one approach to the scenario.

Do it again: You can also get to the Drow Citadel by questioning prisoners from Scene 2: The Black Tree. You can get to the Black Tree by talking to (or stealing intelligence from) the elven retaliation squads operating in the area. So here we have a path that follows a trail of misery.

Do this two or three times (or more for more complex scenarios) and you'll get a pretty good feel for the contours of the scenario structure.

As you begin exploring and creating larger and more complex node-based scenarios and campaigns like this, what you'll eventually find waiting for you is the **node cloud**, in which there is no predetermined and often not even a clear path of progression (like that of the layer cake). Instead, there are just locations, people, organizations, and events linked to each other in a multitude of ways, and how the PCs choose to navigate those connections and what their goals are will, ultimately, be driven by the players.

THE DUNGEON CLOUD

For a simpler example of a node cloud, consider a region in which there are a bunch of ruins belonging to a primeval empire. In other words, a bunch of dungeons. Each of these dungeons has clues and treasure maps pointing to other dungeons in the region, but there's no particular sequence or escalation to these dungeons. The PCs might find any one of them at random, and then follow the leads to explore the rest in any order.

✦ HOMEWORK ✦

5 NODE MYSTERY

Let's pull our heads out of the clouds for the moment and focus on designing our first node-based scenario. We'll get started by using the 5 Node Mystery adventure recipe. This is a very powerful recipe. It's one that I use all the time while prepping adventures, and its versatile simplicity makes it incredibly easy to deploy, even in the middle of a session. The players declare out of the blue that they're going to do something completely unexpected? ("Let's figure out who's selling silverweed!") With a little practice, you'll be able to whip up a 5 Node Mystery so fast that you won't even have to take a break from play.

This straightforward simplicity, of course, also makes this recipe ideal for your first node-based scenario. It's particularly appealing because you can use almost any adventure ingredients while building your mystery.

It works like this:

STEP 1: THE SCENARIO CONCEPT
This works just like the scenario concept for a mystery chain (see page 226): Was someone murdered? Was something stolen? Who did it? Why did they do it?

STEP 2: THE HOOK
Again, just like the mystery chain. How do the PCs get involved? How do they get pulled (or pushed!) into the initial node? This will be where the investigation starts and it'll be your Node A.

STEP 3: THE ENDING

And, once again: What's the conclusion? Where do the PCs learn the ultimate answers and/or get into a big fight with the bad guy? (Big fights with bad guys are still a really easy way to manufacture a satisfying conclusion.)

This will be your Node E.

STEP 4: THREE COOL NODES

Brainstorm three cool locations or people related to the mystery. A seedy tavern down by the docks? Drug den filled with werewolves? The doppelganger who has replaced the sultan's vizier? These will be your nodes B, C, and D.

As we've done before, I recommend brainstorming more than three items, picking the three coolest ideas, and then seeing if you can combine the other ideas with the three you picked before throwing them out.

STEP 5: CONNECT THE NODES

You've got five nodes. Connect 'em with clues like this:

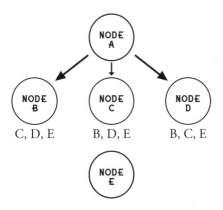

The basic idea here is that Node A points you in three different directions (although, remember, the PCs might find only one of the clues). Then those three locations point to each other and also point to the big conclusion. Simple.

OPTIONAL: ANCILLARY REVELATIONS

The default 5 Node Mystery is a simple, procedural mystery: Follow the clues from Node A, collect your conclusion at Node E.

But if you'd like, you can, of course, layer in any ancillary revelations that make sense or would be cool to have.

RUN IT

Wait . . . is that it?

That's it.

I wasn't kidding when I said that the 5 Node Mystery was simple and fast.

In running your 5 Node Mystery, of course, it's possible for the PCs to go from Node A to Node B to Node E (skipping Nodes C and D). In some cases, the scenario will be modular enough that this means the conclusion isn't what you thought it was. (You thought the conclusion was a big showdown with a bad guy in the violet tower at the center of the graveyard. Turns out, it was actually a rooftop chase as the badly injured PCs try to escape the werewolves from the drug den.) In other cases, the nodes left behind the PCs will metastasize into new adventures—either because the werewolves end up causing trouble or because when the PCs go back to mop up the werewolves they'll find clues pointing them to other scenarios.

ALTERNATIVE NODE STRUCTURES

It's pretty easy to start experimenting with the default structure of a 5 Node Mystery. For example, you might decide that Node A only contains clues pointing to Nodes B and C. Those nodes would then contain clues pointing to each other and Node D, while Node D would be loaded up with a whole bunch of clues pointing to the conclusion.

(Make sure to still include at least three clues in Node A!)

Or maybe Node A includes clues pointing to all the other nodes, which form a loop. Or you add an extra node (which could be a dead end). Whatever seems interesting or needed for the scenario you're working on.

✦ HOMEWORK ✦

5 X 5 CAMPAIGN

Up until now, you've likely been running linear campaigns: The PCs play one scenario (a dungeon, a mystery, or whatever), finish it, and then you hook them into the next scenario.

This linear structure, however, is not the only way to run a campaign. In fact, the same node-based scenario structure we've been using to design complex mystery scenarios can also be expanded to a campaign structure, allowing you to use your mastery of node-based design to build an interwoven campaign of interconnected scenarios.

STEP 1: DESIGN FIVE 5 NODE MYSTERIES

As you're designing these five mysteries, you might have some idea of how they all relate to each other, but maybe not. Discovering how seemingly unrelated things are actually connected to each other is a great way to make both things richer and more interesting.

STEP 2: CONNECT EACH SCENARIO AS A NODE

Arrange the five mysteries into the same node pattern as a 5 Node Mystery. In other words:

- ⚙ Mystery A will have clues pointing to Mysteries B, C, and D.
- ⚙ Mystery B will have clues pointing to Mysteries C, D, and E.
- ⚙ Mysteries C and D will follow the same pattern as Mystery B (pointing to each other and Mystery E).

If you didn't already know how the mysteries related to each other, the process of figuring out how clues for Mystery D ended up over in Mystery B is the part where you figure that out. The possible links between Mysteries can span the gamut of human experiences:

◎ The victim in Mystery A was an employee of the werewolves in Mystery B.

◎ The "villain" in Mystery A was only doing what she did because she was being blackmailed by someone in Mystery C.

◎ The mercenaries in Mystery A have also been hired by the reclusive millionaire in Mystery D.

◎ The werewolves in Mystery B were created by the warlock in Mystery E.

◎ The blackmailer in Mystery C was investigating the warlock in Mystery E.

◎ The reclusive millionaire in Mystery D is murdered by the warlock in Mystery E.

And so forth.

Each clue linking one Mystery to another will, of course, appear in a specific node of the Mystery, and it's usually a good idea to mix this up a bit. Some clues will appear in Node E and serve as the "payoff" for solving the Mystery: You've taken out El Pajarero, but who was he working for?!

But don't fall into the trap of *always* putting the clues in the concluding node. Spread 'em around a bit.

This may mean that the PCs don't necessarily finish one scenario before bouncing into another: They encounter a clue in Node B of one Mystery and follow it into a completely different Mystery. This is great! In fact, because the nodes between scenarios are linked in the same way that the nodes within a scenario are linked, the players will often not even notice that this is happening. They won't know that there's a difference between Mystery A and Mystery B, and the entire campaign will unify into something greater and more complicated than the sum of its parts.

EXPANDING THE CAMPAIGN

Because your 5 x 5 Campaign is using a node-based structure, you can expand it in all the ways that you can expand *any* node-based structure—funnels, layer cakes, free-form clouds, etc.

For example, you can take Mystery E of one 5 x 5 Campaign and treat it as Mystery A of a second 5 x 5 Campaign, creating an easy funnel. This structure can be ideal because it segments the campaign into clearly delineated chunks, each of which is relatively easy to prep.

It can also be great for D&D because a 5 x 5 Campaign is roughly the perfect length for a single tier of play, so you can design one 5 x 5 Campaign for Tier 1, another for Tier 2, and so forth.

SWAPPING ADVENTURES

While building a 5 x 5 Campaign, you can take any or all of the 5 Node Mysteries and simply swap them out for a different type of scenario. That might just be a larger node-based scenario, but it could also be a dungeon (see page 41), raid (see page 268), or heist (see page 307).

You still need to include the clues linking those scenarios to the other scenarios in the campaign, of course, but this is easy to do. For example, in a dungeon you can just key the clues to various rooms.

PART 3

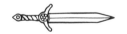

RAIDS AND HEISTS

THE **WORLD**—any world—is filled with locations. That's why location-based scenario structures are so useful. Dungeons, also known as location crawls, are one example of a location-based adventure, but they're not the only one.

Dungeons are primarily based on exploration. When the PCs first enter the dungeon location, its layout and features are unknown, and the focus of play is on discovering the hidden wonders that the dungeon contains. Raids and heists, on the other hand, transform the room-and-key structure by replacing exploration with tactical and strategic planning. At the beginning of a raid scenario, the expectation is that the players will know much or all of the location's layout and defenses, and the focus of play is on how they can use that knowledge to plan their operation.

Because raids and heists are still location-based scenarios, we'll be using many of the same tools and techniques that we use while running dungeon scenarios, but often in slightly different ways and enhanced with a selection of new tools that help us fill these scenarios with thrilling moments and unique challenges.

✦ THE RAID ✦

A raid scenario begins when the PCs identify an **objective** inside a **secure location**. Arriving at the location, the PCs will be able to perform a rapid **survey** to learn the **floorplan** and **defenses** of the location. This information is not necessarily complete (with the PCs still often encountering hidden elements and unexpected surprises during the scenario), but it should be comprehensive enough that the PCs can make a plan for how they'll assault the location. They will then execute their planned raid, most likely facing active opposition that will strategically respond to the PCs' actions.

OBJECTIVE

Every raid needs an objective. This makes a raid a great scenario structure to pull out of your pocket when your players say they want something: Just put the thing they want inside a secure location and point them in the right direction.

Objectives will often be focused on a specific **object**:

⬡ Steal a valuable object.

⬡ Sabotage enemy material (or disrupt a dangerous ritual).

⬡ Plant evidence, install a listening device, or deposit some other item.

⬡ Gather intelligence.

⬡ Secure or destroy infrastructure.

Other objectives will be aimed at a **target**:

⬡ Kill

⬡ Capture

⬡ Rescue

A common variant of this is **clearing hostiles** from a location by killing, incapacitating, arresting, or otherwise neutralizing them. There are also **diversions**, in which the goal is to distract some or all of the denizens in a location for some period of time. (Diversions will often also be part of the tactics used in other raids, but this is slightly different from when the diversion itself is the objective.)

RAIDING THE MONSTER MANUAL

Instead of a human target, it can be fun to flip through the Monster Manual: *Identifying and assassinating a doppelganger, rustling blink dogs, or rescuing an aboleth all pose unique challenges.*

You can complicate a raid by introducing **multiple objectives**. This can be done as a simple copy-and-paste (instead of killing one target, you need to kill six of them; instead of stealing one data-ruby, you need to steal three of them), but having objectives of different types can often be more dynamic (you have to rescue Gabriela and also kill Luisa Fernanda Pérez Rodríguez). A slight variant of this is the **multi-part objective** (you need to steal the hard drive, but first you need to use the location-locked security USB that will decrypt its contents).

Generally, having multiple objectives is only meaningful if the objectives are located in different areas. (It's not more challenging to steal three rubies than it is to steal one ruby if all three rubies are sitting next to each other in a display case.) Other logistical complications can also be effective, though. For example, if all the targets are initially in one location but they'll split up and go in different directions when the alarm is raised, it either has the same effect or provides a great motivation to the PCs to make sure they don't trigger any alarms.

You can also add a **timing component** to an objective.

- A deadline requires the PCs to accomplish their objective by a specific time (e.g., at midnight the lunar vault will vanish until the next blue moon).

- A time limit can begin at the same time as the raid or be triggered during the raid (e.g., once the alarm is raised you'll only have five minutes before the data banks are automatically wiped).

- A time requirement might be built into the objective (e.g., you need to keep the USB plugged into the computer for 5 minutes to complete the download, or your diversion has to last for 10 minutes).

As you prep the rest of the scenario, it will also be useful to consider how an objective will impact the tactics the PCs can employ while conducting the raid: If they need to rescue a hostage, then stealth will probably be vital so that they don't alert the kidnappers and get the hostage killed. If they need to create a big diversion, on the other hand, then stealth will probably only take them so far.

FLOORPLAN

In designing the secure location that will be raided, you're going to use the same mapping techniques and symbols that you used for the dungeon (see page 100). There are, however, a few specific things you'll want to keep in mind while designing your raid map.

First, remember that the location must be **surveyable**. The PCs have to be able to observe the location from outside and figure out the details of its floorplan and defenses so that they can formulate a tactical plan. This will guide your design of the location because for each feature you add, you'll also want to think about how a survey could reveal that feature.

⬦ Windows are your friend. Simply counting windows and knowing their locations can tell the PCs a lot about a building's floorplan, and obviously looking through the windows can tell them even more.

⬦ Try to avoid featureless square-block buildings. More varied building outlines can, once again, let the PCs intuit a lot more about the interior layout of the location (particularly in combination with windows). If you use more varied buildings in general, the occasional use of a square-block building when it's appropriate (e.g., a warehouse) will be revealing in its own right.

⬦ High vantage points, like a nearby hill or clock tower, can give blueprint-style overviews of a location that would otherwise be screened from view (e.g., the courtyard of a castle).

⬦ Keep the scale of the raid scenario manageable. The larger a secure location gets, the more difficult it is to keep it surveyable. (Although as the PCs become more skilled at executing raids, they may discover surveying techniques that make larger complexes more viable.)

With all that being said, it's also true that a survey does not need to reveal every single detail, so don't feel like you need to add a window to every room. We'll discuss the details of a good survey starting on page 274.

Second, where are the objective(s) of the raid located? Answering this question might even provide the core scenario concept. (Where *would* the Lytekkas Hypercorp store their DNA records?) It can be useful to build out from the **objective locations**, making sure to include multiple layers of defense that the PCs will need to bypass or work their way through in order to reach their objective.

Keep in mind that an objective can also be mobile: It might be a person or carried by a person. Or it might be periodically moved, either as part of its function, as a security measure, or because preparations are being made to ship it to another location.

Third, there should be **multiple entrances**. The core experience of the raid scenario is making a tactical plan, and by putting the choice of entrance front and center, you're immediately framing the scenario in those terms for the players. They literally *have* to make a tactical choice to begin the scenario, which will naturally draw them into thinking through the tactical consequences of that choice.

To that end, each entrance should be either secured, hidden, or both.

A **secured entrance**, in this sense, just means that there's some form of obstacle or cost required to use the entrance. This might be:

◎ security guards
◎ security cameras
◎ a trap
◎ a skill check required to use the entrance (climbing, picking the lock, etc.)
◎ an entrance that can only be used one-way (e.g., sealing behind the PCs after they enter), forcing the raid to find a different means of egress

A **hidden entrance** is one that may not be detected during the site survey. To discover it might require:

◎ a skill check
◎ a specific action
◎ a special resource or ability

Finding a hidden entrance will usually be beneficial. It might have lower security (or no security), or it might provide access to a shorter or more advantageous route to the PCs' objective.

As far as entrances are concerned, it should be noted that **windows are entrances**. So if your raid locations offer a realistic number of windows (or skylights or the like), the requirement to have multiple entrances will usually take care of itself.

Fourth, once the PCs are inside the location, there should continue to be **tactical choices**. You can largely accomplish this by xandering your raid location, just like a dungeon (see page 150). If there are multiple routes that can be taken to the objective, varied defenses along each route, and any form of imperfect information (either because features are hidden or because of a failed survey), interesting tactical choices will tend to materialize. (And that's even before taking into account the varied actions of security forces during actual play.)

Finally, since the goal is for the PCs to be able to learn the floorplan, it can be useful to prep **blueprints** that you can give to the players. These might represent actual blueprints obtained by the PCs (although this is more common in heist scenarios, see page 308), but they can also just be a convenient player reference for what their characters learn during their survey. Either way, having the physical blueprints at the table will encourage and enable the players to make their tactical plan.

MOBILE LOCATIONS

Staging raids on mobile locations—military convoys, cruise ships, trains, airships, etc.—is a fun twist that can also be used to create unique challenges for your players.

DEFENSES

The defenses securing a raid location can be either **passive obstacles** (locks, traps, physical challenges, etc.) or **active forces** (guards, patrols, response teams, etc.). The experience you had designing similar elements for your dungeon scenarios will transfer pretty much directly into your raid scenarios, but there are a couple bits of good praxis that can be useful.

First, because the success or failure of a raid scenario often hinges on managing and manipulating the active forces onsite, defenses that raise an **alarm** can be very effective, and are likely to be more common than in most dungeon scenarios. Alarms might be a loud noise (or similar alert) that will attract active forces in the immediate area, or they might be a signal to remote security personnel that will bring them from their area of operations to the area of the alarm. Alarms can include having active forces who detect the PCs and respond by shouting for help or sending a runner.

Second, I highly recommend including a **patrol** in almost any raid scenario. As alarms are raised and adversaries are activated (see page 299), the raid scenario will become increasingly dynamic, forcing the PCs to respond to an ever-evolving tactical situation. Having one or more patrols designed into the scenario will bake this dynamic aspect into the scenario from the very beginning. Patrols are also something of a unique challenge, however, because they will usually have regular cycles of movement, allowing the PCs to survey them, figure out their patterns, and use those patterns to avoid or even subvert the patrols.

SURVEY

At the beginning of a raid scenario, the PCs will perform a survey of the secure location in order to determine the floorplan and defenses. We can break this down further into four specific lists:

- Entries
- Rooms
- Passive Obstacles
- Active Forces

You may not need to literally make lists for each of these. (They're already detailed in your prep notes, right?) But you might find listing them a valuable exercise the first couple times you design a raid scenario, and thinking of them as a list can be conceptually useful regardless: Before the survey, it's a list of things that the PCs don't know, and the goal of the survey is to slide some or all of those items onto a new list of known elements.

CHALLENGE RATING BUDGET

If you're designing a raid scenario for D&D, you generally want to do the following:

◎ Have the total XP of all active forces in the raid equal at least three times the budget for a Deadly encounter.

◎ Divide that XP budget into a larger number of Medium or Easy action groups, rather than Hard or Deadly action groups.

Due to the dynamic flow and active response of a typical raid scenario, it will be *very* common for multiple action groups to flow together into larger encounters or arrive in the middle of an encounter as reinforcements. You want the flexibility to have two, three, or maybe even four of these action groups join together into a larger tactical action without simply curb stomping the PCs.

At the same time, if there isn't enough total opposition at the raid location, the optimal strategy will be to simply let all the bad guys run to your position and wipe them out in one big encounter. Which is boring, particularly if it becomes the default for every raid scenario.

The sweet spot is for the PCs to (a) potentially be able to take out isolated bad guys fast enough that the alarm doesn't get raised (i.e., Easy encounters); (b) be able to deal with armed conflict when it does break out (i.e., stand up to several action groups attacking at once); and at the same time (c) not trivialize the raid (i.e., not defeat everybody in one big fight).

This advice can be generalized to other RPGs: Identify the toughest encounter the PCs can handle in the system, then triple the strength of that encounter to determine the minimum force profile for the raid location.

Learning about each element will be either

◎ trivial,
◎ challenging, or
◎ impossible.

In a typical raid scenario, most of the elements will be **trivial** to survey. This is the foundation of the scenario, providing the fundamental knowledge of the tactical arena that will allow the players to create their tactical plan. Trivial surveys are often essentially automatic: As the PCs approach the raid location, you might simply draw the outline of the building while describing it to them, along with the doors, windows, and guards they can see. In some cases, though, completing the trivial survey may require some minor but deliberate effort by the PCs—e.g., needing to walk around a building to see the back door in the alley or keeping the fortress under surveillance for at least 20 minutes to notice the guard patrol.

A **challenging** element, on the other hand, requires some extra effort by the PCs to survey. This might be a clever action or a skill check, but it doesn't have to be terribly elaborate or onerous. "Can I find some high ground nearby or maybe climb a tree to look down into the compound?" is a good example, as is, "Do I recognize the electronic locks? Maybe there's a manufacturer's override code we could use." This can also include reactive skill checks for stuff that the PCs *might* notice during a trivial survey, but which require particular knowledge or sharp perception.

Finally, there may be some elements that are **impossible** for the PCs to survey before breaching the location. For example, it's hard to imagine how a typical group would be able to figure out the precise layout of a sub-basement by looking at a building from outside. (Of course, you never know how you might be surprised by player ingenuity during actual play.)

Impossible and even challenging elements are not required for a raid scenario to work, but the enigmas they present can play merry havoc with the PCs' plans. On the other hand, if the players figure out how to rip away the engima from a challenging element before the raid begins, they'll enjoy being rewarded with the advantage of their hard-won knowledge.

Special abilities or technology can make the impossible challenging or even trivial. Can a PC see through walls? Do they have access to a drone, a *clairvoyance* spell, or a *gem of seeing*? These are all great resources to have for a raid scenario! They allow you to design more complex and intricate raid locations while still being able to provide a comprehensive survey to the PCs.

Even when the PCs learn about an element, of course, that element may still have undiscovered **secrets**. For example, they can spot a patrol without knowing its exact movements or see a door with an electronic lock without knowing the code to open it.

A particularly useful version of this is that it's possible for the PCs to know that a room exists while having no idea what's inside it. For example, if they look through a window and see a closed door, they don't need to know exactly what's on the other side to intuit that there's a room there. You get the same effect with windows on the outside of the building that they don't look through, and the players can even draw similar inferences about the presence of a room by noting that there's a space on the floorplans they can't account for.

FAMILIAR RAIDS

If a raid takes place in a location the PCs are already familiar with, then the "survey" is actually just their memories of the place (although additional observation may be required for active forces or recent alterations). For example, the PCs might return home to find that goblin shadowstalkers have taken hostages in the inn where they've been staying.

This familiarity can also be outsourced to an NPC for a similar effect. For example, the patron hiring them for a job may be able to provide them the intel they need to plan their raid.

If the PCs are doing actual legwork to pull together information like this, though, you're probably crossing the line into a heist (see page 307).

You also want to be aware of **survey risks**. The most basic of these is pretty simple: What if the bad guys notice the PCs staking out their location?

This common risk is likely resolved with some kind of Stealth-type test. If the PCs *are* noticed, then the bad guys might shoo them away (preventing a more detailed survey), immediately attack them, and/or increase their security. (Their actual choice will depend on both the scenario and the specific circumstances.)

Other survey risks are, of course, also possible, and will often be tied to particular actions taken to reveal challenging survey elements. For example, the PCs might trigger a booby trap or simply fall and injure themselves while trying to climb up to some vantage point.

⊹ RUNNING THE RAID ⊹

Although very similar to running a dungeon scenario, running a successful raid poses some unique challenges. Before you get started with your first scenario, therefore, we're going to dive into a few new techniques for making rulings that are particularly useful during a raid, and then we'll lay out a procedure for managing raid turns that will help keep your scenario on track.

INTRODUCING THE RAID

One of the potential pitfalls of running your first raid scenario is their similarity to other location-based adventures. Players who have only experienced dungeon scenarios will see the raid location and, without knowing that raids are an option, simply default to treating the scenario as if it were a dungeon. This won't necessarily render the scenario unplayable, but it's very likely to become a suboptimal or even deeply frustrating experience for them.

What you need to do, obviously, is introduce your players to the concept of a raid scenario as part of their first raid scenario. The key thing, in my experience, is to make sure that the survey happens. Once the players have a floorplan and details of a location's defenses in hand, it takes only a minor amount of survival instinct for them to use that information to their advantage by forming a plan of action.

One option is to use the PCs' **patron**. In other words, whoever hires them to do the job can give them suggestions or even explicit directions on how the job should be done. ("The target has highly responsive security, so you'll probably want to get in and out as quickly as possible.") Some mission objectives, like planting a listening device or assassinating a target with no collateral damage, can more or less mandate the job be approached as a raid. Such patrons can even perform the survey for the PCs, providing a briefing packet that includes blueprints and security details.

Another option is to design their first raid scenario so that it features an **ultra-trivial survey**. Basically, as soon as the PCs approach the location, you just automatically provide them with a complete set of blueprints and a bunch of obvious security details. ("The entrances are here and here. You can see security guards here, here, and here. Looking through this window on the second floor you can see that Rodríguez is working in her office.")

You can also use **equipment loadout** as a gentle prompt to encourage raid-style play. The scenario's patron could, once again, provide this equipment or you might just stock the appropriate treasure hordes with it. In a science fiction game, for example, if you give the PCs access to T-ray goggles that can look through walls, knockout gas, and a missile launcher with one shot before pointing them toward a heavily armored compound on Ganymede, they might figure it out all by themselves.

Of course, you can also just **tell the players** that the scenario is designed for a raid-style approach and what that entails (surveying the target, putting together a tactical plan, and then successfully executing it). This blunt approach may prove alienating for some players, who will resent having the GM "force" them to do something, but as long as you don't make a habit of it, there's a lot to be said for open, clear communication at the gaming table.

The great thing is that once the *players* have added raiding to their tool kit, they'll naturally start looking for opportunities to perform a raid. They may even surprise you by approaching future dungeon scenarios using raid-style techniques. The difference between a dungeon scenario and a raid scenario is often almost entirely about how the PCs choose to tactically approach the scenario, and as the PCs add additional tools to their repertoire, you'll actually find *all* of your scenarios being enriched as a result.

FAILING FORWARD

When making rulings, we often default to simple binary outcomes: You either pick the lock or you don't. You climb the wall or you fall. You hit the orc with your sword or you miss. You either succeed on the check or you fail.

Failing forward is an alternative technique in which the mechanical result of failure (e.g., rolling below the target number) is described as being a success-with-complications in the game world.

When we first discussed making checks (way back on page 28), we talked about making failure meaningful by disallowing retries. A simple rule of thumb for when you should use failing forward is whenever disallowing a retry feels a little weird to you: Why *can't* the PC just try to pick the lock again?

In our foundational technique, the intended path fails and the PCs need to find an alternative path. Failing forward is a different way of making failure meaningful because you don't annihilate the intended route (whether you prepped it or the players chose it). You just complicate it.

Coming up with interesting complications on the fly, though, can feel intimidating. So, when in doubt, just impose a cost: You succeed, but . . .

- ⊘ You have to pay extra.
- ⊘ You took damage.
- ⊘ Your equipment broke.
- ⊘ It took extra time (if that's relevant).
- ⊘ Someone knows you did it whom you didn't want to inform.

If you have an idea for a better complication, great. But if not, these five broad categories can cover like 90 percent of fail forward checks. In fact, you'll usually have multiple options. When picking a lock, for example:

- ⊘ You open the door but trigger the security trap. (You take damage.)
- ⊘ You open the door, but your lock pick snapped off in the lock. (Your equipment broke.)

◈ You open the door, but it took 20 minutes and now you only have 10 minutes before the Count returns home. (It took extra time and that was relevant.)

If none of these options seem to work and you can't think of something outside of the box, that's fine: Either don't make the check in the first place (just let them automatically succeed) or default back to No Retries Allowed and move forward in a different way.

OFFER COST

Instead of just imposing the cost of a failed fail forward check, you can get a little fancy by offering that cost to the player and allowing them to choose between paying the cost or failing the check. For example, "You've almost got the safe open, but the hacked security camera is going to come back online. Do you stay and open the door or GTFO before the camera spots you?" or "Damien agrees to do it, but he wants an extra 500 gold pieces."

Failing forward is particularly useful when running raid scenarios for a couple reasons.

First, it allows tactical plans to survive contact with the enemy . . . or, more accurately, survive contact with a bad dice roll. If the players spend time making a tactical plan that starts by breaching the back door of the compound, having the whole plan fall apart because their skill check to open the door failed probably isn't the best option. It would be more interesting if, for example, forcing the door damaged the lock in such a way that the next security patrol passing this way would be alerted to the intruders.

On that note, the second reason failing forward works well during raids is that the presence of active security forces provides a rich source for complications. Any fallout from a failed check that alerts security immediately makes the raid more interesting, and lost time is *always* relevant in a raid.

SIMPLE SUCCESS CHECK

A simple success check is kind of the opposite of a fail forward check. It's typically used in situations where the characters are skilled professionals doing a routine task and, therefore, there's no meaningful chance of failure. In most cases, of course, we'd default to yes and the character would automatically succeed, but sometimes success can be assured while still leaving uncertain exactly how good the outcome will be. In other words, success is simple, but we make a check to see if the character excels and achieves a higher-quality result.

So for a fail forward check, a mechanical success indicates the character has achieved their desired goal and a mechanical failure indicates they've done so, but only with a complication. In a simple success check, on the other hand, a mechanical failure means the character achieved their desired goal (they succeeded) and a mechanical success indicates they've gained an extraordinary success or boon.

LET IT RIDE

Something you want to avoid as a GM is **rolling to failure**. This is when a PC attempts to accomplish something, but a successful check doesn't actually let them do it. Instead, a successful roll—for whatever reason—just results in them making another check. This then repeats until the player rolls a failure, at which point the attempt fails.

It sounds a little crazy when you just describe it like that, but it's a surprisingly easy trap to fall into.

For example, it often occurs when the PCs are trying to use stealth. GMs will have the PCs roll a new Stealth check every single time they move or every single time they encounter a new opponent. Even if a PC has a 75% chance of success on their first Stealth check, after just three checks their chance of success will have dropped to 42%. After five checks, it's dropped to 24%. And the first time they fail a check, of course, their attempt at stealth is over as their enemies raise the alarm.

Under these circumstances, of course, failure becomes more or less assured and the players will simply stop trying to be stealthy. Seeing a broad swath of awesome experiences get summarily junked from your campaign kinda sucks, and it's particularly unfortunate for raids because a lack of stealth-based options will really flatten those scenarios.

The solution is to **let it ride.**

When the PCs set a specific goal for themselves, make a single check and let the result of that check ride forward: If they're trying to climb a cliff, make a single Athletics check to determine whether they get to the top (even if it would take them several rounds or minutes or hours to do so). If the intention is to "sneak through the enemy base," then you make one Stealth check for the entire op and it determines how stealthy they're going to be for the whole thing. (And the answer may be, "Not very stealthy, so someone is probably going to spot you." And that's okay.)

This doesn't mean, however, that you roll the dice and then immediately skip to the end. The cool thing about letting a skill check ride is that other actions and choices can intersect with the attempt.

HEATHER (LAEVRA): Okay, I'm going to slip inside and gently ease the door closed behind me.

JASON (GM): Give me a Dexterity (Stealth) check.

HEATHER (LAEVRA): 17.

—⊁ *Jason notes that no one inside the building heard the door open.*

JASON (GM): You're in a back hallway. To your left there are a number of doors. To your right the hall leads to a stairway heading up to the second floor.

HEATHER (LAEVRA): I'll check out the stairs.

JASON (GM): Give me a Wisdom (Perception) check.

HEATHER (LAEVRA): 14.

JASON (GM): You notice that there's a security camera positioned to film anyone coming up the stairs.

HEATHER (LAEVRA): Is there any way to avoid it?

⊶ *Jason knows that the camera is rated at DC 21, so Laevra's riding Dexterity (Stealth) check of 17 will fail if she tries to sneak past it. She doesn't know that, of course.*

JASON (GM): You might be able to slide under the camera and avoid its field of view.

HEATHER (LAEVRA): Hmm. It's too risky. I'll turn around and head back the other way.

JASON (GM): (*rolls some dice*) As you head back down the hall, one of the doors ahead of you suddenly opens, but you manage to quickly duck into a broom closet and out of sight. Looking through a crack in the door, you see two security guards emerge and start walking in the opposite direction.

⊶ *Jason rolled a random encounter and then a Wisdom (Perception) check for the guards. He got a 13 on the check, which was lower than Laevra's riding Dexterity (Stealth) check of 17, so she easily hides from the guards.*

As you can see in this example, these choices can have an impact on the success or failure of the riding check. For example, if Laevra had attempted to sneak past the security camera, she would have been noticed and the alarm raised. Her choice *not* to do that preserved the infiltration.

It's also possible, while riding a check, to **seek bonuses**. For example, if Laevra sneaks into the locker room and steals a guard's uniform, she could make a Charisma (Deception) check to disguise herself. Jason might then give a +2 bonus to her riding Dexterity (Stealth) total until someone sees through her disguise. The Charisma (Deception) check, of course, would *also* be a riding check.

Similarly, certain actions or outcomes could **apply penalties** to the initial check result. For example, after Laevra frees the prisoner she came to liberate, Jason might apply a -4 penalty to her riding check result to reflect the additional difficulty of shepherding the prisoner on their way back out of the complex.

So how does a ride end? Obviously you don't just make a single Dexterity (Stealth) check and then live with it forever. Broadly speaking, there are four possibilities:

◎ Success
◎ Failure
◎ Change of Approach
◎ Change of Circumstance

Success mostly speaks for itself. If the PC accomplishes their goal—they sneak into Rodríguez's private office; they reach the summit of the mountain; they negotiate the peace treaty with Ostranya—then the ride comes to an end in triumph.

Failure is also fairly obvious. If you're riding a check and hit a point where the check fails, then that ride is over. This is straightforward if the riding check is being compared to opposed checks from NPCs, since the ride simply continues until one of those NPCs rolls high enough (if they ever do).

If the riding check is being compared to static DCs, on the other hand, it can get a little trickier. For example, if all the security cameras in the building have the same DC and Laevra rolls high enough, does that mean she just "automatically" bypasses all the cameras? Quite possibly, yes, although we need to quibble on calling it "automatic": It wasn't automatic. She succeeded on her check. She was skilled enough that the security cameras weren't a challenge for her. This does, however, suggest that it's important to have multiple security measures (with, among other things, different DCs and different consequences) and give Laevra meaningful choice in navigating her way through those paths, and this is a lesson that can be generalized to other riding checks. (For example, if the PCs are climbing a mountain, the riding Strength [Athletics] check only becomes relevant if (a) the DCs are escalating, (b) there are multiple paths with some promised advantage for taking riskier paths, and/or (c) other events or opportunities interrupt the journey.)

If you'd prefer to reintroduce some randomness, though, you can convert the static DCs into random ones. (In D&D, you can do this by subtracting 10 from the static DC and then adding 1d20.)

A **change of approach** happens when the PCs riding a check abandon the strategy or actions covered by the check and do something completely different. For example, if they decide it's time to stop sneaking around and instead noisily ambush a group of orcs. Or they decide they're running out of time and drink the *potions of flying* they were saving rather than continue their climb. In some circumstances, you may also decide that changing the focus of the goal ("let's sneak into his bedroom instead of his private office") is enough to warrant a new check.

A change of approach is not the same thing as an **interruption**, however, which is when something unrelated to the goal being attempted momentarily intrudes. For example, attacking orcs ends a riding Dexterity (Stealth) check because it means the PCs are no longer sneaking (and if they choose to go back to sneaking after the fight, it's time for a new check). On the other hand, attacking a tribe of yetis on the side of the mountain probably doesn't end the Strength (Athletics) check for the ascent because the fight is merely interrupting the climb, not abandoning it.

Finally, a **change of circumstance** means that something in the environment has significantly shifted. This involves a judgment call because, technically, you could argue that each individual guard is a different circumstance and you should make a new check! (Which would, obviously, negate the whole concept of letting it ride.)

What you're looking for is something radical enough that it fundamentally alters the nature of what the PCs are doing. For example, if the PCs are sneaking through an orc camp at night and a group of fire giants suddenly attack, you might decide that "middle of a battlefield filled with flame" is so sufficiently different from "sleepy orc camp in the dark" that a new check is called for. Alternatively, maybe the PCs are sneaking through the orc camp, discover a transdimensional portal in the shaman's tent, and jump through it into the Feywild. They can keep sneaking, but things have changed enough that it's probably time for a new check.

POINT OF UNCERTAINTY

When a riding check would fail, you can instead choose to create a **point of uncertainty**. This is the moment at which the riding check is at risk, but the character has an opportunity to save the result by taking some sort of action. This lets you add complications while the overall resolution continues pushing forward.

For example, Laevra is searching an office when a security guard approaches. The guard's Wisdom (Perception) check is higher than her riding Dexterity (Stealth) check, so she's at risk of being discovered. The GM could simply have the guard slam open the door and shout, "Freeze!" ending Laevra's check.

But the GM could instead say, "Someone's approaching the office door. You can see the beam of a security guard's flashlight waving around through the frosted glass."

Laevra now has the opportunity to do the following:

◎ Leap out the window and hang from the side of the building while the guard sweeps the room. (A Strength [Athletics] check.)

◎ Ambush the approaching guard and hope she can take him out before he can raise the alarm. (Resolved through combat.)

◎ Bluff the guard into believing she's authorized to be there. (A Charisma [Persuasion] check.)

◎ Drink a *potion of invisibility*. (Using equipment, which in this case the GM might rule gives her a bonus to her riding check . . . which may or may not be enough to avoid the guard's notice.)

The key thing is that the response to a point of uncertainty should generally not be "make the same skill check again." If Laevra's Dexterity (Stealth) check is at risk, her response can't just be "I hide harder" while making another Dexterity (Stealth) check. You might make an exception if Laevra comes up with a particularly clever idea specific to her current situation, but what's really required is some out-of-the-box thinking.

ENDURANCE TESTS

Sometimes rolling to failure IS the goal. These are situations where an eventual failure is guaranteed and the question is not whether a character can succeed, but rather *how long* they can succeed before the failure happens. Imagine someone trying to stay afloat in stormy waters or holding a door shut while monsters try to batter it down from the far side.

Having the character roll once per round (or hour or whatever period of time is appropriate) until they fail can be a very good fit for these types of endurance tests.

THEATER OF OPERATIONS

When you ran your first dungeon scenario, the encounters were keyed to specific rooms: As the PCs entered Area 15, you checked the key and saw that (a) it was a Cryptic Library and (b) there was a cloaker hiding on the ceiling.

When a fight breaks out in the library, you've learned to make combat encounters memorable by leveraging the environment, so bookshelves topple over on top of people and maybe the injured cloaker retreats back up to the ceiling and starts throwing books. But the cloaker is keyed to Area 15, so that's where the cloaker is met and that's where the fight happens.

As you became more confident as a GM, though, you started looking beyond the current room. When the PCs start fighting the cloaker, you look around the map and use your adversary roster to check nearby areas to see if there are any other monsters who might come join the fight. Over in Area 17 you notice a barracks with five goblin blood warriors and make a check to see if they hear the fight. They succeed on the check, and so a couple rounds later they come rushing over and join the melee in the library!

Tools like adversary rosters and random encounter checks also mean that combat encounters are no longer limited to specific, predetermined areas. They can happen in any room! Maybe the PCs are poking around the orrery in the observatory in Area 30 when a gloomcaster stumbles across them or they're checking out the armory in Area 18 when a group of shadowstalkers arrives to equip themselves.

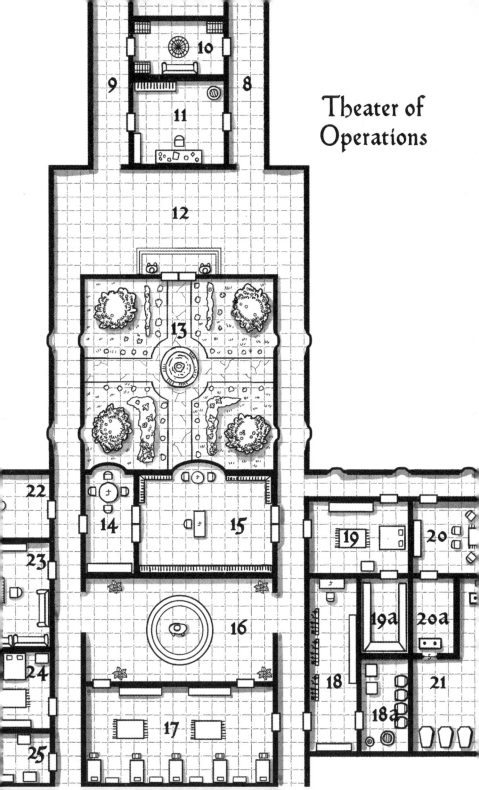

Theater of
Operations

At this point you've accomplished a lot. Your dungeons are no longer static complexes filled with monsters who patiently wait for the PCs to show up and slaughter them. They feel like living, dynamic spaces that respond to what the PCs are doing.

But many GMs who reach this point still have one preconception that they're clinging to. When the goblins came rushing over to join the fight in the library? It was still the fight *in the library*. When the gloomcaster discovered the PCs in the observatory? Many GMs will still be thinking of that fight as somehow "belonging" to Area 30.

One of the reasons this happens is because our method of mapping and keying a dungeon is *designed* to do it: We conceptually break the map into discrete chunks and then number each chunk specifically to firewall each section of the dungeon. As we've seen, it makes it easier to describe the dungeon and it makes it easier to run the dungeon, allowing the GM to focus on the current "chunk" without being overwhelmed by the totality.

But the next step is to go through that abstraction and come out the other side. We don't want to abandon the advantages of conceptually "chunking" the dungeon, but we also don't want to be *constrained* by it. We want clearly defined rooms that we can easily pick up and play with, but in actual play we want to recognize that each room is just one part of an interconnected location.

It's a little bit like juggling. You may start out by just having one room in play, but as you become more skilled you'll want to learn how to keep several of them in play at the same time. For example, check out the map on the previous page and consider our Cryptic Library in Area 15.

If you're only playing with Area 15, then characters can leap up onto the table and you can even have the reinforcements from Area 17 show up in the doorway. But when you can take one step back and start thinking of the dungeon as a **theater of operations**, then you'll see stuff like this:

◎ A character getting thrown through the bay windows into the garden in Area 15.

- A PC slipping across the hall into Area 19 so that they can *pincer* the blood warrior reinforcements in the hall.

- One of the blood warriors breaking off and shouting in goblin, "I'll get Orok and the troll!"

- The ranger activating her *boots of speed*, cutting through Area 14, and racing around to cut the goblin off in Area 12.

- The goblins in the rear simultaneously circling through Area 16 to try to mount an assault on the PCs' flank.

- Other goblins moving down the hall to the windows, and then shooting through Area 13 into the library.

The best part is that, as you introduce moments like this, you'll also be opening the door to your players to start doing the same thing. They'll start engaging in strategic decision-making not only in combat ("Let's fall back into the hallway!"), but also for the exploration and engagement of the dungeon as a whole ("Can we draw them back into the room with the poison traps and use those to our advantage? Can we circle around them? Can we split them up?"). These kinds of actions, which can turn an entire complex into a playground, are particularly valuable in creating dynamic, exciting raid scenarios, whether you're in a combat situation or just trying to avoid one.

Make no mistake: This is hard to do! But it's a skill that can be learned and practiced.

Before you begin working on the theater of operations, make sure to get completely comfortable running just one room. Just like a juggler, you're going to want to be confident in throwing one ball before you try to keep a bunch of them in the air all at once. That's the bedrock everything else is built on.

When you're ready to take the next step, start with **hallways**— the spaces between the rooms. When the PCs are standing in a room, just keep the hallway(s) immediately outside the room in mind. Think of them as spaces where characters are standing in your mental picture of the scene. If a fight breaks out, include them—and the chokepoints formed by the doorways leading to them—in the tactical choices being made.

If you're using some form of a battlemap, make a point of including the hallways in addition to the PCs' current room. This can be relatively easy if you're using a virtual tabletop, since the whole map is usually accessible on the computer screen. If you're using an erasable mat, printing out the map, or building 3D terrain, though, just make sure to take the extra effort.

If you're using theater of the mind, on the other hand, simply make a point of not framing your scenes to the door. You can use random encounter distance (see page 85) to vary the engagement point and push yourself out of your comfort zone. Importantly, this is true whether the PCs are approaching a room or the PCs are in a room that's being approached by an action group.

BREACHING THE DOOR

Even though you're often pushing the initial engagement point out of the room, this doesn't mean that every fight should have the bad guys rush out the door to fight the PCs in the hall. Think about who's aware of who; think about preparation vs. rushing in vs. withdrawing vs. sending help vs. going out the back door and encircling them vs. any number of other possibilities. Expanding your scope should result in more variety, not less.

Once you start getting a feel for the options offered by the hallway, it's time to think about **neighboring rooms**. You can start by just looking at the ring of rooms that are just one room away from the current area. For example, if we're in the Cryptic Library (Area 15), that would include Areas 13, 14, 16, and 19. I think of these rooms as lying within the current "penumbra" of the action.

Using an adversary roster (see page 177) will continue to help you here. Even though you're looking at multiple rooms simultaneously, the individual rooms remain firewalled: The active elements (i.e., the denizens) are still summarized on and can be run from the adversary roster. This means you don't need to dive deep into every detail of every room key to manage the theater of operations. You only need a very broad, high-level understanding of the room's concept (which is often summarized in the room's name), and can use that to choose the moments when you need to do a deeper dive.

As you get more comfortable juggling rooms, you can slowly expand the size of this penumbra as needed. In practice, though, I find that you rarely need to push more than a couple rooms away from the current area. (For the Cryptic Library, that would mean adding Areas 12, 17, 18, 22, and 23.)

THE ROOM LIST

Because the name of the room is often all the context you need to effectively manage the theater of operations, you may find it useful to keep a separate list of the room names for easy reference. In fact, you might include that list right on the map or on the same page as your adversary roster for easy access.

A slightly more complicated methodology than the ring of rooms is to use **line of sight**. More specifically, if the PCs can currently see a door leading to a room, you should add that room to your penumbra.

I find the utility of this method to be very situational, but it can be particularly useful in hallways. For example, if the PCs are standing in the hallway outside of Area 15 (instead of inside the Cryptic Library), then using line of sight would suggest that the rooms you need to care about at the moment are Areas 12, 15, 16, 17, 18, and 19.

As you can see, there's not "one true list" of rooms for you to keep track of. It's more about developing an adaptable situational awareness of which rooms are significant in a particular moment, and learning a slightly different way of looking at a scenario map that allows you to play the totality of the environment almost as if it were a gameboard.

What you *don't* want to do is start trying to prep specific "theaters of operations" in your scenarios. Not only will you end up wasting a lot of prep, but you're probably just creating another inflexible preconception of the environment. The true theater of operations arises out of and is defined by the circumstances of play: What do the PCs know? Where do they go? How have they tipped off the NPCs? What decisions do the NPCs make (often based on imperfect information)?

The point isn't to try to anticipate all of those things. The point is to learn how to actively play the campaign world and to let the campaign world live in the moment.

OTHER THEATERS OF OPERATIONS

Think about your house. Imagine standing in the kitchen and talking to someone in the living room. Or shouting something down the stairs. Or looking up from the couch and seeing what's happening in the next room.

When we're talking about the totality of the environment, that's all we're talking about. It's that simple, and it can be found in even the most intimate of spaces.

On the other end of the scale, there are wilderness environments. (You can read more about them in Part 5, starting on page 363.)

The sheer scale of the wilderness can, paradoxically, cause the theater of operations to collapse into a one-dimensional scope: The forest is vast and, therefore, an entire fight just happens generically "in the forest." There's no place for reinforcements to come from and no capacity for strategic decisions because everything is, conceptually, in a single place—a "forest" that's functionally a haze of trees.

The use of tabletop battlemaps locked to a 5-foot scale can exacerbate this one-dimensionality, limiting the field of battle to a scale that tends to blot out the true theater of operations in the wilderness.

The solution is to instead *embrace* the scale of the wilderness. You're traveling across the plains, but there's a tree line a few hundred yards to the north. There's a family of deer grazing 50 feet over there. There's a ravine to your right perhaps a quarter of a mile away that you've been paralleling for a while now. And the goblin worg riders just cleared the horizon behind you.

What do you do?

THE RAID TURN

A raid turn is, unsurprisingly, very similar to the dungeon turn (see page 66).

1. Mark **ticks**.

2. Make an **activation check**.

3. Declare **actions**.

4. Resolve **adversary actions**.

5. Make **Perception-type checks** as necessary.

6. Resolve actions, including tracking movement on the map.

Whereas a dungeon turn is 10 minutes long, however, a raid turn is only 1 minute long. During a raid scenario, the focus isn't on exploration, so our time scale shifts to reflect the fast-paced tactical focus of the PCs (and also the bad guys who are potentially hunting them).

RAID ACTIONS

Raid actions are generally equivalent to dungeon actions (see page 74), but the shorter duration of the raid turn means that some actions are modified.

Movement is usually done at **raid pace**, which is equal to a character's speed. (This assumes that they are moving cautiously, but with tactical purpose.) Characters can move at **combat pace**, which is equal to speed x 10 per raid turn, but they suffer disadvantage on Perception and Stealth checks.

Ritual casting, which takes 10 minutes, obviously can't be completed in a single raid turn and must instead be done over the course of several raid turns.

Searching, similarly, cannot cover as much area during a raid turn and will require the PCs to be much more focused in targeting their searches. A character can generally search two 5-foot squares (or 50 sq. ft.) as a raid action. This does mean that thoroughly searching a room will chew up a lot of relevant time in a raid scenario, and during those turns the active adversaries will be hunting the PCs.

RAID PERCEPTION

The trick to running an exciting raid scenario without becoming overwhelmed by the potential complexity is efficiently managing the action groups on your adversary roster in a structured way. It's also important to do this in a fair and fun way: If all of your action groups omnisciently know what the PCs are doing (because as the GM, of course, you know it) and immediately swarm them, that's neither fun nor fair. In a raid scenario it's more important than ever that you actually roleplay your action groups: Step into their shoes, think about what they know and who they are and what their priorities are, and then have them act accordingly.

On the other hand, telling you to "just roleplay everyone in the building!" would be ridiculous. There's gotta be a better way.

The better way I recommend is the Triple-A procedure:

- Active
- Alert
- Aware

To better understand these three categories, let's first think about the "default" action group that is currently located in a specific area of your map. This stationary action group is neither active, alert, nor aware.

An **active** action group is one that's taking raid actions, usually moving from one location to another: She leaves the party, she goes to the lab, she gets some dinner, etc.

An **alert** action group is one that knows the PCs (or some form of threat) is present in the location and are taking actions accordingly. (That might be hunting for the PCs, alerting other action groups, moving a VIP to a secure location, setting up barricades, or whatever action seems appropriate to the situation.)

An **aware** action group knows where the PCs are, either precisely or, at least, to some actionable level of precision (e.g., "I heard someone moving around downstairs"). This might be due to line of sight, security cameras, noise, *clairvoyance* spells, etc.

For most purposes, these act as a hierarchy: An alert character is likely to be active, and an aware character will be both alert and active. This mean that you can track the status of each action group on your adversary roster with a single symbol, for example ☆. An active group would have one ☆ while an aware group would have three ☆☆☆.

When it's time to resolve adversary actions, this will allow you to quickly scan down your adversary roster and instantly identify which action groups need to have their actions resolved.

The way an action group actually becomes alert or aware, of course, is through Perception-type checks. These checks should be more difficult, of course, the farther away an action group is from the PCs. Some RPGs will include guidelines for this sort of thing, but if I need to create a rule of thumb I like to simply count rooms. For example, in D&D:

⊘ If the source is on the far side of a wall or door, the Perception-type check is made at disadvantage.

⊘ Apply a cumulative -2 penalty to the Perception-type check for each additional room between them and the source.

If we take a look back at our sample raid map on page 289, for example, if the PCs were making a bunch of noise in the Area 13 gardens and there was an action group in Area 17, I would quickly count the rooms between them (Area 15, Area 16) and then make the Wisdom (Perception) check with disadvantage and at a -4 penalty. (Or you could use the rules for passive Perception at a -9: a -4 penalty for the room count and a -5 penalty for disadvantage.)

Make sure you don't make a lot of noise in a hallway, because that's directly adjacent to a bunch of different rooms!

You could alternatively base your rule of thumb on linear distance (e.g., a -1 penalty for every 50 feet of distance) if you find that more intuitive than room counts.

As you're making Perception-type checks for the bad guys, keep in mind that the target of the check might not be the PCs: It can also be **evidence**. For example, if the PCs kicked down a door or blacked out a security camera or tossed an office while looking for the jade idol, those are all things that enemy action groups may notice.

DUNGEON TURNS VS. RAID TURNS VS. COMBAT ROUNDS

If you're running a raid where the PCs are carefully exploring a compound and the bad guys haven't been alerted yet, you might want to start out using dungeon turns and then swap to the faster pace of raid turns once the action starts heating up.

You might do the opposite, too: If you're running a dungeon scenario and the PCs have stirred up a hornet's nest of enemies on high alert, it could be useful to swap to raid turns.

If it seems like things are happening too fast for the raid turn to handle it, you also have a third option: Drop into combat rounds.

Remember that these are all tools: Use whichever one is most useful for the situation you're currently resolving.

PERCEPTION ON THE ROSTER

Putting the Perception modifier or passive Perception score of an action group on the adversary roster can be very useful in raid scenarios!

WHAT DO THE BAD GUYS ACTUALLY DO?

What the opposition in a raid scenario does is highly dependent on the specific situation, so a comprehensive answer to this question isn't really possible. But here are some things you can quickly default to if you don't have a better idea.

If an action group is directly engaged with the PCs (i.e., they can see the PCs), they'll either

⬡ attack; or

⬡ run away.

If an action group is alert, they'll either

⬡ look for the intruders (i.e., pick a direction and have them move one room over); or

⬡ go for help (i.e., alert nearby action groups).

RAID ACTIVATION

Within the raid turn procedure, there are three ways for a currently passive action group to become active. (But the procedure isn't everything. You can just arbitrarily decide to activate an NPC because it feels like the right thing to do in the moment.)

First, **patrols** begin the scenario activated. (They're basically defined as action groups that are moving around the map.)

Second, you may choose to activate an action group as a **complication** in response to a player failing an action check while using fail forward techniques. ("Oh no! Lady Sablehawk is heading our way!")

Third, they activate on a successful **activation check**.

Broadly speaking, there are two ways you can resolve activation checks, and you'll want to choose the one that you prefer or works best for the current scenario.

The method that's usually simpler is a **site activation check**. Make a single 1d6 roll. On a result of 1, pick one random action group and activate it.

The other alternative is a **group activation check**. Roll 1d12 for each passive action group. On a result of 1, that action group is activated. (This method obviously allows multiple groups to activate simultaneously, which can be much more complicated to run.) If you have a lot of action groups, it's usually easiest to roll for all of them at the same time.

In practice, you'll also want to periodically deactivate groups. In other words, an active group arrives in a new location and then stops moving. You can often do this based on the perceived goal of the action group being accomplished. For example, if a scientist activates and leaves their lab to go to their private quarters, then when they arrive at their quarters they'll probably deactivate.

If you'd prefer a procedural method, you can also make a **site deactivation check** or make a **group deactivation check** for each currently active group. This might include deactivating patrols (who could be taking a break) or even alert action groups (who might be giving up the search or simply bunkering down).

ALARM CASCADES

A phenomenon that can occur in a raid scenario is the **alarm cascade**: One action group becomes alert or aware of the PCs and they alert another action group (or set of action groups). Then those action groups alert another set and the situation cascades until every single action group in the scenario has been activated.

This isn't necessarily a bad thing. It's actually quite logical for security forces to respond like this. ("Sound the alarm! Intruders on Deck Six!") But it can be useful to keep a few things in mind.

First, it can be more effective if the PCs are given an opportunity to prevent it from happening (i.e., shooting the terrorist before he can use his walkie-talkie to alert the others).

Second, even if it's an alarm cascade, it usually doesn't happen all at once: It might involve shouting at a distance (in which case Perception-type checks would be called for). Or it might require movement. After movement, the action groups need to actually interact with each other to pass along information. All of those are likely raid actions, during which the PCs can also be taking actions.

Third, information can rapidly become obsolete in a raid scenario. (Patrol Team A thinks the PCs are on Level 4, but they've actually split up and are on both Levels 5 and 6 now.) If the PCs take an action that could throw the hounds off their scent, roll with it and let the bad guys spread out as they try to track the PCs down again.

✦ HOMEWORK ✦

EXECUTE A RAID

In order to run a raid, you need to prep a few straightforward tools:

- ⬡ Floorplan (entries, rooms, objective)
- ⬡ Defenses (passive obstacles and active forces)
- ⬡ Blueprint (depicting the results of a trivial survey, to which additional information can be added)

The process for doing this will be very similar to how you design your dungeons (see page 93):

- ⬡ Brainstorming
- ⬡ Mapping
- ⬡ Keying
- ⬡ Adversary Rosters and/or Random Encounters

As you're doing this work, you'll usually want to dial down the number of featured rooms compared to a dungeon. Remember that featured rooms are defined by having multiple elements for the PCs to interact with and explore. A raid scenario, however, isn't about exploration. It's still great to have cool discoveries and nifty details in your scenic rooms, but during a raid the PCs will be much more focused on tactically navigating the theater of operations. When you do have a featured room, it's quite likely that its primary focus will be on defensive elements (traps, alarms, etc.).

Raids are a fantastic tool to have in your tool kit because, as we've noted, any time the players say that they want something, you can respond by simply putting the thing they want inside the raid.

This also means that you may find it useful to whip out an unplanned raid in the middle of a session when the PCs unexpectedly go looking for something. This can be tricky, though, because even with a lot of experience a raid can be difficult to improvise. The biggest hurdle is usually the floorplan: It's of vital importance to a raid scenario, but very challenging to gin up on the fly.

RANDOM FLOORPLANS

So we'll start by rolling up a random floorplan, which can also be useful in any number of other situations. (PCs have a terrible propensity for deciding to duck into random buildings at the drop of a hat.)

STEP 1: ROLL CORNER DICE

This is a **table mat generator**, which means that the position of the dice you roll is part of the random generator. In this case, take a handful of d4s and roll them onto a sheet of paper. Most buildings are square, so you can just consider the edges of the paper to be the outer walls of the building.

The location where each die lands is a **corner** with a number of walls extending from that corner equal to the number rolled on the die. The more dice you roll, the more complicated the interior of the building will be (and complexity generally equates to size). For a simple cottage, a single d4 would be sufficient. Below you can see an example using 3d4.

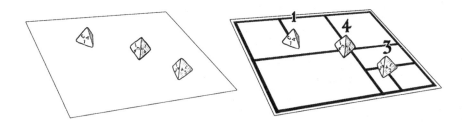

If a die rolls outside the "walls" of your building, you can ignore it, reroll it, or use it as an indicator of an irregularity in the otherwise square profile of your building. Whatever works.

OPTION: STAIR DICE

You can roll a six-sided die as a d3 (1 or 2 = 1, 3 or 4 = 2, 5 or 6 = 3) in addition to the corner dice to determine the number of floors in the building. If there are multiple floors, where the stair die lands can be treated as the location of the staircase if you'd like. If the raw number on the d6 is odd, then the building has a basement (included in the total number of floors). If it's even, then the building does not.

OTHER STAIR DICE

You can increase the maximum number of floors, of course, by increasing the size of the die used and interpreting the results in the same way. (Rolling a d8 as a d4, a d10 as a d5, a d12 as a d6, and so forth.)

Rolling 2d3-1 produces a nice bell curve for the number of floors and a building with multiple stairs. (You can limit the number of buildings with multiple stairs by including multiple stairs only if the dice roll doubles, and otherwise placing the stairs at whichever die rolled higher.)

Rolling 2d3-2 (minimum 1) produces the homes found in a mid-twentieth-century American Midwest suburb if you assume there's always a basement when there's more than one floor.

STEP 2: ADD DOORS & ENTRIES

After drawing your walls, you can remove the dice and add doors and windows wherever it seems appropriate. For a raid, keep in mind that you want at least two entries and that each entry should be either secured, hidden, or both.

For example:

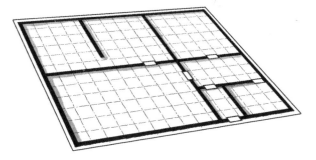

I placed the doors here while imagining a residence (with a short entry hall leading from the front door and a master suite in the upper left corner; you can fill in the other rooms easily). But we could also imagine generating the same walls when we need a small business and, therefore, making different decisions about the doors:

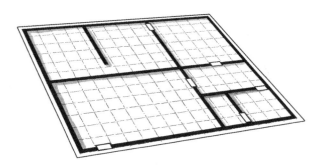

Here you can see how the same randomly generated walls can just as easily give us a shop front with a door leading to a private residence at the back of the building. The master suite remains in the upper left, but here we find a bedroom with a large closet in the lower right. (Or maybe your imagination might make that a kitchen with an attached larder.)

STEP 3: PLACE THE OBJECTIVE

With your floorplan in place, you can now place your objective (or objectives). I generally look for the locations that are farthest away from the entrances so that the PCs need to scheme their way past layers of security.

On the other hand, placing an objective directly behind a heavily secured entrance can also be an effective variant: If you can bypass the last trip wires, scale the wall of the château, disable the guards on the balcony without raising the alarm, and open the door (which is actually a mimic) . . . Congratulations! You've gained entrance to Duke Endo's study (and the vault hidden behind the painting of his dead wife and daughter) without having to worry about the rest of the château!

PRACTICING YOUR PREP

Of course, you don't have to wait until the middle of a session to use this random floorplan generator as the seed for a raid scenario. In addition to using it as a resource while prepping any scenario, it can also just be a fun exercise to roll up random floorplans and quickly start sketching in what the resulting raid scenario might look like.

⊹ THE HEIST ⊹

A heist scenario is very similar to a raid but adds a layer of complexity and opportunity in the form of **legwork**. Unlike in a raid, where the PCs can quickly figure out the floorplan and defensive measures through direct observation, in a heist discovering these elements requires additional effort and planning.

Running a heist, therefore, consists of five phases:

1. Identify the Score

2. Gather Information

3. Onsite Surveillance

4. Prep Work

5. The Operation

INTRODUCING HEISTS

The heist structure is very player-driven, but if the players haven't done proper heists before, they may assume—due to its similarity to location crawls—that they're "supposed" to engage the heist in the same way that they engage a typical dungeon (by storming the door and stabbing everything in sight).

So the first few times you run heist scenarios, just like raid scenarios, it may be a good idea to explicitly let the players know that they have opportunities they might not normally consider.

Once players get comfortable with heists being part of their tool kit, though, things can start to get really interesting: They'll start using heist techniques even with location-based scenarios you hadn't specifically thought of as being heists!

PHASE 1: IDENTIFY THE SCORE

The heist is initiated when the players identify the objective. This might be something that they want or it might be a job offered to them by a patron.

What they're trying to get, of course, is only half the equation. *Where* is equally important. It's possible they'll learn both halves at the same time ("I need you to steal the Frazelka Diamond from the dwarven vault"), but some extra effort may be required ("Where are we going to find an EMP device?!").

PHASE 2: GATHER INFORMATION

The next step is for the PCs to gather information about their target. This should include being able to gain access to some or all of the **blueprints** and **defenses** of the targeted location. It may also include an **event schedule**, which will often feature one or more opportunities for performing the heist (by either providing unique access to the target and/or providing cover for the operation).

Architectural and security details can potentially be found by the following means:

- ⊚ Reconnaissance (similar to a raid survey)
- ⊚ Accessing public records
- ⊚ Hacking the database of a security company
- ⊚ Questioning current and former staff

And so forth.

In prepping the heist scenario, you should give some thought to what form the Gather Information phase might take for the target, but you should always remain open to alternative thinking from the PCs. Remember that the expected outcome is for the PCs to succeed in getting this information. That doesn't mean it's guaranteed: The expected outcome of combat in an RPG is for the PCs to win, right? But that doesn't mean it always happens. The point is that you shouldn't get too enamored with keeping your cards close to your chest here: 90 percent of the fun in a heist scenario comes from seeing a problem and coming up with a solution for it. Only about 10 percent comes from being surprised by the unknown in the middle of the heist (and that will usually arise organically as the heist plays out).

PHASE 3: ONSITE SURVEILLANCE

After the initial gathering of information, most heist stories will give the protagonists an opportunity to conduct onsite surveillance *before the heist happens.* This surveillance allows them to gain information they missed or were unable to gather earlier, clarify the information they already have, and/or discover that some of their information was inaccurate or outdated (and now they have a whole new set of problems to solve!).

In some cases, this will be easy because the PCs will be targeting a public place (e.g., a museum or casino). They can just show up and scope the place out at their leisure.

Other targets, however, may require the PCs to take advantage of special circumstances (or create those circumstances for themselves). The event schedule they found in Phase 2 can provide opportunities not only for the heist itself, but also for surveillance. In other cases, they may need to interact with the target under false pretenses or use forged credentials in order to carry out their initial surveillance.

In prepping a heist, it can be useful to figure out explicitly what information can *only* be obtained through onsite surveillance. One really easy division is to make it easy to obtain floorplans of the target, but to only be able to ascertain limited information about the security measures in place without being onsite.

When running the **surveillance opportunity**, once again remember that the expected outcome is for the PCs to succeed in carrying out their surveillance. Barring complete and utter catastrophe, the worst outcome for the PCs should only be one of the following:

◎   They only get *some* of the information they need.

◎   They get misleading information.

◎   They do something sufficiently suspicious that security is heightened or changed.

◎   One (but not all) of the PCs gets IDed, making their participation in the heist more difficult or impossible.

Generally speaking, failure in a surveillance opportunity should not result in the entire heist failing unless the PCs deliberately take an action that would obviously cause that to happen.

PHASE 4: PREP WORK

Possibly running in tandem with onsite surveillance, the team will also need to make preparations for the job. This prep often takes the form of *altering* the information the PCs have received—creating new entrances, blinding security cameras, subverting guards, etc. It may also involve creating bespoke resources (or simply shopping for necessary supplies).

In modern or science fiction heists, prep work almost always includes figuring out some way to tap the security feeds so that the PCs can monitor the entire facility. If you're not comfortable improvising what they see, prep the appropriate adversary rosters and also **daily schedules** so that the PCs can figure out the "usual routine" at the site.

PHASE 5: THE OPERATION

Finally, the heist itself. The PCs try to carry out their plan.

To run the heist, you'll use the same procedure as a raid. One key difference, because a heist will usually feature a more detailed plan and preparation, is the inclusion of one or more **twists**: unexpected circumstances that the PCs didn't anticipate or that they missed in their research. These twists can either be **gotchas** (twists that you prepare ahead of time and that the PCs have no way of anticipating—"Oh crap! Mrs. Roberts came home early!") or **complications** arising from failed checks (either during their legwork or during the operation itself).

In my experience, you're generally going to want to rely more on complications rather than gotchas. First, skipping gotchas will save you from unnecessary prep work. Second, it's simply more interesting for the players to look back and understand where the complications are coming from.

(Which is not to say you should never use a gotcha: One really great gotcha can elevate a scenario to the next level.)

To break this down more explicitly, successfully executing a heist will usually involve a series of skill checks. A single failed check should not cause the entire plan to immediately fail. Instead, you'll use fail forward techniques to generate complications. These complications on failed skill checks are why you can get away with giving the PCs "perfect" information in Phase 2 and Phase 3: Among other things, you can use complications to introduce "oh no, he got a new safe" obstacles on the fly that effectively alter or reveal gaps in the information the PCs acquired.

Finally, to reiterate something of primary importance: Avoid twists of any type that automatically scuttle the entire job and/or negate all the PCs' planning. They not only suck but will also strongly discourage your players from pursuing heist strategies in the future. It's much more interesting to create a new problem and let the players figure out how to solve it.

IT'S HEISTS ALL THE WAY DOWN
Sometimes while making their plan, the PCs will discover that they need some special resource. How can they get it? Another heist, of course! This might be a full-fledged scenario in its own right, but often a micro-heist (or a simple raid) will suffice.

PREPPING THE HEIST
So what, exactly, should you prep for a heist scenario?

- Blueprints (both the GM's and those intended for PCs to discover)
- Defenses (most likely including adversary rosters, security cameras, traps, etc.)
- Event Schedule (including surveillance and heist opportunities)
- Gotchas (optional)

It's actually a very short list. Everything else flows from your procedure and active play.

HEIST OPTION: THE FLASHBACK

A common motif of heist stories in other mediums is the audience twist: Something goes horribly wrong for the team and it seems as if their whole plan is falling apart . . . but then it's revealed that the "problem" was actually part of the plan the whole time!

These kinds of audience-focused twists generally don't work in an RPG because the players aren't passive audience members. They aren't just watching the heist; they're actively participating in it and they know everything their characters know. And that's okay. RPGs offer different rewards than passive viewership does.

If you'd like to add something similar to these twists to your heist scenarios, however, you can do so with a **flashback** mechanic.

The basic concept is that, at some point during the heist, a player can choose to initiate a flashback—a scene that took place in the past and reveals a plan and/or preparation that the PC made. For example:

- They find themselves trapped in a room with only one exit. "It's a good thing I planted those C4 charges to blow open the wall for our exfiltration!"

- A guard suddenly comes around the corner and spots them! So the players frame a flashback where they bribe the guard and it turns out he's actually here to help them.

- They've upgraded their safe to a Diablo J34! "Perfect. I was actually a security consultant for Diablo during the design of the J34 and I know an exploit."

There are some RPGs—like *Blades in the Dark*, *Leverage*, and *Night's Black Agents*—that are specifically designed to incorporate flashbacks, but this mechanic can be incorporated into other RPGs as long as you follow a few core principles.

First, the use of a flashback must either have a **cost** or be **limited**. In D&D, for example, you might limit the group to a total number of flashbacks equal to their highest proficiency bonus. In addition, a proposed flashback must be somehow associated with a skill or tool the character is proficient with, their background, or a class ability.

Second, the flashback can **change context but not continuity**. A player can frame a scene to bribe the guard who just spotted them, but they can't frame a scene where they assassinated the guard the night before (because the guard has already been established as being in the scene). They can plant C4 to blow a hole in the wall, but they can't simply declare that they had an extra door built into the room (since the room was already described as not having another exit).

Third, the flashback must be **plausible**. Is it really possible that they could have brought in contractors to build an extra door in Rodríguez's mansion? As the GM, you may need to simply veto a proposed flashback scene if it's impossible that the PCs could have done it, but you'll often get better results asking the players to explain how the seemingly impossible could have actually been achieved.

Fourth, the flashback scene must be **resolved**. Just because the PCs want to plant C4 or bribe the guard doesn't mean they actually succeeded. A flashback scene should generally be kept short and sweet, but it should still be framed and played through as a scene. It will likely involve skill checks, and if those checks are failed they can (and should) create complications for the heist—the C4 doesn't go off, the guard took the PCs' money but is planning to betray them, security changed the code on the door locks, etc.

If you choose to implement flashbacks in your heist scenarios, you should also be aware that some players won't like them: The atemporal resolution may feel weird to them or, even more importantly, the ex post facto discovery of information that would've been known to their character and affected their decision-making can be game-breakingly alienating for some players. For some of these players, it may be useful to keep in mind that there are all kinds of stuff that happen in their characters' lives that aren't actually played out at the table, and flashbacks simply assert that some of these events were more significant than others. But for many players, the problem is more fundamental than that and it really can ruin the game for them, so make sure to discuss this technique with your players before (and after!) implementing it.

"PLANNING SUCKS!"

A lot of the fun of a heist scenario comes from creating and executing a plan. ("I love it when a plan comes together!") But for some groups, the actual planning *isn't* fun. In some cases, this is because they've had bad experiences with their plans immediately getting blown up (which is why we don't do that!); in other cases, planning just isn't something they enjoy or it can get bogged down in analysis paralysis.

For groups like this, you'll often be better off running more action-packed raids than heists. But you can also create heist-like (or heist-lite) scenarios by doing the following:

- ⚅ Streamlining the Gather Information phase by having each PC make a single skill check of their choice to learn information.

- ⚅ Setting a short timer (perhaps 10 or 15 minutes) to limit the time spent planning the operation.

- ⚅ Using flashbacks to simulate more elaborate planning during the heist.

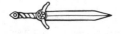

PART 4

URBAN ADVENTURES

THERE ARE A million stories in the city," as the saying goes. The city itself is rarely the adventure, but it is nevertheless a vital part of many campaigns. In campaigns that focus primarily on exploring dungeons or venturing forth into the wilderness, the city serves as the party's home base—the place of refuge and security where they can rest and resupply.

In urban campaigns, of course, the city itself plays host to dungeons, raids, heists, mysteries, and more. The PCs might be

- investigating strange conspiracies,
- a criminal crew securing territory or performing scores,
- engaging in faction-based intrigue, seeking political economic dominance,
- secret agents locked in a cold war drama,
- police detectives solving episodic mysteries, or
- noble scions treating the city and its people as their playthings.

The city is, therefore, not one thing but many, and here you'll find a suite of tools for bringing your city to vivid life, not only creating a vibrant backdrop for your campaign but also integrating adventures into the urban environment and creating others that are uniquely born from the city.

✦ THE CITY ✦

As we get ready to create our city, our assumption in this chapter is that the city is either the setting for the entire campaign or, at the very least, a place that the PCs are going to be exploring for a while. If that's not the case—if the PCs are just flying in for a single adventure—then the techniques in this chapter are overkill. You may still find some of them useful, but you can—and should!—get by with two or three paragraphs broadly describing the city, plus whatever material is immediately relevant to the adventure you're running.

But for a city that's either the focus of play or simply pervasive in your campaign, we'll be prepping a **city map** and **gazetteer** to detail the city, and then using a handful of simple techniques to immerse the players in the setting.

SMALL TOWNS

For the most part, this chapter is also going to be assuming that you're making a full-fledged city. For smaller communities— villages, remote space stations, etc.—you can use some of these same techniques, but you'll want to scale them down. (For example, a small village may only have one roadside inn or it might lack one entirely; you don't need to try to stuff additional options into a community if it's not right for the setting you're designing.)

THE CITY MAP

First, we need a map. If it's a city in the real world, track down a street map. Google Maps or Apple Maps will be invaluable resources, but I wouldn't recommend relying on them as your primary map. You really want something that lets you come to grips with the city in its totality, so buy a paper street map or do an image search for something comparable. The real world has done a whole bunch of development work for you here, so you'll want something that captures all of those little details (like individual street names).

If it's a city that you're creating, you'll obviously need to draw the map. (Or generate one. The tools for this are getting better all the time.) If you use the maps of real-world cities or those typically published for fantasy cities—like the sample map of Anyoc on the next page—as guides, however, you'll be overwhelmed with details: Every single street is shown! Many of them are named! Look at all those buildings!

But you don't need all those details to get started. In fact, I would argue that you definitely *shouldn't* try to include all those details right now. Instead, give yourself some space to develop and learn more about the city. If you try to lock yourself into specific streets and

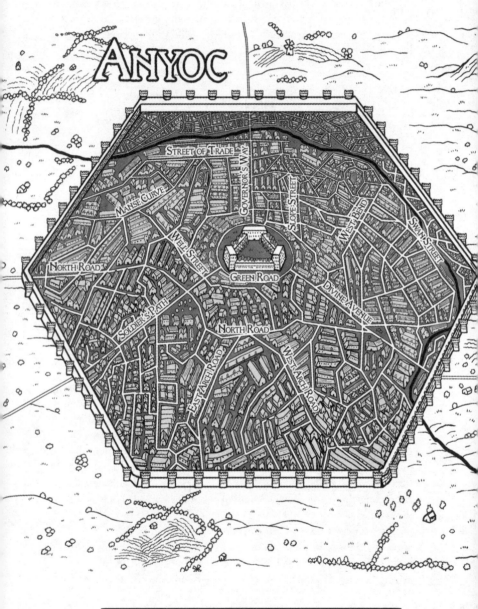

buildings right away, you're far more likely to end up with something generic while leaving yourself with no room to innovate.

Your map only needs two things right now:

◈ the city's districts, and

◈ the major connecting routes.

Let's start with the city's **districts**. We'll refer to these as "districts" for convenience, but they can go by any number of names:

◈ neighborhoods

◈ quarters

◈ zones

◈ precincts

◈ vicinages

◈ boroughs

◈ wards

◈ enclaves

◈ regios

◈ spires

◈ rayons

◈ fùjìn

And so forth. In fact, it's not unusual for cities in the real world to have multiple designations (districts divided into neighborhoods, zones split into quarters, etc.). The labels you choose for these can tell you a lot about the city's character.

As you're slicing your city into pieces, the sweet spot you're aiming for is somewhere between six and twelve districts. You want enough divisions to give the city texture—so that being in Ausbury feels different from being in Northbridge or the Groves—but not so many that either you or the players are overwhelmed.

If you're working from a real city, you can immediately run into problems here because they'll frequently have dozens and dozens of "neighborhoods" or "boroughs" or whatever. Manhattan, for example, has fifty-three different neighborhoods. That's almost certainly too many! It would be exhausting to develop them all for play, and unless the players were already familiar with Manhattan, that amount of detail would just turn into noise.

So what you'd want to do with Manhattan is take a step back and look at broader divisions. Perhaps something like this:

- Washington Heights
- Harlem
- Upper West Side
- Upper East Side
- Midtown
- West Side
- East Side
- Lower Manhattan

You might go with a slightly different division: Maybe Harlem should be split into East, West, and Central. Maybe Central Park should be added as its own district, or Chinatown is important enough in your campaign to be its own district alongside Lower Manhattan.

The flip side of this is that you can come back later and say, "We're spending a lot of time in the Upper East Side, so let's get more specific and talk about Lenox Hill, Carnegie Hill, and Yorktown." And you can obviously do the same thing with a city of your creation, diving into a district and revealing the local neighborhoods (or whatever the local label is).

With districts in place, you can now add the **major routes**. You basically need to answer two questions here:

- First, how do you enter and leave the city?
- Second, how do you travel to and from each district?

Basically, when the PCs are in Lower Manhattan and they say they want to go to the Upper East Side, you want to be able to say, "You take Lafayette Street to Midtown and then follow Park Avenue to the Upper East Side."

At a bare minimum, you'll likely end up with a loose network of major roads. You can stop there, but you'll often want to push on. A city's unique character can often be defined by its transportation. You can also emphasize the fantastic nature of your speculative settings with fabulist transportation routes: Zeppelin towers. Etheric railways. Fairy roads. Spaceports.

(Again, you don't need to develop a complete subway schedule: Where are the major tunnels? What's the biggest or most important station in each district?)

THE GAZETTEER

A gazetteer is a geographical index or directory, used in conjunction with a map to describe an area and its features. For a roleplaying game, it's an encyclopedic description of the setting that's separate from the notes for any specific scenario (although this distinction can get a little muddy in actual practice). That might include locations, characters, history, etc. For example:

SOUTH BRIDGE

South Bridge is a wide, fixed-arch bridge about 30 feet across that carries the traffic of the North Road as it crosses the Anya River southeast of the citadel.

South Bridge is located at the center of the University of Anyoc. As part of the university, an effort has been made to make the bridge particularly appealing to the eye. The bridge is constructed primarily of *anlos* and paved with *vaylos*—a beauty of pale blue and violet. Indeed, the sight of the South Bridge is famed along the North Road, and the structure stands as an emblem of pride for both the university and the city as a whole.

For a real-world example of the type of content found in a city gazetteer, take a peek at any travel guide. In fact, if you're prepping a real-world city for your campaign, a travel guide is a great resource, allowing you to spend as much or more time culling key content as you are creating new stuff.

To begin creating the gazetteer for your city, we'll start by keying each district.

First, describe the district's **general character**. This can be as simple as a couple of sentences, but you can dive into more detail like so:

◎ What types of businesses are found there?

◎ What's the architecture?

◎ What ethnicities or other population types live there?

◎ What's the history of the district?

Once you've sketched in the broad strokes of the district, make a list of specific **landmarks** and briefly describe them. You might be able to get away with just one, but you'll probably want to have at least three per district by the end of your initial prep. (You'll likely be adding more later, though, so it's okay to leave a few gaps for now.)

The term *landmark* may trap you into thinking about statues or big, famous buildings. Those definitely count, but for our purposes a landmark is really any location in the district that could be casually noticed by someone traveling through it. So if you put the Lion's Purr tavern in a district, you can put it on the landmarks list.

If your city becomes detailed enough, you may want to eventually break out a separate list of "major landmarks" for each district for the sake of utility, but even this list will likely be (and arguably should be) esoteric, focusing at least as much on the sites that have become relevant to you, your players, and the campaign as it does on the big stuff that would make a generic tourist's guide.

With the raw foundations of your districts in place, you'll bring the city fully online by prepping a list of **services**.

Exactly which services you'll want to list is going to be very dependent on the campaign you're prepping. If the PCs are wandering adventurers coming to the city for the first time, for example, you'll likely want to have a list of inns. If the PCs live in the city, on the other hand, maybe that's not so important.

Some common service categories, however, include the following:

- Hotels/inns
- Bars/taverns
- Shopping
- Banking
- Hospitals/healing
- Legal services
- Gambling
- Entertainment
- Specialists (locksmiths, magi, assassins, sages, bodyguards, etc.)

Before you get too lost in the weeds here, though, it's important to remember that you're not trying to list every single example of each service in the city. In many cases, you probably can't. Take Galveston, Texas, for example. This modest town with a population of 50,000 has dozens of hotels and more than a hundred bars. Even if you wanted to prep all those options, would it really be useful at the table? What *is* useful at the table is having enough options that the players can make a meaningful choice. A rule of thumb might be to have three options for each service. With inns, for example, I'll often prep a high-class, middle-class, and low-class option. For entertainment, I might offer a theater, a dance hall, and a gladiatorial arena. The goal, of course, is for each option to be clearly distinct from the others in a way that is (or could be) relevant to the PCs.

You may have already placed some of these services as you were designing landmarks for your district. As you add more services to fill in the gaps, place them in specific districts and (unless they're some sort of hidden, underground operation) add them to your landmark lists, too.

ADVENTURE SITES

It's very likely that at some point you'll be adding an adventure location to your city: the entrance to a forgotten dungeon. A bank vault to rob. A haunted mansion.

Some adventure sites might be a landmark. ("The abandoned house up on the hill? That's the Old Tannerly manor. No one lives there now. Not since the Incident.") Often, though, the PCs will only learn about these locations as the result of a scenario hook.

You should certainly know where on the map these adventure sites are located, but should they be added to your gazetteer? Personally, I don't want my references for running the city getting choked up with a lot of ephemeral stuff (Ruby's House, Bob's Wheelchair Factory, A Random Warehouse). So, for me, it's fine if a lot of adventure sites are only detailed in my notes for a specific adventure.

In other cases, though, a location developed for an adventure is important or becomes so: Maybe I create the Terwilliger Vaults, a major banking service in the city that I just didn't know existed previously. Or the PCs become close friends with Ruby. Or they get a job at Bob's Wheelchair Factory. Or they buy the warehouse.

Ultimately, there's no hard-and-fast rule: It's what works for you.

THE LOCATION KEY

You can key locations to your city map with numbers the same way you do rooms in a dungeon, although you may want to assign letters to different districts to create an alphanumeric system that will keep locations easily grouped in your notes. (For example, locations in the Kadbury neighborhood could be K1, K2, etc.)

This key may include landmarks, adventure sites, services, and other locations (like an important NPC's house). Even with everything grouped together like this into a single key for easy use, you'll still want to maintain separate index lists for landmarks (by district) and services (by type of service), as you'll find these references essential while running the city.

SCENIC ENCOUNTERS

A key thing that makes the urban environment feel distinct from other adventure locales is the constant activity: The streets and businesses are bustling with activity, and you want the players to feel like there's stuff happening all the time and just out of sight. We achieve this at the table through the use of **scenic encounters**.

Scenic encounters are similar to the random encounters we use in dungeons (and we'll talk about how they get triggered in a moment), but they don't involve hostile denizens trying to stab the PCs with sharp, pointy things. (Well, not usually . . .) Instead, they provide little slices of life from the city streets:

- An out-of-town messenger has become lost. They stop the PCs to ask for directions.
- 1d6 elves are standing in the middle of the street, arguing loudly with a half-orc.
- A woman is selling broadsheets.
- 2d6 kids are playing stickball in an alley.

- ⬡ An out-of-control wagon is barreling down the street. (The driver has suffered a heart attack.)
- ⬡ A **bandit** attempts to pick a random PC's pocket. If the pickpocket is caught in the act, 1d4 + 2 bandits and a **bandit captain** emerge from a nearby alley.

As you can see, scenic encounters provide a broad range of interactions. It's not unusual for the PCs to simply walk on by, the encounter having served as just a bit of local color to paint the scene.

You can, of course, design these to be either bespoke encounters or procedural ones. Either way, there are four broad approaches to prepping scenic encounters.

BASIC CITY ENCOUNTERS

Prep a single table of scenic encounters for the entire city and use them regardless of where the PCs are in the city. You'll probably want about 20 encounters to get started, and you can also spice things up by using improvisation to "color" an encounter to the current situation. ("Ruffians" at the Docks might be a group of drunken sailors, while the same encounter in the Merchant District might be gangsters shaking down a local businesswoman for protection money.)

DISTRICT ENCOUNTERS

Prep a separate set of encounters and encounter table for each district, customizing the encounters to reflect that district's demography and unique flavor. Each district encounter list will be shorter than a citywide list (perhaps only six or eight to get started), but obviously prepping a separate list for every district will require more prep.

HYBRID ENCOUNTERS

To split the difference between flavor and prep load, you could include "District Encounter" on your citywide encounter table (likely filling multiple slots). This will reduce the number of such encounters you need to prep, and you'll need to prep only a couple of unique encounters for each district that can be used when the District Encounter result is rolled.

SHARED DISTRICT ENCOUNTERS

A more complicated method of reducing (or, perhaps, maximizing the utility of) prep is to use separate district encounter tables, but have certain "shared" encounters that appear on multiple lists. (For example, perhaps Ruffians can appear as random encounters in the Docks, Ironleaf, and the Merchant District, but not in the Gilded Ward.)

LIFE IN THE CITY

With your city sufficiently detailed, it's time to bring it to the table. If at all possible, I recommend that this include **showing the players the city map.** (This might involve prepping a player version of the map.)

The key to running the city during play is that virtually all actions in the city boil down to either **finding information** or **going to a location** (and doing something there). But it turns out that when the PCs are looking for information, that *also* almost always involves going to a location (a library, a sage's tower, etc.). Even if the players aren't certain where they can find the information and are just canvassing the city looking for answers, ultimately you'll need to figure out where they finally find that information (and that will, of course, be a location). Plus, the information that the PCs are looking for will often be, either directly or indirectly, a location, too—a service they need, a resource, the place where their enemy is hiding out, etc.

So it turns out that almost everything the PCs do "in the city" (as opposed to in a specific location) can be broadly summarized as going to a location.

Once the PCs are heading to a location, look at your notes for the district they're heading to. (This may be the same district they're currently in.) Then:

1. Name the **district** and point to it on the map. ("You head over to the Docks.")

2. Mention a **landmark**—a major street they travel down, a building they pass, an art installation, etc. ("Passing down Fishwives' Lane, the smell of gutted tuna thick in the air . . .")

3. Roll 1d6 for a **scenic encounter check**. On a roll of 1, generate a scenic encounter for the district they're heading to. (". . . you see a dragonborn fishmonger offering to sell freshly harvested oyster pearls. He says one of them is a rare rainbow pearl, a sign of good luck.")

4. Describe the **location** they arrive at. ("Dominic's hovel is tucked into a narrow side street just past the red docks. There's smoke coming out of the crooked chimney, so somebody must be home.")

And that's all it takes.

The districts and landmarks weave together the geographical fabric of the city. The encounters provide a low level of activity not directly connected to the PCs or what they're immediately engaged with, creating the sensation that the city is in constant motion.

PLACING SCENIC ENCOUNTERS

A scenic encounter can occur anywhere en route to the PCs' destination. That can be any random street (or subway tunnel or teleportation hub), but consider placing it at either the district's landmark or their destination. It's a convenient way of adding context to procedurally generated content, and it can also be a great way of adding unexpected complications to whatever location the PCs are heading to.

Of course, this procedure doesn't need to be a straitjacket. Maybe you mention two or three landmarks instead of just one (perhaps one per district they pass through?). Maybe you complicate things by checking for encounters in each district the PCs pass through. Or, conversely, once you've established the life of the city as a pervasive presence at the table, you may find that effective pacing demands fast-forwarding past an encounter and cutting straight to the action.

I recommend following this procedure rigorously for a couple or three sessions to really get a feel for it and make sure you've internalized the rhythms of the city, but then do what feels right, knowing that you can always return to this procedure as a safe and effective foundation.

TIME MANAGEMENT

How long does it take to do stuff in the city? This question becomes particularly important if the PCs are facing time pressure or if they've split up (see Splitting the Party on page 525).

I usually think in terms of

◎   the hour,

◎   the watch (4 hours), or

◎   the half day (morning/afternoon).

Which mental construct I find most useful depends on how "meaty" the PCs' planned actions are. If someone is planning to gather information down at the Docks, I might think to myself, "That'll take about half a day." And so the active question becomes, "What is everyone else doing during that half day?" (Or, alternatively, "What are the bad guys doing with that time?")

Even in the absence of other factors, keeping the passage of time concrete—even if it's only in the broadest strokes—will give the actions of the PCs more weight and their choices more meaning. It also prevents each individual day from becoming overburdened with action, which will help make each day (and what was done during that day) more memorable.

INTRODUCING THE CITY

Now that we've established our basic procedure, let's take a closer look at our first session: How do we introduce a new city to the players?

If one or more of the PCs live in the city or are otherwise familiar with it, particularly if it's going to be the focal setting for the entire campaign, I will prep a short **player's briefing packet** to orient them. These are described in more detail as part of the Creating Your Campaign extra credit (see page 439), but will include:

◎ the map,

◎ two or three sentences describing each district, and

◎ maybe one page of common services (list of taverns, list of weaponsmiths, etc.).

You may note that this material conveniently mirrors the material you've prepped for yourself. You can often just strip out your encounter tables, make a couple of other minor changes, and be good to go.

Try to give the player their briefing packet ahead of time if possible; that way they can familiarize themselves with it. If only one (or some) of the PCs are from the city, the great thing is that they can now introduce the city to the other players in character!

But what about the **adventurer at the gate** scenario, where the PCs are coming to the city for the first time?

Generally, I will still give them the map. Even if the PCs technically wouldn't have one, it's just too useful as an easy point of common reference at the table. I find it very effective to

◎ describe the countryside around the city,

◎ describe the city as they approach it,

◎ roleplay a short encounter at the gate (with guards, other travelers, or whatever else makes sense), and

◎ describe their first sight of the city as they step through the gate and I hand the map to them.

If the city isn't walled or they're arriving via an airship or it's an underwater city and they're arriving on the back of a whale, you'll obviously need to adjust the specifics here!

POSTER MAPS

If you've got a city map that's detailed enough or just looks slick enough to support it, I heartily recommend printing out a poster-sized version and hanging it on the wall of your playing space. I'll use a laser pointer to indicate locations from my seat during play.

At this point, as they're standing just inside the city gate (or the local equivalent of this liminal space), **focus on the players' goals**, but use those goals as a **vector for the player briefing**.

For example, if the players say that they're going to spend a day or two getting to know the city, that's super simple: You can just give them the player briefing.

But maybe they say something like, "Let's find an inn."

If it's a common service, present them with the multiple options for that service you prepped earlier. (You can frame this as what a friendly local or their smartphone tells them, or follow their lead if they propose some other means for finding whatever they're looking for.) Specifically call out the different districts these services are in. If they went looking for a weapons shop, for example, you might say, "There's an elven bowyer in Dovecote or dwarven crafters in Kadbury." Now you're not just saying, "These districts exist." You're inviting the players to make a choice *based on these districts*. That's significant. The districts are now an *active* part of the players' thinking about the setting. The more they do that, the more the city will come alive in their imaginations.

At this point, the PCs are going to pick a location to go to—either a common service they've selected or whatever specific location brought them to the city in the first place (e.g., the tower of the High Mage Ghulak). This is simple: Just use the urban procedure we detailed above . . . but with one important addition!

For the district of the location they choose, include the description of the district from the player briefing. You can probably work these two or three sentences into the description of their journey to the inn or tower or whatever.

As the players work their way through their shopping list (or whatever brought them to the city), you'll be organically building up their understanding of the city over time. The scenic encounters, landmarks, and locations found in the scenarios you're running will gradually draw them further into the setting, resulting in them setting goals that are increasingly specific: "Let's find the leader of the Red Bandit pickpockets who tried to rob us" or "That abandoned lighthouse looks cool, let's go check it out!"

In play, the scenario might look something like this:

◎ The PCs enter a new town and go looking for an inn.

◎ "People milling around the gate suggest three choices: The Lion's Purr in Midtown, the Wandering Sword in the Merchant District, or the Wallowed Pig in the Penury Ward."

◎ The players select the Wandering Sword.

◎ "You head south into the Merchant District. Most of the buildings here are two stories high—small businesses with apartments for the owners above them. You notice that there's an abandoned lighthouse standing in the middle of the district . . . which is a weird place for a lighthouse to be. You find the Wandering Sword on Southward Street."

◎ At this point you can describe the Wandering Sword and have a short scene there while the PCs arrange for their rooms. They decide to check out that lighthouse.

◎ On the way to the lighthouse, you describe them passing through the Market Square (another landmark in the Merchant District). As they leave the market, they have a random encounter with Red Bandits who attempt to waylay them.

◎ After dispatching the Red Bandits, they proceed to the light-house (which is a small adventure site you've prepped).

◎ When they return to their rooms at the Wandering Sword, the encounter check is negative, so you simply describe them passing through the Market Square again (it's night now, so the stalls are deserted).

◎ Discussing their plans for the next day, the PCs decide to find the Red Bandits' gang house. So the next morning you call for a Gather Information check and, when they succeed, say, "You ask around and discover it's an open secret that the Red Bandits control a dilapidated apartment building in Penury Ward, which is officially known as Laketon but has been riddled with poverty for generations." (You've snuck in a little extra district briefing there.)

◎ The PCs head for the apartment building.

(continued)

⬡ "You head down Tabernacle Way [landmark] into Penury Ward. Passing the Church of the Bloody Saint [landmark], you're approached by several of the beggars who camp in the church's yard." The beggars here are a random encounter and inspired you to think that the Church of the Bloody Saint would be a good landmark to use here. After a short roleplaying scene with the beggars (during which you might seed other rumors or information about the city), the PCs continue to the apartment building.

And so forth.

Once the players are familiar with a district, of course, you can obviously stop briefing them on the district. At this point, the newcomers have acclimated to the city and you simplify back into the standard urban procedure.

BACKGROUND EVENTS

Another great way to add life to a city is through the use of **background events**. *These are described in more detail in the Extra Credit section, on page 456.*

✦ DOWNTIME ✦

What happens to the heroes between one adventure and the next?

We refer to this as **downtime**, and a city often lies at the heart of it: If the PCs are venturing forth to loot strange dungeons and save the world, they return home to the city for rest and respite before the next call to adventure sounds. If the campaign is based in the city, then the long-term agendas of the PCs will obviously become embroiled with urban affairs.

It's possible to run downtime at the same pace we use for adventures; it's also possible that the PCs will be kept so busy with thrilling action that they never get a break. But often there are projects and goals that need to be resolved at a different scale—stuff that takes weeks or months rather than hours or days. To accommodate this, we use a special downtime structure.

PROGRESS CLOCKS

To handle downtime actions effectively, we'll first need an advanced technique for making rulings called a **progress clock**.

Progress clocks are a simple, visual way of tracking how close a particular outcome is to happening. There are a lot of different ways that you can use a progress clock, but for right now we'll focus on two: failure clocks and project clocks.

Set up a **failure clock** when the PCs begin an extended or multi-step endeavor (e.g., sneaking into a mansion, tracking a band of orcs, investigating a cult's activities in Dweredell).

1. Create a progress clock by drawing a circle and dividing it into four, six, eight, or ten parts. More parts mean the task will take longer to accomplish.

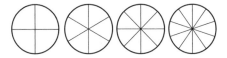

2. Set a significant consequence or overall fail condition. (For example, security at the mansion realizes there are intruders and the alarm is raised; the PCs lose the trail of the orcs and can no longer follow them; or the cultists succeed in summoning a demon who begins rampaging through the Great Market.)

3. Whenever the PCs fail a relevant check, fill in one section of the progress clock.

4. When the progress clock is filled, trigger the consequence or fail condition.

A failure clock can be used for any type of check, but can work well as the default consequence of failing forward on a check, as described on page 280: If you can't think of any other consequence for the failed check, just fill in the next section of the progress clock and explain the connection.

A **project clock** is similar, but inverted:

1. Create a progress clock.

2. Define what the successful outcome of the project is.

3. Whenever the PCs succeed on a relevant check, fill in one section of the progress clock.

4. When the progress clock is filled, the project has been successfully completed.

Multiple characters can collaborate on a project, of course, with each separate success being tracked on the same clock.

Failed checks while pursuing a project should have meaningful consequences. (That might include filling in sections of an opposed failure clock, which could result in the project's ultimate failure if completed.)

EXCEPTIONAL SUCCESSES

If a check on a project clock is exceptionally successful, you may fill in more than one section of the progress clock. For example, in D&D, for every 5 points by which the check result exceeds the DC of the check, fill in an additional section.

Progress clocks should always **follow the fiction**, by which I mean that if something in the game world should affect the progress of the clock, then it *does*, even if a check isn't involved. This can include the use of spells, special resources, or the like, and it can work both ways, by either adding or removing sections of the clock.

For example, Granger flubs his lock-picking check while the group is trying to infiltrate the Sael family estate. The GM rules that Granger has gotten the door open, but he's damaged the lock in the process, and so the GM fills in one section of the Alert the Guards failure clock. But then Katalina uses her *mending* cantrip to repair the damage to the lock, and so the GM erases that section. As they slip through the door, the sorcerer Gorin casts *invisibility* on the group, and the GM decides that could also reasonably decrease the clock.

In other situations, this might even mean bypassing the clock completely. For example, a PC has been working to build a longboat, but then they get access to a *wish* spell and use it to get the longboat they've always wanted. The clock is, obviously, no longer relevant.

At the table, progress clocks can exist in one of three states:

⊚ **Open Clock:** When you create the clock or fill in a section, you show it to the players. This is often the easiest method, making it crystal clear how much progress they've made or what the consequences of a failed check are with no fuss.

⊚ **Hidden Progress:** When you create the clock, you either directly or indirectly tell the players that it exists. (For example, when they're sneaking into a mansion you can clearly state that there's a risk the security team will detect them.) But then the clock itself remains hidden. The players don't know how large the clock is or exactly what the progress on the clock is. Because the clock's progress is hidden from them, however, you'll need to clearly communicate progress and the consequences of failure to them. (For example, describing to Granger how he damaged the lock while opening the door. In the case of a failure clock, such explanations will likely also inform exactly how the failure plays out—in this case, the alarm possibly sounding because someone noticed the signs of tampering on the lock.)

⊚ **Secret Clock:** With a secret clock, you create the clock without telling the players it exists and it serves strictly as a tool for you to keep track of things. As with a hidden progress clock, of course, it's your responsibility to continue clearly communicating the consequences of the clock's progression to the players in your description of the game world.

FINDING DOWNTIME

During each period of downtime, each PC will get to take one down-time action, but you first have to define how long each period of down-time is in the campaign world: A week? A month? A season? A year?

You want this to be consistent across the entire campaign, but which duration is the right one for your current campaign will depend on the natural pace of that campaign. Are the PCs wrapped up in a constant flurry of conspiracy and counter-conspiracy? Then you'll probably want a very short duration, like a week. Are they thieves who carefully research and prepare for every job? Then measuring down-times in months or seasons may be perfect. Are they monster hunters who only have to go forth from their village when the summer thaws free the eldritch horrors from the ancient glaciers? Then a yearlong downtime would seem to sync flawlessly with their adventures.

The other trick, in my experience, is making sure that the transi-tion to downtime actually happens. Adventures are exciting! It can be very easy to go rushing from one adventure headlong into another, particularly as a campaign develops over time; the stakes start to rise, and one adventure leads directly to the next. (You might even have multiple adventures happening at the same time!)

DOWNTIME IN THE BACKGROUND

As a variant, instead of taking a break from adventuring to perform downtime actions, you can instead assume that the downtime is happening in the background. This works partic-ularly well in urban campaigns, where you can just assume that downtime activities are happening in the evenings or during unexamined moments of play.

You probably won't get a lot of downtime this way—since adventures tend to be fast and furious compared to lengthy downtime projects—and you won't have the same focus on downtime, but it's an option if you really want to include downtime-type aspects of play even when the rest of the cam-paign isn't well structured for it.

Having meaningful downtime, however, is great for allowing both characters and the campaign world to develop at a more realistic pace and in greater depth. So, to make sure it happens, there are a couple broad approaches.

First, you can **mandate it**. This generally takes the form of limiting the number of adventures per downtime period, For example, "Characters go on one adventure per year," and then you resolve either yearlong or perhaps season-long downtimes between each adventure.

This approach generally requires a really clear distinction between one adventure and the next. If the PCs are exploring a megadungeon, for example, or switching back and forth between two different dungeons, it can be hard to figure out where one adventure ends and the next begins. (And these lines tend to only get blurrier with other scenario types.)

You'll also need to make sure the adventures remain self-contained. You can't wrap up an adventure by saying, "Oh no! The Onyx Prince has kidnapped the princess!" and then tell the players they have a mandated one-year waiting period before they can go in pursuit. Even if it's mandated at the table, the downtime still has to feel natural and justified in the game world.

The other option is to **motivate it**. Here the players consciously choose when to begin downtime because it's the only way to gain some form of reward or advantage. Two common variants for D&D are:

- **Extended Long Rests:** You can only gain the benefits of a long rest by taking a weeklong downtime.

- **Training:** Even if they've gained the experience points required, a PC can't level up unless they spend one week/one month/ one season/one year training. (To be clear, the training is not the character's downtime action: The training period is defining the downtime period, providing the opportunity to perform a downtime action.)

Alternatively, you could, for example, set the training period to a year, but then resolve monthlong downtime actions. (Or set the extended long rest to a month, but resolve weeklong downtime actions.) In this way, each time downtime is motivated, the PCs will have the opportunity to take several downtime actions in a row.

In some cases, you'll just have players and/or PCs who are particularly interested in what downtime can provide. In those cases you won't need to mandate it or motivate it: The players will take care of it for you!

DOWNTIME PROJECTS

Downtime is about achieving long-term projects. PCs will choose the projects they want to pursue and the players will work with you to define those projects. Successfully completing a project will usually require multiple downtimes to achieve, although this can be considerably sped up if multiple PCs collaborate on the same project.

STEP 1: DEFINE THE PROJECT

Downtime projects are intentionally flexible. You should be able to use them to accommodate any long-term goal or ambition the PCs might have. Examples include:

- Find a patron
- Recruit a contact
- Gain a title
- Craft a magic item
- Bring in the harvest
- Build a robot
- Learn a language
- Brew mead
- Spread rumors
- Research an original spell
- Decode an ancient language
- Convert the godless
- Build or improve a stronghold
- Run a business
- Compete in a tournament
- Woo the marquess
- Perfect a religious ritual
- Raise a child
- Create a work of art

The player should start by telling the GM what they want to accomplish. This outcome should be specific, and the GM and player should both make sure they have a clear (and mutual) understanding of what completing the project will mean. If the project feels too large or ambitious, then the GM should work with the player to split it up into multiple projects. Otherwise, the GM will proceed with designing the scope of the project.

MULTIPLE PROJECTS

There's rarely any reason a PC can't have multiple unfinished projects floating around. They'll just need to choose which project they want to work on with each one of their downtime actions.

STEP 2: SETTING THE CLOCK

Some projects are resolved with a single downtime action and a successful check, but in most cases you'll want to set up a project progress clock. Based on the difficulty and scope of the project, the GM should set the number of clock segments and the default DC for the project.

To set the **number of clock segments**, you should primarily focus on how long you think the project should take to complete. Then simply divide that by the duration of your downtime periods to get a rough estimate for the number of segments the clock should have. (Remember that you're clocking a best-case scenario. The worst-case scenario is what happens if the PCs keep missing their checks.)

If the resulting clock has more than eight sections, then you should probably break the project down into multiple steps (each of which is its own project with its own clock).

The **default DC** for the project can be determined the way you normally determine DCs. Note that this is explicitly a *default* difficulty, and the GM can exercise their discretion to vary it depending on skills, resources, or other variables during each downtime action.

STEP 3: RISKS & PREREQUISITES

Many downtime projects will be straightforward, but others will be complicated with risks and prerequisites.

A **prerequisite** is either:

◎ A **requirement** before the project can be attempted. This might be a different task or project that must be completed first, or a resource (usually rare, expensive, or otherwise unusual). It's not unusual for these requirements to be adventure-based (e.g., you must do an acclaimed deed before you can attempt to earn a knighthood or you must retrieve ruby berries from the Fungal Forest before you can make that potion), providing a great hook for scenarios and wedding the PCs' downtime activities to the rest of play (and vice versa).

◎ A **cost** that must be paid each time a downtime action is taken in an effort to resolve the project. This might, again, be some rare resource that gets expended, or it can be as simple as paying a specific gold-piece value for supplies. (If the project is crafting an object with a known value, divide half its market price by the number of clock segments to determine the cost.)

A **risk**, on the other hand, is a predetermined complication or consequence for failure—either failure of the project as a whole (which can be determined by setting up an opposing failure clock) or of each individual check. This could include options like:

◎ An additional cost or the destruction of a vital resource
◎ Alerting enemy agents of your activity
◎ Gaining the enmity of an NPC or faction
◎ A flaw that debilitates the intended outcome of the project (e.g., you risk creating a robot that doesn't obey your commands)

Risk might also include active opposition from another NPC or faction, whose checks will be used to fill the opposing failure clock.

EXPERIENCE FOR PROJECTS

Completing a project can be its own reward, but you might also consider assigning an XP reward to the PC (or PCs) when they successfully finish their project.

STEP 4: RESOLVE THE DOWNTIME ACTION

When a PC chooses to spend their downtime action on a project, make an appropriate skill check—a tools check for crafting an item; a Charisma (Persuasion) check for recruiting a contact; an Intelligence (Investigation) check to decode a cipher; etc.—and resolve the project clock accordingly.

Remember that a failed check should have consequences or create complications, even if the project doesn't have a predetermined risk. (Use an opposed failure clock if no better option presents itself.)

Although you aren't playing out every moment of the downtime period, it's still a good idea to **roleplay downtime**. This will usually take the form of a short, representative scene. If a PC is wooing a marquess, for example, you might roleplay a short scene of them walking through her gardens on a moonlit night.

Ask the players to describe their efforts before rolling the dice, and if multiple PCs are all working on the same project, you might present that as a little montage.

OTHER DOWNTIMES

Many RPGs, like D&D, Blades in the Dark, *and* Ars Magica, *feature some form of downtime mechanic. When these mechanics already exist, you may be able to use them in addition to, as part of, or instead of the structure for downtime given here.*

⊹ FACTION DOWNTIME ⊹

In an urban campaign, the PCs aren't the only ones pursuing their agendas during downtime. While they're resolving their downtime projects, you'll be taking actions with your factions.

CREATING FACTIONS

A **faction** refers to any group or organization—whether formal or informal—that has its own agenda, beliefs, and goals. They can include:

- Government agencies
- Religious orders (or cults)
- Orders of knighthood
- Military factions (including mercenaries)
- Assassins' and thieves' guilds
- Criminal gangs and syndicates
- Artisan guilds
- Arcane sisterhoods
- Adventuring guilds
- Cabals and secret societies
- Consortiums, corporations, and cartels
- Covens
- Rebel groups
- Schools and universities
- Racial enclaves
- Sodalities, cadres, and coteries

A typical city will have dozens or, more likely, hundreds of factions. In your campaign, however, you're likely only going to be focused on somewhere between four and eight of them at a time, and so that's how many you're going to prep to get started.

For each faction, prep:

- **Short Description:** One or two paragraphs ought to be enough to get you started.

- **Tier:** You want to be able to make action checks for the faction, so you'll need to give them some form of default rating in whatever RPG you're using. For D&D, you'll rank them by **tier** and list the faction's **proficiencies**. If a faction is opposing another faction or character of a lower tier, they gain advantage on their checks. If they're opposing a faction or character of a higher tier, they suffer disadvantage.

- **Leader:** The person (or perhaps small council of people) who are in charge of the faction. You don't need to do a full write-up of these NPCs yet—a couple of sentences should suffice.

- **Agents:** These are the members of the faction the PCs are most likely to interact with or run afoul of. This is not a comprehensive list of every single person who works for the faction, but you want two or three different operatives or small action groups to play with.

- **Allies & Enemies:** Pick at least one other faction that this faction is allied with and at least one other faction to be this faction's enemy. (These do not necessarily need to be from the list of factions that you're currently focused on and, therefore, prepping. If that's the case, you can just leave them as a name on the page for now.)

- **Faction Clock:** Each faction should have at least one (and almost never more than three) faction clocks representing their current agenda.

D&D FACTION TIER TABLE

FACTION TIER	PROFICIENCY BONUS
Tier 1	+4
Tier 2	+6
Tier 3	+8
Tier 4	+10

As your campaign continues, other factions will likely become important—they'll gain your focus and/or the focus of the PCs. That's great! You can flesh them out with full write-ups (and continue expanding them) as needed. You'll also want to pay attention to which factions are becoming less important and allow them to fade into the background, generally aiming to keep the factions you're actively tracking and running in that sweet spot between four and eight. If a faction that's lost focus suddenly becomes important again, you can always bring them back into the spotlight!

A MIX OF FACTIONS

Particularly as you're prepping your first batch of factions, it's a good idea to make sure that you've got several different types of factions: If all of the factions are government agencies, for example, your city will feel very one-dimensional.

On the other hand, it's also a good rule of thumb to include more than one faction in each sphere of influence to create rivalries: Two criminal gangs can fight each other for territory. Three religious orders can feud over doctrine. And so forth. Not every faction needs a direct rival, but including at least a few will certainly liven things up.

FACTION CLOCKS

Creating a faction clock works just like any other progress clock, with you choosing four, six, or eight segments depending on the complexity of the project. A faction's clock is a quick, easy, and effective way of tracking what their current agenda is and what their current activities are.

The goal of the clock can be almost anything, but examples could include:

- Destroy a rival faction
- Increase drug production
- Secure territory
- Acquire an ancient artifact
- Retrieve valuable intel
- Conduct a dark ritual
- Raid a rival gang's base

- Assassinate a high-profile target
- Establish a homeless shelter
- Reclaim artifacts stolen from their homeland
- Establish a new business
- Forge an alliance with another faction

Large factions are likely doing lots and lots of stuff all at the same time, so you once again have to choose your focus. The faction clock you select might be literally the most important thing the faction is doing right now, or it might just be the thing most likely to affect the PCs or the thing the PCs care most about.

RESOLVING FACTION CLOCKS

During each downtime period, roll 1d6 for each active faction clock. On a roll of 1, fill in one segment on the clock. Once all segments have been filled, the faction has achieved their goal. You should determine the fallout from that and then immediately create a new faction clock for the faction: What's their next goal?

ALTERNATIVE RESOLUTION

For a more complicated resolution, you can assign each faction clock a DC and make an appropriate skill check using the faction's Tier proficiency. This will likely cause faction clocks to resolve faster, and failed checks should also create complications for the faction, resulting in a far more hectic pace.

For a blended approach, roll 1d4 for each faction clock, resolving a skill check only on a result of 1.

AFFECTING A FACTION CLOCK

PCs may affect a faction clock, either assisting (by adding segments) or opposing (by removing segments). This may be the result of an adventure (the Morthbrood were trying to claim a powerful artifact, but the PCs destroyed it) or a PC may choose to use their downtime action to similar effect.

In some cases, it may also make sense for other factions to similarly assist or oppose another faction's clock instead of their own. (Although this may also be represented by setting up an opposing clock.)

INTERSECTING THE PCS

Each time a segment on a faction clock is filled in (or removed), that represents the faction making tangible progress (or suffering a significant setback) in achieving their goal: They've acquired an asset, destroyed an obstacle, gained an ally, achieved a breakthrough, and so forth.

You need to make that concrete—what, exactly, happened?—and then you need to figure out how to make those events intersect the PCs. That might be

- reading about it in the newspaper,
- getting a job offer,
- witnessing the aftermath (hey . . . where'd that crater come from?),
- hearing about it in casual conversation,
- becoming targets,
- getting caught up in the action, or
- having their own downtime actions affected.

The resolution of your faction clocks gives life to your city, generates a plethora of scenario hooks that you can offer to the players, and provides a constant churn of activity for the PCs to respond to and get involved with.

⊹ URBANCRAWLS ⊹

The urbancrawl is a campaign structure born of the city. You can run episodic campaigns (see page 448) or node-based campaigns (see page 263) in a city—node-based campaigns, in particular, are great in an urban environment!—but with an urbancrawl, the city is no longer merely a backdrop, but becomes the core experience and focus of your game.

We've actually already created the scaffolding on which the urbancrawl is built: the district map of the city.

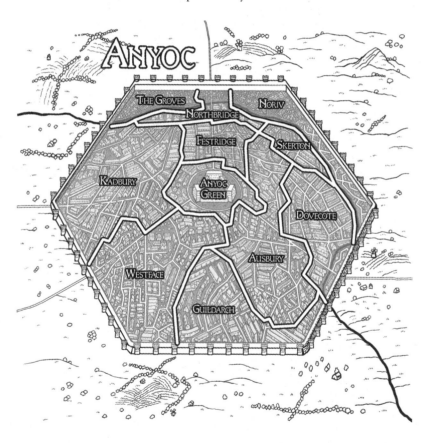

You're going to **key** content to each district, which the PCs will then access by taking **investigation actions**.

The urbancrawl is designed to work in tandem with the other urban structures we've already discussed: So the PCs will be moving between districts, having encounters, taking downtime, reacting to faction actions, and so forth, all the while delving deeper into the city's secrets and going on exciting adventures.

KEYING DISTRICTS

The content you'll be keying to your city's districts will generally be **scenes** and **scenarios**. In fact, in this context, you can probably think of a scene as just being a very, very short scenario, where the beginning, middle, and end all play out in a single interaction.

Using Anyoc as an example, you might key the following:

- **The Groves:** A vampire den has taken root in the saelleys. (A dungeon adventure.)

- **Noriv:** The city guard are hiring muscle to help clear out the squatters around the North Well. Will the PCs sign up for the paycheck or help protect the locals?

- **Northbridge:** Jonas River of River Reagents is looking to hire adventurers to fetch wyvern eggshells. (A patron, hooking to a dungeon scenario located outside of the city.)

- **Skerton:** Ramshackle urchins have been disappearing. (A mystery scenario, see page 201.)

- **Anyoc Green:** Several nobles have gathered outside the Council and are engaged in political debate. (A scene.)

- **Kadbury:** Lady Legat has recently returned from Seyrun with the Imperial Ruby. (A heist scenario, see page 307.)

- **Festridge:** A strange magical curse has infected the denizens of a house with glowing purple energy. (A raid scenario, see page 268.)

- **Ausbury:** The Noir Mantilla gang has been threatening proprietors in the East Market. (A node-based scenario, see page 239.)

- ⊚ **Dovecote:** A professor at the University of Anyoc has been murdered. (A mystery scenario, see page 201.)

- ⊚ **Westface:** A farmer in the West Market has found a strange meteorite in his field. He's looking to hire some bodyguards to help him transport the meteorite safely to town, where he's hoping to sell it to a blacksmith. (A route-based scenario, see page 374.)

- ⊚ **Guildarch:** The Noir Mantillas have stolen an adamantine anvil from one of the smithies. (A mystery scenario, see page 201.)

As you can see, the district is a very flexible container. You can key almost any type of scenario to it. The key content will usually be contained within the district where it's encountered, but sometimes the district will only be where the scenario begins, with the action potentially taking the PCs anywhere in the city (or even beyond it).

URBANCRAWL LAYERS

In a **basic urbancrawl** you simply key each district with one piece of content and you're done: The urbancrawl is fully playable and the PCs will be able to find adventure wherever they look.

You can think of this basic urbancrawl as a "layer" of content that lies on top of the city gazetteer. It follows from this, however, that you could actually key a city with multiple urbancrawls. Each 'crawl acts as a separate **layer** and can be thought of as a sort of "metascenario" or a themed collection of scenarios.

For example, you might key Anyoc with separate layers for:

- ⊚ Vampire blood dens
- ⊚ Noir Mantilla gang activities
- ⊚ Potential targets for lucrative heists
- ⊚ Patrons looking to hire the PCs for various jobs
- ⊚ Local contacts who could potentially be recruited by the PCs

Each layer would have interesting material keyed in every district of the city, so if the PCs go poking around in Guildarch, for example, they might find the local vampire den. Or get contacted by agents of Lord Mekayle Ansella. Or run into Noir Mantillas harassing local businesses. Or discover that a local merchant family holds the Neferelli Diamond.

You could (and probably should) still have a "base layer" for the city, which can serve as a catchall for content that doesn't fit into a citywide category. You can also, of course, add new layers to the urbancrawl as the campaign progresses, while likely retiring layers that are no longer useful (e.g., the PCs have killed all the vampires).

THE INVESTIGATION ACTION

How do the PCs actually access the content we've keyed to the urbancrawl layers?

They investigate.

The **generic investigation action** is pretty straightforward: The player points to a district and says, "I want to investigate there." Then you look at the urbancrawl key and you tell them what they found:

- ◎ "Keeping your ear to the ground in Guildarch, you hear the Noir Mantillas have stolen an adamantine anvil. The smithies are offering a rich reward for its return."
- ◎ "You're in the university library when you hear a woman screaming!"
- ◎ "While making your way through the twisted streets of Noriv, a small boy comes up and tugs on your coat. 'Excuse me, sir,' he says. 'But I remember you helping Almie get his cat out of a tree last month. Now Almie's missing and I don't know what to do.'"

If you're running an urbancrawl with multiple layers, then you can randomly or arbitrarily choose which layer the PCs encounter. The investigation action effectively creates (or triggers) a scenario hook (see page 498), pulling or pushing the PCs into the scene or scenario you've keyed to the district.

In practice, as the campaign evolves, the PCs will start poking around the city with definite goals in mind. They'll start saying things like, "Let's try to find the vampire den in Noriv" or "I'm going to ask around Guildarch and see if I can get any leads on the Noir Mantillas." These are **specific investigation actions**, and they're resolved exactly like a generic investigation action except you don't randomize the layer they interact with—you just pull content from the layer appropriate for whatever it is that they're investigating.

(Although if the PCs are looking for something that isn't there, you might still resolve this as a generic action and have them stumble across something else. Alternatively, if they're looking for stuff you haven't prepped, that might be an indication that it's time to add a new layer to your urbancrawl.)

It's also possible that the players will declare **nonspecific investigation actions**, which can be either totally generic ("I wander the city looking for something interesting to do") or topically targeted ("We'll search the city for vampire dens"). When this happens, the best thing to do is simply ask, "What district are you starting in?" (or otherwise get them to focus on a specific district). You can then resolve the investigation action normally.

While it can be good to let the players know that "pick a district and see if there's anything interesting there" is a default action that they can always take in the campaign, I do recommend keeping the separate layers of your urbancrawl as a player-unknown structure. The players shouldn't be saying things like, "I'd like some content from the Heist urbancrawl layer, please." You want them to be saying, "We need another big score real bad. I'm going to hit up my contacts in Kadbury and see if I can find something lucrative."

In some or all cases, you may also want to add a mechanical component to resolving an investigation action (like a Charisma [Investigation] check). In other cases, there might be a monetary cost (e.g., spreading gold around for bribes or hiring a sage). Different layers, obviously, could have varying difficulties or costs to access.

TRIGGERED DISTRICTS

In some cases, you might want to key an urbancrawl layer with a triggered district. This just means that the PCs automatically encounter the keyed content when they enter the district (or perhaps have a random chance of doing so) and don't need to perform an investigation action.

In practical terms, the distinction between "random encounter" and "triggered district" is often thin at best. You can get a similar effect from either, so it will largely depend on what seems to be most useful to you.

RUNNING THE URBANCRAWL

As I mentioned before, you'll be running an urbancrawl as one part in the grand tapestry of your city. The PCs will be discussing their plans while sipping athsai at the Purple Lotus in the Kadbury district and decide that they should try to find the vampire den in the Noriv district.

The first thing they'll have to do, obviously, is go from Kadbury to Noriv. Using Life in the City (see page 326), you'll mention the landmarks they see along the way and make a scenic encounter check. An encounter is indicated, so you roll one up and describe the goblin urchins playing stickball in the street. (Do the PCs notice that one of the urchins is picking their pocket?)

Now that they're in Noriv, they can take their investigation action. They've decided on two approaches: Granger is going to ask among some of his underworld connections and Talbar is going to talk to the local churches. The vampires are well hidden, so you've assigned their urbancrawl layer DC 20. Granger rolls 15 on his Charisma (Investigation) check and comes up empty (the criminals down here take a real "it's best to ignore it" attitude toward murder, even—or particularly!—ones where the bodies have been drained of blood), but Talbar rolls 22 on his Charisma (Religion) check and finds a very frightened priest who can point them at the sewer entrance he saw one of the creatures slither into as the sun was dawning.

The PCs head into the sewers, raid the vampire den, and reemerge several hours later covered in corpse dust and gore. They head back to their rooms at the Purple Lotus to recuperate (so you can describe another trip and check for another scenic encounter) and then take care of some downtime activities.

In addition to the urbancrawl blood den layer, the vampires are also a faction in Anyoc. You decide that the loss of the Noriv den has set back their plans to conduct a dark ritual, so you erase a segment of the clock, but you also decide to add a new four-segment clock: Identify the PCs.

What will happen when the vampires figure out who's been targeting them?

We'll play to find out!

DISCOVERING LAYERS

How do the PCs discover new urbancrawl layers to interact with? For example, how do they first discover the vampire blood dens in Anyoc so that they can start investigating and raiding them?

There are actually *lots* of ways for this to happen:

- A generic investigation action might have the PCs randomly discover vampire activity.

- The layer could feature a triggered district, so that the PCs only need to enter that district to discover the layer.

- A random encounter could feature vampires.

- The faction actions of the vampires might create events that hook the PCs.

- The PCs might find clues (see page 219) in other scenarios, pointing them toward a location or NPC on the layer.

✦ SOCIAL EVENTS ✦

Urban campaigns are filled with social events. It only makes sense given the constant swirl of people through every nook and cranny of the city.

Small social events are pretty straightforward: Grab a few NPCs, throw them into a room with the PCs, and start roleplaying. Things get trickier, though, as the size of the social events grows: How many NPCs can you really roleplay at the same time? And how many of them can the players really keep track of?

Which is a shame, because big social events are great set pieces for any RPG campaign: They're hotbeds of intrigue. If violence needs to break out, the innocent bystanders raise the stakes. If there's to be a murder, they provide a wealth of suspects. If the PCs are trying to pull a heist, they delightfully complicate the proceedings.

They're also a great way to escalate the stakes in a campaign and signal that the PCs have changed their sphere of influence: You rescued the mayor's daughter from a dragon? Chances are you're going to be the belle of the ball, and you're going to discover that powerful and important people have become very interested in making your acquaintance.

There are so many different social events like this you can run, too:

- Soiree on a flying ship
- Dinner in a mystic castle
- Journey on a long-haul space freighter
- Political caucus

- The royal masquerade
- A jousting tournament
- The pirate's ball
- A wizards' conclave
- The lunar regatta

Fortunately, there's a very simple scenario structure you can use to run these events. To use it, you'll have to prep four tools: the **location**, the **guest list**, the **main event sequence**, and the **topics of conversation**.

LOCATION

Where is the social event taking place?

You've got a lot of flexibility with this. I've run these types of events in everything from a simple ballroom to multiple airships (with the event moving back and forth between vessels). What you want to avoid, however, is making the location too small or too simple. The key to any good party is having multiple zones of activity, so that social groups can form and break apart freely. Similarly, as we'll see, what makes this scenario structure tick is the PCs are *not* simultaneously engaged with every single NPC at the event.

This doesn't necessarily mean that you need lots and lots of different rooms. Consider this tap room, for example:

Tap Room

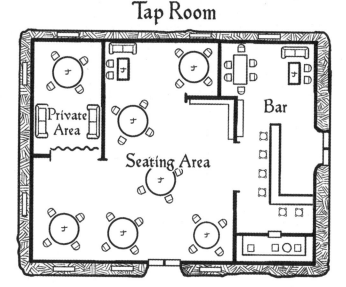

It has a seating area, a bar, and a small private area. All of these are within view of each other, but they're distinct areas that people can congregate in and move between.

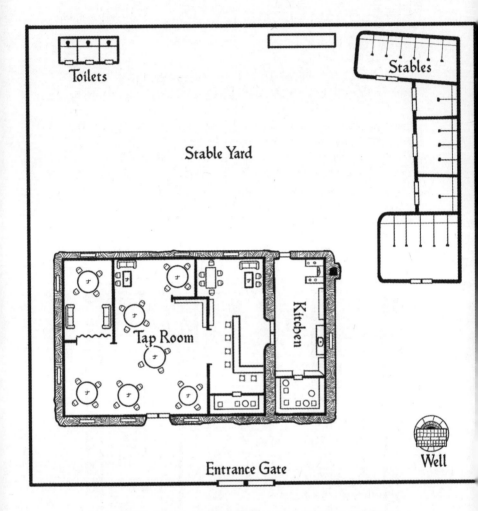

On the other hand, it doesn't hurt to incorporate a holistic environment, either. For example, let's zoom out a bit from that tap room: You could consider this five distinct areas:

- Tap Room
- Kitchen
- Stable Yard
- Stables
- Entrance Gate

The essential distinction being that characters in one area can no longer be seen from another and it will take more deliberate effort to move between these locations or track down specific people. Of course, while using this larger scope, you could still consider the tap room at the heart of the event as three distinct areas on a smaller scale.

Either way, including some specifically private areas can also be a good idea, not just for the opportunities they provide the PCs to seclude themselves, but because seeing NPCs slipping into or out of such private areas can immediately invoke intrigue.

GUEST LIST

Next, you'll want to prep the guest list. In my experience, you'll usually want ten to twenty people. Fewer than ten and the event isn't dynamic enough and doesn't really feel "big." More than twenty and the lack of focus just devolves into noise. Fifteen or thereabouts feels like a pretty good sweet spot to aim for.

Note that the event itself might be much larger than that! There may be dozens or even hundreds of people there. But the guest list you're prepping is focusing on the circle of NPCs that are immediately relevant to the PCs.

First, you'll want to prep a **master list of names** to use as a quick reference while running the event.

Next, prep notes for each of these important NPCs. I recommend printing out one NPC per sheet and keeping them loose-leaf. That will let you quickly pull out the sheets for each NPC participating in a particular conversation for easy use. If you've got the time and resources, it can also be rewarding to prep a visual handout for each NPC. During each conversation, you can quickly display these, making it easier for the players to track who they're talking to and enhancing their memory of each character as a separate individual. (They'll also serve as a handy visual reminder for you!)

I strongly recommend using the Universal Roleplaying Template for these characters. This tool is presented in the Supporting Cast extra credit on page 507 and is specifically designed to make it easy for you to quickly pick up each NPC and seamlessly slip into their role. If you're using this template, the Key Info section is designed for scenario-essential information. For social events, this could include:

- ◎ The character's relationship with or attitude toward other NPCs. ("Despises Susannah" or "Will enjoy swapping war stories with the naval officers.")

- ◎ Specific reactions they might have to stimuli. ("Is angered by anyone suggesting her father is dying.")

- ◎ Particular actions or interactions that should be triggered. ("Will try to poison Cassandra's drink" or "Wants to sell the PCs' timeshares in Venice Beach.")

- ◎ Clues that can be gleaned from them. ("Knows the knife belonged to Cassandra" or "DC 20 Wisdom [Perception] check to notice that her dress has been torn.")

- ◎ Scenario hooks.

- ◎ Cross-references or common experiences that they share with particular PCs. ("Was raised in the same orphanage as Bella" or "Was a friend to the duke they killed in Session 3.")

- ◎ Unusual or important gear they might be carrying. ("Her glass eye allows her to see through walls" or "The golden cross she wears is made of aurum [true gold].")

Obviously some of these categories overlap with each other, and there are plenty of other essential details that will be scenario- or character-specific.

MAIN EVENT SEQUENCE

Now you're going to prep the main event sequence for the event. For example:

- ◎ Announcing Guests of Special Honor
- ◎ Merlin Appears
- ◎ Galahad Arrives
- ◎ Guinevere Arrives
- ◎ The Green Knight Issues his Challenge
- ◎ Duel of Verse

- ◎ Argument Regarding Morgan le Fay
- ◎ Debate of the Knights
- ◎ Merlin's Prophecy
- ◎ Galahad and Gawain Seek Out the PCs
- ◎ Guinevere's Song

I usually prep these as a linear sequence (A happens, then B happens, then C happens), but you can also

⊚ prep a grab bag of events that could happen in any sequence,

⊚ stock a random table and roll to see what happens next, or

⊚ prep multiple linear event tracks, swapping between them flexibly as appropriate.

The PCs can also initiate alternative "major events," or they may end up derailing (or transforming) the events that you'd originally planned. More power to them. The main event sequence should be seen as a tool, not as destiny.

It can also be tempting to think of the main event sequence as the Story of the Party™. But it isn't. It's more like the piece of string that you dip in a saturated sugar solution to make rock candy. The experience of the party—the cool and unique events that you and your players are going to remember—will crystallize *around* the string. If you're eating the string instead of the candy, you're doing it wrong.

TOPICS OF CONVERSATION

The last tool to prep is the list of conversation topics. These might be momentous recent events, fraught political debates, or just utter trifles (like the series finale of a television program that aired last night). An example from a campaign I ran included:

⊚ a recent riot

⊚ a magical battle that the PCs had been involved in

⊚ a string of terrorist attacks that had been plaguing the city

⊚ rumors of war to the south

⊚ the health of a guest who canceled at the last minute

⊚ a magical STD that had been afflicting merchant families

⊚ the recent prison escape by a criminal the PCs had arrested

⊚ a new restaurant that recently opened in the Nobles' Quarter

I recommend mixing in a few "irrelevant" topics of conversation to camouflage (or at least contrast) the "important" stuff.

The topics of conversation can also pick up elements from the main event sequence as they happen. ("Did you see Astoria rush out in tears? What could Rupert have possibly said to her?!")

In some cases, you may want to reference topics of conversation in the Key Info section of the NPCs from your guest list (i.e., what they think about or can contribute to a particular topic), but for the most part you'll probably want to simply improvise what various people have to say about each topic. What can be more useful than prepping custom responses for every NPC, though, is figuring out two or three different *general* viewpoints on a particular topic (supporting the new Ironworkers' Guild vs. thinking it's a front for criminal activity), and then you can just have each NPC ad-lib within that debate.

RUNNING THE EVENT

To get the ball rolling, the first thing you'll want to know is what happens in the moment that the PCs show up for the event.

⬡   What will immediately attract their attention?

⬡   Who will they see?

⬡   Is there a major announcement (about them or otherwise)?

⬡   Is there something big and loud going down?

⬡   Is there something subtle that only they might notice?

This will generally be the first event on your main event sequence. It's the initial hook and it should give the players enough context to begin taking action in the scene—reacting to what they see, going to speak to someone they know, etc.

From that point forward, running the event is largely a matter of picking up the various toys you've built and putting them into play in different configurations.

⬡   Which NPCs are talking to each other? (Consult your guest list.)

⬡   What are they talking about? (Look at your topics of conversation.)

⬡   Who might come over and join a conversation the PCs are having? (Again, guest list.)

Encourage the PCs to split up. Cutting back and forth between various conversations is extremely effective in large social events, and you'll want to use crossovers (see page 528) between various interactions to make the party feel like a unified whole. (For example, if one of the PCs gets involved in a huge shouting match with the Barundian diplomat, the other PCs should either hear it directly or hear people talking about it.)

Keep the social groups circulating. You don't have to completely use up everything interesting about a particular NPC in a single interaction. In fact, you shouldn't. Reincorporate characters that the PCs met earlier in the event. Similarly, reincorporate topics of conversation—let the players discuss similar things with different people in order to get (and argue) different points of view.

Pay attention to which NPCs "click" with the players (whether in a positive or negative way). In my experience, there's really no way to predict this: Part of it is just random chance. Part of it is which character traits particularly appeal to your players. Part of it will be which NPCs are clicking for you (and therefore providing stronger and more memorable interactions). Regardless, make a point of bringing those NPCs back and developing the PCs' relationships with them.

If things feel like they're lagging, either cut to another group of PCs or trigger the next event in the main event sequence.

Don't hog the driver's seat. Allow the PCs to observe things that they can then choose to react to. (For example, instead of having every NPC come to them, allow them to notice NPCs walking past or overhear a group talking about a topic of interest. Let them choose whether and how to engage.) Make a point of asking them what they want to do (and, if they don't have an answer, trigger the next event).

What essentially makes this scenario structure work is that you have not prepped a dozen specific interactions for the PCs to have. Instead, you've prepped a couple dozen different toys—people, topics, events—and you're going to constantly remix them into new configurations for as long as they hold the players' interest.

QUICK-AND-DIRTY SOCIAL EVENTS

The full scenario structure presented here obviously requires preparation to run to full effect. But what if the PCs have just spontaneously decided to crash the society debut of the governor's daughter? Is there any way to use this scenario structure on the fly?

Here's the 5-minute version for emergency use:

- Make a list of three to five places people can congregate.
- Make a list of ten characters.
- Make a list of five events.
- Make a list of five topics of conversation.

Don't go into detail. Just list 'em.

If this social event is growing organically out of game play, then you've probably already got the NPCs and the topics of conversation prepped—you just need to pull them into the lists for this event.

Finally, if the PCs are going to the social event to achieve some specific goal, figure out three ways they can do that and notate it in the appropriate places (whether the location keys, the event track, the guest descriptions, or the topics of conversation).

For example, if they're trying to figure out who in the Governor's circle of friends might have assassinated Marco's sister, you might identify a couple guests who can point them in the right direction and maybe one of the events is an opportunity to witness the Governor's chief of staff slipping off to talk to a known gangster. Of course, when you're actually running the event, the PCs may discover a bunch of other ways to accomplish their goal. Follow their lead.

PART 5

INTO THE WILD

ONCE YOU STEP outside the walls of the city or dungeon, you'll find yourself confronted by the wilderness.

It's a dangerous business, Frodo, going out of your door. You step into the Road, and if you don't keep your feet, there is no knowing where you might be swept off to. Do you realize that this is the very path that goes through Mirkwood . . . or even further and to worse places?
—Bilbo, The Lord of the Rings (*J. R. R. Tolkien*)

One wilderness can be quite different from another, however. It depends on where you are and also what you're trying to do there. Some wildernesses are quite tame, having been domesticated by roads and towns and suchlike. Others are anything but, turning even basic navigation into a challenge and inviting only the bold to explore their savage depths. Do you have a map? Are you sticking to the road? What dangers lurk among the trees or prey upon unwary travelers?

So as your campaign enters the wilderness, the first thing you—and your players—will have to figure out is what you want the wilderness to be. Or, to put it another way, why (and how) you're going there.

One way of looking at the wilderness is as the obstacle between where you are and where you want to go. It's the challenge that interrupts your vector and must be overcome to achieve your goal. (Even if your goal is just, "I want to get to the next village.")

Another way of thinking about the wilderness is that it's a map with keyed adventure sites. In this mode, it acts almost like a menu that the PCs can order their next scenario from. (Even though sometimes they'll be "reading" that menu with a blindfold on.)

Another is a playground, where the wilderness itself is the adventure. Here the map works more like the map of a dungeon, linking individual experiences and challenges that can be encountered through navigational choices.

In addition to being varied, the nature of the wilderness is also ever-shifting. It can—and almost certainly will—change over the course of a campaign, depending on the current goals of the PCs, their location, and the evolution of current events.

So as we step into the wild together, I won't be showing you the One True Way™ of running the wilderness, because that doesn't exist. Instead, we'll look at a constellation of options you can use.

◎ Routes (see page 374), for when the PCs are heading from Point A to Point B.

◎ Hexcrawls (see page 391), for campaigns focused on exploration, particularly on the edges of civilization.

◎ Pointcrawls (see page 420), for exploration in regions with more established routes of travel.

There is, perhaps unsurprisingly, a fair degree of overlap between these different structures. In fact, it's not unusual to use all three simultaneously as different "layers" or ways of interacting with a specific region. So whichever structure would be most useful for your current needs, it will probably still make the most sense to start by reading through this section from beginning to end (as concepts are introduced, for example, in the discussion of hexcrawls that will later be referenced for pointcrawls).

✦ WATCHES ✦

No matter how you're traveling through the wilderness, you'll need to keep track of time and movement. A **watch** is the basic unit for tracking time and actions while traveling through the wilderness, and is used regardless of whether you're using routes, a hexcrawl, or a pointcrawl. Each watch is equal to 4 hours, which means there are six watches per day. During each watch, a character can take one **watch action**. The type of watch action taken by a traveler will determine what type of watch it is for them.

There are three **types** of watches:

◎ Active
◎ Rest
◎ Travel

It's generally assumed that travelers are spending two watches per day traveling, two watches per day resting, and two watches per day engaged in other activities.

The rules below are designed for use with the current edition of D&D, but the mechanical structure should be relatively easy to adapt to other roleplaying games as needed.

FORCED MARCH

If a character spends more than two watches traveling in one day, they must make a Constitution saving throw each hour (DC 10 + 1 per hour of additional travel). On a failure, they suffer one level of exhaustion.

LACK OF SLEEP

If a character does not spend at least one full watch per day resting, they must succeed at a Constitution saving throw (DC 16 - the number of hours they slept, if any) or suffer a level of exhaustion.

STANDING ORDERS

It's often a good idea to get an expedition's "standing orders" (e.g., who's navigating? who's riding sentinel?) instead of asking everyone to declare their watch action during every single watch. If the ranger has been doing the navigating for the last 8 days, he's probably going to continue navigating for the next 4 hours and you don't need to bog things down by confirming that.

TRAVELING

While taking a travel watch action, a traveler chooses a **travel pace** (see page 367) and can move up to a maximum **distance** determined by that pace and any **speed modifiers** inflicted by **travel conditions** (see page 368) or **terrain** (see page 369). Speed modifiers (e.g., ¾ speed, ½ speed, etc.) are applied by simply multiplying the base speed by the modifier.

TRAVEL PACE

Travelers can choose one of four paces of travel.

Normal: An expedition traveling at normal pace cannot use Stealth checks to avoid detection.

Slow: While moving at a slow pace, the expedition is being purposefully careful. An expedition traveling at slow pace:

◎ Gains advantage on navigation checks.

◎ Can make Stealth checks to avoid detection.

◎ Has its chance for a non-exploratory encounter halved. (If a non-exploratory encounter is generated, there is a 50% chance it doesn't actually happen.)

Exploration: While exploring, an expedition is assumed to be trying out side trails, examining objects of interest, and so forth. While exploring, an expedition:

◎ Can't use Stealth checks to avoid detection.

◎ Gains advantage on navigation checks.

◎ Has its chance for encounters doubled.

Fast: While moving quickly through the wilderness, an expedition traveling at fast pace:

◎ Can't use Stealth checks to avoid detection.

◎ Suffers disadvantage to Wisdom (Perception) checks.

◎ Suffers a -5 penalty to navigation checks.

PACE	PER HOUR	PER WATCH	PER DAY
Fast	4.5 miles	18 miles	36 miles
Normal	3 miles	12 miles	24 miles
Slow	2 miles	9 miles	18 miles
Exploration	1.5 miles	6 miles	12 miles

Note: Per Day on this table is based on traveling for two watches (8 hours); i.e., a full day of travel without a forced march.

TRAVEL CONDITIONS

Certain climate conditions and activities modify the speed at which an expedition can travel.

CONDITIONS	SPEED MODIFIER
Cold or hot climate	x ¾
Giant terrain	x ¾
Hurricane	x $\frac{1}{10}$
Leading pack animal	x ¾
Poor visibility (fog, darkness)	x ½
River crossing	x ¾
Snow cover	x ½
Snow cover, heavy	x ¼
Storm	x ¾
Storm, powerful	x ½

⊘ **Leading Pack Animal:** Under normal circumstances, a pack-puller can lead a file with a number of animals equal to their passive Wisdom (Animal Handling) skill.

⊘ **Poor Visibility:** This condition also gives disadvantage to navigation and forage checks.

⊘ **River Crossing:** This penalty applies to any watch during which a river must be crossed. This does not apply if the characters are following a road that has a bridge on it, but does apply if they're traveling cross-country and must seek out a bridge.

TERRAIN

The type of terrain an expedition is moving through modifies the speed at which they can travel.

- **Highway:** A highway is a straight, major, paved road.
- **Road:** A road is a dirt track or similar causeway.
- **Trail:** A trail is an irregular byway. Probably unsuitable for most vehicles and may only allow for single-file travel. Most off-road travel follows local trails. A **known trail** does not usually require navigation checks, although a known trail in poor repair requires a DC 10 navigation check to follow.
- **Trackless:** Trackless terrain is a wild area with no paths. +2 to navigation DCs.

TERRAIN	HIGHWAY	ROAD/ TRAIL	TRACKLESS	NAVIGATION DC	FORAGE DC
Desert	x1	x ½	x ½	12	20
Forest, sparse	x1	x1	x ½	14	14
Forest, medium	x1	x1	x ½	16	14
Forest, dense	x1	x1	x ½	18	14
Hills	x1	x ¾	x ½	14	12
Jungle	x1	x ¾	x ¼	16	14
Moor	x1	x1	x ¾	14	16
Mountains	x ¾	x ¾	x ½	16	18
Plains	x1	x1	x ¾	12	12
Swamp	x1	x ¾	x ½	15	16
Tundra, frozen	x1	x ¾	x ¾	12	18

WATCH ACTION

WATCH ACTION: FORAGER

Characters can forage during an **active watch** or while traveling at **slow pace**. Foragers make a Wisdom (Survival) check against the Forage DC of the terrain (see page 369). On a success, the forager either gains 1 ration of food or finds a source of fresh water (allowing the expedition to drink their daily ration of water and waterskins to be refilled). An additional ration of food or source of fresh water can be found for every two points by which the check result exceeds the DC.

FOOD & WATER

Food: Small or Medium creatures require 1 ration of food per day. They can go without food for a number of days equal to 3 + their Constitution modifier (minimum 1) before suffering 1 exhaustion level per day thereafter. A normal day of eating resets the count of days without food to zero. A creature on half rations counts as going a half day without food (and these half days accumulate until they can eat full rations).

Water: Small or Medium creatures require 1 gallon of water per day, or twice that in hot weather. A creature on a half ration of water must succeed on a DC 15 Constitution check at the end of each day or suffer a level of exhaustion. If they drink less water than that, they suffer a level of exhaustion automatically. If the character already has one or more levels of exhaustion, the character takes two levels instead of one level in either case. Waterskins hold a half ration of water.

Recovery: Any exhaustion suffered from lack of food or water cannot be removed until after a full day of normal consumption.

Large and Tiny Creatures: Tiny creatures require one-quarter ration of food and water per day. Large creatures (like horses) require four rations of food and water per day.

WATCH ACTION: MAKE CAMP

During an **active watch**, a character can establish a camp suitable for four creatures if they have tents or similar equipment to shelter them. (Horses and similar creatures do not require tents, but must still be accounted for in camp preparations.) If the expedition does not have equipment for shelter, the character can only establish a camp suitable for one creature (either themselves or someone else) per watch action. Multiple characters can, of course, work together to make a larger camp.

WATCH ACTION: NAVIGATOR

During a **travel watch**, the expedition's navigator is responsible for making navigation checks. A second navigator can assist, granting advantage to the navigation checks.

WATCH ACTION: PACK-PULLER

A pack-puller is responsible for managing an expedition's pack animals during a travel watch. A pack-puller can lead a number of animals equal to their passive Wisdom (Animal Handling) score. (This number includes the pack-puller's mount, if any.)

WATCH ACTION: RESTING

A character must take the Resting action for two **rest watches** in a row in order to gain the benefits of a Long Rest. (See the rules for Long Rests in the D&D rulebooks regarding which types of interruptions are possible without disrupting the Resting action.)

Characters without a proper camp or similar conditions (e.g., a roadside inn) require an additional Resting action to gain the benefits of resting. (In other words, it would take them three Resting actions in a row to gain the benefits of a Long Rest.)

WATCH ACTION: SCOUTING

A scout can be sent out to chart a course or learn the lay of the land during an **active watch** or, if they are traveling at a speed faster than the rest of the expedition, during a **travel watch**. When scouting, a character can choose one of two actions:

- ⬡ **Reporting:** If the navigator receives a scout's report, they gain advantage on their navigation checks during the next travel watch.
- ⬡ **Pathfinding:** The scout attempts a Wisdom (Survival) check using the area's Navigation DC. On a success, the expedition can treat trackless terrain as if it had a trail for the next travel watch.

If encounter checks are being made, an additional encounter check is made for each scouting group. (They are effectively a separate expedition while engaged in scouting.)

WATCH ACTION: SENTINEL

A member of an expedition acting as a sentinel during any watch can make Wisdom (Perception) checks and use their passive Wisdom (Perception) score to detect threats or notice anything else out of the ordinary.

WATCH ACTION: TRACKER

A Tracker can either find tracks or follow tracks as a watch action.

- ⬡ **Finding Tracks:** Searching a significant wilderness area for tracks is an active watch action. The tracker makes a Wisdom (Perception) check against the appropriate Track DC.
- ⬡ **Following Tracks:** Once tracks have been found, a tracker can follow the trail during a travel watch by making Wisdom (Survival) checks against the appropriate Track DC. A new check must be made each time the trail enters a new hex (or once per watch if not using a hexmap). If a trail is lost, it may be possible to reacquire it using the Finding Tracks action.

SURFACE	TRACK DC
Very soft ground (snow, wet mud)	5
Soft ground (sand)	10
Firm ground (fields, woods, thick rugs, dusty floors)	15
Hard ground (bare rock, indoor floor, stream-beds)	20
CONDITION	MODIFIER
Multiple people	-2
Large group	-4
Very large group	-8
Creature is bleeding	-4
Every day since the trail was made	+1 per day
Every hour of rain since the trail was made	+1 per hour
Fresh snow cover since the trail was made	+10

WATCH ACTION: OTHER ACTIONS

This list of watch actions should cover the most essential activities for organizing and managing an overland journey, but the road is long and there are many forms of mischief that the PCs can get up to. This is particularly true around the campfire at night. If a PC takes an action that feels like it would take at least an hour or two of focused attention, that probably counts as a watch action.

The PCs may also make pit stops: buying supplies in a village. Exploring a dungeon they stumble across. Resting at the Nuinë Springs. You can assume that any such stop takes at least one watch action, although in some cases the break from traveling may be long enough that you're effectively just putting the journey on hold until the PCs resume it.

PREPARING SPELLS

In D&D, you'll need to decide whether a caster needs to spend an active watch preparing their spells or if that can be bundled into a Resting watch action. The amount of time required tends to be fairly low for a full watch of activity, but it's an activity that requires focused attention, so you can make the argument either way.

A JOURNEY OF 1.000 DAYS ON ALIEN WORLDS!

What if the PCs are traveling on an alien world where there are only 16 hours per day? Or what if you want to run a mega-epic journey that lasts for 1,000 days? Do you really need to resolve 6,000 watches of activity one by one?

Well . . . no. For extraordinary expeditions or environments, you'd want to adapt the guidelines given here. Similarly, although the specific mechanics described here are for D&D, the structures can be easily adapted to other roleplaying games.

⊹ ROUTES ⊹

Let's imagine that the players are in the city of Kingsdeep and they need to go to the border town of Maernath to study the ancient crypt of the founder of the Verdigris Order. How does that trip play out at the table?

The first option is the easiest: **Skip it**. Look at your map to figure out the distance between Kingsdeep and Maernath, consult the table of wilderness travel speeds to calculate how long the trip will take, and then say something like, "Okay, having journeyed northwest across the Great Basin, you arrive in Maernath on the seventeenth."

There's nothing wrong with this approach. It's often exactly the right way to handle travel. You've determined that there are no interesting choices to be made during the journey, so you're framing past that empty time (see page 204) to the next set of interesting choices. But this may also leave you feeling vaguely unsatisfied. Among other things, you might remember any number of fantasy stories you've read or watched in which journeying from one location to another is a significant feature of the narrative and feel like you're missing out on an opportunity. (These stories aren't limited to fiction, either. Xenophon's March of the Ten Thousand would be really boring if the *Anabasis* was just, "We left Cunaxa and, long story short, we were back in Greece two years later.") Travel is an opportunity to expand your game world and create novel experiences for your players.

CHOOSING A ROUTE

When beginning a new journey, the first thing the PCs must do is choose which **route** they're going to use. This choice is only possible, of course, if the PCs know what routes they can use and where they're going. They might gain that information from things like

⊚ maps,

⊚ local guides,

⊚ mystical assistance, or

⊚ personal experience.

If the PCs *don't* know of any routes from where they are to where they want to go (and can't find one before departing), then what they're actually doing is exploring and you're going to want to use a hexcrawl (see page 391) or pointcrawl (see page 420).

In order for the choice of routes to be interesting, there must be some meaningful distinction between them. "Meaningful" in this case means that it's something that the PCs care about.

This can include stuff like:

- **Speed:** One route is faster than the other. (You'll always need to calculate how long each route will take to travel in any case.)
- **Difficulty:** One route is more difficult to navigate. It might require special knowledge, special tools, or special skills to successfully traverse. (E.g., climbing through the mountains or being able to answer the riddle of the gate-sphinx.)
- **Stealth:** One route will make it easier for the PCs to avoid detection. This can either be in general or a particular route that might make it more difficult for one specific NPC or faction to detect them. (You can also conceptually invert this and think of it as a route making the PCs *vulnerable* to detection from a particular faction: If you take the High Road you might be press-ganged by the king's army. On the other hand, the army's recruiters don't go into the Bloodfens, but if you go that way you'll be at risk from the goblin rovers instead.)
- **Expense:** The cost of traveling the route. (This can be as simple as the price of a ticket.)
- **Advantageous Landmarks:** A route can have beneficial pit stops along the way, making it potentially more appealing than other options. (E.g., visiting the Oracle of Delphi or seeing an old friend.)
- **Hazards:** Conversely, there might be a significant hazard along one of the routes. (You can enter Mordor this way, but you'll have to figure out some way past Minas Morgul.)

In order for this to be a **choice** rather than a **calculation**, the two routes must be distinguished by at least two incomparable characteristics that the PCs care about.

PLAYER: How can we get from Kingsdeep to Oathsaken?

GM: You can take the High Road or you can travel by sea.

PLAYER: What's the difference?

GM: Well, you'll get there faster by sea.

This is obviously not a choice. It's a calculation: The routes are identical except for the speed at which the PCs will get to Oathsaken, and so they'll take the route that is faster. But if you instead say, "Well, it's faster to sail, but there are reports of pirates hitting ships in Carmine Bay," this is no longer a calculation. Instead, the PCs have to *choose* whether speed or safety is more important to them.

One solid set of incomparables is all you need for this to work, but you can always add more (and you'll generally find them arising naturally out of the given circumstances of the game world in any case). Watch out, though! There's a risk that you can inadvertently turn the choice back into a calculation as you add complexity. For example, you might say:

- The sea route is faster and is dangerous due to pirates.
- The High Road is slower and is dangerous because of orc bandits.

If the pirates and bandits are known to be equally hazardous, then you're back to a straight-up calculation: There's equal danger on both routes and one route is faster.

(This doesn't happen if the PCs can't be sure of the relative hazard posed by the pirates and bandits. In that scenario it becomes an **incomplete information problem**, in which a calculation is turned into a choice because the player lacks the information necessary to make the calculation. Basically, they have to trust their gut: Do they think the pirates are more dangerous than the bandits and, if so, how much more dangerous and is that worth the extra speed?)

This is also why the PCs need to *care* about the distinction between routes. If speed isn't actually important to them (e.g., they need to be there before June and either route will get them there by April), then Faster + Hazardous vs. Slower + Safer is still just a calculation, this time of which route is safer.

The point here is not, necessarily, to create stuff to make a particular route a viable choice. Just recognize that it's *not* a choice and don't present it as such (or explain why it isn't if the players are curious for some reason). For example, if you're trying to get from Chicago to Indianapolis, you wouldn't consider "first drive to St. Louis, then turn around and drive back to Indianapolis" as an option. (Because why would you?)

So while there will likely be many possible routes that the PCs could hypothetically take, in practice only a few of these (possibly just one of them) will be a **meaningful route**—i.e., a route that the PCs might have some reason for choosing. These are the routes that you'll need to design for play.

DESIGNING A ROUTE

A route is fundamentally defined by a sequence of **landmarks** that are spaced along its length. These might be permanent structures (cities, statues, bridges, etc.) or they might be programmed encounters that only apply to this particular journey (a broken-down wagon, an ambush by orc bandits, etc.). Either way, these landmarks will be encountered at specific points along the route.

Routes may also have **features**, the most common of which is a **speed modifier**. If there's a chance of getting lost while following the route, then it would also include a **Navigation DC**. Some routes might also have bespoke features, like a faerie road that can only be followed if you wear a sprig of mistletoe in your hair.

At your discretion, you might also design a **random encounter table** for the route. These are made in the same fashion as the random encounter tables for a dungeon (see page 160), although obviously the nature of the encounters will depend on the nature of the route.

ROUTES THROUGH HEXCRAWLS

Random encounters are a good example of how the different structures for wilderness play can overlap with each other. If a route passes through a region you've already designed as a hexcrawl, for example, you could easily use the region's existing random encounter table.

CROSS-ROUTE ELEMENTS

One drawback of the route system is the choice between multiple routes, which creates a Choose Your Own Adventure structure in which you can end up wasting your time prepping a bunch of material for routes that the PCs don't take.

There are a few ways to mitigate this in practice, however.

First, there may not actually be a choice between multiple routes. In any situation where the choice of route boils down to a calculation, as we've discussed, the only route you'll need to worry about is the best route.

Second, you can often minimize wasted prep by having the players choose their route at the end of a session. You'll still need to broadly prep each route so that a meaningful choice can be made between routes, but this is fairly minimal and the details only need to be prepped for the route that's actually chosen. (In other words, you need to be able to say "there are pirates in Carmine Bay" for the PCs to make their choice, but you only need to actually prep pirate ships and pirate stats if the PCs choose the sea route.)

Third, if the PCs are repeatedly traveling through the same area over the course of the campaign, it becomes more likely that they'll take different routes at different times, which allows you to eventually use the material you prepped for those other routes.

Fourth, material can be prepped that applies to multiple routes. There are several forms these **cross-route elements** can take.

Traveling companions are a good example. If the PCs are traveling with a larger group, then that group will go with them regardless of which route they choose. You can prep various roleplaying interactions or even full scenarios (like a murder mystery, for example), so that the PCs literally carry the adventure with them.

Hunters, i.e., bad guys who are pursuing the PCs, are another easy example. Think about the Nazgûl of Middle Earth or the Terminator cyborgs. Whether the PCs take the road to Rivendell or leave it to go via Weathertop, you'll still be able to actively play the Black Riders as a threat.

Broadly speaking, you're looking for **proactive elements** that can come to (or come with) the PCs no matter where they go. You may also note that these elements can also make the choice of route more interesting, just as the Ringwraiths forced the hobbits—and later Strider—to make a number of route choices balancing speed, safety, and stealth.

ADVANCED ROUTES

If once we shake off pursuit, I shall make for Weathertop . . . It is a hill, just to the north of the Road, about halfway from here to Rivendell . . . Gandalf will make for that point, if he follows us. After Weathertop our journey will become more difficult, and we shall have to choose between various dangers.

—*Aragorn,* The Lord of the Rings *(J. R. R. Tolkien)*

The basic route system described above assumes that the route follows a clear and unmistakable path—a road or river, for example. Some routes don't follow paths, however. These **unpathed routes** generally take the form of a landmark chain: Head north to Archet, then turn east to Weathertop. Turn south from Weathertop, cross the road, and then head west until you hit the road again.

To handle unpathed routes, you'll need mechanics for (a) getting lost, (b) realizing that you're lost, and (c) getting back on track after you become lost.

Hidden route elements are those unknown to the PCs before they begin their journey: The *gansōm* bridge was washed out by the spring floods, releasing howling water spirits into the Nazharrow River. Before arriving in the Bloodfens, the PCs were unaware of the presence of goblin rovers. They're pleasantly surprised to discover that the Imperial checkpoint at the Karnic crossroads has been abandoned, its regiment summoned north to deal with peasant rebellions.

These elements can include both landmarks and features. They are often something that *cannot* be known before the journey begins (barring extraordinary effort), but in other cases the PCs may have just not done their research. Although I mentioned before that the PCs need to be aware of distinctions between available routes, that doesn't necessarily mean that they need to know *everything*.

Forked routes feature route choices that are made after the journey has already begun. These can include **detours**, in which the fork in the route eventually collapses back into the original route.

Detours are often made in response to hidden route features discovered along the way (e.g., the *gansōm* bridge has been washed out, so you need to figure out a different way across the river). PCs can be both pushed and pulled by detours, however: In addition to trying to avoid bad things on the original route, they might also choose to turn aside to gain some benefit (from an advantageous landmark, for example), usually at the cost of time.

RUNNING A ROUTE

Routes are run by the watch. Every character gets to choose one watch action per watch, you resolve the actions while introducing any events or landmarks encountered along the way, and then you start a new watch and do it again.

During each watch:

1. Mark the **watch** and tick **durations** and **daily resources** (food, water, etc.).

2. Make an **encounter check**.

3. Declare **watch actions**.

4. Resolve **travel** by:

   A. Declaring **pace**.

   B. Making a **navigation check**.

   C. Tracking **movement** on the route map.

5. Resolve **encounters**, including Perception-type checks (which may interrupt travel).

6. Resolve **other watch actions**.

Unlike the dungeon turn (see page 66), which I've found generally works best as a player-unknown structure, overland travel seems to work best when players are aware that time is being tracked in watches and are able to select the specific watch actions that they're taking.

TRACKING TIME

With a little practice, you'll find that most watches get resolved very quickly. I recommend tracking the passage of watches using **tally marks**, beginning a new grouping of marks at the end of each day. (That way you won't have to track multiples of six to know which day you're on: You can just count tally groups.)

In practice, the members of an expedition will usually be mostly unified in the type of watch actions they're taking: They'll all travel together for a couple of watches, make camp, and then do a little shuffling of active and rest actions to make sure a watch is kept. This can be made routine with standard marching order (see page 395), and usually the most important question will be who's on watch when an encounter happens.

There are only a handful of spells and abilities that have a duration longer than one watch, but you'll want to track those with ticks just as you would while running a dungeon (see page 72).

Usually of more importance are **daily resources**, like rations and water. If the PCs are traveling along a road with regular inns or similar services, this can likely be ignored. When supplies do become important, it's generally best to have one person at the table be responsible for tracking them. That's something you can do as the GM, of course, but it's often more efficient to have a specific player as the expedition's **quartermaster**. If the latter, make sure to clearly communicate the passage of days to them so that they can tick supply usage.

ROUTE ENCOUNTERS

Making an **encounter check** while traveling is resolved using the same procedure as dungeon encounter checks (see page 73), except for the **encounter distance**:

- ⬡ **Open Vistas:** 2d6 x 60 feet
- ⬡ **Obstructed Visibility:** 2d6 x 20 feet
- ⬡ **Limited Visibility:** 2d6 x 10 feet

Because watches tend to be resolved really quickly, you can save a lot of time at the table by making all of the encounter checks for a single day at the same time. Instead of rolling a single d8, roll six eight-sided dice at the same time and read their results from left to right (for the first watch of the day, the second watch of the day, and so forth). Mark which watches will have an encounter and then begin generating them. (You can often do this while the players are making navigation checks, discussing their options during a previous encounter, or the like.)

WHEN DID THAT HAPPEN?

If you want to randomly determine a specific time within a watch, roll 1d8 to determine the half hour. You can get even more specific by rolling a d30 to determine the exact minute within the half hour.

ROUTE NAVIGATION

While traveling, the navigator should declare the expedition's travel pace.

If the expedition is following a road, river, or similarly obvious path, no **navigation check** is required. If the route is unpathed, however, the navigator must make a navigation check—a Wisdom (Survival) check with a difficulty determined by the terrain they're traveling through (see page 369). The terrain-based DC assumes that there are local trails that are being followed, but in a trackless waste, add +2 to Navigation DCs.

If the navigation check is failed, the expedition has become **lost**. Begin counting the number of watches the expedition has been lost for and continue making navigation checks during each watch. On the next successful check, the navigator will realize that they've become lost. Assume that the expedition must spend as many watches backtracking to return to the correct route as they spent lost in the first place (although, if additional navigation checks are failed, they could end up becoming lost again).

In addition to being lost, groups failing navigation checks may suffer other complications, such as

- ending up somewhere they didn't want to be,
- encountering a regional hazard like quicksand or the black vapors,
- an increased risk of random encounters, or
- discovery by enemies they were seeking to avoid.

The appropriate complication, if any, will depend on the current situation and is at your discretion.

If the navigation check succeeds, or was not needed, on the other hand, use the group's travel pace to determine how far they moved along their route. This may, of course, include encountering one or more **landmarks**.

THE TRAVELOGUE

A route is not inherently interesting. It's the experiences that you fill the journey with that will make it entertaining and memorable. (This is just like a dungeon: Moving through some lines drawn on graph paper isn't inherently interesting, either. It's what you key into the dungeon rooms that make or break the experience.)

By default, the route system will lead you toward a generic travelogue (" . . . and then we went to X and then we went to Y and then we went to . . ."). But the best travelogues find ways to elevate the sequence of events. You want your game to resonate with the vibes of a great road trip movie or the epic journeys of *The Lord of the Rings*.

You might think about what kind of story you want the journey to be: exploration, a race, escape, survival, self-discovery, edification. Or is the journey simply a convenient framing device for a bunch of individually interesting and complete short stories? Journeys can set mood (think of the emotional toll of Frodo and Sam's long trek across Mordor), emphasize a theme (sure are a lot of goblins in these fens), reinforce current quests (passing caravans of refugees from the war), or provide hooks to side quests.

As you describe a journey, your travelogue will include pit stops and passage.

Pit stops are the landmarks and encounters that are framed into full-fledged scenes and played out as scenes. (Or, in some cases, across multiple scenes.) These are travelers you meet along the way and roleplay a conversation with or the small roadside shrine where the PCs might choose to make an offering, but it's also the significant challenges—like a washed-out bridge or even a full dungeon—that they encounter along the way.

The **passage**, on the other hand, is how you describe the journey between each pit stop. This can also include landmarks ("You pass by the Red Spire of Anauroch around mid-afternoon, and then by dusk . . ."), but will largely be painted in broader strokes ("You enter the cool shadows beneath the gabled boughs of Silverwood, a blessed relief from the scorching sunlight").

When we talked about describing dungeon rooms, we had some rules of thumb for creating awesome descriptions (see page 107):

⚅ Three of Five
⚅ Two Cool Details
⚅ Three-by-Three

Even though the passages of a travelogue are vastly different in scope and purpose from the rooms of a dungeon, it turns out these same rules of thumb will continue to serve us well in describing them: Invoke multiple senses, add a couple cool details, and sprinkle your descriptions with a little depth.

To make the journey truly come to life, you'll also want to make sure that the players have an opportunity to actually play through the experience. Some of this will come from the pit stops, but you'll also want to **frame roleplaying opportunities** between the PCs. A good way to do this is to simply listen for the moments when the players at the table are talking to each other—whether they're planning their next move, checking their supplies, or speculating about who the Faceless Riders work for—and interject a frame for where and how that conversation is happening in the game world: chatting while they ride their horses side by side. Gathered around the campfire at night. Huddled inside their tents while the blizzard rages outside.

You may also get good results from periodically prompting the players with an open-ended roleplaying opportunity. For example, you might say, "After making camp, you gather around the fire for your dinner. What do you talk about?" Or even make it more specific by asking something like, "Cleotha, what tale do you tell to entertain your companions?" This sort of thing will become quite taxing if you try to do it every single time the PCs make camp, but applied as a light spice it can have great results.

DO I NEED THIS ROUTE AT ALL?

If you're having difficulty making a route interesting, it might be a good time to take a step back and say, "Should we skip this?" If a route is boring, it's probably because there are no meaningful choices being made. If no meaningful choices are being made, you should probably cut forward to the point where interesting choices will be made.

✦ HOMEWORK ✦

THE ROUTE MAP

The next time the PCs need to go to an adventure site in your campaign, prep the journey as a route.

STEP 1: IDENTIFY THE ROUTE

Look at the **map** of your campaign world. Where are the PCs now and where are they going to?

- Is there a road, river, or trail they could follow?
- Can they get there by boat?
- What about exotic methods such as an airship or magic portal?

If you don't have a map yet, this is a great time to start one: Grab a blank sheet of paper, then write down the PCs' current location in one spot and the location they're going to in another spot. Select a type of route (road, river, train tracks, etc.) and use it to connect the two locations.

I WANT MORE MAPS!

If you'd rather get started with a more elaborated map, check out the Quick-and-Dirty Worldbuilding extra credit (see page 471) and also the guide to making hexmaps (see page 406).

STEP 2: ADD LANDMARKS

Define the route by listing the landmarks the PCs will encounter while traveling along it. If you're referencing an existing map, it will likely provide some of these landmarks for you (river crossings, villages, etc.). Start with those and then fill in the gaps.

If these are new landmarks, you may want to add some or all of them to your map for future reference.

Some of these landmarks may only be mentioned as scenery during the travelogue, but if you're focusing on a particular journey I recommend including at least one or two landmarks that are more interactive and can form the basis for a small scene. On the other hand, for your first route I'd keep things fairly simple and probably cap the interactive landmarks at no more than three or four.

STEP 3: ADD ENCOUNTERS

Finally, add encounters and an encounter table, whether bespoke or procedurally generated. (Remember that you can borrow existing regional encounter tables if you've got them!) Since this is likely a relatively short route, you probably don't need more than a handful of encounters, unless it's a site the PCs are likely to be visiting repeatedly.

RE-RUNNING A ROUTE

Even if the PCs aren't going back and forth to this adventuring site, you'll likely use this route at least once more when the PCs head home.

When this happens, pay attention to the **transitory landmarks**: the wagon with a broke wheel. The farmers bringing in the harvest. The traveling bard who offers to sing them a song for a silver piece.

These transitory landmarks won't repeat, so you'll need to remove them and will likely want to replace them with new transitory landmarks. (Unless transitory content like this is tightly tied to a specific location, you might also want to think about encoding it into your encounter table, where it's easier to manage.)

THE SECOND ROUTE

When you're ready (or the opportunity naturally presents itself), you can offer the players a choice between two different routes.

◎ **Step 1: Identify the Routes:** This is usually easier if the two routes are of different types (e.g., by road or by sail), but this isn't strictly necessary. Add the locations and routes to your map if they aren't there already.

◎ **Step 2: Create the Choice:** Choose a characteristic that would be significant to the PCs from the list of examples on page 376 and make one of the routes better (e.g., taking the airship is faster than riding along the road). Then pick a different characteristic and make it advantageous for the other route (e.g., a ticket on the airship is expensive, but riding on the road is free).

◎ **Step 3: Make the Choice:** Present the two options to the players and let them choose which route they want to take. You can then prep that route using the procedure above.

THE ROUTE MAP

Over time, if your campaign regularly features travel, you'll begin to accumulate a collection of routes that crisscross the local region. It's likely, in fact, that this **route map** will evolve into a pointcrawl (see page 420): As the routes intersect and overlap with each other, the map will develop enough depth that the players can make complex navigational decisions and begin charting their own routes in detail.

For example, months ago the PCs passed through Black Larch on their way from Kingsdeep to Maernath. Later they went from Maernath to Oathsaken, a trip that also took them through Black Larch. Now they want to go from Oathsaken to Kingsdeep . . . and the route already exists! You just need to patch together pieces of the two previous routes.

It may be tempting to imagine sitting down and planning this elaborate route map ahead of time as part of your campaign prep. But while there may be a few major, obvious routes where it would make sense to do this, for the most part I recommend resisting the temptation. Partly because the thought of all that wasted prep makes the little winged GM on my shoulder wince, but mostly because it's intrinsically more effective to let the players (by way of their PCs) tell you where they want to go and what the important routes in the campaign are.

This doesn't mean that you shouldn't draw roads or rivers on your map! It just means that you shouldn't feel compelled to flesh out every road and river into a full-fledged route with detailed landmarks, encounter tables, and the like (any more than you would feel compelled to map out the floorplan of every single building in a city).

In transportation planning there's a concept called the **desire path**: These are the paths created by the erosion of human travel across grass or other ground covering. It's the way that people *want* to travel, even if the planned or intended paths are telling them to take a different path.

It has become quite common for urban planners to open parks, college campuses, and similar spaces without sidewalks, wait to see where the desire paths naturally form, and only *then* install the pavement.

You're doing the same thing here: following the players' paths of desire and developing the campaign along the lines they have chosen.

✦ HEXCRAWLS ✦

The prototypical hexcrawl is a small outpost on the borders of civilization: It's the lonely castle on the trackless heath; the small town of the American Old West; the Roman fortress of Camulodunum; the pirate's cove clinging to the edge of an unknown isle. When the PCs pass through the gates of that final refuge, they journey into the unknown, uncertain of what they might find (or what might find them).

The hexcrawl campaign structure is quite flexible and can be used for other settings, but the key feature is that the PCs will be explorers. If they have a map at all, they won't be sticking to the established roads and byways. (You'd use a pointcrawl, page 420, for that.) Nor will they simply be passing through on their way to somewhere else. (You'd want to use the route system for that.) Instead, they'll be repeatedly throwing themselves into the wild; crisscrossing the land in an effort to tease out its deepest secrets and most hidden treasures.

A hexcrawl is based around a **hexmap**, like the one on the next page.

The numeric or alphanumeric references for each hex on the map allows locations to be easily **keyed** to the map. During play, the GM can determine which hex the PCs are starting in and then use travel mechanics to determine how far they can move and where they move. When they enter a new hex, the GM will tell them the terrain type and determine whether or not they discover the keyed content of the hex.

From the players' perspective, the hexes themselves are usually a player-unknown structure. In other words, the GM **hides the hexes** from the players, instead describing the world to them as their characters would perceive it and letting them declare their actions accordingly. (This is because the abstraction of the hexmap is useful and convenient for the GM as they track navigation, key encounters, and so forth, but tends to have a negative impact for the players, distancing them from their characters if they engage strictly with the abstraction.)

The basic form of play in a hexcrawl is that the PCs are standing in a hex and they **choose a direction** they want to travel. As they travel, they'll experience the encounters and locations keyed to the hexcrawl.

Sample Hexmap: Maernath

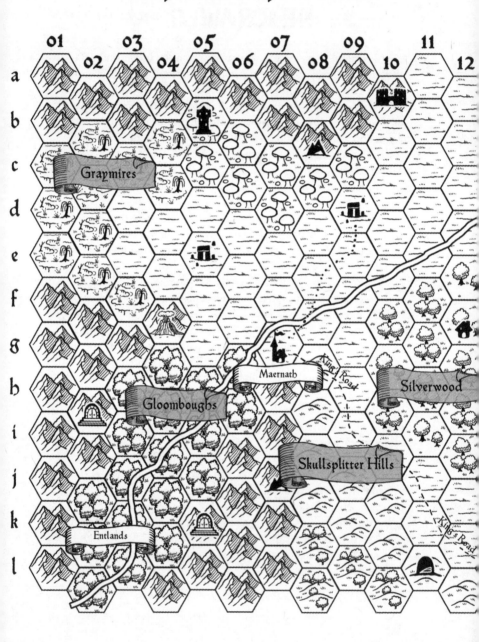

Sometimes their navigation will be guided by their growing knowledge of the area and the goals they've set for themselves, but often (particularly early in a campaign where they're still gaining that knowledge) they may just choose a random direction into the unknown to see what they can find.

RUNNING THE HEXCRAWL

Hexcrawls are run by the watch. Every character gets to perform one watch action per watch, you resolve the actions while introducing any events or landmarks encountered along the way, and then you start a new watch and do it again.

During each watch:

1. Mark the **watch** and tick **durations** and **daily resources** (food, water, etc.).

2. Make an **encounter check.**

3. Declare **watch actions.**

4. Resolve **travel** by:

   A. Declaring **pace.**

   B. Making a **navigation check.** On failure, determine **veer.**

   C. Marking **progress** and tracking **movement** if entering a new hex.

5. Generate and resolve **encounters,** including Perception-type checks (which may interrupt travel).

   A. **Exploration encounters** are the keyed location of the current hex.

   B. **Wandering encounters** are rolled on the random encounter table, including a lair/tracks check.

6. Resolve **other watch actions.**

   . . . wait a minute. Are you experiencing déjà vu?

That's intentional. Exploration in a hexcrawl is run on the same basic chassis as traveling via a route. This allows you to seamlessly transition between them during play: The PCs can hack their way through the trackless wastes of the Viridian Jungle, emerge onto the Emeraude Highway, and gratefully follow that back to civilization.

WHEN ARE WATCH ACTIONS RESOLVED?

- **Forager:** Other Watch Actions
- **Make Camp:** Other Watch Actions
- **Navigator:** Travel
- **Pack-Puller:** Travel
- **Resting:** Other Watch Actions
- **Scouting:** Travel
- **Sentinel:** Encounters (Perception-type checks)
- **Tracker:** Finding Tracks (Other Watch Actions)
- **Tracker:** Following Tracks (Travel)
- **Other:** Usually under Other Watch Actions

HEXCRAWL RUNNING SHEET

On page 396 you'll find the Hexcrawl Running Sheet. You can make copies of this sheet and use it for your own hexcrawl adventures, but it's also easy to duplicate its functionality using a sheet of scratch paper.

Party Name provides a convenient label for the sheet. This might be the "T-Skulls" or "Unit 457."

Duration Tracker provides a few slots for tracking effect durations. To keep everything unified, these are measured in watches, so an effect that lasts 24 hours, for example, would be ticked six times before expiring.

Watch Tracker provides a space for marking off watches and tracking days, including a space for listing the starting date of the expedition.

Marching Order provides a template for tracking the current or standard positioning of the PCs. It works just like the Marching Order section of the dungeon running sheet, as described on page 69.

Standing Orders provides space for listing the PCs in your party and their standard or current watch actions during travel watches, while the **Watch Tracker** lets you list which PCs are keeping watch, if any, during non-travel watches.

Hex Tracker lets you keep track of the expedition's movement. Write down the current day and watch in the left-hand column (for example, 3-1 is the first watch of the third day), then mark the hex the party is currently in and their intended direction of travel. Add information on the veer if the party gets lost, and use the check boxes to mark off progress.

Mark off progress in miles, and when you reach the end of one row of check boxes (for near hex faces) or run out of check boxes entirely (for far hex faces), the expedition has left the hex. Reference their intended direction of travel and veer to determine what hex they've entered and write that down in the next row. Repeat.

HEXCRAWL RUNNING SHEET

Party Name

DURATION TRACKER

EFFECT	DURATION	TRACK
		☐☐☐☐☐☐ ☐☐☐☐☐☐
		☐☐☐☐☐☐ ☐☐☐☐☐☐
		☐☐☐☐☐☐ ☐☐☐☐☐☐
		☐☐☐☐☐☐ ☐☐☐☐☐☐
		☐☐☐☐☐☐ ☐☐☐☐☐☐

STANDING ORDERS

PC	CURRENT	TRAVEL

WATCH TRACKER

1	2	3	4

MARCHING ORDER

Front

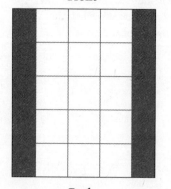

Back

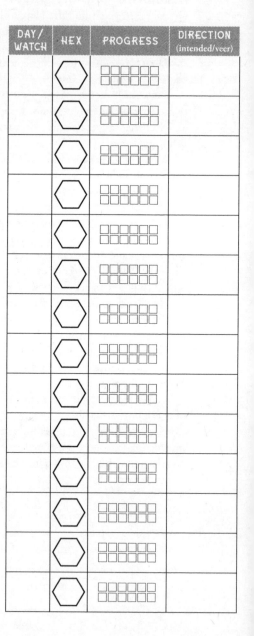

DAY / WATCH	HEX	PROGRESS	DIRECTION (intended/veer)
	⬡	☐☐☐☐☐☐ ☐☐☐☐☐☐	
	⬡	☐☐☐☐☐☐ ☐☐☐☐☐☐	
	⬡	☐☐☐☐☐☐ ☐☐☐☐☐☐	
	⬡	☐☐☐☐☐☐ ☐☐☐☐☐☐	
	⬡	☐☐☐☐☐☐ ☐☐☐☐☐☐	
	⬡	☐☐☐☐☐☐ ☐☐☐☐☐☐	
	⬡	☐☐☐☐☐☐ ☐☐☐☐☐☐	
	⬡	☐☐☐☐☐☐ ☐☐☐☐☐☐	
	⬡	☐☐☐☐☐☐ ☐☐☐☐☐☐	
	⬡	☐☐☐☐☐☐ ☐☐☐☐☐☐	
	⬡	☐☐☐☐☐☐ ☐☐☐☐☐☐	
	⬡	☐☐☐☐☐☐ ☐☐☐☐☐☐	
	⬡	☐☐☐☐☐☐ ☐☐☐☐☐☐	
	⬡	☐☐☐☐☐☐ ☐☐☐☐☐☐	

HEXES

1 Hex = 12 miles (center to center/side to side) = 7-mile side = 124 square miles

The fundamental unit of the hexcrawl is, naturally, the hex. The measurements above give the mathematical dimensions of a 12-mile hex—in other words, a hex that is twelve miles across if measured from one side to the opposite side. This measurement also, conveniently, is the measurement from the center of one hex to the center of a neighboring hex. So whether you imagine someone standing in the center of a hex moving to the center of another hex or someone starting on one side of the hex, traveling across it, and then entering the hex on the far side, the distance traveled will be 12 miles. That's a concrete measurement that we can perhaps rely on as a foundation.

In most ways, however, a hex in a hexcrawl should be considered an abstraction. If the PCs are "in" a hex, we don't actually know where, exactly, in the hex they are. The same thing is true for locations keyed to the hex. In fact, we don't *want* to know. By embracing the abstraction, we make it easier to key content, to manage movement, and to make meaningful navigational decisions without the unmanageable complexity of detailed navigation across specific topographical maps.

The one thing we need to know is whether or not we've left the current hex and entered a new one. To do this, we keep track of an expedition's **progress** within the hex.

STARTING IN A HEX

⊚   If an expedition starts movement from a location within a hex, assume that it requires 6 miles of progress to exit any face of the hex. (We are effectively assuming, for the purposes of our abstraction, that the location is in the exact center of the hex.)

CROSSING A HEX

⊚   It requires 12 miles of progress to exit a hex through one of the three faces on the opposite side.

⊚   It requires 6 miles of progress to exit a hex through one of the two nearest faces.

BACK THE WAY WE CAME

If an expedition doubles back along their own trail, simply reduce their progress until they exit the hex.

CHANGING DIRECTION

Changing direction more than once within a hex will result in the loss of 2 miles of progress each additional time the expedition changes direction. (You can imagine them circling back and forth through the hex.)

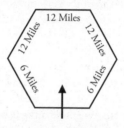

WHAT CAN YOU SEE IN A HEX?

A 12-mile hex is large enough that if you're in it we can—within our abstraction—broadly assume that you can't see into neighboring hexes. This means you don't have to juggle a gaggle of hexes: You only need to look at the key entry for the hex the PCs are currently in.

If you want to get a little fancier, PCs with less than 6 miles of progress can observe the terrain type of the hexes behind them. PCs with more than 6 miles of progress can begin to discern the terrain type of the hexes in front of them.

Mountains: Mountains can be seen from up to 6 hexes away (72 miles).

HEXCRAWL NAVIGATION

In general, an expedition can navigate through the wilderness by **landmark** or they can navigate by **compass direction**.

NAVIGATION BY LANDMARK

It is trivial to follow a road, river, or other natural feature of the terrain. It's similarly easy to head toward a visible landmark. The landmark or terrain feature will determine the route of travel and there's no chance of becoming lost, so you can simply track the number of miles traveled.

NAVIGATION BY COMPASS DIRECTION

Navigators trying to move in a specific direction through the wilderness must make a navigation check using their Wisdom (Survival) skill once per watch to avoid becoming lost. The DC of the check is primarily determined by the terrain type of the current hex (see page 369), though other factors may also apply.

Characters who fail the navigation check become **lost**.

LOST CHARACTERS

Characters who become lost may veer away from their intended direction of travel. Roll 1d10 on the diagram below:

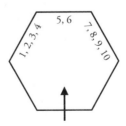

When lost characters exit a hex, they will exit through the face of the hex indicated by the die roll.

FINDING LOCATIONS

The difficulty and complexity of finding a specific location within the wilderness varies depending on the character's familiarity and approach.

Familiar Locations: If a navigator is in the same hex as a location they've previously visited multiple times, they automatically find the location. (Within the abstraction of hexmapping, they've demonstrated sufficiently accurate navigation.)

Unfamiliar Locations: Unfamiliar locations, even those a navigator has been to once before, are found using encounter checks. In other words, when a navigator has gotten the expedition into the correct hex and an encounter for that location is generated (see page 402), that indicates that the navigator has found the location they were looking for.

Visible Locations: Locations designated as visible are automatically spotted by anyone in the same hex.

Hidden Locations: Even when encountered, hidden locations require a skill check or some special action to actually discover them. This might be as simple as a Wisdom (Perception) check or it might require the PCs to be carrying a specific magical item that can reveal the location.

On Road: If a location is on a road, river, or trail, then a character following the road, river, or trail will automatically find the location. (Assuming it isn't hidden.)

Characters who are lost remain lost. In the next hex neither their intended direction of travel nor their veer will change. If characters who are already lost fail another navigation check, their veer can increase but not decrease. (If they have not yet begun to veer—i.e., they rolled a 5 or 6 on their initial veer check—then their veer can increase in either direction.)

EXAMPLE

A lost party is already veering to the left when they fail another navigation check. A roll of 1-4 on 1d10 would cause them to exit the next hex two hex faces to the left of their intended direction, but any other result would not change their veer at all.

RECOGNIZING YOU'RE LOST

Lost navigators continue making a navigation check once per watch. If the check succeeds, they will recognize that they are no longer certain of their direction of travel.

Navigators who encounter a clear landmark or unexpectedly enter a distinctly new type of terrain can make an additional navigation check to realize that they've become lost. (It's also possible that some situations will make it obvious to a character they've become lost without requiring any check.)

REORIENTING

A navigator who realizes that they've become lost has several options for reorienting themselves.

They can **backtrack** by following their own tracks using the Finding Tracks action (see page 372). While tracking allows them to retrace their steps, they must still recognize the point at which they went off-track. If a character is successfully backtracking, they can attempt a navigation check each watch, using the Navigation DC of the terrain type, to correctly recognize whether they were on-track or off-track. If the check is a failure, they reach the wrong conclusion.

A character can determine a **compass direction** ("I want to go east") with a DC 10 Wisdom (Survival) check. On a failure, randomly determine the direction the navigator thinks is true north.

A navigator can attempt to precisely determine the direction they should be traveling in order to reach a known objective by making a navigation check at the Navigation DC of the terrain type + 10. If the navigator fails this check, they immediately become lost again. Determine the direction of travel like any other lost character.

USING A COMPASS

Compasses grant advantage to navigation checks. In addition, they automatically eliminate veer at hex borders even if the user doesn't recognize that they were lost. (Even if you don't recognize that you ended up off course, the compass constantly reorients you toward your intended direction of travel.)

HEXCRAWL ENCOUNTERS

Generating a random encounter in a hexcrawl is slightly more complicated than it is for dungeon scenarios or route-based travel.

Make an **encounter check** by rolling 1d12. A roll of 1 indicates that a **wandering encounter** should be generated. A roll of 12 indicates that the expedition has encountered a **keyed location** within the hex as an exploration encounter.

When a keyed location is encountered, refer to the hex key and describe the location to the players.

To generate a wandering encounter, follow this procedure:

1. Roll on the **random encounter table**.

2. Make a **lair/tracks check** by rolling 1d6. On a roll of 1 or 2, this becomes an exploration encounter with the creature's **tracks**. On a roll of 6, it's an exploration encounter and the creature(s) are found in their **lair**. Otherwise, continue generating a wandering encounter.

3. Determine the encounter distance (based on the terrain type of the hex):

   - **Open Vistas:** 2d6 x 60 feet
   - **Obstructed Visibility:** 2d6 x 20 feet
   - **Limited Visibility:** 2d6 x 10 feet

4. Make a **reaction check** by rolling 2d6 and consulting the reaction table below.

5. Determine **surprise**, if any. (In D&D, this will usually be done with opposing NPC vs. PC Dexterity [Stealth] and Wisdom [Perception] checks.)

REACTION TABLE

2D6	REACTION
2-3	Immediate Attack
4-5	Hostile
6-8	Cautious/Threatening
9-10	Neutral
11-12	Amiable

EXPLORATION ENCOUNTER

Exploration encounters only occur during watches in which the characters are traveling or otherwise exploring an area. They do not occur during watches in which the characters are resting or otherwise stationary.

WANDERING ENCOUNTER

A wandering encounter can occur during any watch. They are usually creatures, whose movement can bring them into contact with the expedition regardless of whether the expedition is on the move or not, but they could also be some similar phenomenon (e.g., meteors falling from the sky, a noxious vapor drifting through a forest, etc.).

TRACKS

When a tracks encounter is indicated, the PCs discover (or have a chance to discover) the creature's tracks as an exploration encounter. Such tracks can, of course, be followed, so you will need to decide where they're coming from and where they're going to. An easy answer to this question is whatever the keyed location in the current hex is (and then you'll just need to figure out why these creatures were going to or from there).

I will also indicate on my random encounter table the hexes that various random encounters might be based out of so that I don't get caught flat-footed—e.g., "1d4 + 4 goblins (Hex A4)," because Hex A4 is a goblin village.

Note that tracks don't necessarily mean foot- and/or paw prints. It can also include stuff like sounds, smells, an abandoned campsite, or a smoke trail rising into the sky to the west.

LAIR

This check functionally generates a new location in the current hex—i.e., the lair of the creature type indicated by the random encounter table. The more time the PCs spend in a particular area, the more content will be added to that area.

This does, of course, leave you in the position of needing to improvise a lair, most likely using some form of location-based scenario structure (e.g., a dungeon). If that seems daunting, you've got a couple of options:

1. Prep four or five small, unkeyed maps. Vary the types, including perhaps a cave, a building, a small campsite, and so forth. When a lair is indicated, simply grab one of these maps.

2. Simply ignore the lair result. You'll end up with slightly more wandering encounters with the PCs directly encountering creatures, but that'll be just fine. (And I promise not to tell anybody.)

CHECK WITH ONE ROLL

Because the encounter check and the lair/tracks check use different types of dice, you can roll both dice simultaneously to save time!

✦ HOMEWORK ✦

DESIGN A HEXCRAWL

Most of the homework you've done in this book has been some form of, "Here's how you can design a quick adventure! Take it for a spin and see what it can do!" That's not the case here. There's no such thing as a quick hexcrawl. It's an inherently prep-heavy format: In order for the hexmap to be large enough that the PCs don't immediately run off the edge of it in the first session, you're going to have a significant number of hexes, and you're going to have to fill those hexes with content.

This heavy prep load is a coin with two sides, though, because all of that up-front prep means that you won't need to do much prep during the actual campaign. Instead of trying to find time every week to prep a new scenario for your Friday night session, you can get away with occasionally doing some light restocking but otherwise just letting the PCs continue exploring what you've already created.

This only works, though, if the campaign involves the PCs repeatedly engaging the region around their home base, venturing forth again and again to explore the area covered by your hexmap. If that's not the case—if, for example, the PCs are just passing through the region—then you'll end up prepping dozens and dozens of hexes with stuff you'll never use at the table. That's a terrible and frustrating use of your time, and you'll almost certainly be better off using a different structure.

So, long story short, this homework is very much a build-an-entire-campaign assignment. It will be an immensely rewarding experience, but not one to be undertaken lightly. When you're ready to take on this challenge, however, let us charge into the breach!

OPEN TABLE HEXCRAWLS

Hexcrawls are excellent for open tables specifically because they require little per-session prep. And, vice versa, open tables are great for hexcrawls because you'll have multiple groups exploring the region. Check out the The Open Table extra credit on page 463.

YOUR FIRST HEXMAP

Starting with a blank sheet of hex paper, you should design a **10 x 10 hexmap**, meaning a map that is 10 hexes wide and 10 hexes tall, for a total of 100 hexes. Alternatively, grab some hexmapping software and do it all digitally.

In a hex at the center of the map, place the **home base** from which the campaign will be based and the region will be explored. (You won't be able to precisely center this on a 10 x 10 hexmap, but you'll want to be as close as possible.) This home base could be any of the following:

- A small village
- A large town
- A border fort
- A dwarven stronghold
- The ancient nexus of portals through which the PCs arrive
- A desert oasis
- A floating island fortress chained to the ground
- A crashed spaceship
- An expedition's base camp

In short, it can be almost anything you can imagine. The only important feature is that it should probably provide the PCs with an opportunity to rest and resupply. (Like larger dungeons, hexcrawls are usually built around expedition-based play, as described on page 140.)

The size of this map is a good compromise between (a) making the map large enough that the PCs can comfortably explore in any direction while remaining on the map and (b) keeping your initial number of hexes manageable so that you don't end up getting completely overwhelmed while filling them.

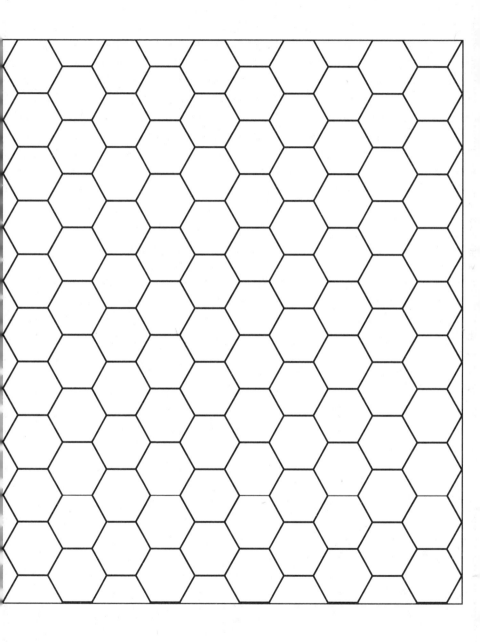

Fill in all the hexes on the blank map on the previous page with terrain types, using the **hexmap key symbols** on the next two pages. As you're doing this, make a point of including at least three or four different terrain types in the six hexes immediately surrounding your home base. Even in the absence of all other information, these different terrains will prompt the players to make an initial navigation decision. ("Do you want to go into the forest, the mountains, or the swamp?")

As you're placing terrain, think about the **regions** that you're creating: What's the name of that forest? How large is that swamp? Who or what do you imagine living in the Skullsplitter Hills? Jot down some notes as these ideas occur to you.

You'll want to place the major **roads and rivers**. In doing this, you'll also need to decide if there are any **other settlements** on the map. As we've discussed, hexcrawls tend to work best where there's a lot of open, unexplored land for the PCs to roam through and . . . well . . . explore. So, particularly for your first hexcrawl, I'd recommend keeping settlements far apart (and, quite possibly, off the edge of your initial map entirely).

With that being said, it can also be a good idea to include at least a couple different routes leading away from your home base (e.g., a couple of roads or a road and a river). Like the different terrain types, these immediately present the players with easy, bare-bones navigational choices.

KEYING A HEX

When you're keying content to a hex, you're keying a location. The distinction between a "location" and an "encounter" can get a little fuzzy if you stare at it for too long, but in practice it's pretty straightforward: If your key says there's "an ogre walking down the road," then the next time the PCs come this way the ogre will presumably be gone (particularly if they've killed it). If the key instead reads "an ogre living in a shack," then even if the PCs kill the ogre, the shack will still be there.

Of course, one might argue that the PCs could do some quick demolition work on the shack and make it disappear, too. (That would be an excellent example of staring at the distinction too long.) But the general point remains: You're keying permanent geography, not ephemeral events. (The latter are handled through the encounter check.)

HEXMAP KEY SYMBOLS

TERRAIN			
	Desert		Jungle
	Farmland		Jungle, heavy
	Forest, sparse		Jungle, with hills
	Forest, medium		Marsh/Moor
	Forest, heavy		Mountains
	Forest, with hills		Hills
	Forest, dead		Swamp
	Forest, dead with hills		Tundra, frozen
	Fungal Forest		Plateau/Cliff
	Plains		

TERRAIN

▲	Cave	🌋	Volcano
	Dungeon		Fortress/ Stronghold
	Ruins		Castle
	Lair		Lake
	Tower		Sinkhole
		Magic Portal	

PATHING		SETTLEMENTS	
......	Trail		Village
- - - - -	Road		City
– – – –	Highway	★	Capital
══════	River	OTHER FEATURES	
	Mountain Pass	†	Point of Interest

Each hex key will feature

- the **hex #**, uniquely identifying the keyed hex,
- the **name** of the hex, providing a summary and reminder of what the hex contains at a glance, and
- the keyed location's **discovery type** (visible, hidden, or on road/river/trail, see page 400), if any.

Then things get a little more complicated.

The hex might contain a **small, specific site**. These sites are pretty similar to a dungeon room, and I'll key them in a similar manner, with boxed text, reactive skill checks, and site elements:

A3-ORLUK TOTEM
A giant statue, worn by weather and depicting an elephantine beast of prey with black- and yellow-striped fur, holds a lonely vigil in the center of the grassy plains.

INTELLIGENCE (NATURE)-DC 16
The statue depicts a creature known as an orluk.

STATUE
The yellow-and-black stone is not painted, but rather two different types of colored granite have been quarried and then shaped to take advantage of the natural strata.

Some sites might be quite large, but with a uniform experience that supports a similar approach:

N15-RECENT FOREST FIRE

Several acres of this hex have been scorched by a wildfire. Foraging checks are made at disadvantage in this hex, but if the check fails due to disadvantage, the forager discovers the burn site.

Larger sites, however, will more commonly be prepped as a **location-based adventure**. This will usually be a dungeon—anything from a micro-dungeon to a megadungeon—but it could also be designed with an alternative structure, like a raid (see page 268) or caravanserai. In my hex key I'll often just include a reminder to check the separate adventure notes, sometimes accompanied by a minimal description of the location:

F15-SKULL ROCK (ON RIVER)
A rock shaped like a skull thrusts out of the center of the river.

SKULL'S MOUTH
Crawling through the mouth leads to a crypt. See adventure notes.

A hex could also be keyed with a community, like a city, kasbah, shantytown, or dwarven citadel. These are, of course, urban adventures (see page 315), but my tip is that, unless it's a community you're really interested in diving into, you can usually get away with keying the results of a single urban investigation action (see page 350) rather than developing a full-fledged city. However the PCs choose to interact with a particular community, you can usually respond by treating it as an investigation action and serving up the prepared response.

STOCKING YOUR HEXES

Ideally, you want to **key every hex**. For a 10 x 10 hexmap, as we've noted, that's 100 hexes. If you're thinking that sounds like a lot of work, you're not wrong. Even with a majority of your hexes being small sites (and, therefore, roughly equivalent to a dungeon room in terms of prep), it can still be a staggering task.

But it needs to be done. If you have a hexcrawl with a bunch of empty hexes, it creates pacing problems. Even more importantly, it results in the PCs being unable to reliably find landmarks, which makes it impossible for them to navigate through the wilderness. The whole structure of the hexcrawl breaks down.

You can also end up with the same problem in the opposite direction: If you get a lot of hexes keyed with multiple locations, the abstraction of the hexcrawl collapses as the PCs engage in lots of navigation inside the hex. This is also referred to as sub-hex navigation, and it can create problems because, by design, when you're running a hexcrawl, you're not worried about where exactly something is located "inside" the hex—you just know that the PCs are in the hex and the location is in the same hex. But if there are multiple locations in the hex, the players are going to expect the geographic relationships between those locations to remain consistent, despite the fact that there's no mechanism in the hexcrawl structure for keeping track of that.

It's best to just avoid this problem by only keying one location per hex, but sometimes multiple locations in a single hex can't be avoided. That's okay, you'll just need a different mechanism for handling the sub-hex navigation. A pointcrawl can be used for this, as discussed on page 420.

But I digress: You have 100 hexes. How are you going to fill them all?

TECHNIQUE #0: KEEP IT SIMPLE

Before we get started, it's important to know that this may not be as much work as you might think. There are a couple of secrets to that.

The first secret, as I've mentioned before, is that when you're prepping material for yourself, **polish is overrated**. (Details are also overrated, with the proviso that *essential* details and *awesome* details should always be jotted down.) If I were writing up a dungeon behind a waterfall for someone else to use, I'd probably take the time to mention how wet and slick the stairs leading down into the dungeon are; the damp moistness in the air of the first chamber (providing a slight haze that can be burned away dramatically by a *fireball* trap); and the way the dampness gives way to a chilled condensation that hangs in glistening drops from the rough-hewn walls as you descend into the dungeon. But if you're prepping for yourself, you don't need to write that down.

Trust your voice as a GM. During play, based on your intrinsic understanding of the scenario and the environment, the circumstances will provide the logical and evocative details you need to flesh things out. And by placing trust in yourself, you can save yourself a ton of prep time.

The second secret is that the amount of detail required by a hex key can vary quite a bit. You can **use minimal keys**. Just because something is geography, it doesn't mean that it has to be elaborate. Don't fall into the trap of thinking that every hex "needs" to have a 20-room dungeon in it. It definitely doesn't. It almost certainly shouldn't! Remember the ogre's shack and the orluk totem? A hex key doesn't have to be any more complicated than that.

TECHNIQUE #1: BE CREATIVE, BE AWESOME, BE SINCERE

We'll get to the tips, tricks, shortcuts, and/or cheats in a moment, but first things first: Do some honest brainstorming and pour some raw creativity onto the page.

The neat ideas you've been tossing around inside your head for the past few days? Everything your players think would be cool? Everything you think would be cool? Everything you wish the last GM you played with had included in the game?

Put 'em in hexes.

Then think about the setting logically: What *needs* to be there in order for the setting to work? For the stuff you've already keyed to work?

Get 'em in hexes.

Bring your creativity to the table. And make sure everything you include is *awesome*, because life is too short to waste time on the mediocre or "good enough" or the "I guess I need to do that." If there's something mundane or generic, give it a twist or add something extra.

Finally, throughout this entire process, be sincere. I think it's really important to stay true to yourself when you're doing design work: You have a unique point of view and a unique aesthetic. Even when you're bringing in material or inspiration from other sources, apply it through your own perspectives and values.

TECHNIQUE #2: JUMP AROUND

It can be useful to start at Hex A1, go to Hex A2, and then systematically proceed on through the As before getting to the Bs.

But if you're working on A3 and you get a cool idea that belongs on the other side of the map, don't hesitate: Jump over there and key up Hex F7.

This is not only useful from a practical standpoint: It also feels great when you get to Column F and discover three-quarters of the hexes have already been filled in.

TECHNIQUE #3: STEAL

Okay, you've filled a couple dozen hexes, but now you're starting to run out of ideas. What next?

Steal.

If your RPG of choice has published adventures, grab the best of them and start dropping them into hexes. If you don't already own adventures and can't afford to buy them, do a search online for fan-created scenarios. The One Page Dungeon Contest, for example, is an all-you-can-eat smorgasbord for this sort of thing.

Not every adventure can be dropped straight into a hex, of course, but even adventures that aren't explicitly location-based will often feature cool locations that can be ripped out and easily adapted. If the adventure has multiple locations, rip them apart and drop each location into a separate hex.

The stuff you steal doesn't have to be fully developed, either. You can find countless free adventure maps online, just waiting to be filled with cool encounters.

As you're harvesting material like this, you may start to notice patterns: Maybe you've grabbed three different adventures featuring fairies. How could they be connected? What other creatures from the Feywild might be found in the region?

TECHNIQUE #4: RANDOM GENERATORS

We started by filling the map with every ounce of creative thought we had. Then we started recklessly stealing everything we could lay our hands on. But we're still staring at empty hexes. Now what?

Now we need to get our creative juices flowing again by rapidly injecting fresh ideas that will break us out of the dried-out box our thinking is currently trapped in. There are a lot of ways to provide this stimuli:

- Roll a random page number in the *Monster Manual*. Do it again. What are these two monsters doing together in this hex?

- Draw four random *Magic the Gathering* cards and use their names and graphics for inspiration.

- Ask an AI text generator to provide a list of 20 fantasy locations and grab the best ones.

- Go over to your collection of fantasy novels and pluck one off the shelf. Flip to a random page: Where are the characters? Can you use that location, or one like it, in your hexcrawl?

There are also a large number of RPGs that actually include random generators designed for exactly this purpose. (Or generators that can be repurposed or used for inspiration.) Sadly, this doesn't include the current edition of D&D, although previous editions did include them (and there are a number of games similar to D&D you could use to generate similar locations if D&D is your game of choice).

TECHNIQUE #5: SPIN-OFFS

Regardless of how you're stocking a hex, you should keep your mind open to other locations that the current hex suggests.

For example, you've got a necromancer in a crystalline spire who's served by a bunch of goblins he's charmed by writing arcane runes on the inside of their eyelids and then sewing their eyes shut. Where'd he get the goblins from? Maybe's there a village of them living nearby. They protect a tree that bears a single bright red fruit each year. The fruit has magical properties and each year the necromancer comes to claim the fruit and take away goblin slaves.

Or you're keying a grotto that a bunch of bandits are using as a hideout. Turns out these bandits have longbows of remarkably high quality. This is because they're trading with a one-eyed troll who lives in a cave that can only be accessed through a green crystal that thrusts up through the forest floor: Lay your hand upon the crystal, say the magic password, and the crystal becomes intangible. The troll is a master bowyer.

TECHNIQUE #6: WALK AWAY

Finally, be willing to walk away from the project and take a break: Watch a TV show. Read a book. Flip through some unrelated game manuals. Power up the PlayStation®.

Give your brain a chance to breathe and your creative batteries a chance to recharge.

This is not, by any stretch of the imagination, a comprehensive catalog or definitive list of techniques for stocking a hexcrawl. But it's stuff that's worked for me while stocking hexcrawls. Maybe it'll work for you, too. Experiment and play around until you find what works best for you.

STATUS QUO DESIGN

Hexcrawls benefit from **status quo design**, which is basically a fancy way of saying that you prep chunks of the game world in a particular situation, but then you hit the pause button and *don't touch it again* until the players' actions interact with the situation. As soon as the players *do* agitate or change that status quo, though, that chunk of the game world becomes active.

It's kind of an inverted quantum state: Until you observe a subatomic particle, it's impossible to know its current state. With status quo prep, on the other hand, you know *exactly* what the state is *until* you look at it.

Status quo design can be useful in a lot of ways when you're running a roleplaying game, but its utility is starkly obvious when it comes to a hexcrawl. When you're done stocking your hexcrawl, you'll have 100 hexes of keyed content. If you tried to reach in after every session and update every single one of those hexes with a running narrative of events, it would be a daunting task. It would also be a pointless one: Your players won't have seen the previous situation in the vast majority of those hexes, and they likely won't see the new situation you're creating, either. In other words, the PCs aren't actually observing or being affected by any of this activity that you're generating. You're doing a bunch of stuff, but it's not producing any value at the actual game table.

Leaving these various locations in a "frozen" state may seem artificial, but it's really just the way that the world works most of the time: Imagine that you go to a diner for lunch today. You see some waitresses and one of them takes your order. They deliver the food.

If you had gone to the diner for lunch tomorrow instead of today, what would've happened? You'd see some waitresses, one of them would take your order, and they'd deliver the food. If you go next month, will it be different? Probably not. Maybe the waitresses will be different or the owner may tweak the menu a bit, but if you'd never been to the diner before, these changes would not meaningfully alter your experience.

Now, let's say that you went to the diner today and *fired a rocket launcher through the window*. Then you go back tomorrow. Is the diner different now?

Of course it is.

When you're prepping a hex, you're generally prepping the diner. If the PCs go to the diner and do some minor interactions (e.g., they meet a waitress and learn her name is Nancy), then the diner is put into motion and the next time they come back there may be some minor differences (Nancy recognizes them, Nancy has been fired, there's a new menu special, etc.). If the PCs go to the diner and blow it up with a rocket launcher, then there'll be big changes and A LOT of motion (as the diner is rebuilt, Nancy goes looking for a new job, etc.).

This same principle can be extended to more dramatic and/or precarious status quos, too.

For example, you might prep the logging village of Caerdheim for a hexcrawl and know that a murder is about to happen there! But that murder doesn't happen immediately as the campaign begins. The village is in status quo. It's only when the PCs show up that you hit the play button and the murder takes place. (Or Nancy gets into a fight with her boss. Or a logging triceratops breaks loose and rampages through town.)

THE ACTIVE QUO

The status quo also doesn't mean "boring." The status quo of a pirate cove, for example, isn't "The pirates are all sitting around doing nothing." The status quo of a pirate cove is a bunch of pirate ships sailing out to pillage the high seas. The best status quo design is usually more like a coiled spring: The lightest interaction from the PCs will cause an *explosion* of activity.

NON-LOCAL EFFECTS

The action that forces a location (or organization or NPC) into "motion" doesn't have to be direct. For example, when the PCs unleash a horrible plague that kills goblins? They don't actually need to visit the dungeon full of goblins on the other side of the map in order for those goblins to be affected by the plague and the status quo of that dungeon to be changed.

These non-local effects don't require cataclysmic scenarios, either. A single NPC being knocked loose from a location can act as a free radical, putting any number of other elements into motion. For example, when the necromancer escapes from the PCs' raid of Bleached Bone Gulley, maybe they end up slaying the goblin chief and enslaving the tribe.

RETURN TO THE STATUS QUO

With that being said, in the absence of continued PC interaction, elements of the campaign world will generally trend back toward a status quo again. (Note that I said *a* status quo; it's usually not likely that things will go back to the *same* status quo. PCs tend to be more disruptive than that.)

For example, the PCs raid a cult compound, wreak a lot of havoc, and kill a couple of the cult's leaders before being forced to retreat. Over the next week the cult calls in reinforcements from some of their other cells to guard against further incursions until they can finish packing up and moving their operations to a new location.

If the PCs don't reengage with the cult within a couple weeks of the original raid, then the new status quo features steampunk cyborg guards (the other cells were up to some wacky stuff), an abandoned cultist compound, and a new operational center set up in the sub-basement of an emir's palace.

WILDERNESS
⟶ POINTCRAWLS ⟶

Now we come to the last of our structures for wilderness play. Where the hexcrawl abstracts a wilderness into small, explorable areas, the **pointcrawl** can abstract the same region conceptually by focusing on how characters navigate and move through the space.

In other words, you create a map of **locations** and you connect them with **paths**, forming a node map. We refer to the locations as **points** (thus the first half of the name) and the paths as **connectors**. During play, PCs in a location can choose one of the paths connected to that location and travel along it to another location. They can thus crawl (there's the other half of the name) through a **pointmap**.

The pointmap on the facing page depicts part of the same region shown on the sample hexcrawl map on page 392. You can see, therefore, how you can use both the pointcrawl and hexcrawl structures in the same campaign, swapping which structure you're using based on how the players are choosing to interact with the world.

As we look at the connections that make up the structure of the pointcrawl, we can start with the **literal paths**: These are trails, roads, rivers, and the like that are literal paths in the game world. (Thus the name.) These are almost always a player-known structure, and they have a one-to-one correspondence with the game world: The line on the pointmap is directly representing a specific highway or the like.

But pointcrawls will usually also feature **abstract paths**, which represent the natural flow of travelers through the world without being one specific route that you could point to in the game world. That might be because there is no path (the PCs are trying to cross the trackless wastes of the Eldlands), but it can also be because there's a multitude of paths and it doesn't matter which one they take. (Are they taking an old deer trail? Following the river? Just trying to cut through the forest as best they can? Small differences in the travelogue aside, they'll all cross the same region, use the same encounter table, and take them to the same place.)

You can see the difference between literal and abstract paths by looking at the Maernath pointmap: If the PCs leave Maernath by the

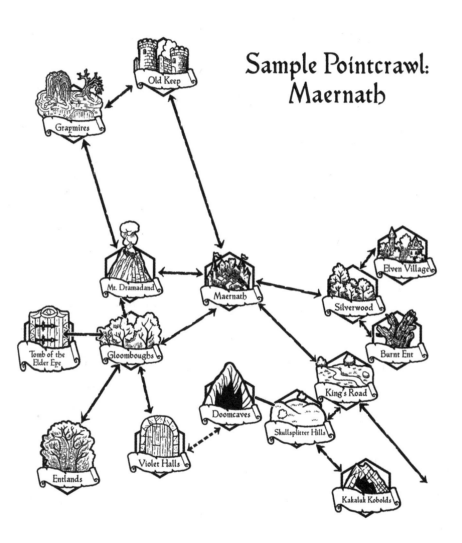

Sample Pointcrawl: Maernath

King's Road, they're following a literal path (the actual road) and if they go that way again, they'll be taking the same road. If they instead head southwest into the Gloomboughs forest, that's an abstract path. The next time they go that way they might take the same path, or they might take another.

You can show the players the pointmap of a region if you want, but this isn't necessary. Assuming the pointmap remains a GM-only tool and a player-unknown structure, the GM will become an "interpreter" where abstract paths are concerned, translating the players' intentions into the pointcrawl system, using the pointcrawl system to resolve it, and then describing the outcome to the players in terms of the fiction.

The players may announce **specific intentions**. This can be a literal path ("let's take the King's Road") or it might be based on a known landmark ("let's head toward Mt. Dramadand!"). Either way, you can simply look at the pointmap, see their destination, and move them along the appropriate path.

Alternatively they might announce a **nonspecific intention**. This will often be a compass direction, such as, "Let's head east from Maernath." Looking at the pointmap you know that east will take them in the direction of Mt. Dramadand, so you select that path.

Finally, they may announce an **indirect destination**. In other words, a destination that is not directly linked to their current location by a path. For example, from Maernath they might say, "Let's go to the Graymires." Once again looking at the pointmap, you can see that the most direct route involves following the path to Mt. Dramadand and then following the path from there to the Graymires. (Alternatively, seeing the other route via the Old Keep, you might ask them if they want to go northwest across the plains or stay closer to the mountains. Or, if they're already familiar with both routes, you might just ask them which route they want to take.)

What you wouldn't do is have them go straight from Maernath to the Graymires while skipping the points in between. In the absence of intentionality (e.g., the players saying that they're going to head northwest, but are going to specifically steer clear of the Old Keep), the pointmap represents the normal "flow" of travel: If you head from Maernath to the Graymires, you will either visit (or at least pass by) Mt. Dramadand or the Old Keep.

MAKING THE POINTMAP

You could hypothetically make a pointmap with no other reference for the game world and run a campaign from just that and nothing else, but it would likely be a struggle at best. There's a lot of information about the world that feels fairly essential (e.g., what's the terrain like between Maernath and the Fungal Forest?) that would require extra effort to key onto the pointmap. I, personally, would find it difficult to even create a pointmap in such a vacuum. (Your mileage may vary.)

I find it useful to think of a game world as being layered. A traditional map, a geopolitical map, an airship route map, a hexmap, a pointmap—these are all different ways of creating, presenting, and accessing information about the world; they're separate "layers" that all coexist with each other (or, at least, *can* coexist with each other). The pointmap, therefore, is one stratum, but it's embedded within the larger strata of the game world.

Therefore, when I'm designing a pointmap, I will start with an existing map of the campaign world and use it to figure out the pathing, like the example on the next page.

The source map doesn't have to be a hexmap; it's just convenient in this case since we already have a hexmap of this region. You might instead use geographical, topographical, geopolitical, or cadastral maps. The key info you need is as follows:

- Where are the points of interest?
- What are the diegetic routes (roads, rivers, etc.)?
- What is the travel time between points (generally calculated from terrain/route type and distance)?

As you're sketching out your pointmap, start with the literal paths: Look at the major roads, for example. What locations do they connect? Draw those connections. Is river travel significant? Add those connections, too. In an "edge of civilization" setting like Maernath, this may not give you very much. In other regions, though, it may give you a lot more structure.

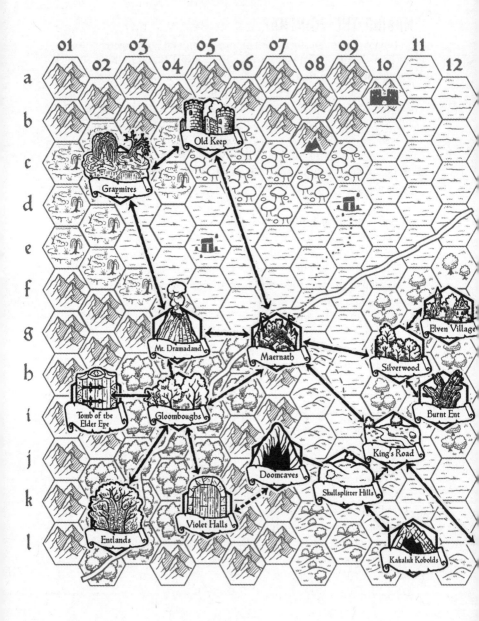

Either way, your next step is, unsurprisingly, the abstract paths. These are trickier, but what I find useful is to just kind of imagine myself traveling the world. Easy pickings at this stage are any points of interest that aren't yet connected to the pointmap: If you wanted to get there, how would you do it? But even points that are located on literal paths may still have abstract links.

You'll also likely be adding additional points that don't appear on your source map—adventure sites, minor landmarks, and the like.

Once you've got all the connections in place, go through and determine the **terrain type** and **distance** for each path. These can be listed directly on the map for easy reference during play.

HIDDEN ROUTES

A hidden route in a pointcrawl is a connection between two points that isn't immediately obvious; i.e., the PCs have to find the route before they can use it. This might be an illusory druid path, a teleportation circle, or perhaps an underground tunnel.

Hidden routes are often discovered as part of a scenario or while exploring a particular location. In other cases, discovering the hidden route might be as simple as making an Intelligence (Investigation) or Wisdom (Survival) check in the right place.

Hidden routes can be indicated on your map using a dotted line. For example, there's a connection within the Violet Halls dungeon to the Doomcaves on the far side of the mountains that's indicated as a hidden route on the Maernath map.

RUNNING A POINTCRAWL

When the expedition leaves their current point, they choose one of the paths connected to their current point and follow it.

Then, during each watch:

1. Mark the **watch** and tick **durations** and **daily resources** (food, water, etc.).

2. Make an **encounter check**.

3. Declare **watch actions**.

4. Resolve **travel** by:

   A. Declaring **pace**.

   B. Making a **navigation check**.

   C. Tracking **movement** on the pointmap.

5. Resolve **encounters**, including Perception-type checks (which may interrupt travel).

6. Resolve **other watch actions**.

When the expedition reaches a new point, describe it to them and let them interact with it. At some point they will choose a path connected to the new point, and the process repeats.

This procedure is essentially identical to running a route, except that the expedition has a choice of paths at each point. This is probably unsurprising, because a pointmap can also be thought of as a map of many individual routes that the PCs can swap between.

OFF POINT

If the PCs are in a point on the pointmap, you can just follow this procedure. If for some reason they've slipped "off" the pointmap, simply funnel them logically into the pointmap and continue from there.

You might be able to assume that they're "at" the nearest point (e.g., they're close enough to Mt. Dramadand that they're basically "coming from the volcano" as far as other points are concerned). Alternatively, if you want to get all formal about it, you could think of their current location as a "temporary point" and think about how it would attach to the pointmap as they begin traveling.

✦ HOMEWORK ✦

THE MANY-HEADED POINT

A wilderness pointcrawl is a great tool, but it really only scratches the potential of the pointcrawl structure, which is incredibly versatile because each "point" can be literally *any* point of interest. Those points may be extremely specific, like "the orluk totem outside of town," but they can also be quite vast, like "the city of Kingsdeep" or "the Empire of Catalac." Even better, the structure is very flexible, with points of different "scale" easily coexisting. (For example, the orluk totem and the city of Kingsdeep can both appear on the same pointmap.) It can even be trivially fractal, with the point on one pointmap being an entirely self-contained pointcrawl in its own right. (This also means that a pointcrawl can be used as either a scenario structure or a campaign structure.)

Pointcrawls can also be adapted to completely different milieus: You can use pointcrawls for a ruined city, a cyberspace network, a galactic star map, or the vast caverns of the Shadow Deep.

And this is, in fact, your homework assignment.

It's actually the last homework assignment you'll find in this book. If you've plowed through the entire volume from the front cover up to this point, then you've already learned (and used!) a bunch of different scenario structures: mysteries and heists and dungeons and social events and more!

(If you haven't done that yet, you may want to hit the pause button here and come back later.)

As you've discovered, every one of those scenario structures can be used to create an almost limitless number of different scenarios. At some point, though, you're going to want to create a scenario and you'll discover that these scenarios structures—even in combination—won't get the job done. When that happens, you'll have to figure out how to create a new scenario structure for yourself, something that will guide both what you prep for the scenario and how you run it.

This homework is about dipping your toes into that pool by taking the pointcrawl structure and adapting it into a non-wilderness adventure or campaign. We'll start by taking the wilderness pointcrawl structure we're already familiar with and boiling it down to the most essential procedure. In doing so, we'll reduce it to its most basic structure, which we can then expand and build upon for our variant structure.

BASIC POINTCRAWL PROCEDURE

Running a basic pointcrawl boils down to a three-step procedure.

STEP 1: FOLLOW A PATH

The PCs choose one of the paths connected to their current point.

> **TIME**
>
> The length of time it takes to follow a path may be standardized for an entire pointcrawl. (For example, you may assume it always takes 10 to 15 minutes to move from one point to another in an urban setting.) Alternatively, different connections may take different amounts of time. If so, this can be indicated directly on the map using either small numbers or dots (with each dot representing one standard interval of time). In setting these times, you'll most likely be taking the strata of the pointcrawl into account (e.g., traveling 1 mile down an open road will take less time than traveling 10 miles through the tangled bracken of a wild forest).

STEP 2: RANDOM ENCOUNTER

Check for a random encounter.

> **PROCEDURE**
>
> Any number of random encounter procedures could be employed here. You might check once per path, once per interval, once per watch, or at any other rate that makes sense for the current 'crawl.

STEP 3: ARRIVAL

The PCs arrive at the next point.

ADAPTATION

What's the non-wilderness milieu of your new pointcrawl? There were a few options listed previously, but you can really go with anything where there are points of interest connected to each other (and a reason for the PCs to explore or travel through them).

At this point, you've got a couple options.

First, you can develop your pointcrawl through play: Create a pointmap, key the points, and set up a random encounter table. Then just start playing. The basic procedure above is fully functional.

As you're running this pointcrawl, you'll start finding the places where you need more support. When problems come up at the table, you'll obviously need to find ways to deal with them and play through them. This often works just fine, but you'll also want to keep notes and maybe even do some postmortems with your players so that they can provide their own feedback on what's working and what's not. For problems or rough spots or questions that you're running into again and again, you'll likely want to develop a formal solution that can be applied again and again.

You can avoid some of these rough spots, of course, by trying to anticipate them before play begins: What types of actions are the players likely to take? Where will they want to go? How will they want to get there? What does the pointmap look like? What do the paths represent?

Imagine running a scenario. What are the things you're likely to say? Here are some examples:

⊚ "Crossing Waterloo Bridge, you head south past the London Eye to Lambeth Palace." (The PCs are leaving a vampire den near Covent Garden. Waterloo Bridge, the London Eye, and Lambeth Palace are all locations on the pointmap. In this case, the players already have some familiarity—or perhaps a great deal of familiarity—with the city, recognizing these locations without the GM needing to describe them.)

(continued)

◎ "Following the bonsai turtles, you pass through an arch in the hedgerow and find yourselves standing at the top of an ancient amphitheater. Benches of worn stone descend to a circular area where three of the bonsai turtles have already gathered. On the far side of the amphitheater you can see two other arches like the one you've just come through, leading to other paths in the Maze." (The amphitheater is a location the PCs have just discovered. The GM is indicating the existence of two other paths, leading to other locations, that the PCs could follow.)

◎ "You're following the gateway IP to the subnet when you see Black-IC approaching." (The PCs are traveling along a connection and a random encounter has been triggered.)

◎ "You exit the gnarl in the Ceti Alpha system. Do you want to dock here, continue hubward to Ceti Beta, or detour spinward via Canopus?" (These are all stellar systems and gnarl-ways the PCs are familiar with.)

Really thinking about how you'll describe the world through the lens of the pointcrawl and how the players will take action within the context of the pointcrawl will tell you a lot about how the adventure is supposed to flow at the table, the types of actions you'll need to be able to resolve, and the like.

As you're putting these pieces together, testing them during play, and revising them, you'll want to make a point of arranging all of your material into a specific running procedure. Literally "do this, then this, then this." (You've seen and used these for almost every scenario structure and campaign structure in this book.)

Once you've got your procedure written down, do a couple imaginary test runs to spot any obvious problems. (You'll almost certainly discover more once you're actually interacting with the players and juggling their actions and responses.) One thing you want to watch out for in particular is **mis-sequencing**: Any point where a step in your procedure requires information you don't have yet.

For example, when I ran my first hexcrawl campaign, I had put together most of the tools described in the Hexcrawls chapter (see page 391), but I'd mis-sequenced the random encounters:

◈   Okay, check for an encounter. (*roll dice*)

◈   There is an encounter, so let's determine what the encounter is. (*roll dice*) A group of 1d12 goblins, so roll the number of goblins. (*roll dice*) 8 goblins, write that down.

◈   Now, where does the encounter take place? First, determine time of day. (*roll dice*) Where would they be at that time of day?

◈   Ask them what direction they're going, then calculate their speed, figure out where they'll be.

◈   Now check to see if they got lost. They did, so go back—this is the first mis-sequencing!—and determine where they actually ended up . . . (*roll dice*)

◈   Hmm. So that means they're in this hex over here. But that means the terrain type has shifted, so I need to go back and recalculate the distance they actually traveled. (Another mis-sequencing!)

◈   Oh! And the encounter table changed. So that means they didn't encounter goblins, they would have encountered . . . Wait, what did I roll?

It was a train wreck. There were lots of painfully long pauses while I fidgeted with my notes.

And that's okay! That's why we playtest and revise and refine.

The other thing I like to keep an eye out for is **busywork**: Where are you expending a lot of effort to generate a result or manage information, but it's not creating value by improving the experience at the table? Pay particular attention to any place where you're doing a bunch of stuff behind your screen that's never perceived by the players.

One way to solve busywork is to simply eliminate it, but the other option is to ask yourself how you can make that material, whatever it is, visible to the players (and therefore relevant).

For example, if you go through all the work of advancing a faction clock (see page 344), but then never complete the process by figuring out how the progress clock intersects the PCs, that would just be busywork: rolling dice and filling in ticks, but never to any real effect as far as the players are concerned. It's when the progress clock impacts the PCs—as a rumor, a strike team, a job offer, a newspaper headline, etc.—that the faction clock becomes meaningful.

Finally, consider **recordkeeping**. The Dungeon Running Sheet (see page 71) and Hexcrawl Running Sheet (see page 396) are both powerful tools that help you keep track of vital information that you'll need to reference repeatedly and/or significantly later. Are you losing track of stuff? Make a point of writing that down. And once you're writing stuff down, is there a way you can systematize that to make it easier or even more useful?

ANNOUNCE THE PLAYTEST

If you're trying out something new, it doesn't hurt to tell the players: "Hey! We're going to be playtesting something new tonight. There'll probably be some rough edges while I figure things out, and I'd really appreciate your feedback after the session."

We're all in this together, right? And if the players know what's going on, they'll help you out.

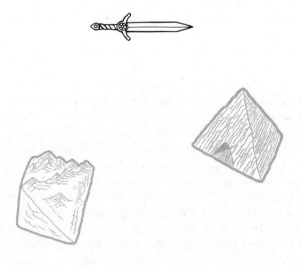

EXTRA CREDIT

WELCOME to your extra credit! Whether you're arriving here after reading the rest of the book cover to cover and running dozens of scenarios for your grateful players or you're just skipping ahead to grab the specific tool or technique you need to enhance your campaign, this is where you're going to find a treasure trove of material for fleshing out your game and taking it to the next level.

Here's a quick guide to the extra credit you can choose to pursue:

- **Creating Your Campaign** (see page 435), including how you can find players, pitch your game, create characters, and learn new roleplaying games.

- **Campaign Status Documents** (see page 448) are a tool for organizing your campaign notes.

- **Learning a New RPG** (see page 458) gives some useful tips for confidently running an RPG you're unfamiliar with.

- **The Open Table** (see page 463) is an alternative way of running a campaign that can make playing an RPG as easy as a board game.

- **Quick-and-Dirty Worldbuilding** (see page 471) has guidance for the essential material you need to start running games in a world of your own creation.

- **Rumor Tables** (see page 476) are a technique for passing information about the game world to the players.

- **Running Combat** (see page 486) is a grab bag of tips and tricks for improving your combat encounters.

- **Scenario Hooks** (see page 498), aka how you get the players to play your adventures.

- **Supporting Cast** (see page 506) is another grab bag of tools and tricks for creating and running memorable NPCs.

- **Splitting the Party** (see page 525), or what to do when the PCs want to do multiple things at the same time.

Whether you're running dungeons, mysteries, heists, or hexcrawls, this is material that will always be useful.

Let's dive in!

CREATING YOUR
─┼─ CAMPAIGN ─┼─

How do you go from saying, "I want to run an RPG campaign" to actually running your first session?

The core skills of designing and running adventures are a large part of that, but in actual practice there are a bunch of really practical tasks that need to be accomplished, starting with the most basic: Who's actually sitting at the table and playing the game with you?

FINDING PLAYERS

In order to play any multiplayer game, you have to start by inviting people to play with you. When it comes to roleplaying games, you can either

A. invite friends, i.e., the people you already know, or

B. find gamers, i.e., people you don't know who share the mutual interest of playing a roleplaying game.

Maybe you have friends who *are* gamers. That's fantastic! Those would certainly be the first people I would talk to. They might even be people who you've played with before in another GM's game or, if this isn't your first rodeo, people who have played in your previous campaigns.

That's recruiting on easy mode! (You lucky bastard.)

Those interested in playing RPGs often seek out fellow hobbyists, so let's start there. In your hometown, you can check out your **local game store**. Some will have bulletin boards where you can advertise your game or find players looking to find a game. Game stores will also host organized play events, like the Adventurers League for D&D or the Society for Pathfinder, where you can meet other players.

You can also do some googling for **local game clubs**, which can offer similar LFG (looking for group) services and opportunities to socialize with other gamers. Online **meetup groups** on Facebook, Reddit, and similar sites can also be good places to reach out, as can **schools**, **libraries**, and **community centers** (some of which may already have game clubs). You may also have luck finding kindred spirits at **board game nights**.

It can be easier to catch something if you throw your net on a national or even global scale, which is something that virtual table-tops, video calls, and similar tools make possible. Check out **forums**, **subreddits**, **Discord servers**, and similar online RPG communities. Many virtual tabletop programs will also offer LFG services and/or online communities through their sites.

Last, but certainly not least, what about your **non-gamer friends**?

In many ways, this should be easy: Just ask them. The same way you'd ask them to watch a movie or play a board game.

But one of the reasons that many would-be GMs try to seek out existing gamers, instead of just asking their friends to play a game with them, is that it's often seen as difficult to get new players to try an RPG for the first time. For a long time, this was largely because of the "geek stigma" around roleplaying games, but the geeks have long since inherited the earth, so what's going on here?

A lot of it has to do with the commitment you're asking these new players to make. As you think about running an RPG, you're likely imagining a grand campaign—perhaps a D&D epic from 1st to 20th level!—but that's a really big commitment for someone who's never played before! It's not really comparable to a movie night or playing a board game at all! "Hey, would you like to spend every Saturday afternoon for the next year doing this thing you've never done before?"

What I recommend, therefore, is recruiting through one-shots. (The Mephits & Magmin adventure on page 46 is a great example of the type of one-shot scenario you can run for new players.) Don't pitch a long-term commitment. Just ask people to hang out for one afternoon. That's a lot more like hanging out at the bar or playing Ultimate Frisbee in the park.

Not everyone who plays an RPG with you for the first time will decide that it's something they want to do long-term. But some of them will! The friends who do? Now they're gamer friends!

And that's recruiting on easy mode.

We make our own luck here.

OPEN TABLE RECRUITMENT

Check out the Open Table extra credit (see page 463) for another
great way to make RPGs more accessible to your friends.

THE CAMPAIGN CONCEPT

With players in hand (or possibly a little before that), you'll want to figure out your **campaign concept**. This can be roughly broken down into the answers to three questions:

◎ Who are the characters?

◎ What do they do?

◎ Where do they do it?

Some roleplaying games are designed to give you answers to some or all of these questions, although the answers can range from the very specific to the vaguely generic.

D&D, for example, provides fairly generic answers:

◎ You're fantasy heroes.

◎ Who go on adventures.

◎ In a Tolkienesque fantasy world.

Despite being fairly vague, these answers are good enough that you can usually just tell people, "We're playing D&D," and they'll be able to create characters that will probably work for whatever campaign you're planning.

Ars Magica, on the other hand, defaults to the following:

◎ You're powerful magi.

◎ Who have banded together to found a covenant.

◎ Somewhere in a fantasy version of medieval Europe.

This example may make it a little clearer that, if you're running an *Ars Magica* campaign, you'll need to nail down exactly *where* in medieval Europe this particular covenant is being founded. By extension, the same thing is true for D&D across all three questions: You want to take all those vague answers and start fleshing them out and nailing them down with specifics.

The creation of a campaign concept—i.e., providing concrete answers to these questions—can be a collaborative process. The question, "What game do y'all want to play next?" is basically the most simplistic form of this, but you can also work with your players to answer the key questions of the campaign concept. Having vague answers (like the ones D&D provides) can actually be quite useful here, since it can help guide the group more effectively than a completely blank slate would.

Some RPGs are more explicitly designed to do this. For example, John Harper's *Blades in the Dark* gives very specific answers to most of the campaign concept questions:

⬡ You're playing members of a small criminal organization.

⬡ Who do scores in order to build their organization into a large and powerful faction.

⬡ In the postapocalyptic fantasy city of Doskvol, cloaked in eternal night.

And then the character creation mechanics prompt the players to choose what type of criminal organization they're running (assassins, cultists, smugglers, etc.) and, therefore, the types of scores they'll typically be performing.

Other RPGs won't give you any guidance at all. They're designed with expansive settings and mechanics that, at least hypothetically, give you the tools to do anything you can imagine in them. Jonathan Tweet's *Over the Edge*, for example, takes place on the Mediterranean island of Al Amarja, where every conspiracy theory is true and every covert organization has converged to fight a proxy battle for reality. You can do and be virtually anything there. Which is incredibly cool! But also really daunting unless and until you and/or your players nail down a more specific concept.

THE CAMPAIGN PITCH

A basic campaign concept can also serve as your pitch when selling a new campaign to prospective players:

◎ You're space pirates trying to scrape together a living among the backwater worlds of the Blue Nebula.

◎ You're wizards who have banded together to form a covenant in the Black Forest of medieval Germany.

◎ You're professional dragonslayers, hunting wyrms among the Greyspire Peaks.

If you're playing with an established group that's looking to start a new campaign, it can be really effective to put together three or four of these concepts and pitch them to the group. Every concept should be something that you're excited about running, and offering them as choices to the group will make sure that everyone else can be equally excited for what comes next!

THE BRIEFING PACKET

The next thing you need is the **player's briefing packet**. This document contains the essential information about the campaign setting that the players will need in order to create their characters and character backgrounds.

The briefing packet is often dependent on the campaign concept, but it's not unusual for them to be developed in tandem. For example, you might give the players broad information about what the Mythic Europe setting of *Ars Magica* looks like so that they can choose what region they want to establish a covenant in, and then, based on that additional aspect of the campaign concept, pull additional information about that specific region that will be relevant to them.

You generally want to keep this briefing packet as concise as possible. I've run campaigns, for example, where the briefing packet was just one paragraph long. The upper limit, in my experience, is about five pages. That's roughly the length at which I can have a reasonable expectation that most or all of the players will read it before coming to the session, and if they don't read it, it's short enough that they'll be able to peruse it at the table without chewing up too much time.

For certain cultural touchstones—if you're playing in Middle-earth or the *Star Wars* universe, for example—you might even discover that a single sentence will work. ("You're human rangers working out of Rivendell" or "You're agents of the Mos Eisley Police Authority.")

The key thing to remember is that you're just looking to provide a baseline. As players get excited about the setting and start developing their characters, they will *seek out* more detailed information (and care a lot more about it as a result).

If you're creating a briefing packet for an original setting of your own creation, check out the Quick-and-Dirty Worldbuilding extra credit (see page 471) for tips.

CREATING CHARACTERS

Now that the players know what the campaign concept is and they know enough about the setting to orient themselves, it's time to create your characters.

You can have all the players create their characters separately, but if you're creating characters for a long-term campaign, I recommend having everyone do it together. You want to give everybody an opportunity to weave their characters together. While this kind of bond can be created over time through actual play, it's often much easier to do it as part of character creation, and it will help get your first session off to a strong start. (This is sometimes referred to as a Session 0, and in some cases—particularly if you're also collaborating on the campaign concept—it can even take a full session. This is usually okay, as long as everyone's expectations have been set up for this.)

This doesn't mean that *everything* needs to be done as a group. One-on-one sessions allow the PCs to have secrets from each other (which can be both dramatic and exciting!), and there will likely come a point in the process, after the initial details have been established and the group dynamic figured out, where it will simply become more practical to continue the work one-on-one via email, a Discord server, or the like, as described below.

In some esoteric cases it may even make sense for the players to all create their characters in complete secrecy from each other, but this creates a much larger burden on you, as the GM, to make sure you end up with a cohesive group.

STEP 1: THE PLAYER'S CONCEPT

Start by turning the players loose to create whatever they want to create. In some cases the strictures of the campaign will tightly curtail their options. For example, if the campaign is about a group of teenagers who have manifested psychic abilities and been drafted into a government special-ops team . . . well, then I'm expecting to get back characters who are teenagers with psychic abilities.

In other cases, like most D&D campaigns, the players can have pretty much carte blanche with their character concepts. (And you'll frequently be amazed by the stunningly original ideas they bring to the table.)

Either way, it's not unusual for a player to challenge the assignment. For example, they might say, "Can I actually create the government handler assigned to the teenage psychics?" or "What if my psychic time-slip ability has prematurely aged me so that I look middle-aged even though my character is only 13?" Sometimes this just won't work (there's a reason why the campaign concept is set up in a specific way), but my inclination is, as it so often is, to default to yes and see if there's a way that we can make it work.

Often this turns out to be to the campaign's benefit in ways that I could never anticipate. For example, I once ran a D&D campaign where one of my few instructions was that none of the characters should be from the city where the campaign was set. I knew that the first session would begin with the PCs waking up with partial amnesia and the first chunk of the campaign, therefore, would be about them exploring the city and trying to find their bearings. I didn't want any of them to already be familiar with the city because I felt the disorientation was important.

During character creation, one of the players was drawn to the background details about the local elves, so her character—an elf named Tithenmamiwen—ended up being from the city after all . . . and it turned out I'd been completely wrong. Having one character who *was* familiar with the city and had contacts there, but who was completely alienated from everything and everyone she knew as a result of the partial amnesia, was *far* more compelling than what I'd originally envisioned.

In any case, once you've got the character concepts back from your players, the next step is integrating those concepts into the campaign. There are actually two parts to this process, which I'll refer to as the **public integration** and the **private integration**.

WHAT ABOUT THE GAME MECHANICS?

The rulebook for whatever RPG you're playing will walk you through the character creation mechanics step by step. Just follow that procedure and you should be fine.

The one thing that may come up is if a player has a strong concept for their character that isn't quite supported by the available rules. As a new GM, you're perfectly justified to say, "Since we're just learning the game, I'd be more comfortable if we stuck with the rules right now." But often it'll be just fine if you tweak things a bit. Another good phrase to remember here is: "We'll try this, but we may need to make adjustments later to get the balance right."

STEP 2: PUBLIC INTEGRATION

The public integration is where I collaborate with the player to work the character more deeply into the cultural and historical aspects of the campaign world. There are a couple reasons for this: First, bouncing ideas back and forth tends to just inherently encourage more deeply imagined characters. Second, the player rarely knows as much about the campaign setting as I do (even if it's a published campaign setting), so the collaboration is both a way of leveraging my own expertise for the character's benefit and also a way of introducing the player to more of the setting.

The actual process of integration will vary quite a bit from one character to the next. Our starting point, of course, is whatever the player's initial concept is, which can be anything from a few sentences to a dozen pages of detailed background or even more. What I'm generally looking for are specific details about the character that can either be made more specific, given a deeper context, connected to other elements of the campaign world, or all of the above.

For example, you might have a player who says, "My character is a knight."

Let's start by making that detail more specific by offering three specific orders of knighthood that the player could choose for their PC to be a member of:

◎ Order of the Adamantine Band
◎ Brotherhood of the Blade
◎ Knights of the Silver Serpent

(In practice, each of these would also be accompanied by a short description so that the player could understand the choice they were making.)

We can also give that detail a deeper context by providing details on the history and beliefs of the knighthood. Here's an example that I've used in my own campaign:

THE WAY OF KNIGHTHOOD

Any order of knighthood has three things in common.

1. They follow the Code of Law as laid down in the *Book of Athor*.

2. They adhere to the Martial Code as laid down in the *Book of Itor*.

3. They honor the Seven Compassions as laid down in the *Book of Crissa*.

The Code of Law is your bedrock "thou shalt not" stuff: Don't murder, steal, enslave your brother, and so forth.

The Martial Code is essentially your standard chivalric ideal: Face your opponent fairly and honorably.

(continued)

The Seven Compassions are a bit more philosophically complex, and are also referred to in some commentaries as the Seven Cares. The compassions are of the self, the companion, the stranger, the task, the thought, the memory, and the true. In other words, care for yourself, for your companions, and for strangers. Take care with what you do and what you think, and it shall be remembered. And if you can do all that, then you will know true compassion. (For most people, the Seven Compassions boil down to "be nice to people" and "think before you act.")

Collectively these are also known as the Way of Knighthood.

You can see how this type of detail can immediately give the player raw fodder for roleplaying their character. Now they don't have to just talk vaguely about chivalric ideals, they can invent quotes from the *Book of Athor* or give their opponent mercy in accordance with the Martial Code.

We can also link these orders of knighthood or the PC's relationship with them to other elements of the campaign world: The Knights of the Silver Serpent might be vassals of the Imperial Church, for example, or the PC could have been recommended to the Brotherhood of the Blade by a noble family with strong ties to the order.

In many cases, particularly if we're playing in a world of my own creation, these are not even details of the setting that previously existed. Prompted by the PC's background, I'm seizing the opportunity to add depth to the campaign world. (And, crucially, it's depth precisely aimed at an area of the campaign world that one of the PCs will be connected to and that the player is likely to be very interested in.)

You also don't need to overthink this. It's often as simple as the player saying, "I want to play the cleric of a god of war." And then you say, "The god of war is Itor."

Just because you *can* add details about how the Church of Itor operates; what the history of the church is; what the religious uniforms of the church are; what the holy symbol of the god is; and so forth doesn't mean that you *need* to or even should.

Crucially, this process is not about me, as the GM, trying to impose my concept on the character. My goal is to work with the player to enrich and enable their concept. It's not a one-sided process, and we'll likely go back and forth several times. If the player wants to develop the details of an original knightly order for their character to belong to, you should absolutely leap at that opportunity. (And the collaboration now becomes a matter of how that knightly order can be integrated into the wider campaign world.)

Similarly, I always try to leave the final say with the player. For example, if they come to me with a knight and I send them back a couple of pages about the Knights of the Silver Serpent, I'll try to make a point of asking, "Does that sound right?"

If it isn't, we'll try to figure out where I misinterpreted the character concept and try to find a solution that works. (This is also why I like to give them options and then develop the option they choose.)

BETWEEN THE SESSIONS

Somewhere early in the public integration phase (after a few key questions and basic options have been resolved, like which order of knighthood the character belongs to) is where I'll usually wrap up in-person character creation and move the process to email or chat. This is ideal because it's a format that allows me to pull chunks of information from my setting documents to share and also one that allows the players to think about and carefully develop their character.

The end goal of this back-and-forth is to produce and/or have the player produce a definitive "Character Background" document. A typical length, with the kind of development process described here, is two or three pages, although it's not unusual for some players to take it further than that.

STEP 3: GM'S INTEGRATION

For all intents and purposes, the character is now ready to go. But as the GM, I'm not finished. At this point, I'll start figuring out how to hook the character into the larger structure of the campaign.

- ⬡ Is there a major villain in the second act? Make it the long-lost brother of one of the PCs.
- ⬡ Is there a kidnapping victim in the third adventure? Make it the mentor of one of the PCs.
- ⬡ Was I planning to have a corrupt order of wizards? Give one of the PCs a chance to join it.

And so forth.

It's about figuring out how to make the campaign about the characters instead of just involving the characters.

STEP 4: BRINGING THE PARTY TOGETHER

Technically, this isn't a separate step. It's something that should be taken into consideration throughout the entire character creation process.

What binds these disparate characters together?

Whether the PCs are delving into dungeons, investigating eldritch horrors, sailing the Astral Sea, or trying to protect the Feyish Court, they need some reason why they are sticking together and working with each other.

Fortunately, it's not solely your responsibility, as the game master, to explain this. As they're creating the group, make sure the players figure out why all these characters are hanging out together.

- ⬡ What background do they share?
- ⬡ What goal do they have in common?
- ⬡ What secret do they all share?
- ⬡ What organization do they all work for?
- ⬡ What emotional connections do they have to each other?

Once you know what makes them a group, you can hang your scenario hooks off it (see page 498). This works even if their connection seems mundane and unrelated to whatever the scenario is. For example, let's say they decide they all work at the same comic book store. Great, now you can threaten the store. Or have some strange person/creature come to the store. Or maybe the whole structure of the campaign becomes tracking down rare issues of comic books for resale, and the weird people, places, and estate sales they go to also get them tangled up in whatever the scenario happens to be.

If they all share a dark secret, then a scenario hook just needs to threaten that secret in some way to pull them all in. Or they can all be blackmailed by the same mysterious patron.

Note that not all of the characters need to be bound together by a single reason. For example, two of the characters might be a brother and a sister, bound together by their family connection, while the sister and all of the other PCs work together.

Also, just because the *players* are all collectively figuring out what binds their characters together, this doesn't necessarily mean that the *characters* all know each other when the game begins! For example, they might all want to find the Ruby Eye of Drosnin or figure out the Truth about the Templars and be actively pursuing that without necessarily pursuing it together. (At least, not at first.)

You may also find it useful to provide the players with a simple, open-ended seed to focus their mutual intent around. The scenario hook for the first adventure is a great place to start. For example, I ran a campaign where I told the players:

◎   The first scene of the campaign will be your characters walking through the doors of the Red Hand tavern in Dweredell to meet a contact who's offering you a job.

◎   You need to figure out how you all ended up there together.

If you were launching your campaign with Mephits & Magmin, you might ask the players to explain how they all ended up together in the small village near Firebelch Cavern.

CAMPAIGN STRUCTURE

As you're developing the concept for your campaign, you'll also want to give some thought to the **campaign structure** you want to use in building it.

Broadly speaking, a campaign structure is the way in which the individual scenarios of a campaign are associated with each other and, importantly, how the PCs are expected to go from one scenario to another.

A simple structure is the **episodic campaign**, in which the GM presents one scenario to the players, they play it, and then the GM presents another scenario. You'll need to give the PCs a scenario hook at the beginning of each new scenario (see page 498). (A common variant is to use one or more **patrons** who either hire the PCs as freelancers or act as their boss to send them on missions, thus creating a default method for giving the group scenario hooks.)

If you want options that are a little more dynamic, or that empower the players, you might also check out node-based campaigns (see page 239), hexcrawls (see page 391), pointcrawsl (see page 420), or urbancrawls (see page 471) as alternative campaign structures.

CAMPAIGN STATUS
+ DOCUMENTS +

Campaigns are a collection of scenarios. There are a lot of structures that can be used for organizing those scenarios—it might be a purely episodic campaign (one scenario after another), a node-based campaign (see page 239), or a hexcrawl (see page 391)—but ultimately what you have, figuratively or literally, is a binder full of scenarios.

A lot of the details of the campaign, therefore, will be found in your scenario notes.

But where do you keep track of all the stuff that *isn't* part of a specific scenario? Or that was part of a scenario that wrapped up, but is still floating around like a free radical affecting the PCs and/or the setting? (For example, a bad guy who escaped and has sworn vengeance on the PCs. Or a demonic plague that was accidentally released into the city. Or an NPC that one of the PCs has fallen in love with.)

There's where the **campaign status document** comes into play. (Literally.)

Rather than keeping notes attached to a dozen different scenarios, you can rope all the active elements of your campaign together into this single document and then update it after each session. In this way, it becomes the default repository for the evolving canon of the campaign. It's arguably the single most important document I have at the table during play. It's always kept close at hand and is ultimately the guide I use to keep the campaign on track.

It's also kind of my secret weapon as a GM. How can I run these huge, sprawling, complicated campaigns without getting lost? I have a road map. I use the campaign status document as a cheat sheet, offloading the mental load to my downtime between sessions so that at the actual table I can stay focused on execution and active play rather than the logistics of continuity.

The campaign status document, however, is not a one-size-fits-all tool. Every single campaign is unique, and I've found that to be reflected in each campaign's status document. It often takes me three or four sessions with a new campaign before I can really start grokking what the status document for that campaign is going to look like.

With that being said, there are three elements that form the core of most campaign status documents:

◎ scenario updates
◎ the timeline of bangs
◎ background events

SCENARIO UPDATES

Once you begin running a scenario, the actions of the PCs will begin to transform that scenario, and then the reactions of the NPCs to what the PCs have done will transform it even further.

A simple example: The PCs kill all the skeletons in Area 7. Now there are no skeletons in Area 7.

Each active scenario in the campaign—i.e., each scenario that the PCs have been interacting with and for which continuity needs to be tracked—gets its own section. If the PCs are currently in the Caverns of Doom, I want to remember that they killed the skeletons in Area 7 last session so that they don't miraculously reappear in this session. If they're leaving the Caverns of Doom but are planning to come back later, it's even more important to keep track of all those little details that could otherwise easily get lost.

Dungeons actually make for a fairly clear-cut example of this, so let's take a peek at how I track dungeon status. There are basically four tools I use:

- ⬢ adversary rosters
- ⬢ updated room keys
- ⬢ scenario timelines
- ⬢ return to a status quo

The first thing is that, as with everything else in the campaign status document, you can and should keep it simple. Just because you have all of these tools available for tracking dungeon status, it doesn't mean that you need to use all of them all of the time. For example, here's what the status looked like for a dungeon in one of my campaigns:

MISTKEEP

- ☐ B5: Ogre killed.
- ☐ B12: Paintings removed from the walls.

That's all I needed given the changes the PCs had made up to that point! The more stuff the PCs do—and the more stuff they change—of course, the more notes you'll need.

Using **adversary rosters** (see page 177) makes it easy to track casualties, reinforcements, or other changes to the denizens of the dungeon. During actual play, you can easily update the roster as necessary (e.g., crossing off casualties) and then, between sessions, simply update the roster, putting the current version in the scenario update and ignoring the original when the PCs return to the dungeon.

The other half of a dungeon, of course, is the **room keys**. We discussed updating these keys in detail on page 165, but the short version is that you simply list each room where something has been changed (destroyed, looted, etc.) and note the changes. I recommend using bullet points to keep this pithy and easy to reference.

If the disrupted scenario is in a highly agitated state but you're not sure exactly when the PCs will reengage with it, a **scenario timeline** may come in useful. Basically, this is just a list indicating that at such-and-such a time the adversary roster and/or room key will be updated. A simple example is when the bad guys have summoned reinforcements but they won't arrive for a little while and it's possible the PCs will come back for a second assault before they get there. In this situation, you would create an adversary roster *without* the reinforcements, and then use the timeline to indicate when they should be *added* to the adversary roster. If the PCs *don't* come back, then the next time you're updating your campaign status document, you can add the reinforcements and remove the timeline entry.

A timeline, therefore, might look something like this:

- ☐ ~~10/05/790: Tee attacks Temple of Dissolution.~~
- ☐ ~~10/06/790: Tee uses Dreaming Arts to unleash nightmare on Arveth, leaving her fatigued next day.~~
- ☐ ~~10/07/790: Arveth hits Tee with Dreamspike.~~
- ☐ ~~10/08/790: Tee unleashes nightmare on Arveth, leaving her fatigued next day.~~
- ☐ ~~10/09/790: Arveth switches sleeping pattern so that she won't be asleep at night.~~
- ☐ 10/10/790 (4 AM): Arveth hits Tee with Dreamspike (forced to watch her friends' eyes ripped out).

(continued)

☐ 10/10/790 (11 PM): Rissien and Santiel are kidnapped from Narred and taken to Temple of Dissolution.

☐ 10/13/790: Santiel is blinded.

☐ 10/14/790: Santiel's eyes delivered to Tee.

☐ 10/15/790: Santiel is killed.

☐ 10/16/790: Rissien suspended in the Prismatic Altar.

☐ 10/21/790: Rissien is killed. (Possibly rescued by the Jade Oak.)

I use strikeout text to indicate events that have already happened, including some events from actual play for easy reference. In some cases I'll simply delete these items (for clarity or to save space), but I've often found it useful to be able to look back and review what's been happening in an evolving scenario.

It follows, of course, that events that haven't been struck out haven't happened yet. They may, in fact, never happen. (If, for example, Tee catches up with Arveth before she can kidnap Rissien and Santiel.)

As you're working with timelines, therefore, there are a couple questions that are useful to keep in mind:

1. When is it likely that the PCs will reengage with the dungeon? (I won't prep timelines much beyond this point because the likelihood of wasted prep becomes high.)

2. If the PCs don't interact further with this dungeon, what will be the new status quo?

The latter question can be easy to overlook, but it's really an essential component of efficient, smart prep. Some situations will continue to spiral out of control, spinning their chaos out into the rest of the campaign, but most scenarios will instead settle down into a status quo (e.g., the mafiosos bring in new muscle to guard their drug operation and then . . . that's it, they've taken the precautions they think they need to take). This means that you can simply prep up to that new status quo, file it in the appropriate section of your campaign notes, and then stop thinking about it until it becomes relevant again.

(For a deeper look at status quo design, see page 417.)

THE TIMELINE OF BANGS

A **bang**, described in detail on page 211, is the explosive moment that you use to start a new scene. Stripping the jargon from it, the timeline of bangs is basically a list of events that are going to happen to the PCs in the future. In other words, the places where the active campaign world is going to seek them out instead of waiting to react to them.

Any type of bang can be put on the timeline, but there are a few types that I find common.

Appointments are added to the timeline when the PCs make an arrangement to do something. They're your reminder that something has been scheduled. The PCs are often aware of the what, where, and when, but that won't always be true: Sometimes you whisper to a butterfly and you just can't be sure when the giant eagle will show up.

Scenario hooks, which are described in more detail in their own extra credit (see page 498), can be dropped into the campaign to pull or push PCs toward a new scenario (or reengage them with a scenario they've been ignoring). For example, a client showing up at the PCs' detective agency with a job.

Roleplaying prompts are a broad category that can be generally understood as "an important NPC shows up for a big scene." Maybe your brother comes looking for cash or your boyfriend calls and says, "We have to talk."

Event fallout covers the myriad ways in which the game world reacts to the PCs.

In many ways, a GM's entire role at the table can be described as providing the world's response to the PCs' actions. "You do X, therefore Y happens. Now what do you do?" This is relatively easy to maintain and keep track of in the normal course of play as reactions happen in more or less immediate succession: You swing your sword at the orc and we immediately learn whether or not you hit them.

But in some cases, the reaction will be delayed. Or the PCs will knock over a chain of dominos that continue to topple off-screen: They leave evidence of their break-in and the Herschfelds begin an investigation. They retrieve a powerful artifact and deliver it to one of the heirs of the throne. They write a letter to their contact in Paris and must wait for a transatlantic response.

If the response is a **single event**, it can just go directly on the timeline of bangs. For example, when the PCs in one of my D&D campaigns fought a demon, got coated in demonic filth, and then teleported directly back to their rooms, they ended up impregnating the rug in their room with some of that filth. I decided that the filth would fester for several days before generating a half dozen demonic maggots. It would have been easy to lose track of this cool idea, since it wouldn't happen for several sessions, but I simply included it on the timeline of bangs. Once there, the event could simply sit and wait until it was triggered at the appropriate time.

If a chain of dominos is falling, on the other hand, then you might want to list that **sequence of events** as a separate, dedicated timeline, with events on that timeline that intersect with the PCs (or could intersect with the PCs) being cross-referenced on your primary timeline of bangs.

In fact, you might create separate, specialized sections like this in your campaign status document for any entry on your timeline of bangs. (For example, those demonic maggots needed stat blocks, which I listed in a separate "Demonic Maggots" section.) In my experience, you want to keep the timeline itself as uncluttered as possible so that it can fulfill its primary function of making sure you don't miss something or forget an event.

These specialized sections can often function like mini-scenarios (e.g., the mini-scenario of your rooms becoming infested with demonic maggots). If these become sufficiently complicated, though, they should be spun off into a full-fledged set of scenario notes (which can, of course, be cross-referenced and triggered in your timeline of bangs). If you're looking for a rule of thumb, anything longer than a single page should almost certainly be spun off, and I'll usually try to keep these to a half page or less.

Timelines of bangs, in my experience, are usually organized **chronologically**, which might look like this:

- ☐ 9/22/2057: Vargas offers a case to Ashlorn. (*Case 8: Vargas Kidnapping*)
- ☐ 9/22/2057 (10 AM): Rachana's press conference scheduled. (*Lytekkas Hypercorp*)

☐ 9/22/2057 (Evening): The Neo-Stasi identify "Ashlorn" as Zubaida. They attack the mansion. (*Ashlorn's Doom*)

☐ 9/23/2057: Olga's Training.

☐ 9/23/2057: Receive invitation from the Hélia Corporation to beta test the *Cryoworld* expansion. (*Case 9: Cryoworld*)

☐ 9/24/2057: Rachana's rocket-propelled grenade launcher delivered.

You can see how events can be keyed to days (in which case they could be triggered at any time on that day), specific times, or something in between (e.g., Evening). You can also see how I use parentheses at the end of a bang to indicate that it's linked to a scenario (e.g., Vargas Kidnapping, Lytekkas Hypercorp, Cryoworld) or subsection of the campaign status document (e.g., Ashlorn's Doom) where additional information can be found.

Another chronological approach is to create a **sequential checklist**. Bangs appear on the list in the order they'll happen, but without assigning specific dates or times to them:

☐ Olga's sister Aliona arrives in town. She needs help finding her husband. (*Case 10: Stanislav's Run*)

☐ Rain of blood polyps falls from the sky. (*Lytekkas Hypercorp*)

☐ Rachana: Check Black-IC installed on her deck.

☐ Neo-Stasi kidnap Lalita. (*Ashlorn's Doom*)

☐ Spyware installed on Rachana's RPG uploads data packet.

As you're running your campaign, you can just move down the list, checking off each bang as you use it.

A final option is to keep the checklist but ditch the sequencing. This becomes a **menu of bangs**, basically a list of proactive elements that you can select and drop into the campaign whenever it feels appropriate.

You could even maintain multiple timelines of bangs if that seems useful to you: one a chronological list of stuff keyed to specific times and another that's a more flexible list of bangs you can choose as fancy and need dictate.

BACKGROUND EVENTS

Background events are a second timeline of future events running in parallel with the timeline of bangs. These are the events that *don't* directly involve the PCs, but that are nevertheless taking place and moving the campaign world forward.

If the PCs are playing FBI agents in New York City in 1944, for example, then the D-Day invasion of Normandy would be a background event. So, too, the race for US Senate between Robert F. Wagner and Thomas J. Curran, and the release of *Rosie the Riveter* in cinemas.

In my earliest campaign status documents, I didn't separate these two timelines from each other: Stuff that would be directly experienced by the PCs and background headlines from the local newspapers would be freely mixed together in a single timeline of dates. This worked up to a certain point, but I eventually realized that:

- The two lists are actually used in distinct ways and at distinct times during play, so having them directly juxtaposed wasn't providing any meaningful utility.

- The timeline of bangs is, in many ways, a list of "things I don't want to forget to have happen." The background events, on the other hand, are factoids that the PCs have to seek out or that are opportunistically used as backdrops. Mixing them together on the same list sometimes resulted in the essential bangs getting lost amidst the reactive background events, thus degrading the utility of the list.

So although they're superficially similar, insofar as they're both lists of ongoing events that are likely to happen as the campaign world moves forward through time, they actually serve distinct purposes and work better when split apart.

I'll often frame background events as newspaper headlines or broadsheet article summaries, with the PCs scooping them up whenever they grab a copy of the paper. But you can also use your background events as topics of conversation with NPCs or as backdrop elements in other scenes (e.g., a chase scene that crashes through a ticker-tape parade for the Mercury 7 astronauts, or a television in the bar broadcasting the inaugural lift of the Kilimanjaro space elevator).

Background events provide depth to the campaign, creating a game world that exists and persists beyond the PCs' immediate line of sight. If the PCs reach a certain level or notoriety or get mixed up in events with a high profile, though, it can be fun to seed in details about how their exploits are being publicly reported.

It's also not unusual for players to become interested in background events and start poking their noses into them. If that happens, you may discover that some background events will blossom into full-fledged scenarios.

BACKDROP FILES

As the complexity of your campaign world grows, you'll likely discover that some of your background events will develop into significant sub-narratives. For example, the D-Day invasion wasn't a one-off: There was a long war before it and plenty of war after it, a whole sequence of background events that build and develop over time (and potentially provide vital context for any number of scenarios).

When this happens, I find it useful to create backdrop files: separate documents that each track a separate sub-narrative. For example, in our hypothetical FBI campaign set in 1944, I might create:

◎ *Backdrop 1: World War II*
◎ *Backdrop 2: Senate Race*
◎ *Backdrop 3: New in Cinemas*

And so forth.

These backdrop files usually consist simply of the same short bullet-pointed items found in the Background Events section of the campaign status document (with the occasional additional detail for PCs who go digging for them), but prepping them separately makes it much easier to coherently weave those events together.

Offloading this material into backdrop files also allows me to archive older events and also far-future events while keeping the campaign status document itself as slim as possible. Then I can simply transfer events from my various backdrop files as needed. For example, the status document for my current D&D campaign reads:

NEWSSHEETS (Backdrops updated through 10/27)

Which is a reminder to myself that, when we get close to the 27th of Nocturdei in the campaign, I should go through all my backdrop files, pull out another 5 to 10 days of material from those timelines, and add them to the campaign status document.

ARCHIVE YOUR STATUS DOCUMENT!

When it's time to update my campaign document for a new session, I make a point of saving the old version of the document in an archive.

To keep your campaign status document functional, you'll be constantly purging irrelevant and out-of-date material from it. Sometimes, though, you'll make a mistake and delete something that's still relevant . . . or that suddenly becomes relevant again 20 sessions later.

Take the hard lesson from my mistakes: Keep an archive of your status documents!

✦ LEARNING A NEW RPG ✦

So you're getting ready to GM a new RPG for the first time. That can be a little intimidating. Maybe it's the first RPG you've ever played. Or it's a little more complex than anything you've run before. Or it's your first time prepping a game you haven't previously played. Or it's just something new.

In any case, you'll obviously want this process to go smoothly, and you'll want to make as few mistakes as possible. (Although Step 0 here is accepting that mistakes _will_ happen, and that's okay. That's part of the process.)

STEP 1: READ THE RULEBOOK

Cover to cover. I'm afraid there's no cheating around this and no shortcuts. If you're lucky, the RPG you've chosen will have a well-organized rulebook, but the process of mentally "touching" every page of the book will not only prevent you from missing a rule entirely, it will also begin constructing a mental map of the rulebook that will allow you to look up information inside it more quickly during play.

STEP 2: CHEAT SHEETS

Make a cheat sheet including the most important rules. I like to include all the mechanics except for character options and format my sheets so that I can display them on my GM screen. It's real easy to fake mastery of a rule system when you have it all laid out six inches in front of your face. The act of creating the cheat sheet also enhances your own learning process: It involves "touching" every part of the system a second time, and also requires you to mentally engage with the system and really understand what makes it tick.

The truth is that a lot of RPGs can be pretty terrible when it comes to technical writing, and the act of boiling messy text into a clear cheat sheet will lead you to pre-solve difficult cruxes that would otherwise booby trap you during play. The cheat sheet will also often susses out those weird rules that RPG manuals leave lying around in dank corners.

You can find examples of these cheat sheets for a variety of systems on my website, the Alexandrian (https://thealexandrian.net).

STEP 3: RUN A ONE-SHOT

If I'm interested in running a long-term campaign in a given system, I'll almost never start by jumping directly into that campaign. Instead, I'll run a one-shot, usually with pre-generated characters (so that we can jump right in).

Running the one-shot allows both me and the players to work out the kinks, and the players gain a lot of understanding of how the game works that will prove invaluable when it comes time to create their long-term characters.

The result is better characters and a stronger first session, both of which will help get the campaign off on the right foot.

STEP 4: CO-OPT PLAYER EXPERTISE

Do this in every way you can. That includes, "Bob, can you look up the rule for pugilating people?" It also includes, "Anybody know the rules for pugilating people?" (instead of defaulting to looking it up yourself).

There's sneakier stuff, too, like, "I can't figure out how to beat the PCs when they use ability X, so I'm going to design a bunch of bad guys who use ability X and I'll see how the players deal with it."

BRIBE YOUR ASSISTANTS!

My editor, Elliot, recommends a technique used by their GM: Give XP to the first player who can find or remember a rule you've forgotten!

STEP 5: RULES HIGHLIGHT SESSIONS

For any game like D&D that has a lot of specialized sub-systems, consider designing sessions that highlight one of those sub-systems over and over and over again so that you can, as a group, get a lot of focused repetition using it.

Often groups struggle with these sub-systems because they only come up once every four or five sessions, which means every time you need to use them you've forgotten the last time you muddled through them, and you end up needing to muddle your way through them all over again. Having problems with grappling? A whole scenario based around grasping gorillas and their pet pythons will usually lock those rules in permanently for the group. (Which also means you'll have increased expertise across the entire group, which you can co-opt in the future.)

STEP 6: SET A REFERENCE TIME LIMIT

If you find yourself getting frequently bogged down in the new rules, set a time limit. If you can't find the answer you're looking for in 30 seconds (or 60 seconds or whatever feels right to you), make an arbitrary ruling and move on. Be open and clear about what you're doing with the players, and make a note to review those rules after the session. Then, before the next session, review the correct rules with the whole group.

STEP 7: IDENTIFY YOUR HIERARCHY OF REFERENCE

As you're prepping your scenario notes, particularly when it comes to stat blocks, try to include everything you personally need to reference *on the page.* Where the system cheat sheet gives you the core rules at your fingertips, this technique puts the relevant class abilities, superpowers, creature features, and similar character-specific abilities that are pertinent to the current situation at your fingertips.

Over time, you will master more and more of the system and no longer need the immediate reference. When that happens, you can simply scale down the reference. For example, when you first start playing D&D you won't have any idea what a *magic missile* spell is. Eventually, though, you'll become familiar enough with it that just seeing the name of the spell will be enough.

This often follows the **hierarchy of reference**:

- ✪ Include the full text.
- ✪ Include a brief summary of the most important factors (and a page reference in case you end up needing to look up the details).
- ✪ Include just a page reference.
- ✪ Simply list the keyword, spell name, feat, etc.

Move down the hierarchy as you gain more and more mastery over the system you're running. It's kind of like using vocab cards to learn a new language (except you never need to spend time memorizing them; just playing the game does that for you organically)—as you master each concept, you simply cycle them out of the rotation.

Including the full text for something has become really easy in an era of copy-and-paste. But having such a large bulk of text is not always the best option for quickly referencing something during play. And if you're dealing with lots of different abilities or effects, including the full text for every single one of them will often bloat your content to the point where it becomes more difficult to use (because, for example, you're having to flip between multiple pages in order to run an encounter).

TEACHING A NEW RPG

As the GM you are likely the one who chose the game you're playing and, therefore, will often have more expertise with the rules than any of the other players. It's your responsibility and your privilege to share that knowledge with the players. (Plus, it's just a good idea because it will make the players feel better and help the game run smoother.)

First, make sure that the players have access to a copy of the rulebook at the table. I'll often try to have a second copy of the rulebook just for the players because I don't want my own access to the book cut off while a player is referencing something, but that's not strictly necessary. In most groups, it won't be unusual for one or more of the players to buy their own copies.

Second, give them a copy of your cheat sheet. I usually make a copy for every player.

Third, prep a 5-to-10-minute introduction to the game, using your cheat sheet as a reference. You don't have to overthink or literally script this. Just make a bullet point list of the topics you want to cover, identifying the core concepts (like how action checks are resolved) that you need to explain.

If it's a relatively simple RPG, you might actually touch on all of the rules in this introduction, but that's not necessary. Focus on getting the key essentials across, and then be aware during the actual game of moments when new mechanics show up for the first time and take the time to explain them (once again referencing the cheat sheet).

⊹ THE OPEN TABLE ⊹

Imagine that you had never heard of baseball before and someone said, "Hey, wanna join a baseball team?"

"What's that involve?" you ask.

"Well, we practice three hours every Wednesday evening and we'll have a game every Saturday afternoon for the next seven months."

You'd have to be really, *really* curious about baseball to take that guy up on his offer, right? And if you actually made that commitment and were on that baseball team, then the quality of your team would probably be really important and you'd need to be really convinced that someone was going to make a great baseball player before you'd invite them to join you, right? Plus, it's such a huge commitment of your time that it would be incredibly difficult for you to commit to two different baseball teams, so at a certain point you'd just play baseball with the people on your team and you'd stop inviting other people to play with you because all the roster spots on your team were full and there'd be no room for anyone else.

If that was the only way people could start playing baseball, it's pretty easy to see that you wouldn't have a lot of baseball players.

Of course, that's not how people start playing baseball. Most people start playing baseball when somebody says, "Hey, wanna play catch?" And playing catch is easy. You pick up a ball and you throw it. There's no commitment, so people will be more open to trying it and inviting others to do it with them. Some people, of course, will never pick that ball up again. But lots of people will find that they like throwing the ball around, and some of those people will eventually find themselves agreeing to spend three hundred hours every year participating in amateur baseball leagues.

THE DEDICATED TABLE

When it comes to roleplaying games, the equivalent to the amateur baseball league is what I've come to call a dedicated table. It's the way most people play RPGs today: They have a regular group of five or six people who plan to get together on a regular or semi-regular basis for ten or twenty or more sessions.

When you agree to join a campaign like this, you're making a minimum commitment of 80 hours or more spread out over months or years of your life. Dropping out or frequently missing sessions is usually considered bad form, since losing a player (and, therefore, their character) can be incredibly disruptive to the tightly woven continuity of the modern campaign.

And that level of commitment can result in truly amazing things. For example, I ran an *Eternal Lies* campaign for the *Trail of Cthulhu* roleplaying game that lasted for 95 hours spread across 22 sessions of play, and that amount of time allowed us to explore a deep and interesting scenario while creating well-rounded characters who changed and grew over time. I've also got a D&D campaign that's been running as a dedicated table for more than 15 years and, once again, the commitment of time and focus unlocks creative options that simply would not be possible in purely casual play. (Just like a baseball team that practices together regularly is going to be more skilled in their collective play than a pickup team that plays for a single afternoon.)

But this mode of play also comes at a cost. Part of that cost can be personal: There are lots of people who talk about how they can't play RPGs anymore because they just don't have the time to commit to them. Another part of that cost comes from the incredible difficulty of inviting new players to join your dedicated table, particularly if they're completely new to roleplaying games (since there's no way to know whether or not they'll like the game enough to stick with the significant commitment you're asking of them).

What's unfortunate is that many people believe that this is a cost that *must* be paid in order to play an RPG, and if they can't pay that cost, they conclude that they can't play RPGs anymore (or at all).

But there is another option.

THE OPEN TABLE

An open table is built around (a) campaign material that's set up so that you can run the game with little or no prep and (b) open group formation, so that you can play a session with any combination of players. In combination, this means that, just like a board game, you can play the game at basically any time. In fact, you can play it on the spur of the moment.

This is awesome.

It's awesome for you because you never have to worry about wrangling schedules. Feel like playing on Thursday? Just send out an email saying, "We're playing on Thursday. Who wants to come?" and you're good to go. Just hanging out with some friends and you're trying to figure out what to do? Normally you'd never suggest an RPG because of the prep time involved, but with an open table you can always just pick it up and start playing.

This also makes an open table the ultimate recruitment tool for finding new players (see page 435). Even if they only play the one time, they can have a great experience without causing any disruption to "continuity." You may even be thinking that you can't make an open table work because you don't have enough players. But when you actually have an open table, you'll be astonished at how quickly you can end up with more players than you know what to do with. For my first open table, I started with an email list of eight or nine players. Within a couple of months that list had grown to more than thirty. Today, I have more than sixty people in my pool of active players. And that's only possible because the open table makes the recruitment of new players so easy.

This is also why an open table can be fantastic even if you prefer the focus and intensity of a dedicated campaign: The open table is how you find the high-quality, enthusiastic players who make truly great dedicated campaigns possible. That awesome *Eternal Lies* campaign I ran? I first played with several key members of that group through my open table. And when I needed a replacement player in my long-running D&D campaign I knew exactly where to find her, because for months she'd been proving herself to be the perfect player for that campaign at my open table.

With an open table I can play with more people, I can play more frequently, I can use it as an incubator for testing out new ideas in a low-risk environment, and it improves *all* of my gaming, both open and dedicated.

If you love roleplaying games, I really believe you owe it to yourself to keep an open table in your back pocket. Here are some ways you can make your table an open one.

INTO THE MEGADUNGEON

There are many different ways that you can set up an open table, but one of the most straightforward is a classic megadungeon (see page 174).

Start with the campaign concept (see page 437): The PCs are dungeon-delving adventurers based out of a town near (or, alternatively, directly on top of) the megadungeon. Each session, a group of PCs will form an expedition that will journey down into the dungeon. (See Expedition-Based Play, on page 140.)

You'll need to create the town. It could be anything from a small village to a sprawling metropolis. A small frontier fort is another option, or you could go for something truly unusual like an airship or a transplanar nexus that can be reached by anyone with the appropriate token.

You'll also, of course, need to create the megadungeon itself. See Starting a Megadungeon on page 174. (Remember that you don't need the full megadungeon, just the first three levels.)

As you're designing this, it may be useful to recognize that the dynamic is fundamentally similar to a gold rush. Over time, players will find a wide variety of personal reasons and goals for delving into the dungeon, but it's very likely that the reason the megadungeon attracts so many different adventurers is the golden allure of treasure. So think about the kinds of communities that are created by gold rushes.

SCHEDULING SESSIONS

With your megadungeon in place, it's time to open your table.

You will, of course, still need to start with some players. Offer the open table to anyone you're playing with or have played with in the past. Do the normal recruitment things (see page 435). Suggest a dungeon delve at your next board game night. Opportunistically ask your geeky friends, "Would you like to try playing D&D?"

I recommend setting up a mailing list, Discord server, social media group, or some similar community for the open table. You'll want to be able to send out session invites to everyone interested, and ideally you also want to give the players a forum for sharing information and chatting with each other away from the table.

TABLE CAPS AND WAITING LISTS

My first forays into an open table featured a simple "We'll play with whoever shows up!" ethos. As the popularity of the open table grew, however, this quickly became nonviable: I had one session in which I GMed for ten players running something like 22 PCs and hirelings.

Then I imposed **table caps**.

The system is pretty simple: I cap the number of players at a certain number. (For me, that's five players and I'll allow a sixth if it's for a couple playing together. Your mileage may vary.) These slots fill up on a first-come, first-serve basis. Once the cap is hit, that's it for that session.

To prevent highly active players from monopolizing the slots at every session, I also use a **waiting list**: If you signed up for a session but couldn't play because of the session cap, then you get preferential placement in the next session. (The waiting list also helps with last-minute cancellations, because you can call up the next person on the waiting list.)

Now you can schedule a session. You can schedule an **open call** by simply announcing the date and time of the game and asking the players to RSVP. You can create a **regular session** by simply having an open call on the same night each week or every other week (e.g., you play every Tuesday night).

Alternatively, specific players (or groups of players) can request a **sponsored session** by approaching you and asking for it. Make sure players know that they can do this. I'll generally tell players that they should offer me a range of dates and then I can figure out which one works for me. It's up to them whether they want the sponsored session to also include an open call to fill any empty seats or if it's an "exclusive" event just for them.

Sponsored sessions can arise because of events in the game world (e.g., "We want to go back to the Temple of Elemental Evil!" or "We should retrieve Varla's corpse" or "We need to go back for the rest of that treasure before somebody else snatches it") or the real world (e.g., because Steve's in town, for a bachelor party, we all happened to be drunk at the time, or just because somebody was bored and wanted something to do on a Thursday night).

RUNNING THE OPEN TABLE

Game night has arrived and the players who RSVP'd are taking their seats at the table.

The first thing you need to do is **form the group**. Returning players will need to choose which of their characters they want to play tonight (they could have several) or if they want to create a new 1st-level character.

This decision will often depend on what characters everyone else is playing (Marko and Alonso have a blood feud, so if Cynthia is playing Marko tonight, then Paul might not want to play Alonso . . . or maybe he'll *definitely* want to play Alonso!), what the players want to do tonight (if they're heading down to the Fields of Black Diamonds, then Cynthia might prefer to play Kaden, who has an interest in finding the Grey-Mantled King), and/or the relative power levels of the characters (if everyone else is low-level, then maybe Colleen tables her 8th-level character and rolls up a new one). So expect a discussion to break out.

New players, of course, will need a new character. If they're completely new, then you'll also need to introduce them to the game system.

In terms of teaching the game, you need to prep a tight 5- or, at most, 10-minute spiel. Check out the Learning a New RPG extra credit on page 458 for some guidance on this, but it's really important that you don't spend too much time on this, particularly since in an open table you've almost certainly got other players sitting there who don't need the introduction.

When it comes to starting a new character, if you're playing a game with lightning-fast character creation that can be done even by a neophyte in 5 or, again, 10 minutes at most, then you can just have players create their characters at the table.

The current edition of D&D, unfortunately, is not such a game. Therefore:

- ⬡ Encourage experienced players to create their character ahead of time and bring it to their first session.
- ⬡ Create a bunch of pre-generated characters (also known as pregens) and have a stack of sheets that other players can simply pick from.

Some RPGs will actually provide a bunch of pregens. Use 'em! For D&D, there are a bunch of online generators that you can use to create a pregen with the push of a button. Some of those could also be used to let players make some basic decisions about their character—e.g., "I'd like to play an outlander tiefling sorcerer"—and then generate the rest.

With the group formed, give them a chance to buy supplies in town if they'd like and then head into the megadungeon! At this point, you're just running the adventure like you would any other.

ENDING THE SESSION

A key element of the open table is that, at the end of the session, the PCs all need to be back at their home base so that they're available to participate in the open group formation at the beginning of the next session.

Make sure to make this expectation explicit. You're not trying to pull a fast one here, and, in my experience, the players will be more than happy to collaborate in making this happen.

Sometimes, of course, this just isn't possible. Back in the real world, people have to get up in the morning and they weren't anticipating getting completely lost after that teleportation trap on Level 3. When this happens, you'll probably just want to wave your hand and say something like, "After a long journey, you manage to make your way back to the surface."

You might want to impose some form of penalty or consequence when this happens, but as long as a good faith effort is made it's usually best to just let it slide.

Another option, though, is to offer a **sequel session**: If the evening is coming to a close and the group is in the middle of something important to them, then you can hit the pause button and pick up where you're leaving off if (and only if!) everyone at the table can immediately agree on a time when everyone in the current group can get together for another session. (I usually require this session to happen within the next 10 days and/or before the next regularly scheduled session, because it can be incredibly disruptive to an open table to have characters unavailable for play because they're stuck somewhere.)

BETWEEN SESSIONS

After the session is done (and before the next one is done), restock your dungeon (see page 165).

As I mentioned, one of the great things about an open table is that it can allow you to just pick up and play a roleplaying game as easily as you would a board game or video game. Megadungeons make great open tables because (a) they're designed to be so large that they cannot be cleared out (so they're always available for play) and (b) their content can be trivially regenerated with some simple restocking procedures.

When I'm running a megadungeon, it usually takes me less than 20 minutes to restock it between sessions (often much less). In fact, with a little practice, you can get a little sneaky and take care of the restocking at the beginning of the next session while the players are picking out their characters and shopping for equipment.

OTHER OPEN TABLES

Megadungeons, of course, are not the be-all and end-all of open tables. You could easily expand your megadungeon into an open table based on a hexcrawl (see page 391), for example, and that's barely scratching the surface of the possibilities you can explore by swapping genres, games, and campaign structures.

A few key things to look for in choosing a system and setting up a campaign for an open table:

◎ Quick character generation

◎ A game system that can be quickly taught to new players

◎ A mechanism for open group formation, explaining by default how a semi-random assortment of PCs comes together for a new mission/expedition each session

◎ A default goal and default action that can set each session in motion

◎ Ideally a method for easily regenerating or extending adventure content (although this can be replaced by a willingness to simply generate a lot of one-shot adventures)

Have fun sharing all your wondrous worlds!

QUICK-AND-DIRTY
✦ WORLDBUILDING ✦

Want to create an entire world?

Sounds intimidating, doesn't it? Just look at published settings like Middle-earth, the Forgotten Realms, or *Star Wars*. Hundreds, often thousands, of pages dedicated to describing a fictional reality. Your first session is on Saturday! You don't have time for that!

Of course, you don't need to do all of that to start gaming in your own setting. A detailed breakdown of the dialects spoken on the Triskan subcontinent might be really fun to explore but is probably not strictly necessary for a new campaign taking place in the Sasharran archipelago.

The real secret is that if you can get your new world to the table, then it will begin rapidly developing through actual play. Every scenario you design and every session you run will build atop the last. All you'll have to do is keep good notes.

So what's the minimum amount of stuff you'll need before the game begins?

In my experience, three to six pages.

Let's break down what those look like.

THE MINIMUM PREP PACKET

Start with one to two pages of **broad detail about the world**. The goal of this high-level summary is to provide context for whatever local scene your campaign will end up starting in. The exact nature of what this overview looks like will vary based on the setting, your preferences, and probably the campaign you're planning.

For example, my personal D&D campaign setting is the Western Lands. If you look at it today, it actually *does* fill hundreds of pages and gigabytes of data. But when I first started creating it two decades ago, I wrote one page summarizing the five major empires of the Western Lands (one paragraph per empire). Then I wrote a one-page timeline of the setting's history.

(I really did have a game on Saturday.)

For an urban fantasy campaign set in an alternative version of the modern day, on the other hand, you might do one page on the true nature of magic and another page on the major fey factions.

Whatever this content ends up needing to be for your campaign, though, keep it to no more than two pages.

CALENDARS & TIMEKEEPING

Make sure to include a calendar, if your setting needs that sort of thing. You'll want to be able to date events and talk about the passage of time in concrete ways.

Next, **what do the players need for character creation?** In D&D, for example, this includes the gods (because clerics need to pick a deity) and languages (because everyone needs to pick those). Do another one to two pages on that.

Finally, we're going to aggressively zoom in and focus on the **local setting**. Obviously, you'll need to start by deciding where the first adventure of the campaign is going to be set.

⬡ A major fantasy metropolis?

⬡ A village on the edge of civilization?

⬡ A lunar space station?

⬡ A lich-infested Rome?

Exactly what you'll be prepping here will depend on the exact nature of the setting, but once again your goal is one or two pages of broad context that will give you a foundation for developing and improvising as needed.

A few things that are often relevant:

⬡ Enough detail to describe local navigation. For a city, this might be a breakdown of neighborhoods. For a village, it might be the local roads (where do they go?) and terrain features (the Old Forest, the Trollfens, etc.).

⬡ Who is politically in charge? That might be a local authority (e.g., the mayor) or a distant one (e.g., Tsarist border patrols periodically pass through the region).

⬡ What are the local factions? These might be businesses, criminal organizations, social organizations, ethnic groups, civic institutions, etc.

Your goal here is not to be comprehensively encyclopedic. It's okay to say, "There's a city council," for example, without specifying every individual councilor. Or to name one or two councilors while leaving the rest as a tabula rasa for later development.

Check to make sure that you've provided common resources that the PCs will go looking for. In D&D, for example, that would typically include:

⬡ the local store(s) where they'll be able to buy supplies;

⬡ an inn or other place for them to stay; and

⬡ a tavern, as a default social destination and/or rumor distribution center. (PCs just love going to taverns.)

A quick way to make your setting feel unique is to look at the essential functions being provided here and, instead of using the generic solution (general store, inn, tavern), come up with creative and unusual solutions. For example:

- There is a strange steampunk machine in the middle of the village. Insert gems or precious metals and it will deliver, within 2d12 hours, the items you request.
- The village doesn't have an inn, but the PCs can find beds in the abandoned—and very, very haunted—military barracks on Blood Hill.
- The locals socialize in a dreamhouse or nobhill, gathering at night in their dreams while they sleep.

With these three parts in place—world summary, character creation needs, and local setting—you'll have your three to six pages of prep. From this point forward, the setting will continue to expand:

- As the players create characters and you/they need to start answering specific questions about where they're from, etc.
- You create your first adventure.
- You create your second adventure.

And so on.

Of course, you can also just continue developing details of your world wherever your whim and fancy take you. Worldbuilding for its own sake is fun! And you can often discover things while delving into the unexamined parts of your setting that can feed back into your adventures in amazing, unexpected, and delightful ways.

MAPS

While working on your initial setting material, you may find it useful to do some maps. To keep things brief, I have a couple tips for this.

First, if you can get away with NOT doing a map, skip doing the map for now.

Second, if you're doing a map, keep it sketchy and try to keep it at roughly the same level of detail as your minimal prep packet.

For example, when I did the first map for my Western Lands campaign, I sketched a coastline, a couple mountain ranges, and the borders of the Five Empires. I eventually added regional maps with more details, but I was still using the original map with very few additions more than 10 years later.

You need less than you think.

THE PLAYER PACKET

The other thing to note is that the three to six pages you've written up can almost certainly, with perhaps just a teensy bit of editing, double as the player's briefing packet for the setting (see page 439).

It not only covers everything they need to know but is conveniently almost the exact length (five pages) that I generally find to be the maximum amount of extracurricular reading I can rightfully hope that players might be willing to do before our first session.

(Or, failing that, it's short enough for them to parse it at the table.)

PUTTING THE WORLD IN PLAY

You may have started this whole thing with an adventure in mind: "I have an idea for a scenario where the PCs are mercenaries hired by asteroid miners to protect their hab from space pirates . . . What setting can I run this in?" Or maybe you just had a cool idea for a world. Either way, it's time to take this foundational material you've developed and put a scenario in it.

There are obviously a whole bunch of different types of scenarios you might choose to launch a campaign with. (See literally everything else in this book.) No matter what the scenario is, though, it's virtually certain it will add more detail to your setting:

- A murder investigation involving the Hephaestus Corporation will add details about Hephaestus to your faction notes.

- A dungeon scenario set in the ruins of the dwarven city of Khunbaral will add details about dwarven culture and the history of the great dwarven kingdoms of the east.

- A heist targeting Solarian blood diamonds may add details about the asteroid mining guilds and the Lytekkas Hypercorp.

Which is great! As you actually run these scenarios, you'll also want to keep track of stuff that develops through actual play. (It's a rare session when you don't discover something new about a character or need to create a whole new location on demand.) A lot of this information will only be relevant to the specific scenario, but there'll also be stuff that you'll want to add to your general notes on the world. If you take the time to do that, it'll make it a lot easier for you to use these details in future scenarios (when the PCs decide to target Hephaestus for a heist or get hired by Lytekkas, for example).

Of course, the amount of setting material you'll need to prep for your initial scenario (and later scenarios) can vary quite a bit. If you're setting up a hexcrawl (see page 391) for an open table campaign (see page 463), for example, then you'll be prepping A LOT more setting material before the first session. If it's a simple 5 + 5 Dungeon (see page 119), then you might be adding very little.

Either way, you'll have taken your first steps into a brand-new world. Your world.

✦ RUMOR TABLES ✦

For an exploration-based campaign like a megadungeon or hexcrawl to come to life, the players need to be able to learn information about the region of exploration so that they can

- ⬡ set specific goals,
- ⬡ ask specific questions, and
- ⬡ plan their expeditions (see page 140).

This is the function of the **rumor table**, which in its most simple form is simply a random table: Roll a die and tell the players a rumor. This gives a default baseline for delivering a basic foundation of lore, with each rumor providing a tangible nugget of information.

d10	RUMOR
1	In the ruins northwest of Maernath, there is said to be a large cache of silver coins.
2	Orc raiders have been attacking caravans along the King's Road.
3	In the depths of Silverwood, there is a tree with the corpse of a vampire staked to it.
4	A dryad's tree can be found along the Mitari River in the Gloomboughs.
5	Flying carpets have been seen in the skies around the volcano west of town.
6	In Silverwood there's a circle of stone sarsens. Stand among them and blow on a horn of mistletoe and you can open a fairy gate.
7	A group of recently executed smugglers supposedly hid their treasures in a cave in the Skullsplitter Hills.
8	The lizardmen of the Graymires are said to treat minotaurs as if they were gods.
9	If you go to the Fungal Forest, it's important to avoid the spore clouds there.
10	On the eastern edge of the northern mountains, an ancient castle stands on the side of a peak. It is surrounded by a dome of red energy through which nothing living can pass.

You can see how the rumors on this table would instruct PCs in a hexcrawl campaign about local regions (Silverwood, Gloomboughs, Skullsplitter Hills, Graymires, Fungal Forest) and interesting adventuring sites (northwest ruins, smuggler caves, the crimson castle) that they can now consciously choose to seek out or use as navigational markers rather than just stumbling around randomly.

If this information is so useful, why not just give it to them all at once? Partly this comes down to effective pacing. In an exploration-based campaign, you really want the players to be discovering things over time. This also avoids information overload: By spreading the information out over time, it becomes easier for the players to process it and use it. (It's the same reason you don't read a textbook cover to cover but instead process each section of the textbook and then apply it through practice problems, classroom discussion, and the like before proceeding to the next section.)

Conversely, if you only want to give the PCs a few rumors at a time, why go to the trouble of stocking an entire rumor table? Why not just design the handful of bespoke rumors that you're going to give them? Well, as we'll see, a good rumor table is an incredibly useful tool for you, as the GM, to have at the table, allowing you to respond to any number of actions that might be taken by the PCs.

STOCKING THE RUMOR TABLE

Stocking a rumor table is pretty straightforward: Figure out what size die you want to roll, list that number of rumors, and number them. (Or, vice versa, make a list of rumors until you run out of ideas or feel like you have enough of them, then count them and assign whatever die size seems most appropriate.)

But how many rumors should you aim to have in your hexcrawl or megadungeon?

There's no one true answer here. Personally, I like to have 20. A d20 is convenient, and it gives you enough rumors to cover the breadth of the hexcrawl without going overboard. (If you own a d30, this can also be a fun way to use that unusual die. But a table of d100 rumors, in my experience, can be a lot of work to prep without really providing anything of extra value.)

In making each rumor, you're going to be looking at its **source** and **focus**.

RUMOR SOURCE

The source for a rumor in a dungeon is likely to be a room or level. In a hexcrawl, things can get a little more varied, including any of the following:

- hexes
- random encounter tables
- roads/paths/trails
- factions
- NPCs

Basically, anything you've keyed or created for the hexcrawl can (and arguably should!) be fodder for your rumor table.

KEY FROM THE HEX

If I start struggling to come up with new rumors to stock my hexcrawl rumor table with, a technique I've found useful is to just pick a random hex, look at what I've keyed there, and then figure out a rumor that could lead the PCs to it. (If you've done a 10 x 10 hexmap, for instance, you can just roll two d10s, cross-reference their position, and look at the resulting hex.)

If you're feeling confident in your improv skills, you can use this same technique to generate random rumors during actual play even if you don't have a prepared rumor table.

RUMOR FOCUS

Potential focuses for rumors can include any or all of the following:

- Location
- Creature
- Object
- Actions/Situations (including threats and upcoming situations)
- Background/Lore

For example, let's consider this simple example hex:

C2-WYVERN SHAFT
A 60-foot-deep shaft that serves as the lair of a wyvern. The wyvern has dug an escape tunnel that emerges from a hill a quarter mile away.

WYVERN
Has a large scar on its left side from a spear wound.

TREASURE
7,000 sp, 5 zircons (50 gp each)

What rumors could we generate from this?

- **Location:** Adventurers exploring the Red Plateau southwest of town report seeing a mysterious 60-foot-deep shaft.
- **Creature:** A wyvern has been seen flying over the Red Plateau.
- **Object:** A wyvern attacked a tax assessor's wagon along the Southway and carried off a lockbox containing 7,000 sp. It was last seen flying east.
- **Situation:** A wyvern has been attacking travelers along the Southway.
- **Lore:** A generation ago, wyvern eggs were taken from the Red Plateau and sent east so that the hatchlings could imprint on imperial wyvern riders. The practice ended because the plateau became depopulated as a result of the egg-harvesting.

Note that, regardless of the rumor's focus, each rumor is **actionable**, in the sense that it gives a clear location for the PCs to go to. The primary function of the rumor table is to guide and inform the PCs' explorations, and it can't do that if the PCs lack the information necessary to do anything *with* the rumor. (For example, a rumor that just said "there's a wyvern in the area" is, at best, very limited in its utility, because there's no way for the PCs to go looking for the wyvern other than just wandering around randomly.)

The actionable specificity of a rumor can vary quite a bit, though. "East of the Southway" is less precise than "check out the Red Plateau," which is less precise than "the adventurers sell you a map indicating the precise location of the shaft for 10 gold pieces." But even the vaguest of these provides some specific direction.

HEARING RUMORS

With a fully stocked rumor table ready to go, it's time to deliver your rumor to the PCs. Broadly speaking, there are three approaches for doing this: proactive, reactive, and opportunistic.

Proactive methods sort of "push" rumors on the PCs without the players taking any specific action to acquire them.

- **Interval Trigger:** At some regular interval, the PCs pick up new rumors. This might be once per week, at the end of each adventure, once per downtime, or any such trigger.

- **Action/Location Triggers:** You might also trigger rumor delivery based on actions the PCs take that are not, explicitly, looking for rumors. For example, they might get new rumors each time they return to town or visit a new town.

- **Character Creation:** It's a very good idea to give any brand-new character one or more rumors to kick things off. Before play even begins, these rumors will give players the knowledge to start setting goals and making navigational decisions.

- **Rumor Check:** At any point where you could have a proactive rumor trigger, you could make a rumor check instead of automatically granting rumors. You'll also want to decide if it's possible to gain multiple rumors at the same time, and whether rumors are gained individually or by the whole group.

For example, in my last open table (see page 463) hexcrawl campaign, every new character would get 1d4 rumors (the stuff they'd heard before the player started playing them) and I would make a 1 in 6 rumor check for each PC at the beginning of each session (representing stuff they'd heard around town since the last time we'd seen them in play).

ROLL FOR RUMORS!

No matter how they actually get the rumor, you can have the players roll for their rumor! It is a fun way for them to feel involved in the process and can increase their sense of "ownership" over the rumor they get.

As players learn how useful rumors can be, they're likely to start actively seeking them out. They may also go looking for other types of information without necessarily thinking in terms of "rumors," but that nevertheless can feed rumors to them. You can be **reactive** to these PC actions:

⬡ **Investigation Action:** The investigation action is part of the urbancrawl scenario structure (see page 350), but this covers any effort by the PCs to deliberately canvass a community for information. This effort might require a Charisma (Investigation) or similar check, with the number of rumors gleaned perhaps being determined by the relative success of the check.

⬡ **Tavern Talk:** Buying a round of drinks and plying others over a cup of grog in the common room of a tavern is another common shorthand for gathering rumors.

⬡ **Broadsheets and Bulletin Boards:** Broadsheets (the antecedents of newspapers) and bulletin board notices are formal packaging for rumors, allowing the PCs to periodically check in and receive a fresh packet of information. (You can imagine any number of similar packages, ranging from town criers to magic mirrors murmuring cryptic prophecies.) The content of each package (broadsheet headlines, job offers on the bulletin board, etc.) can be bespoke creations, or it's just as easy to roll them up randomly from your rumor table.

⬡ **Research:** Delving into tomes at the local library or digging through the musty scrolls of the official chronicles may not turn up rumors dealing with purely current events, but there are any number of rumors that can nevertheless be delivered through PC research (e.g., the trade in wyvern eggs a generation back).

Regardless of the precise method pursued by the PCs, you might consider **adding a cost** (for buying a round of drinks, well-placed bribes, access fees at the university library, etc.). I'd recommend against making this a particularly large fee, since obviously you don't want to discourage players from pursuing rumors. Something like 1d6 gp in D&D is quite reasonable.

Another option is to make the fee optional, but have it grant a bonus to the PCs' skill check (making success more likely or improving the quality or number of rumors gained). In this case, since it's not essential, you can elect to make the cost more substantial.

ADD RUMOR COST TO THE EQUIPMENT LIST!

Once a cost, optional or otherwise, has been attached to rumor gathering, one cool thing you can do is add this cost to the equipment list for your campaign. Now every player rolling up a new character and every returning character looking to resupply for their next expedition will have an in-their-face reminder that hunting for rumors is something they can do!

Of course, because the whole point of the rumor table is to impart information to the players, you should also **seize opportunities** during play that you can use to leverage your rumor table. For example:

◉ During any broad social interaction (e.g., the players say, "We spend the evening drinking at the tavern"), you might mention one or two interesting things they pick up in the general conversation.

◉ During interactions with specific NPCs, the rumor table can be used to generate topics of conversation. ("Did you hear about the wyvern sightings?")

◉ NPCs could also be deliberately questioned or interrogated about the area.

In practice, the rumor table is an incredibly versatile tool, and whenever a dollop of information would be useful or provide a bit of spice, you can simply roll or select an appropriate rumor for the situation.

CONTEXTUALIZING RUMORS

When giving a rumor to a player, you can simply drop it in their lap: "You've heard that a wyvern has been attacking travelers along the Southway." It works. There's nothing wrong with it. In fact, it may often be the best way to present that particular rumor. (For example, if you're handing out a bunch of rumors at one time—e.g., at character creation—there's no need to get fancy with it.)

Frequently, though, you'll find it more effective to contextualize the rumor—to explain exactly how the PCs came by the information and perhaps even give them an opportunity to play through it. This is when you frame up a scene at the local tavern where the PCs have noticed a young man with a freshly bandaged wound on his shoulder. Now they can strike up a conversation with him, learn his name, and hear from his own lips the tale of how the wyvern attacked his caravan and carried away his sister. They can see the haunted look in his eyes as he describes how her screams still echo in his ears.

Now those wyvern attacks have been given a face.

There are many ways, of course, that you can contextualize rumors. Here are a few options if you're struggling:

- ◎ Talking in a tavern. (Is it a quiet conversation? Or do they hear someone boisterously boasting at the next table?)
- ◎ Saw the information posted somewhere (a wanted poster, a bulletin board, etc.).
- ◎ Chatting with a friend. (Which friend? Ask the player if you don't know.)
- ◎ Performing research. (Where?)
- ◎ A letter. (From whom?)
- ◎ A tarot reading, fortune telling, or divine vision.

REPEATING & RESTOCKING RUMORS

When you give a rumor to the PCs, cross it off the rumor list. If you roll the same rumor again, you may want to reroll until you get a new rumor, but another option is to make a point of finding a different spin or variation on the information the PCs already have. (For example, if they've previously heard that a wyvern has been attacking travelers along the Southway, they might hear about a different group of travelers being attacked. Or maybe the wyvern has expanded its range and is attacking people near the logging camps. Or maybe there's a group of adventurers who saw it flying over the Red Plateau.)

As rumors get chewed up, though, you'll eventually want to restock the rumor table. Simply repeat the same process you used to create the rumor table originally, but also keep in mind current events and evolving situations (e.g., the wyvern expanding its range or stealing something valuable to add to its hoard).

A particularly effective technique is to reflect the PCs' actions in the rumor table. PCs tend to do lots of big, splashy stuff (like killing wyverns) that are exactly the sort of thing people gossip about. So when they do something notable, add it—or the situations that evolve out of it—to the rumor table.

Players love this. ("Hey! That was us!") It makes them feel important and it's a great way of showing that their choices are meaningful and their actions have consequences. The possibilities are almost limitless:

- With the wyvern slain, trade along the Southway has boomed. The caravan activity has outstripped the capacity of the Patrol Guild and they're looking for freelance guards willing to ride with the smaller caravans.

- Lord Erequad has issued a bounty for the adventurers who are believed to have stolen the tax assessor's lockbox (which was originally taken by the wyvern).

- Four hungry baby wyverns have been seen hunting on the Red Plateau.

In a great campaign, the adventure never ends and the rumor table is constantly driving the world forward.

✛ RUNNING COMBAT ✛

Most roleplaying games include a very specific procedure for running combat. You usually can't go too far wrong just following that procedure. If the game doesn't include a cheat sheet, though, you might want to prep one—summarizing the combat sequence and the combat actions each character can take—to keep you on the right track.

This extra credit is all about taking your combat to the next level—not just running it, but excelling at it. We'll start with a core set of best practices and then expand with a selection of tips and tricks.

I don't recommend trying to put all of this material into practice at the same time. Instead, just pick one or two things and really focus on incorporating them into your sessions. Once you feel like you've really mastered those techniques, grab another one to focus on. Add tools to your tool kit over time.

What I'll do is write the thing I'm working to improve onto a Post-it® note and attach it to my GM screen. That way the reminder to focus on combat descriptions or putting players on deck (or whatever it might be) is always in my peripheral vision. I call these practice points, and they really help me make sure I'm not losing track of that stuff during the hectic chaos of the game.

BEST PRACTICES FOR COMBAT

Before combat even begins, set yourself up for success by prepping a **combat cheat sheet** for your group. This is just a list of the PCs along with key information like

- armor class (AC),
- spell save DC, and
- Wisdom (Perception) modifier.

You don't want to have to track the full character sheet of every PC (you've got too many other things to worry about), but stuff like this is the absolute death knell for fast-paced, action-packed combat:

GM: The orc attacks you! What's your AC?

MALIKWA (ELWYNN): 18.

GM: (*rolls some dice*) The orc hits! They do 6 bludgeoning damage. Frank, what's Reinhart's AC?

FRANK (REINHART): 15.

GM: (*rolls some dice*) The other orc hits you! 5 damage.

As opposed to:

GM: One of the orcs attacks Elwynn and the other Reinhart. (*rolls some dice*) You're both driven back half a step under their bludgeoning blows. Elwynn takes 6 damage and Reinhart 5. Reinhart, what are you doing?

Particularly when you consider that this is happening over and over and over again. So much more focus and flow can be achieved if you just jot down the numbers you're constantly needing to reference. It's also a great idea to put this info on a Post-it note and attach it to your GM screen, so that you always know exactly where it is.

Unfortunately, this doesn't work well if a PC has an ability that is constantly changing their AC (or other target number). In D&D this is comparatively rare and you can usually just suck it up for that specific character, but these target numbers can be much more fluid in other RPGs. An alternative you can use here is to give each player a tent card: They can put their character name and the key target numbers on the tent card. If the player takes an action that changes their AC, it's their responsibility to update their tent card. (You can even buy whiteboard tent cards that can be easily updated.)

On the other side of the battlefield, you can also prep **combat stat sheets** for your bad guys. If I'm running an RPG with minimalist stat blocks, I will frequently be able to fit all of the stat blocks for an entire adventure on one page. (Which is, of course, fantastic.) For games like D&D with more elaborate stat blocks, I'll try to make sure all the bad guys in a specific scene or, alternatively, each action group from my adversary roster (see page 177) are grouped onto a single sheet.

What I want to be able to do is lay the stat sheet (or all the relevant stat sheets) on the table in front of me. That way I don't have to go flipping through books looking for stats; I can just flick my eyes from one piece of information to another.

THE GM'S TV TRAY

Whether I'm running at a table or from my computer, I find it super useful to put a TV tray next to my chair. Sometimes I'll use two! It gives me a dedicated space for my rulebooks, adventure notes, campaign status document (see page 448), miniatures, and the like. Only the material that is immediately relevant to the scene I'm currently running goes on the table in front of me, making everything easier to manage and reference.

Continuing the theme of keeping good notes, once combat starts, **write down the initiative order**. You can do this on a piece of paper, you can use a digital tool to keep track of it, you can put each combatant on a separate note card and flip through the stack, you can write it on a whiteboard, you can erect an initiative tower, or you can drop small tent cards in order across the top of your GM screen. Whatever works for you. Just never, ever be this guy:

GM: Does anyone go on 18? . . . No? Okay, what about 17? 16? 15?
MALIKWA (ELWYNN): I go on 15!

When one combatant wraps up their turn, you should know whose turn is next and go straight to them. Keep combat moving!

As you're running combat, even though the rules are likely making everything a little more formal, remember that you're still just making rulings. Don't forget your basic principles: Default to yes. Roll to find out. Have meaningful failures. And so forth.

This includes **narrating outcomes**. In the constant back-and-forth of combat, it can be easy to fall into a rote exchange featuring only the bare-bones mechanics:

GM: The orc hits you. 6 points of damage.

MALIKWA (ELWYNN): I attack the orc. (*rolls some dice*) I hit for 3 damage.

GM: Okay, the ogre is attacking now, too. He misses. Reinhart?

FRANK (REINHART): I hit the orc. (*rolls some dice*) 8 damage.

GM: The orc dies.

The mechanics reflect, model, and even prompt the game world, but it's ultimately your responsibility to bring that world to life.

GM: The orc slams Elwynn back into the wall. Take 6 points of damage.

MALIKWA (ELWYNN): I'll shove him off me and swing my sword. (*rolls some dice*) I hit for 3 damage.

GM: The orc takes a nasty cut to his arm. Green blood trickles onto the floor as he backs away cautiously. (*rolls some dice*) You take a step after him, but then leap back as the ogre's club crashes down between you! Reinhart?

FRANK (REINHART): I'll attack the orc. (*rolls some dice*) 8 damage.

GM: Penned in by Elwynn and the ogre, the orc can't scurry away fast enough. Your sword pierces through its belly, pinning it to the wall. It squirms haplessly on your blade and dies.

By setting the tone, you'll also be encouraging the players to get more descriptive and creative in their actions. Failing that, you can prompt them by asking, "What does that look like?" (E.g., "You've killed the orc. What does that look like?")

Providing awesome combat narration is tough, though. Even keeping in mind that less is usually more (you only need one or two small details to bring the scene to life, not a short story), the constant stream of action is very demanding, particularly since so much of the action is fundamentally repetitive. (How many different ways can you describe Reinhart hitting something with his sword?!)

Fortunately, the more you practice combat narration, the better you'll become. (It's a skill, just like any other.) In fact, you can even practice this away from the gaming table. An exercise I've found to be effective is to watch an action movie that you love while describing the action on-screen as if you were narrating a game session. You might feel a little silly, but this will build your repertoire of fight moves and challenge you to find ways to describe new types of action.

If you're still getting ready to run your first few sessions, pause here and take some time to get comfortable with this basic foundation. Then you can start layering in the advanced tips that follow when the time is right.

ROLL INITIATIVE LAST

D&D and many other RPGs you play will tell you that:

1. Combat starts.

2. You roll initiative.

But this often doesn't produce optimal results.

What I recommend is that you have your players roll their initiative at the *end* of combat. Write those numbers down and then use them for the *next* combat. When it looks like the PCs are about to encounter something, you should also roll for its initiative and slot it into the initiative order before combat actually breaks out.

Using this technique, by the time combat starts, initiative is already completely resolved, so there's no delay where you have to ask for initiative, the dice are rolled, your players tell you the results, then you sort those results in order . . . etc.

By having initiative ready to go, you can start combat off with a bang and keep the ball rolling with that same high intensity. It means that when the players are ambushed, you can maintain that adrenaline rush instead of immediately undermining it with the mundane task of collecting initiative. Instead of "Eight goblins drop out of the jungle canopy! . . . Let's wait three minutes while we all shuffle numbers around," it's "Eight goblins drop out of the jungle canopy! Reinhart! What do you do?!"

Rolling initiative at the end of combat is convenient because that's typically a time when other bookkeeping chores are being done anyway: After the heat of battle, wounds are being healed, corpses are being looted, equipment lists are being updated, and options are being discussed. Juggling a few extra numbers doesn't detract or even really distract from that. It just becomes part of the ambient noise. You can also achieve a similar effect by setting up a digital tool that lets you generate an initiative order by pushing a single button. (Technology is fabulous!) But here, too, I recommend anticipating the moment a bit: You really want to be able to flow directly from the moment hostilities break out into the fast and furious action with zero distractions.

PUT THE PLAYERS ON DECK

To keep the action flowing once you're in the thick of combat, put your players on deck.

As I mentioned above, there are lots of ways to track the initiative order. Some of these methods will allow the players to see the initiative order at all times (whiteboards, initiative towers, and so forth), while others won't. But in either case, make a habit of periodically saying, "Okay, the goblins are going to attack now, and then Malikwa you're on deck."

This will get annoying if you do it every single time, but with practice you'll find the moments when you *should* do it by watching for when the attention of the players has wavered, and it will speed up combat by making sure players are ready to go when their turn arrives.

The even more advanced version of this tip is **multitasking**. While Malikwa is deciding what Elwynn is going to do or, later, as she's making her attack roll against the goblins, you can look ahead and see that the hell hound is going next. If Elwynn is on the other side of the battlefield—or otherwise unlikely to affect what the hell hound is going to do—you're free to decide that it's going to attack Reinhart and make its attack roll. Now, when Elwynn's turn ends, the hell hound's action has already been resolved and you can simply declare what happens!

With practice, you can sometimes get the players to multitask, too. It's a little trickier and not every player is comfortable doing it, but if, say, Reinhart was going immediately after Elwynn in the initiative order and was, similarly, on the opposite side of the battlefield, there's no reason he couldn't start resolving his attack against the hell hound.

(If Reinhart is planning something that *could* interfere with what Elywnn is doing, or vice versa, it's obviously also fine to just say, "I'm going to wait until she's done.")

THE FISTFUL OF DICE

Another way to speed up combat resolution is rolling lots of dice at the same time.

You can start simple: Instead of making your attack roll, checking to see if you hit, and then rolling your damage, simply roll your attack and damage at the same time. If you hit, the damage is ready to go. If you don't, just ignore the damage die.

You can, once again, suggest that your players do the same. Some players won't like it, for any number of reasons, and that's just fine.

Back on your side of the screen, when you're dealing with an entire squad of bad guys, you can make all their attack rolls at the same time. For example, if I've got six goblins all attacking on the same initiative count, I'll roll 6d20 and then resolve the goblins in order from left to right as the dice fall. (I usually don't combine this with simultaneously rolling damage dice. I know it's sacrilege to suggest it, but there is such a thing as too many dice.)

SHARE TARGET NUMBERS

Remember how you're writing down the PCs' target numbers so that you don't have to keep asking for them during play?

You can do the same thing for the players by sharing your monsters' ACs and saving throw DCs!

If it's convenient, you might actually write these down for them. (If the initiative tracker is visible, perhaps you could jot it down next to their initiative entry.) But even just telling Reinhart, who's currently fighting the hell hound, what the hell hound's AC is can have much of the same effect. (If Reinhart's player is forgetful, perhaps suggest that they write it down on some scratch paper.)

Now, there are many situations in which it may feel more appropriate for the players to not know the bad guy's specific AC or saving throw DC or whatever. If that's the case? Don't share it!

But frequently that's not the case: Reinhart, the seasoned combat veteran, should have a pretty good idea how difficult it is to hit guards wearing plate armor. Plus, after a round or so the players will probably be able to reverse engineer the numbers anyway, so you might as well openly declare them and reap the benefits of saved time.

DESCRIBE YOUR TOKEN PLAY

If you're playing with a battlemap—whether physically on a table or virtually on a screen—a bad habit you can fall into is to move your miniatures (or tokens or standees or whatever) and *then* describe what happened. (Or not describe it at all. Or describe it and then move.) What you should try to do is move the miniature and describe the action at the same time.

And, specifically, try to describe the action in terms of the game world. Not, "I'll move over here" but "The goblin scurries past the brontosaurus."

You should also do this when you're setting up your miniatures! (Or peeling back the fog of war in your VTT.)

> **GM:** (*starts sketching the scene on the battlemap*) Suddenly you hear the mournful baying of wolves and the battle horns of orcs. Reinhart, what are you doing?
>
> **FRANK (REINHART):** I'll draw my sword and move in front of the spellcasters!
>
> **GM:** (*places Reinhart's miniature and continues sketching*) What about Elwynn?
>
> **MALIKWA (ELWYNN):** I'll activate my *ring of invisibility*.
>
> **GM:** (*as she places miniatures*) Over the top of the ridge, a dozen worg riders suddenly surge into view! Reinhart, it's back to you. (*continues placing miniatures as Reinhart declares his next action, then continues smoothly into action resolution*)

The point, of course, is that you're not putting the action on pause. In fact, this can turn the placement of the miniatures into a dramatic moment in its own right. "How many worgs *are* there?" the players whisper. Or, later, you reach down into a drawer and declare, "Suddenly, out of the black abyss, a black dragon emerges!" as you pull the miniature out, swoop it across the table, and drop it onto the battlemap.

USE GENERIC PROXIES

"I don't have an umber hulk miniature, so we're going to use this ogre miniature instead."

I understand the impulse, but I've found that for many players the constant visual input of the proxy miniature will override the description of the game world: No matter how many times you say "umber hulk," they will literally remember fighting an ogre.

If you've got something that's close ("We're going to use goblin miniatures for these orcs" or "We're going to use this red dragon for a black dragon"), you're probably fine, but anything further afield I think is a bad idea.

I'm not, of course, suggesting that you're not allowed to use an umber hulk in your game until you can afford the appropriate miniature. That would be absurd. What I'm saying is that if you're using a battlemap and you don't have the right miniatures, you should use completely generic tokens.

I've found that for most creatures, colored glass beads (like the ones often used for life tokens but that can usually be bought much cheaper in a crafts shop), numbered tokens, or poker chips work great. For larger creatures, I've got a stack of templates I've cut from colored card stock and I'll simply place one of the generic tokens on top of it.

Similarly, when using a virtual tabletop, I'll make sure to have a set of generic tokens (usually numbered) that I can use when needed. You don't want to be limited to only the specific tokens you have prepped, particularly if the PCs do something unexpected in the middle of a session.

QUEUE ACTIONS FOR DESCRIPTION

Instead of describing each individual action as it's resolved, you can mechanically resolve several actions, group them together, and weave them together into a single dynamic description.

GM: The orc hits you. 6 points of damage.

MALIKWA (ELWYNN): I attack the orc. (*rolls some dice*) I hit for 3 damage.

GM: Okay, the ogre is attacking now, too. He misses. Reinhart?

FRANK (REINHART): I hit the orc. (*rolls some dice*) 8 damage.

GM: As the ogre comes thundering in with his massive club raised above his head, the orc lunges forward with his bloodstained blade. Elwynn has no choice but to actually step forward into the orc's attack, twisting her body so that she only takes a glancing blow. The ogre's club smashes into the ground where she was just standing, sending a plume of dust into the air. As Elwynn propels herself forward, the orc falls back in a panic, only to be caught between you and simultaneously skewered from the front and back!

You don't need to do this every time, but this technique can make it a lot easier to keep the description of combat fresh and engaging. We asked earlier, "How many different ways can you describe Reinhart hitting something with his sword?" Well, the number increases exponentially when his attacks can be woven into and through the actions of others.

As you weave this action together, remember that combat turns are an abstraction we use to make resolving combat easier and more straightforward. They aren't the reality of the characters' experience. In that reality, the combatants aren't all standing around politely waiting to take their turn. Everything is happening at the same time!

THE MOP-UP

We've reached the end of combat and the last bad guy is down to the dregs of his hit points. One of the players makes an attack roll . . . She hits!

And the GM says, "Don't bother rolling damage! He's dead!"

Don't do this.

Before we delve into why this is a bad idea, let's first talk about why the impulse exists: The combat is clearly coming to a conclusion and the remaining combatant poses no meaningful threat to the PCs, so there's no longer any tension or meaningful stakes in the scene; it's been reduced to a rote resolution. Heck! The bad guy might only have one or two hit points left, so the outcome really *is* predetermined, so why bother rolling damage dice?

This is pointless! Let's wrap it up!

The impulse is not necessarily wrong. It's just mistimed.

The key thing here is the ownership of the win. When a player rolls a successful attack, deals damage, and the bad guy dies, that's something that THEY did. They own that moment.

If you, as the GM, interrupt that process and declare a fiat success, you take that moment away from them: They didn't kill the monster; you did.

It's a subtle distinction, and it won't always result in the moment getting deflated, but it'll deflate often enough that it's worth steering clear of this technique. Particularly since the benefit you're getting is so minor: You're saving . . . what? 15 seconds by having them skip the damage roll?

The obvious alternative is to just **let them roll damage** and then announce the result.

That works if the damage kills the bad guy. But what if the attack doesn't *quite* deal enough damage to finish the job? This fight is boring! It's time to be done with it!

First, double-check to make sure that's actually true. As the GM, the fight has become boring because you can see the numbers and the outcome has become certain. In roleplaying the bad guys, you've lost meaningful agency and that's boring. But your experience here may not mirror the players', they haven't lost agency. In fact, they're about to reap the rewards of their agency! They're going to win! Winning is exciting!

If it is time for the fight to be done, however, you can **fudge the bad guy's hit points**. After the PC deals damage, the bad guy still has 2 hit points left. You can just round that down to 0 and call it a day. (Fudging the results of a roll is usually a really bad idea, but it's probably fine here. You're not actually changing the ultimate outcome, which is where all the various problems with fudging come from. You're just speeding it up.)

Alternatively, you can do the exact opposite: If the combat is lagging and you're concerned the current PC's attack may not deal enough damage to end it if they roll poorly on the damage dice, **tell them how many hit points the monster has left** before they roll. This obviously blocks you completely from using the fudging technique.

The reason this works, however, is that knowing the damage needed puts the table's intense focus on the damage roll: Everyone knows exactly what needs to be rolled, the tension builds as the dice are picked up, and then explosively releases—whether in triumph or failure!—as the result is revealed. If the bad guy dies: Great! You've injected that moment with a little extra oomph. If they don't? Great! You've still clearly framed this as the final countdown and that focus will tend to carry forward to the next PC's attack.

Taking a step back, we might also ask ourselves how we got to this specific moment: How could we have avoided getting to the point where a combat encounter is ending in a whimper?

The obvious answer is to **end combat sooner**.

There are several ways to do this, but the easiest is to simply have the bad guys run away. The PCs take out the Bandit Queen and that's the sign for all of her mooks to hightail it! Or, alternatively, the PCs take out a bunch of mooks and the Bandit Queen decides discretion is the better part of valor.

(Also check out The Principles of RPG Villainy, on page 515, for a lengthier discussion of how and why having your bad guys run away is a good idea in any case.)

It's really important, though, to make sure that there's actually been a conclusion! And that the players can feel ownership of that conclusion! The example of the PCs taking out the Bandit Queen and then the mooks panicking works because the combat ending is a clear result of the PCs doing something decisive and significant.

(Fortunately, having the bad guys run away is a decision that player agency can persist through. So you've got a wide margin for error here.)

As you're trying to find the sweet spot here, it can be useful to understand some of the problems that arise when GMs end combat prematurely:

- ◈ Characters built to enjoy their spotlight time during combat are being punished.

- ◈ Strategically clever players often spend the first few rounds of combat setting up an advantageous situation, and it's frustrating if that gets prematurely negated.

- ◈ If players feel that encounters are being summarily dismissed in a way that isn't affected by their agency, their uncertainty about which encounters are actually being determined by their actions and which are being determined by GM fiat will make it difficult for them to determine when and how to spend limited resources. (Burning a one-use potion or once-per-day ability only to have its use become irrelevant because the GM got bored is incredibly frustrating. If the use of that ability is what effectively ended the threat of the combat, make sure you're emphasizing that in framing the end of the scene so that the player's agency is given its due.)

It can help to remind yourself that you should be the PCs' biggest fan: Them trouncing your bad guys should, paradoxically, fill you with as much joy as it does the players! When that's true, you'll be on the same page as the players and it'll get a lot easier to accurately judge how a scene is playing out (and how it needs to end).

To wrap up with the big takeaway here: Make sure the players feel ownership over what happens: that *they* were the ones to win the fight. As long as that remains true, everything else will work out.

✦ SCENARIO HOOKS ✦

Scenario hooks are the methods by which PCs become aware that a scenario exists, are enticed to engage the scenario, and/or are forced to engage the scenario.

Let's say that you have a scenario featuring a pack of werewolves that have taken up residence in a ruined castle a few miles away from a small village. What scenario hook could you use to get the PCs involved in this scenario?

Perhaps:

- The villagers could ask them for help, or a local burgher could offer to pay them to root out the werewolves. (This is an example of **patronage**; an NPC is requesting that something specific be done.)

- They could hear rumors in the local tavern about the spate of recent werewolf attacks, or see bounty notices posted by the local sheriff. (This is an example of an **offer**; the GM is simply offering information and it's up to the PCs to determine what they want to do with that information, if anything.)

- As they ride past the ruined castle, a couple of the werewolves come racing out to attack them, or they hear screams of terror emanating from a farmhouse. (This is a **confrontation**; the scenario is directly encountered by the PCs.)

In each case, the PCs generally come away with a basic understanding of the situation and an understanding of what action they're expected to take: There are werewolves in the ruined castle and they need to get rid of them. (With some hooks they might only know that there are werewolves in the area and need to do some investigation to identify the ruined castle as their den, but that would still involve a general understanding of the situation. It's also possible, of course, for the PCs to choose a course of action that doesn't involve getting rid of the werewolves, but when you design a scenario with slavering werewolves who are killing innocent people, it's fairly clear what the *expected* decision will be.)

In order for a scenario hook to work, it must be **actionable**. In other words, there has to be an identifiable vector that will allow the PCs to engage with the scenario—to explore its locations, interact with its characters, and so forth. It doesn't matter how much tantalizing information you give the PCs about the Lost City of Shandrala; if they have no way of *finding* the city, then it's not a scenario hook. It's just backdrop and foreshadowing.

MULTIPLE SCENARIO HOOKS

If you think in terms of quest-givers in video games or the plot hook of a typical film or book (or even the example given by many published RPG scenarios), it can be easy to think that each scenario in your campaign should have a single, distinct scenario hook. As our example with the werewolf den demonstrates, however, it's quite easy for a single scenario to have multiple scenario hooks connected to it. In fact, I would argue that virtually every scenario *should* have multiple scenario hooks.

First, this follows principles similar to the Three Clue Rule (see page 217). In fact, if you're using a node-based campaign structure (see page 239), it's literally the Three Clue Rule. By including multiple scenario hooks for each scenario, you make it much more likely that the PCs will be enticed by one of the hooks and engage with the scenario.

Second, each additional hook provides a unique angle—of opportunity, of knowledge, of responsibility—on the scenario. Like a multifaceted gem, these angles enrich a scenario, increasing its depth and variety.

Third, multiple hooks can be set in direct conflict with each other. These are referred to as **dilemma hooks**, and their contradictions inherently empower the players by forcing them to make meaningful choices about what they're doing and why they're doing it.

One of my favorite techniques for setting up a dilemma hook is to use opposing patrons: If Patron A asks them to murder the CEO of Abletek and Patron B asks them to work as the CEO's security detail during an upcoming business conference, the players immediately need to really *think* about the scenario they're being hooked into: What do *they* want to have happen to the CEO? They can't just do what they're told. They're going to have to decide what *they* think should be done.

The really cool thing is that once this empowers the players—once they understand that they're the ones in control of how the scenario will play out—they'll often end up deciding they want something completely different from either patron. They'll set their own agenda and take the game to places none of you could have imagined before play began.

Simply having multiple hooks can also result in dilemmas emerging during play, even if they weren't designed with that in mind. ("Do we chase after the assassin to claim the bounty or do we save the Jewel of Erthasard from the river of lava?") If you've got multiple goals, it's not unusual for circumstance to put those goals in conflict with each other.

The only real drawback to having multiple scenario hooks is that you have to create them. But in truth, this is no hardship. Once you have a fully developed scenario, it's easy to hang scenario hooks off it. In fact, as an RPG producer, I tell my writers to design the scenario hooks *last*, even though it's the first thing the players will experience: It's infinitely easier to hang a hook when you already have something to hang it on, and it almost always results in stronger and more compelling hooks.

As a final note, you ideally want each scenario hook to be distinct: They should come from different sources, include different (although probably overlapping) information, and be driven by different motives. (It's less interesting for three different villagers to all follow the same basic script in asking the PCs to help get rid of the werewolves. It's more interesting if they see werewolf tracks in the forest and then a villager asks them for help and then they spot a poster offering to pay a bounty on werewolf pelts.)

TWISTED SCENARIO HOOKS

A typical scenario hook will give the PCs a basic understanding of the situation and an understanding of what action they're supposed to take, but this is not actually a necessary characteristic of a scenario hook. Or, more accurately, it's not necessary that their understanding of the situation or the action they're supposed to take is *correct*. You can instead twist the scenario hook by misleading the PCs about one or both of these things.

You might mislead them regarding the **nature of the threat**: The villagers, discovering dismembered limbs and unfamiliar with lycanthropic activity, think that the attacks signal a return of the tribe of cannibalistic ogres who plagued the region a generation ago. That's what they tell the PCs, who will be unpleasantly surprised—and perhaps wish they had stocked up on silver weapons!—when they head out to the ruined castle and discover the truth.

PLAYER-PROVIDED HOOKS

As you're running a campaign, it's not unusual for the players to create their own scenarios. "I really want a lavender *Ioun stone*," they say, or, "I think it's time to kill Sebastian."

This, of course, is fantastic. All you need to do is find the right scenario structure, fill in the blanks, add some challenges that need to be overcome for them to achieve their intention, and you're good to go.

Such scenarios usually don't need a scenario hook. (The PC is, obviously, already invested and engaged. They've really created their own scenario hook.) The exception is when their intention isn't actionable. For example, they want a lavender *Ioun stone*, but have no idea where one might be.

When that happens, you'll need to create an actionable vector. That's functionally a scenario hook and so it works like any other scenario hook. One thing to note, though, is that sometimes you can actually just add that scenario hook to an existing scenario—e.g., it turns out the Ewing family owns a lavender *Ioun stone*, so I guess that's another reason to stage a heist on their vault. Now you don't even need to create a new scenario!

You could also mislead them about the **motives** of the various NPCs involved. For example, it turns out that the werewolves in the ruined castle have actually come to the area to END the attacks by hunting down their former packmate who's suffering from silvered rabies.

Or when the werewolves come rushing out of the castle toward the PCs, it's because they've just escaped from the hidden torture dungeons of the local baron, who's transforming innocent villagers into werewolves to build a powerful, supernatural army. **Reversing good guys and bad guys** like this is an extreme example, but an instant classic.

When NPCs are involved in delivering the misleading scenario hooks, it can be useful to distinguish between whether the **NPCs are deceiving the PCs** or if it is, in fact, the **NPCs being deceived** (or mistaken) about the situation: If the villagers know that the werewolves are just peaceful nature lovers and they want the PCs to eliminate them so that they can claim the werewolf clan's ancestral property in the valley, that's a very different story from the villagers honestly believing that the werewolves are guilty of horrible crimes. The possibilities are basically endless, and can obviously vary a lot depending on the actual details of the specific scenario.

The reason to use a twisted scenario hook is to create a **reversal**: The players enter the scenario thinking that it's one thing, but when they discover the truth *the entire scenario changes into something new.* In practice, delivering a strong reversal like this can turn even an otherwise pedestrian scenario into a truly memorable one.

Twisted scenario hooks also work great when you're using multiple scenario hooks, particularly if they're misleading in interesting and different ways. It's not only easier to vary the hooks; it immediately creates a sense of mystery that will tantalize the players and encourage them to engage with the scenario to figure out what the heck is going on.

MEANINGFUL SCENARIO HOOKS

A mysterious cloaked figure in the corner of the tavern beckons the PCs over. He wants to hire them to retrieve the Ruby of Kardalia from a shipwreck near Stormhaven Cove!

This sort of scenario hook is fine, but it's not really meaningful: The PCs undoubtedly like money, but they've never met this guy before and they've never heard of the Ruby of Kardalia before. You could swap the nouns out and nothing would change.

Video games have normalized generic scenario hooks like this, with NPCs sending you on countless quests to kill wild boars, collect wolf gizzards, or deliver meaningless letters while you grind XP.

(The gizzards, in particular, seem zoologically suspect.)

You'll also find generic scenario hooks in most published adventures, for the simple reason that the authors of those adventures don't know your PCs, don't know what's happening in your campaign, and have no way of making the scenario hooks meaningful to you. But you *do* know your PCs and what's been happening in your campaign, so it can be quite trivial to do a lot better than this.

Start by simply listening to your players and **making it personal**. What do they *already* care about? People, places, things, goals. Whatever it is, simply tie your hook to that and your work is already done.

- Instead of a mysterious stranger, what if it's a family member or longtime ally of the PCs?
- Instead of the Ruby of Kardalia, what if it's a magic item that one of the PCs has been longing to get their hands on?
- What if the shipwreck the stranger has identified is actually the one that claimed the lives of a PC's parents?

You can also **increase the stakes**. Put important stuff—including people's lives—on the line. "Hey, can you deliver this letter to my wife?" is just a menial task. "You need to deliver this medicine or my wife will die!" or "Deliver this letter to Stormhaven! They must be warned of the Frostmancer's return!" have a lot more meat on their bones.

LONG-TERM SCENARIO HOOKS

On a similar note, video games and published scenarios have also conditioned us to think of scenario hooks as bang-bang interactions: The mysterious stranger wants to hire you, and so you immediately leave to retrieve the Ruby. A dire wolf attacks you on the road, so you immediately follow its tracks back to the pack's warren.

Again, nothing wrong with a bang-bang hook. If you're running a campaign, though, you have the opportunity to do more than that, by building up scenario hooks over the long term:

- The Ruby of Kardalia was mentioned in that arcane text you recovered from the Frostmancer's tower.
- The dire wolf attack isn't just random; you've been hearing reports of dire wolf attacks throughout the valley for months. In fact, your sister was mauled and nearly killed by one last week.

Weaving the threads of your campaign together like this across several adventures will make the whole experience feel more cohesive, and it'll naturally add extra layers of meaning to your scenarios. In fact, making a scenario hook meaningful by making it personal often has this same effect in reverse: Such a scenario is emerging from the long-term interests and relationships that the PCs have.

You can also **foreshadow** future scenarios by dropping information that's not actionable. For example, the PCs can spend weeks hearing about dire wolf attacks without having any clear way of responding to them, allowing information to build up over time. (In some cases, the PCs *could* take action but don't realize it. The effect is similar.)

Giving the PCs **simultaneous scenario hooks** for multiple adventures at the same time also inherently means that some of them won't be immediately pursued. In combination with having multiple scenario hooks per scenario, this also allows lore to accumulate.

BAIT HOOKS

Some scenario hooks don't actually point to scenarios. Instead, these **bait hooks** only exist in order to put the PCs in a position where they can be confronted with the *real* scenario.

For example, the PCs might be hired to guard a package of diamonds that's being delivered to a bank vault, but the only reason the job exists (and it might even go off without a hitch) is to put the PCs in the bank when the bank robbers show up.

The bait hook is usually a device of the GM, but it can also be diegetic when an NPC gives the PCs a false job offer in order to maneuver them into a location or situation for an ulterior purpose. This plot conceit is quite common in pulp fiction, for example, when detectives are hired to keep a person or location under observation and end up being framed for a crime.

TREASURE MAPS

Treasure maps are worth calling out as a specific type of scenario hook because they mesh so well with exploration-type scenarios like a typical dungeon (see page 65) or hexcrawl (see page 391).

The default action of these types of scenarios is basically "pick a direction and see what you find." In other words, if you're ever uncertain about what you should be doing in a dungeon, you can never go too far wrong by just picking a random door and seeing what's on the other side.

That's fine as far as it goes, but if the players remain limited to random choice, then they can't make meaningful choices (and that's where the real meat of the game is). Fortunately, all scenario hooks create specificity. In other words, they give the players a specific goal to pursue instead of a generic one. They're no longer opening doors or picking directions at random; they're trying to find one specific place or find one specific thing.

Treasure maps do the same thing, but they do it particularly well in exploration scenarios: Once the PCs spot a landmark depicted on the map, they'll be able to start orienting themselves using the map as a guide. Possibly a riddling or imperfect one, but a guide nonetheless.

The best part is that a treasure map can take almost any form and it can be used to point at almost *anything*.

✦ SUPPORTING CAST ✦

Your worlds will be filled with countless nonplayer characters, a vast panorama of roles covering the gamut of humanity and beyond. These roles—and playing these roles—are the lifeblood of a truly great RPG campaign, literally bringing it to life for you and your players.

I'm not going to pretend that this is easy. It's a challenge just roleplaying *one* character, let alone a legion of them. (A *fun* challenge, but a challenge nonetheless.) So this extra credit is going to focus on some tools and principles I've found useful in creating and running my supporting cast.

THE UNIVERSAL NPC ROLEPLAYING TEMPLATE

The more important an NPC is, the more detailed they become. But the more detailed they are, the more their description becomes an unwieldy mass that's almost impossible to parse during the pressure of actual play. And so, ironically, the more important an NPC is, the more difficult it becomes to run them smoothly and effectively at the table.

You do your best, of course, but how are you going to fish all the little details out of that wall of text? And three scenes later you realize that everything has spun out of control because you forgot that the NPC was supposed to tell the PCs about the properties of the Starstone, but that was hidden away as a single sentence in the fourth paragraph!

Which also means, as you create your own NPCs, that you'll find yourself wasting a lot of time writing up lengthy descriptions that never seem to have any real impact at the table. You need to figure out a better way of organizing your NPCs so that you can just focus on the important stuff. (Plus, it would be great, when the players decide to spontaneously visit the guy they met 12 sessions ago, if you could quickly pick that NPC up and start playing him again.)

Or maybe you're really good at juggling all those little details, but you struggle when it comes to really getting into character or making each of your NPCs a unique, distinct, and memorable individual.

Well, that's what the Universal NPC Roleplaying Template is all about.

The template is designed so that it doesn't take any extra effort to prep compared to the traditional "wall of text" presentations, but it structures the NPC's description into utilitarian categories that will (a) focus your prep and (b) make it incredibly easy to use during actual play. I've found that I can design NPCs with this technique, lay them aside for months at a time, and then pick them back up again in the middle of play without any review: Instead of trying to parse several paragraphs of dense text, the template will guide you directly to the information you need.

NAME

Self-explanatory. (Or, at least, I hope it is.)

APPEARANCE

Essentially a boxed-text description that you can use when the PCs meet the NPC for the first time. Get it pithy. One or two sentences is the sweet spot. Three sentences is pretty much the maximum length you should use unless there's something truly and outrageously unusual about the character. Remember that you don't need to describe every single thing about them. Pick out their most interesting and unique features and let your players' imaginations paint in the rest.

You can also include a picture of the NPC at the top of your briefing sheet. This image can also be shown to the players, of course, but is also useful for quickly finding the NPC you're looking for during play.

BRIEFING SHEETS

When I'm using this template, I'm often thinking of and using the NPCs as briefing sheets: I only put one NPC on each page. (And, in fact, it's usually just one NPC per sheet, so that the opposite side of the page is blank.)

When setting up a scene, this allows me to quickly "cast" the NPCs in it by simply grabbing the appropriate sheets and laying them out in front of me. That way I can just swap between characters with a flick of my eye. (I usually keep my campaign notes in a three-ring binder, so I just pop out the relevant pages.)

When running a scenario using the social event scenario structure (see page 354), I can similarly just pull all the guests' briefing sheets and then quickly riffle through them, making it easy to quickly mix and remix the social situations the PCs are in.

ROLEPLAYING

This is the heart of the template, but it should also be the shortest section. Two or three brief bullet points at most. You're looking to identify the essential elements that will "unlock" the character for you.

There are no firm rules here, but I will always try to include at least one simple, physical action that you can perform while playing the character at the table. For example, maybe they tap their ear. Or are constantly wearing a creepy smile. Or they arch an eyebrow. Or they speak with a particular accent or affectation. Or they clap their hands and rub them together. Or snap their fingers and point at the person they're talking to. Or make a point of taking a slow sip from their drink before responding to questions.

You don't have to make a big deal of it and it usually won't be something that you do *constantly* (that gets annoying), but the mannerism is your *hook*: You'll find that you can quickly get back into the character by simply performing the mannerism. It will also make your players remember the NPC as a distinct individual. And it can even make playing scenes with multiple NPCs easier to run (because you can use mannerisms to clearly distinguish the characters you're swapping between).

You'll generally only need *one* mannerism. Maybe two. More than that and you lose the simple utility of the mannerism in unnecessary complexity. It's not that the character's entire personality is this one thing; it's that the rest of the character's personality will flow out of you whenever you hit that touchstone.

Round this out with personality traits and general attitude. Are they friendly? Hostile? Greedy? Ruthless? Is there a particular negotiating tactic they like? Will they always offer you a drink? Will they fly into a rage if insulted? You may find that a properly crafted quote can be a very effective way of capturing the NPC's unique voice. But, again, keep it simple and to the point. You want to be able to glance at this section, process the information almost instantaneously, and start playing the character. You don't need a full-blown psychological profile and, in fact, that would be counterproductive.

PSYCHOLOGICAL GESTURE

If you want to do a truly deep dive into the power of using gesture and mannerism to assume character, check out Michael Chekhov's On the Technique of Acting.

BACKGROUND

This section is narrative in nature. You can let it breathe a bit more than the other sections if you like, but a little will still go a long way. I tend to think of this in terms of **essential context** and **interesting anecdotes**. Is it something that will directly influence the decisions they make? Is it information that the PCs are likely to discover about them (e.g., in conversation with them, talking to other people, or doing a background check)? Is it an interesting story that the NPC might tell about themselves or (better yet) use as context for explaining something? Great. If it's just a short story about some random person's life that you're writing for an audience of one, refocus your attention on prepping material that's relevant to the players.

BACKGROUND BOLD

Use bold text to call out key concepts in the "Background" section. For example:

Background: Bhaltair is Ariadnan of **Caledonian** stock. During the frontier conflict between Caledonia and Rodina, **his father fought in the war and never came back.** Bhaltair **lost himself in drink** for a while but got clean and made a pledge that he would work to never see his home world torn apart by such senseless violence again. He has **recently arrived** to take part in the Alliance Summit.

KEY INFO

Finally, in a bullet point format, lay out the essential interaction or information the PCs are supposed to get from the NPC (if any). The nature of this section will vary depending on the scenario and the NPC's role in it, but the most obvious example is a mystery scenario (see page 201) in which the NPC has a clue. Rather than burying that clue in the narrative of the NPC's background, what you want to do is yank it out and place it in this list to make sure you don't lose track of it during play.

(The Three Clue Rule applies, of course, so just because something appears in this section, it doesn't mean that the PCs will *automatically* get it. You're just making sure they don't miss it because *you* screwed up.)

You could also use this section to lay out the terms of employment being offered by the Mysterious Man in the Tavern. Or to list the discounts offered by a shopkeeper. It's a flexible tool. In some cases, it could get quite long, but it's essential that you keep it well organized (which is why you're using bullet points). If it just becomes a giant wall of text, its essential function has been lost. To this end, you may sometimes find it useful to split voluminous material into multiple Key Info sections, such as:

- Key Info—Clues
- Key Info—Topics of Conversation

With the former, obviously, listing all the clues, while the latter has any notes pertaining to the various topics of conversation being bandied about at the party.

Divisions based on topic may also be useful. For example, an NPC might have some information on werewolf sightings and also a lengthy account of the Haunting of Greybear Mansion, and thus:

- Key Info—Werewolf Sightings
- Key Info—Greybear Mansion

Of course, just because one NPC has their information broken up like this, it doesn't mean that every other NPC in the scenario needs their Key Info broken up in the same way (or at all). Most of the time, a single Key Info section with a couple bullet points is all you need.

LONG-TERM RELATIONSHIPS

If the PCs have a long-term relationship with an NPC, it's not necessary for them to divulge every piece of key information they have the first time they meet. In fact, it's probably a bad idea! You can pace out those interactions. You could even create a custom rumor table (see page 476) for very important NPCs, allowing you to randomly determine which bit of info might be dropped each time the PCs interact with them.

STAT BLOCK

If you need stats for the NPC, put 'em on the bottom of the briefing sheet in whatever format makes sense for the system you're running. (If your system uses a particularly long stat block format, you might need to put the stat block on the opposite side of the sheet.)

VIVID & MEMORABLE NPCs

Now that you have a template for your NPCs, what do you actually pour into that template? How do you create fully realized characters that will captivate, infuriate, and enthrall your players? The types of characters that they'll remember for the rest of the campaign, or even the rest of their lives.

First, give your NPC a **distinct mannerism**. I already called this out specifically in the Roleplaying section of the template, but it's so vital as a touchstone for both your roleplaying and the players' memory of the character that I'm mentioning it again.

Second, give the NPC a **strong agenda**. Make them *want* something. Better yet? A pair of agendas. If they're agendas that partly conflict with each other, even better.

TEMPLATE EXAMPLE: SYR ARION

Appearance: A man in the flush of youth: Short-cropped, jet-black hair sets off his piercing blue eyes. His frame is only lightly muscled, but toned and trained. The weight of his office, however, has left bags beneath his eyes, and his shoulders stoop with responsibility.

Roleplaying:

◎ A passionate man, but—increasingly—a weary one.

◎ In desperate need of friends, but years of experience and loss have taught him not to trust lightly.

◎ Rests his chin heavily into the palm of his hand.

Background: Arion's mother died in childbirth, and he was reared as the last scion of the Erradons by his father, a man whose faculties were already deserting him when Arion was born. Arion's father believed that his brother had been killed by the Guild, and the one edict he never wavered from was that Arion should be strictly sequestered. As a result, the only true friend Arion had while growing up was Celadon, the Captain of the Prince's Guard—a man 30 years his senior.

Despite this, or perhaps because of it, Arion dedicated himself to rigorous self-perfection: When he was not learning swordplay from Celadon, he was spending hours poring over the musty tomes in his father's library. He saw that his father was a poor ruler and believed it was his place to restore the honor of the Erradons by restoring the glory of Dweredell.

It actually works best if this agenda is not aimed directly at the PCs. "I want to destroy the PCs!" is nice and all, but something that simply overlaps the PCs' areas of interest is usually more effective. If the PCs' actions/knowledge/connections/whatever could help (or hinder) the NPC, having the NPC discover that during their interaction with the PCs (or having the PCs discover it and then decide what they want to do with that knowledge themselves) instantly makes for a powerful scene.

This is not a universal rule, obviously. There's nothing wrong with a patron showing up and simply wanting the PCs to do something for them. But the less the players think "X exists because the GM wants us to do Y," the more they will think of X as an actual person.

Third, throw out a **plethora of NPCs** and then pay attention to which ones "click" with the players. Focus on those and be okay with letting NPCs that aren't clicking move on with their lives. (This is discussed a bit more in the Social Events section starting on page 361, but it's equally true as a general principle.)

Fourth, along these same lines, apply Neel Krishnaswami's **Law of the Conservation of NPCs**: Whenever you're designing a scenario and need to include an NPC, rather than designing a new NPC, start by checking to see if any of the existing NPCs in the campaign could be used to fill the role.

There are several major benefits to reincorporating NPCs like this:

- It limits the cast of characters in your campaign, giving both you and your players fewer characters to keep track of.
- It allows NPCs to appear more frequently, giving you more practice playing them and the PCs more time to develop deep, complex relationships with them.
- It reveals and develops multiple facets of the character over time, turning them into more interesting and well-rounded individuals.

Fifth, **connect the NPCs** to each other and give them **strong, contradictory opinions** about each other. If everyone thinks Lord Bakersfield is a pompous asshole, eh, whatever. That's fine. If some people think he's a pompous asshole and other people think he's the greatest man they've ever met (and they both have cause to think so), Lord Bakersfield is a much more interesting character.

This also basically *forces* the players (and their PCs) to make up their own minds about Lord Bakersfield: Is he an asshole? Is he a great man? Both? And, if so, which is more important? That means they'll need to think meaningfully about him as a character, and that's step one to memorability.

REINCORPORATE EVERYTHING!

Reusing an NPC isn't the only way you can reincorporate elements of the campaign into new scenarios. If you're designing a dungeon scenario set in a ruined monastery, for example, it could be just any old monastery. But what if the monastery once belonged to the same religious faction as the party's cleric? Now the adventure is more personal for the PCs, and can develop the lore of the cleric's faith in a way that will continue paying dividends for the rest of the campaign.

Characters, locations, events, organizations, and even esoteric knowledge like history or arcane metaphysics can all become richer by virtue of being reused.

THE PRINCIPLES OF RPG VILLAINY

It's a classic scene from countless pulp adventures: After taunting the heroes, the villain swoops out of the scene. Our protagonists watch impotently as he escapes, building the rivalry between them and whetting our appetites for the finale of the story!

It's an effective trope—and guided by the books, movies, and graphic novels we love, it's not unusual for new GMs to try to include it in their adventures . . . only for the PCs to shoot the villain dead.

"You can't do that!" the new GM thinks. "You're ruining the story! My bad guy simply *must* get away!"

Maybe the new GM even cheats, negating the choices and accomplishments of the PCs in order to force their preconceived outcome. The problem, though, is that when you push your thumb on the scales of fate in order to predetermine the outcome of your game, you deflate the value of that outcome. If you do it poorly (or simply do it often enough), the anger and frustration of the players will stop focusing on the NPC villain and it will start focusing on you!

The core truth is that roleplaying games—unlike books or movies or graphic novels—aren't linear media with predetermined outcomes. They're interactive media with emergent narratives that are created through active play.

Does this mean that we can't have long-term villains in a roleplaying game? Of course not! It just means that villains don't work the same way in an RPG as they do in other mediums.

Here are the three Principles of RPG Villainy:

PRINCIPLE #1

Build tension between the PCs and the villain without using direct confrontations between them. Give the bad guy minions and introduce other NPCs who have a relationship with them (an ex-boyfriend, a family member, a victim, etc.). Have the bad guy do horrible things off-screen to people, places, and organizations the PCs care about. Staging social interactions in situations where the PCs won't be able to simply shoot them in the head without serious consequences also works well to build a personal relationship, as do taunting communiqués and phone calls.

PRINCIPLE #2

When you're prepping your scenarios, include *lots of bad guys*. You're probably doing this anyway, so the real key here is to simply refrain from pre-investing one of these guys as the "big villain." Basically, don't get attached to any of your antagonists: Assume that the first time they're in a position where the PCs *might* kill them, the PCs will *definitely* kill them. (You'll be right more often than not.)

PRINCIPLE #3

Remember that people in the real world usually don't fight to the death. Have your bad guys run away. And not just your "big villain" (since you won't have one of those anyway): Unless their back is truly to the wall, *most* of the people your PCs fight should try to escape once a fight turns against them. Most of them will probably still end up with a bullet in the back of their heads, but some of them will manage to escape.

The ones that escape?

Those are your memorable villains. They're your major antagonists.

This is the crucial inversion: Instead of figuring out who your major bad guy is and then predetermining that they will escape to wreak their vengeance, what's happening here is that the guy who escapes to wreak their vengeance becomes the major bad guy.

Consider *Die Hard* for a moment. As written, the film is a great example of our first principle in action, with the antagonism between John McClane and Hans Gruber being established almost entirely without any interaction between the two of them.

◎   Gruber takes McClane's wife hostage.

◎   They talk to each other through notes and walkie-talkies.

◎   Gruber sends his thugs to fight McClane elsewhere in the building.

The exception to this is the scene where Gruber pretends to be one of the hostages. This is a really clever device that heightens the conflict between McClane and Gruber by allowing them to directly interact with each other. But if this was a game table, what would happen if the PCs saw through Gruber's bluff and put a bullet through his forehead right then and there?

It doesn't matter.

Remember our second principle? Lots of bad guys. So now *Die Hard* becomes the story of the hotheaded Karl Vreski taking control of Gruber's delicate operation and blowing it up in a mad pursuit for vengeance. Maybe he starts killing hostages and becomes the most memorable villain of the campaign when he throws McClane's wife off the top of Nakatomi Plaza.

Okay, so cycling through the org-chart of Villains, Inc., works if you're using a team of bad guys. But what if the PCs really are facing off against a single nemesis?

First off, remember that not every challenge needs to be of epic proportions: Sometimes you run into some goblins in the woods and you kill them and you move on. You don't need every goblin to murder the priestess's cousin or become the blood-sworn enemy of the paladin.

Second, even the most memorable villains from fiction are often part of Villains, Inc., even when that isn't immediately obvious. For example, consider *Dracula*: Wouldn't it be really unsatisfying if Jonathan Harker snuck into Dracula's tomb at the beginning of the book and staked him through the heart before he ever went to England? I mean . . . this is *the* Dracula, right?

Remember, though, that Dracula only became *the* Dracula because that didn't happen at the hypothetical gaming table. If we were running this as an actual scenario, then we wouldn't know that he's "supposed" to become obsessed with Harker's wife and kill Mina's best friend in pursuit of her. We would discover that during play. So let's pretend that play had gone a different way: Harker stakes Dracula and heads back to England, satisfied that he's destroyed an ancient evil. It's a beautiful, happy ending to a short pulp horror adventure story.

. . . until the Brides of Dracula pursue him back to England seeking bloody vengeance.

Dracula? Schmacula.

He was just the appetizer.

Our hypothetical GM has included lots of bad guys, allowed them to die indiscriminately, and let a major villain naturally emerge in a way that's delightfully/horrifically surprising for everyone at the table.

Fake examples like this from other forms of media can be useful due to the common understanding we have of the source material, but can also be misleading because the official version of events from the original media lends a patina of canonicity that shouldn't be true of actual tabletop scenarios. So let me offer a couple of examples from an actual D&D campaign that I ran.

Silion was a cult leader. Using our first principle, I built her up in a variety of ways: Her name was referenced in early foreshadowing. The PCs tangled with her thugs and were targeted for retaliation by her organization. She was also incorporated into the background of a new PC joining the campaign, becoming responsible for murdering the PC's family and destroying their village.

Eventually, the PCs managed to track down her lair. They snuck in, found her digging through a box of archaeological artifacts, rolled a critical hit, and put an arrow through the back of her skull. She literally never even got a chance to look them in the face.

My players gleefully tell this story at almost every opportunity. They love it. It's one of their favorite moments from the entire campaign.

Why did it work?

Because when you heavily invest in a villain through foreshadowing, the payoff for defeating them is massively satisfying. It can be argued that this sort of thing might not work as well in other media (although consider that Luke's physical confrontation with the Emperor in *Return of the Jedi*, after building up to it over the course of three films, lasts almost no time at all), but in a roleplaying game the audience is synonymous with the protagonist. Your players don't want to be handed their quarry on a plate, but a quick kill shot isn't a gimme: It's a reward for all the work that got them to the point where they could take the shot.

Here's another example from the opposite end of the spectrum.

Arveth was a mook. She was captured by the PCs, questioned by Tithenmamiwen, and then cut loose. When Elestra, another PC, tried to sneak back and slit Arveth's throat to stop her from warning the other cultists, Tithenmamiwen stopped her.

But then the cultists caught up with Arveth: Believing that she had betrayed them to the PCs, they tortured her and even cut out her eye. Eventually concluding that Arveth was still loyal to their cause, however, the cult gave her a team of assassins and sent her to kill Tithenmamiwen.

This was our second principle: Use lots of bad guys and develop the ones who survive. In some other campaign, Arveth could have easily been cut down randomly during combat and completely forgotten by the next session.

Targeting Tithenmamiwen when she was alone, Arveth nearly succeeded in her assassination attempt before the rest of the party showed up. While the rest of her team held the party at bay, Arveth managed to escape (barely evading Tithenmamiwen's angry pursuit). This was our third principle: When they're losing a fight, have your bad guys run away.

At this point, things transitioned back to the first principle: Arveth used a magical artifact to send horrible nightmares to Tithenmamiwen, often featuring Arveth cutting out Tithenmamiwen's eye. She issued threats to Tithenmamiwen's friends. She placed a bounty on Tithenmamiwen's head.

Tithenmamiwen responded, hiring spies to hunt down Arveth and leaving Arveth messages on the bodies of cultists she killed along the way.

The PCs would eventually fight Arveth again. This time Arveth was teamed up with a medusa who turned two of the party members to stone. Arveth carved an eye out of each of the statues before making her escape once again.

By this point, of course, the PCs were absolutely furious. Tithen-mamiwen, in particular, had a rage that burned so white-hot that her alignment actually shifted: She had shown this bitch *mercy* and she was repaid with endless torment. I don't think I've ever seen such intense hatred focused toward an NPC before. It reshaped the entire course of the campaign.

Arveth was a mook no more.

When she finally died, the cheers of the players rocked the house. They literally took her miniature as a trophy so that it could never be used in a game again.

These are the villains that will be remembered forever by your players.

And by you.

ROLEPLAYING IN COMBAT

Roleplaying your bad guys during combat is tough. There's a ton of stuff you're keeping track of, with a bunch of rules flying back and forth. Plus, the action is broken up in a weird, semi-artificial way through the initiative count. It's just really easy for roleplaying to slip through the cracks.

There are a couple key ways to patch up those cracks.

First, remember that combat decisions ARE roleplaying. Seeing your mentor cut down, roaring in rage, and throwing yourself at her killer is every bit as much roleplaying as a scene filled with witty repartee. So make those combat decisions *as the character*; don't just treat them as playing pieces in a melee simulator.

Second, make a point of having characters talk on their initiative count. That might be:

◎ Dialogue directed at the PCs.
◎ Leaders shouting orders to their minions.
◎ Cries of pain or anguish.
◎ Chunks of an ongoing monologue.

And so forth. These are all things that can be directly associated to the actions they're taking on their turn, but they don't have to be.

If you're still struggling, turn the initiative count entirely to your advantage by literally adding "NPC Says Something" to your initiative tracker in one or more spots. When you hit that entry on the tracker, be compelled to actually do it.

If you make a point of setting an example for the players, you'll likely be able to draw them out and get them roleplaying through combat, too. And that back-and-forth will make it easier for all of you.

IMPROVISING YOUR SUPPORTING CAST

No matter how many NPCs you prep, at some point the players will say, out of the blue, "Hey! Let's talk to this random guy on the street!" or "We need to find a mercenary. Let's go ask around at the Irontooth Arena." And in that moment, you will need that random NPC to spring full-blown from your brow like Zeus giving birth to Athena.

Improvisation is tough (although it's something you can practice and get better at), and improvising an entire character on the fly and out of nothing is even tougher. What you need is a minimum profile—a simple template—that you can quickly snap into place. What you need is:

◈ a name,
◈ a descriptive detail,
◈ a roleplaying mannerism, and
◈ an agenda.

Names are usually tough for people to come up with on demand and off the top of their heads, so I recommend always keeping a list of random names in your notes. On the facing page you can find a list of fantasy names that I've used in basically every D&D campaign I've run for the past 15 years. When the PCs approach a random NPC, I just pick up the list, pick a name, and cross it off. At the start of a new campaign, I print off a new copy and start over again.

The best part is that the process of picking up this piece of paper and looking at it, if handled properly, is indistinguishable from looking at any of your other notes. It buys you a valuable breath of time in which to brainstorm the unexpected NPC and then put your thoughts in order before opening your mouth. Plus, your players won't be able to distinguish between the NPCs you prepped and the NPCs you didn't (since you're "checking your notes" either way).

You may find real-world names easier to come up with, but I still recommend prepping a list, particularly if your campaign or scenario is set in a culture you're unfamiliar with.

As far as a **descriptive detail** and a **roleplaying mannerism** goes, you can prep or find similar random lists that you can use. But a quick and effective shortcut is to mentally "cast" your NPC as an actor or actress you're familiar with.

You're bad at impersonations? Perfect! The players won't even recognize where you're pulling the character from.

Genre flips can have a similar effect: Ian McKellan's Gandalf is basically an archetype at this point, so you could easily have a wizard show up smoking a pipe, waggling their eyebrows, and speaking cryptically in dramatic whispers and no one's going to bat an eye. But use those same mannerisms for a mafioso or Luke Skywalker's characterization for a petulant halfling and your players will probably never realize where you drew your inspiration from.

LIST OF NAMES

- Gassan
- Arcutela
- Westhuis
- Canellis
- Richelle
- Davlin
- Virtucio
- Vijeh
- Maneja
- Francia
- Tulka
- Mendelyn
- Bulbuena
- Kennard
- Delev
- Eidem
- Shiarla
- Starai
- Benaitis
- Belorit
- Paiva
- Opalach
- Mederos
- Cordero
- Radu
- Malak
- Cargle
- Zorek
- Hatami
- Shirish
- Saralyn
- Leka

- Lukaj
- Rukaj
- Deakin
- Istvandi
- Nardis
- Isett
- Tanquary
- Tortorano
- Quaransa
- Niccore
- Jacczak
- Hamma
- Gavino
- Narala
- Harianto
- Geotina
- Filatova
- Paylicek
- Alstine
- Gimello
- Elsbury
- Tele
- Hamilla
- Rubino
- Vollmer
- Fishel
- Babaian
- Oliva
- Nauta
- Klepperich
- Machelle
- Hitech
- Soukaev

- Elatab
- Ryba
- Klacik
- Bilcaglia
- Leunissen
- Misra
- Opet
- Swanciger
- Folloni
- Churco
- Paterno
- Paoletti
- Mrafa
- Koetya
- Santouiero
- Stacho
- Gassan
- Addis
- Siress
- Dupere
- Grinstead
- Siddiqui
- Oberempt
- Komatina
- Tyronda
- Nodarse
- Galardo
- Raeder
- Opalach
- Bachtell
- Jeddry
- Garriel
- Ja-Juna

Figuring out an **agenda** for a bit character can be the toughest thing to do, and some will even argue that it's not really necessary. But figuring out what a character *wants* and what they're trying to achieve, even if it's completely tangential to the scene, is the best way, in my opinion, to bring them vividly to life.

The agenda is highly dependent on the specific circumstances of the character and the scene, but it can be useful to remember that it doesn't have to be of earth-shattering importance. The NPC might just be here to buy soap. That can be enough.

Assuming that your setting is already well stocked with NPCs, however, another thing you can do is basically just co-opt an existing NPC's agenda. This makes sense: In the real world, after all, there's not just one guy who's pro-Brexit or trying to buy real estate in the Guildsman's District or aligned with the Mafia or engaging in anti-android-apartheid activism.

So add this new NPC to one of these existing factions of interest.

It works best to then give their agenda a twist so that it's providing a different angle or insight into the agenda. The easiest twist is to simply flip the agenda and have them opposed to whatever the other NPC is trying to accomplish: So they're anti-Brexit, trying to protect middle-class property rights in the Guildsman's District, a gangbuster, or an android-tester enforcing the apartheid.

⊹ SPLITTING THE PARTY ⊹

"Never split the party."

It's a popular maxim, and for good reason.

First, splitting the party divides its strength, making each group weaker and more vulnerable. (Which is particularly problematic if you're playing in a paradigm where adventures are primarily combat encounters and those combat encounters have all been balanced to leave your full group poised on the edge of total destruction. Nothing good can come from splitting up in those conditions.)

Second, it places an undue burden on the GM, who now needs to keep track of two separate tracks of continuity while also making sure to juggle spotlight time between the groups.

There's some truth to both of these concerns, which is why "never split the party" is great advice for newbies.

But once you have a little experience under your belts, things get slightly more complicated.

Let's start with the PCs: If you're in hostile territory . . . yeah, splitting the party is probably a bad idea. But once your adventures leave the dungeon, there are going to be lots of times when you're *not* operating in hostile territory and can gain huge benefits from multiplying your active fronts.

Think in terms of action economy: If you all stick together, you'll be stuck doing one thing at a time. If you split up, on the other hand, you can often be doing two or three or five things at the same time, stealing a march on your opposition or just moving quicker toward your goals. Being able to pursue multiple leads at the same time in a mystery scenario—particularly if you're trying to wrap up the case before the serial killer can strike again!— is a great example of this.

This can also make it easier for different characters to pursue actions that play to their unique strengths, making it less likely for a player to get stuck in "passive mode" watching other players do everything important. When two actions of the same type need to happen at the same time, it's also a great opportunity for someone who's second-best at something to get a chance to showcase their skills, whereas normally the group likely defaults to having the character with the best modifier always make the check.

Splitting up can also be good for personal scenes: It's hard to woo your lady love with four wingmen/women/people hovering over your shoulder all the time.

On the GM's side of the screen, I *love it* when the PCs split up. Not out of malevolent glee, but because once you know what you're doing, running the game for a split party is GMing on Easy Mode™. The trick is that when the whole group is together, you have very limited control over pacing: You can end a scene and frame a new one, but that's about it. As soon as the PCs split up, though, you're immediately inundated with a deluge of new options.

TALKING ABOUT SCENES

If you haven't already, you may want to check out the chapter on framing Scenes (see page 203). It may make some of the techniques we discuss here a little clearer.

CUT IN THE MIDDLE OF SCENES

For the GM, almost every advantage of splitting the party flows from the simple fact that instead of being limited to cutting to a new scene only when the previous scene has come to an end, you can now cut away in the *middle* of Group A's scene, jump to Group B's scene, and then jump back to finish Group A's scene. In fact, you can do this repeatedly between simultaneous scenes.

It takes a little extra juggling to keep track of the continuity between the two groups, but there are so many ways you can use this new power.

- ⬦ **Cut on a new bang.** "The door is suddenly blown open with plastic explosives! Colonel Kurtz steps through the mangled wreckage, the firelight gleaming on his monocle! Meanwhile, on the other side of town . . ."

⊘ **Cut on the choice.** Remember that a roleplaying game is, ultimately, a conversation of meaningful choices. When a doozy of a choice comes along, cut to the other group.

⊘ **Cut on the roll of the dice.** This leaves the outcome in suspense, but it also has the practical effect of eliminating the mechanical pause while the dice are rolled and the modifiers are added. The players are doing all of that while something exciting is happening to the other group, and when that other group gets to their own action check—BAM! You cut back to the first group, collect the result, and instantly move forward with the action.

⊘ **Cut whenever a player is preoccupied.** This is purely a practical cut, but at any point where a player needs to look up a rule or perform a complex calculation or read through a handout, you can eliminate dead air at the gaming table by swapping over to the other group.

⊘ **Cut whenever you're not needed.** Are the PCs in Group A discussing their options or reviewing their notes? Cut to Group B! I love this cut, because the players in Group A are still roleplaying even while I'm doing stuff with Group B. Because you're doubling up this time, literally everyone at the table is getting to play more than they normally would. Splitting the party actually increases spotlight time! It's like you're stealing fire from the gods.

CLIFFHANGERS

In practice or effect, a lot of these cuts between split groups create cliffhangers: The players *want* to know what will happen next, but you're denying that to them. You're making them wait for it.

This is great, because if I could only give one tip to GMs about pacing in RPGs, it would be to do a cliffhanger every single time the opportunity presents itself. It's virtually impossible to have too many of them.

The trick, though, is that when EVERYONE wants to know what will happen next, that includes you! You'll be just as eager and excited as the players, so it'll be really tempting to just keep playing and find out the answer.

But this is why you're sitting in the big seat: You've got to recognize that desire and then resist it, so that everyone—including you—can enjoy it even more!

CROSSOVERS

Once you've mastered the basic juggling of simultaneous scenes, you can enrich the experience by tying those scenes together through **crossovers**.

The simplest type of crossover is a **direct crossover**. This is where an element or outcome from one scene appears immediately in a different scene. For example, if one group blows up the arms depot, then the other group might hear the explosion from across town. Or Colonel Kurtz flees from one group of PCs and ends up running back to his office . . . which the other PCs are currently searching.

Indirect crossovers are both subtler and more varied. These are common or related elements in each scene that are not identical. For example, you might have Franklin discover a cult manual bearing the sign of a white cobra while, simultaneously, John sees a white cobra painted on the face of his murdered wife.

An indirect crossover might not have any specific connection in the game world whatsoever: For example, Suzy might ask Rick out for a date at the Italian Stallion on Friday night. Simultaneously, in a different scene, Bobby gets ordered by his police lieutenant to arrange surveillance for a mob boss meeting at the same restaurant at the same time. Suzy and Rick have no connection to the mob or the police, but that's still a crossover.

This also demonstrates how crossovers can be used to weave disconnected narratives together: Suzy, Rick, and Bobby are all going to end up at that restaurant at the same time. Franklin and John are both going to be launching separate investigations into the white cobra. It's still not clear exactly how their paths are going to cross, but they've definitely been set on a collision course.

This technique can be particularly effective at the beginning of a scenario or campaign: Instead of having the PCs all meet in a bar, you can instead launch them all into separate scenes and then seed crossovers into those scenes to slowly and organically draw them all together.

Another way of using these techniques is to strengthen the role of player-as-audience-member. You know that moment in a horror movie where the audience doesn't want a character to open a door because they know something the character doesn't? Hard to do in an RPG . . . unless the *table* knows it (because it was established in a different scene), but the PC doesn't. (This assumes, of course, that your players can handle a separation of PC and player knowledge.)

THE TIME CRUNCH

The party doesn't have to be constantly facing do-or-die deadlines, but putting the PCs under a time crunch can be effective in a lot of different ways. It makes every choice between A or B significant, because they may not have time to do A and then also do B.

You don't even need to set a plethora of explicit deadlines to make time relevant. Just having a campaign world that is active—in which the players can see that significant things happen over time and that situations evolve even when they're not directly interacting with them—will create not just the perception, but the reality that time matters, and that's all that's needed to feel the pressure of time.

A natural result of this time pressure is that it will encourage the party to split up: Facing a difficult choice between A or B, they'll cut the Gordian knot by breaking into two groups and doing both.

So have multiple things happening at the same time: Two different patrons wanting to hire them for jobs on the same day. An unexpected crisis breaking out just as they're getting ready to go do a thing. When they're in the middle of doing something, use a cell phone or a *sending* spell to have a desperate friend call them for help.

WHO'S FIRST?

When a group splits up, whose scene should you frame first?

I recommend usually looking for the group whose scene is most likely to be interrupted the fastest. This interruption might be

- a complicated decision,
- a skill check,
- some sort of logistical calculation,
- a dramatically appropriate moment, or
- a rules lookup.

Basically any of the reasons you'd normally cut from one scene to another.

The reason you're starting with the scene most likely to be interrupted the fastest is pretty straightforward: You're dipping your toes in the first scene, and then as quickly as possible cutting away to another group. Not only does this keep everyone engaged, but you're getting to the time-saving advantage of multitasking as quickly as possible (with Group 1 continuing to resolve stuff or discuss stuff in their scene while you've turned your attention to Group 2).

LOOK FOR CROSSOVERS

The slightly more advanced technique here is to look for effective crossovers between the scenes and then make sure you're sequencing the scenes to set those up for maximum effect.

BALANCE SPOTLIGHT

Regardless of splitting the party, you generally want every player to be contributing equally and to have an equal amount of time in the "spotlight" (i.e., getting to show off the cool stuff they can do, being responsible for the group's success, etc.).

Once the group splits up, therefore, you want to avoid what I call the "lone wolf spotlight," in which one PC wanders off by themselves and ends up getting fully half of the GM's attention. This can sometimes be a symptom of disruptive play (with the lone wolf's activities interfering with the other players' fun), in which case the increased spotlight time is actually rewarding the bad behavior, but this is usually not the case. (There are lots of reasons why one PC might head off to take care of something by themselves.)

Solving the problem is just a matter of keeping in mind the general principle of everyone getting an equal share of the spotlight. Instead of splitting your attention equally between groups, split it evenly between players: If one group has four PCs in it and the other group has one PC in it, you should usually spend four times as long focusing on the larger group.

(There can be lots of exceptions to this. Juggling spotlight time is more art than rigid turn-keeping. Maybe the smaller group is doing something much more important and gets a lot of focus in the first half of the session, and then you can make sure the other PCs get extra spotlight time in the second half of the session or at next week's session.)

A related pitfall is thinking you need to keep time between the two groups strictly synced. So if Group A is staying put while Group B is driving 15 minutes across town, you would need to resolve 15 minutes of activity with Group A before you could even *think* about cutting to Group B.

This can very easily make it impossible to effectively split spotlight time or cut between groups.

The solution, of course, is to simply not keep time synced: Start running the scene with Group A, then cut "forward" to Group B arriving at their destination. Run a bit of that interaction, then cut "backward" to Group A.

This can sound complicated, but in practice it really isn't. You can stress yourself out thinking about all the ways the PCs could hypothetically violate causality, but you either (a) say that isn't an option or (b) perform a simple retcon or flashback to resolve the conflict (whichever is most appropriate to the situation). Your players will help you do this in a way that makes sense for everyone. (Plus, in practice, timekeeping in the game world isn't that precise to begin with, so you've usually got a pretty wide margin of fuzziness to fudge things around.)

CONTINUOUS COMMUNICATION
What if the PCs have cell phones or earpieces or some other form of continual communication unlimited by distance that can trivially breach the continuity between the two groups? Often, the net effect here is that the party isn't actually split: Even though they're in two locations, each group is able to participate in what the other group is doing (by offering advice, etc.). This makes it substantially less important to balance spotlight time between the groups, since players can grab a slice of spotlight for themselves over the comms line.

JOINT INITIATIVE LISTS

If the PCs split up and get into two fights simultaneously, make a single initiative list, then just swap between the fights whenever the initiative order tells you to.

Running two combats at the same time is often seen as the worst-case scenario for a split party, but the structure of the initiative list can actually act like training wheels and make it the easiest. If you're trying to get a feel for what running simultaneous scenes should feel like—cutting between groups, balancing spotlight time, etc.—running simultaneous combat can be a *great* way to do it.

TO THE FUTURE!

YOU'VE COME TO the end of *So You Want to Be a Game Master* and I hope that many of you have already begun running your first campaigns, sharing your amazing worlds and ideas with your players, and creating memories of the fantastic that will last a lifetime.

So what's next?

Run more games!

I once told you that I've run entire campaigns using nothing but dungeons. Now you have dungeons, mysteries, node-based campaigns, raids, heists, conspiracies, social events, urbancrawls, hexcrawls, and pointcrawls. With the secrets you've unlocked here, there's really no limit to the scenarios you can create and the games you can play.

So you should design more scenarios, mastering the intricacies of the various scenario structures.

As you're running those scenarios for your players, take the time to really master the extra credit. Get a feel for the rhythm of the table. Check in with your players and get their feedback on how the campaign is going, then use that feedback to keep improving.

Try to play in some games, too. Game mastering is fun, but it's only half of the experience! Sitting in a player's chair will also teach you a lot about the type of game master you want to be and the types of experiences you want to create for your players.

Finally, start thinking about how you can create new scenario structures and unlock even more adventures. How would you run:

- ⚅ A natural disaster like a tsunami or Pompeii?
- ⚅ An election campaign with the PCs as candidates?
- ⚅ An Edwardian household drama like *Downton Abbey*?
- ⚅ A coast-crawl inspired by the journeys of Hanno?
- ⚅ A football team playing a full competitive season?

For some of these you might be able to use or hack the scenario structures you've already mastered, but for others you'll likely need to create a new structure suited to the task. The most exciting part of that, is that each new scenario structure unlocks not just one adventure, but—like mysteries and dungeons and heists—an endless variety of new adventures.

Good gaming! I'll see you at the table!

JUSTIN'S FAVORITE RPGs

UP **UNTIL NOW**, statistically speaking, you've probably only played one RPG. If you're having a good time, that's great! But the day will likely come when you'll want to try something different—a different genre, a different focus, a different experience—and that's great, too. One of the best ways to challenge yourself as a game master is by running and playing new games, bringing what you discover back to your favorite games, and maybe finding a few new favorites along the way.

Here are a dozen of my favorite games, in no particular order, that you might want to check out, too.

Numenera (Monte Cook): A science-fantasy game set one billion years into the future. Earth has seen eight megacivilizations rise and fall, and a neo-Renaissance now picks through the ruins, rediscovering what was lost.

Ars Magica (Jonathan Tweet & Mark Rein·Hagen): Everybody plays the wizard! Your powerful magi have banded together to found a covenant in Mythic Europe, a fantasy version of the continent's thirteenth century.

Pendragon (Greg Stafford): Step into the legends of King Arthur, playing knights of Camelot in a campaign designed to span decades.

Technoir (Jeremy Keller): A cyberpunk game with a radically inventive game system in which you change the world by using Verbs to push Adjectives. Also features conspiracy-driven plot mapping.

Blades in the Dark (John Harper): Everybody plays the rogue! The players craft not only their characters, but also the criminal crew they all belong to. Features mechanics specialized for carrying out heists and other scores that are tightly integrated with downtime development of the crew.

Night's Black Agents (Kenneth Hite): A vampire spy thriller, in which retired secret agents discover that vampires are real. After creating your own unique vampire variant, very creative tools like the Conspyramid empower the GM to run a vast, global conspiracy.

Eclipse Phase (Rob Boyle & Brian Cross): A transhuman kitchen-sink space opera set ten years after the Fall of Earth. With elements ripped from the pages of cutting-edge science fiction, *Eclipse Phase* is a multitude of games in one.

Call of Cthulhu (Sandy Petersen): Based on the horror fiction of H. P. Lovecraft, the players take on the roles of investigators seeking to unravel eldritch mysteries.

You might also enjoy these storytelling games, which are tabletop narrative games similar to roleplaying games, but distinctly different (and not all of which even have a GM):

The Quiet Year (Avery Alder): A map-based storytelling game in which the players collaboratively create a postapocalyptic civilization using prompts generated from a deck of playing cards.

Microscope (Ben Robbins): Explore an epic history entirely of your own making, using the rules of the game to build an ever-expanding, non-linear chronology.

Shock: Social Science Fiction (Joshua A. C. Newman): A game intensely focused on the *speculative* in speculative fiction, in which each player takes on the roles of both their Protagonist and also the Antagonist for the player sitting to their right.

Ten Candles (Stephen Dewey): Ten days ago, the sun went out. And then They came. The survivors have learned to stay in the light. You play this game by candlelight, snuffing out one of the ten candles at the end of each scene . . . until the last candle goes out.

ACKNOWLEDGMENTS

DAVE ARNESON created the modern roleplaying game. Gary Gygax and Frank Mentzer taught me how to run a dungeon. Jennell Jaquays is the ultimate guru when it comes to xandering the dungeon. John Tynes (*Three Days to Kill*) taught me how to run a raid. D. Vincent Baker (*Apocalypse World*) and John Harper (*Blades in the Dark*) gave us progress and faction clocks. The importance of Scott McCloud, particularly his *Understanding Comics*, must also be acknowledged.

SPECIAL THANKS TO
Sarah Holmberg, Seth Gupton, Preeti Gupton, Sarah Heller, Andrew Holmberg, Jacqueline Leach, Chris Malone, Dave Blackmer, and Sasha Myhrom. This book would not be what it is if I had never played with you.

At Page Street Publishing I would also like to thank Elliot Wren Phillips, the champion who fought endlessly to make this book great; Sarah Monroe who believed in it; Juliann Barbato for countless error corrections; and Laura Benton and Meg Baskis, for making it gorgeous.

PLAYTEST CREDITS
- ◈ **Group 1:** Pyram King, Leland Tankersley, Matt Mason, P. E. "Beef" Larsen
- ◈ **Group 2:** Peter Heeringa, Heather Burmeister, Allen Voigt, Erik Malm, Kristina Fjellman

ABOUT THE AUTHOR

JUSTIN ALEXANDER has been a game master for over 30 years and has been designing RPGs professionally since he was in high school. He's currently the RPG developer at Atlas Games and has previously worked with Fantasy Flight Games, Modiphius, Goodman Games, Steve Jackson Games, Dream Pod 9, and many others. In addition to more than 200 published books, articles, and reviews, he's the co-creator of the *Infinity* roleplaying game and the second edition of *Magical Kitties Save the Day*.

Justin is also the creator of the Ennie Award–winning Alexandrian, a website perhaps best known for the Gamemastery 101 series, dedicated to exploring the many arts of running and playing roleplaying games. (Drop by when you're ready to take your game to a whole new level!)

He can also be found on YouTube and Twitch as The Alexandrian, and on Twitter as @hexcrawl. At home, he's the proud daddy of a little girl and the happy husband of a wonderful wife.

INDEX